Man, Climate and Architecture

SECOND EDITION

ARCHITECTURAL SCIENCE SERIES

Editor

HENRY J. COWAN
Professor of Architectural Science
University of Sydney

Previously published

Thermal Performance of Buildings
by J. F. VAN STRAATEN

Fundamental Foundations
by W. FISHER CASSIE

Models in Architecture
by H. J. COWAN, J. S. GERO, G. D. DING and R. W. MUNCEY

Principles of Natural Lighting
by J. A. LYNES

Electrical Services in Buildings
by P. JAY and J. HEMSLEY

Architectural Acoustics
by ANITA LAWRENCE

Fire and Buildings
by T. T. LIE

Psychology for Architects
by D. CANTER

Spatial Synthesis in Computer-Aided Building Design
edited by C. M. EASTMAN

Wind Loading on Buildings
by J. MACDONALD

Design of Building Frames
by J. S. GERO and H. J. COWAN

Building Services
by P. R. SMITH and W. G. JULIAN

Sound, Man and Building
by L. H. SCHAUDINISCHKY

Man, Climate and Architecture

by

B. GIVONI
B.Sc. (Arch.), M.Sc. (Hygiene), Ph.D. (Public Health)

Building Research Station
Technion, Israel Institute of Technology

SECOND EDITION

APPLIED SCIENCE PUBLISHERS LTD
LONDON

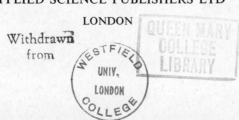

APPLIED SCIENCE PUBLISHERS LTD
RIPPLE ROAD, BARKING, ESSEX, ENGLAND

First edition 1969

Second edition 1976

ISBN: 0 85334 678 X

WITH 65 TABLES AND 78 ILLUSTRATIONS

© APPLIED SCIENCE PUBLISHERS LTD 1976

Printed in Great Britain by Galliard (Printers) Ltd Great Yarmouth

Preface to Second Edition

Six years have passed since the publication of the first edition of this book and the whole perspective with regard to relationship between Man, Climate and Architecture has been changed drastically. A new awareness of the need to conserve energy and to minimize energy needs for heating and air-conditioning of buildings has arisen, as a result of the energy crises. In addition, an interest in the utilization of natural energies as substitute for conventional fuels has been renewed and intensified.

During the period which elapsed since the first edition has been published, additional research has been conducted by the author in the physiological effects of the thermal environment. This research, which was conducted as a joint programme with Dr. R. Goldman of the U.S. Army Research Institute of Environmental Medicine in Natick, Massachussets, has resulted in several biophysical predictive models of various physiological responses to work, the thermal environment and clothing properties. Some of these models are summarized in the new version of Chapter 3.

Additional research has been done also by the author, together with Dr. M. Hoffman, on the prediction of the indoor temperatures in buildings under their "natural" state, without air-conditioning. This research is summarized in a new chapter, written by Dr. Hoffman.

Chapter 10 has been re-written, by Professor M. Milne of UCLA, with emphasis on the description of the motion of the sun and architectural methods of sun control.

And finally, a new chapter has been added, dealing with the utilization of natural energies for heating and cooling of buildings and analyzing the suitability of different systems to different climatic conditions and building types.

v

Preface to First Edition

The increasing interest, on the one hand, in the effect of climatic environment on man and, on the other hand, in the relationship between climate and architecture, is reflected in the numerous books and other publications, as well as in the growing research activity, on these subjects. Although most of the books dealing with the climatic aspects of architecture contain some references to the physiological aspect, and some of the publications dealing with environmental physiology contain remarks concerning the physical environment, the emphasis in each of them is placed on only one of these subjects.

The research in recent years has been directed mainly towards the problem arising in the hot, tropical and sub-tropical regions. There are two main reasons for this trend. First, these regions contain most of the developing countries and most of the world's population and, secondly, most of the existing knowledge has been gained in Europe and North America, with their temperate climate and the specific problems associated with it. Only in relatively recent years have the developing countries started to develop their scientific institutions and research activity, and the developed countries to pay more attention to problems of hot climates.

In the present work an attempt has been made to discuss in one volume with equal emphasis and detailing the physiological, the physical and also the architectural aspects of the relationship between climate, man and architecture which, in reality, are inseparable. It is hoped that in this way it would help to base decisions concerning one aspect on the implications involved which are related to the other aspects as well.

This book is outlined according to the syllabus of a graduate course in Bio and Building Climatology given by the author at the Israel Institute of Technology in Haifa. It is based to a great extent on the research work carried out in the last ten years at the Department of Building Climatology of the Building Research Station of the Institute. An attempt has been made, however, to give an account of this work, and to base the analysis of the problems and the conclusions drawn on the research work and publications in other research institutes. The fact that most of the author's research work is concerned with the physiological and building problems of hot climates is of course reflected in the book.

An idea underlying this book is that it is impossible to consider the effect of any of the various factors influencing either human thermal comfort or the indoor climate by itself, as the effect of each one of them, and the requirements with respect to it, depend on the level and conditions of other factors. Therefore an emphasis has been placed on the interactions between the effects of the various factors.

The monograph is divided into five main parts, each containing several chapters. The first part deals with the description of the climatic elements, their physiological, sensory and biophysical influences, and methods for the evaluation of their combined effect on man. The second part deals with the thermophysical properties of building materials and their effect on the indoor climate and wetness conditions. The third part is concerned with the impact of solar radiation on buildings and the design implication of its control. The fourth part deals with ventilation problems, such as physiological requirements, physical factors involved and the design factors which influence indoor ventilation conditions. The fifth part is devoted to the integration of the material presented in the preceding parts into design principles and details, for different climatic types.

Acknowledgements

It is with great appreciation that the author wishes to thank his colleagues at the Department of Building Climatology for their assistance in the research work which served as basis for the book, and in its actual preparation for publication: in particular Mrs. E. Nir and Mr. M. E. Hoffman, who participated as investigators in the various research projects; Mrs. N. Arad, who drew the Figures; Mmes. N. Seanger and N. Oren, and Mr. J. Carmeli, who helped in carrying out the projects; Miss S. Maguire, who assisted in the preparation of the manuscript for publication and Mrs. P. Nussbaum who typed it.

Particular thanks are due to Professor M. Milne and Dr. M. E. Hoffman, who wrote new chapters for the second edition.

Thanks are also due to all the authors and publishers of the works which were cited and reproduced, for their willingness to permit these quotations.

And last but not least the author extends his gratitude to UNESCO, U.S. Public Health Service, Ford Foundation and the Israeli Ministry of Housing for their invaluable financial help to the research projects without which the present book could not have been written.

Contents

Chapter 1

The Climatic Elements

The purpose of the first chapter is to provide the reader with a general understanding of the nature of the factors which affect climatic conditions over the earth.

The "climate" of a given region is determined by the pattern of variations of several elements and their combinations. The principal climatic elements, when human comfort and building design are being considered, are solar radiation, longwave radiation to the sky, air temperature, humidity, wind and precipitation (rain, snow, etc.). The present chapter briefly describes these elements, their inter-relations and their distribution over the earth. An attempt has been made to give for each factor the data related directly to human comfort and to the aspects of building design which affect this.

Standard climatological books assess the climate of a region according to the long-term averages for the levels of each of the factors, but, as conditions may vary greatly from day to day and from year to year, deviations from the average should be taken into account for a more realistic view when dealing with climatic prob-lems. For many applications the extreme conditions and their expected frequency may be of greater importance than the average conditions.

This chapter draws for information primarily on three books by Ashbel [1.1], Miller [1.4] and Trewartha [1.5] and the author gratefully acknowledges the kind permission to quote from these works, granted by the authors and publishers.

1.1. Solar Radiation

Solar radiation is an electromagnetic radiation emitted from the sun. The different wavelengths included (solar spectrum) range, on the surface of the earth, from about 0·28 to 3·0 microns (thousandths of a millimetre). The solar spectrum is broadly divided into three.

1

regions: the ultra-violet (u.v.), the visible and the infra-red (i.r.). Only the small section of the spectrum between 0·4 and 0·76 micron is light visible to the eye; waves shorter than 0·4 micron are u.v. radiations and waves longer than 0·76 micron are i.r. Although the peak intensity of solar radiation is in the visible range, over one-half of the energy is emitted as i.r. radiation.

The solar energy at the upper limit of the atmosphere varies from 1·8 to 2·0 cal/cm^2/min according to the earth's distance from the sun and the solar activity. On average it is 1·97 cal/cm^2/min [1.1], and this value is known as the solar constant. As radiation penetrates the earth's atmosphere its intensity is decreased and the spectral distribution is altered by absorption, reflection and scattering.

Radiation is selectively absorbed in the atmosphere, according to wavelength. Most of the u.v. rays and all wavelengths below 0·288 micron are absorbed by ozone and an appreciable part of the i.r. rays are absorbed by water vapour and carbon dioxide. Reflection takes place mainly from water droplets and is effectively non-selective; thus the spectral distribution of reflected radiation is similar to that of the source radiation, and hence the reflected light is white. When impinging on molecules and particles of dimensions similar to or smaller than the wavelength, radiation is refracted and diffused in space. Thus light is diffused, providing illumination even in the absence of direct sunlight. This is a selective phenomenon and the amount of scattered radiation of each wavelength is proportional to the fourth power of the reciprocal of the wavelength. Thus the air molecules scatter more of the shorter wave, blue and violet light, giving the blue colour of clear sky. But when the atmospheric content of larger dust particles increases, increasing the turbidity of the air, the proportion of the longwave yellow and red light scattered is increased and the sky becomes a whiter colour.

Clouds reflect back a significant fraction of the solar radiation to outer space, but the remainder reaches the earth's surface in a diffused form.

The diurnal and annual patterns of solar energy incident on a given region of the earth's surface depend on the intensity and duration of irradiation by the sun. The potential intensity of the radiation depends on the thickness of air through which the rays must penetrate, which is determined by the earth's rotation about its axis, its revolution about the sun and the inclination of the axis to the plane of revolution, all of which can be accurately computed. However, the amount of solar energy actually reaching the earth depends also on the sky clearance with respect to cloud, and the purity of the air with respect to dust, carbon dioxide and water vapour; these are factors which have to be estimated rather than calculated exactly.

The thickness of air through which the rays penetrate to reach a point on the earth depends on the angle of the sun above the horizon, or the altitude of the sun, and on the height of the point above sea-level. The altitude of the sun varies with the geographical latitude of the point, from a maximum in the tropics, decreasing towards the north and south poles. The duration of sunlight, however, increases in summer and is reduced in winter, with increasing latitude. Thus in

Table 1.I

Cross-section from pole to pole of the mean monthly global*
solar radiation at the 40°E meridian during the I.G.Y.
$(cal/cm^2/day)$ *(after D. Ashbel [1.2])*

Latitude	January	March	June	August	Yearly average
85–N	0	30	650	200	100
80–N	0	75	580	220	120
70–N	15	150	400	260	180
60–N	40	200	430	300	220
50–N	85	250	480	470	300
40–N	160	280	600	590	370
30–N	280	450	740	670	530
20–N	360	530	570	550	600
10–N	500	600	500	500	500
0	500	500	500	450	500
10–S	480	480	500	450	480
20–S	600	550	430	450	470
30–S	700	600	330	400	450
40–S	500	380	180	260	400
50–S	450	280	80	150	300
60–S	510	230	20	70	210
70–S	560	180	0	10	160
80–S	610	130	0	0	110
90–S	700	120	0	0	80

* Global solar radiation is the total of direct and diffused radiation falling on horizontal surfaces.

summer the greater length of the day in high latitudes partially compensates for the low angle of the sun.

The conditions of humidity and cloudiness also vary with latitude. These factors combine to give the highest intensity of solar radiation, during summer and on a yearly average basis, not in the tropics but in the sub-tropical arid regions.

On the basis of the world-wide measurements of solar radiation during the International Geophysical Year (1957–1958), Ashbel [1.2] has prepared maps of world distribution of solar radiation. Table 1.I is based on these maps and shows a cross-section of global solar radiation from the north to the south poles through the 40°E meridian, for January, March, June, August and for the yearly average.

The procedures for quantitative determination of solar impact on man and buildings are dealt with in Chapters 4 and 10 respectively.

1.2. Longwave Radiative Heat Loss

Longwave radiation is emitted by the surface of the earth to the atmosphere and to outer space. According to the Stefan–Boltzmann Law, the intensity of emitted radiation is proportional to the difference between the fourth powers of the absolute temperatures (°K) of the emitting and absorbing points. It therefore depends on the difference between the temperatures of the earth's surface and the medium absorbing the radiation (in the atmosphere or outer space). Longwave radiation is also emitted in all directions by the gases in the atmosphere and of this the earth absorbs the downward components.

The gases comprising the atmosphere absorb and emit radiant energy, not as a black body (through a continuous spectrum), but in a selective way; while only a small part of shortwave solar radiation is removed, most outgoing longwave radiation is absorbed in the air. However, only certain wavelengths are affected and the remainder continues to travel into space.

Of the atmospheric gases, water vapour is the principal longwave absorber; carbon dioxide is also important, but to a lesser extent.

The difference between the amount of radiation discharged from the earth's surface and that emitted back to earth by the atmosphere is the net radiative heat loss. When the sky is overcast, this is reduced to a very low level. This is because the water particles in the cloud absorb and emit the whole longwave spectrum emitted by the earth, in contrast with the selective absorption by water vapour, and so all the earth radiation given out is fully absorbed at the base of the cloud. Thus the net radiative heat loss is highest when the atmosphere is clear and dry, and it decreases as the amount of water vapour, dust and particularly cloud, increases.

Geiger quotes the following formula for the net radiative heat loss from a given surface [1.3]:

$$R = 8 \cdot 26 \times 10^{-11} \times T^4 \, (0 \cdot 23 + 0 \cdot 28 \times 10^{-0 \cdot 074P})$$

where R is the net radiation from the horizontal surface in cal/cm^2/min, P is the water vapour pressure in millimetres of mercury (mm Hg), measured close to the ground, and T is the absolute temperature (°C + 273). This formula applies only to a cloudless sky.

The effect of vapour pressure on the longwave radiation heat loss is illustrated in Table 1.II, which was prepared from Geiger's nomograms and which gives the values of R, for surface temperatures of 10°, 20° and 30°C, as a function of the vapour pressure.

Table 1.II

Net longwave radiative heat flow
(cal/cm²/min) (after Geiger [1.3])

Temperature	Vapour pressure (mm Hg)						
	4	6	8	10	15	20	30
10°C	0·197	0·175	0·160	—	—	—	—
20°C	0·225	0·200	0·183	0·160	0·153	—	—
30°C	0·260	0·230	0·210	0·195	0·163	0·155	0·150

Geiger remarks that the values obtained from the above formula may be too high, by about 17%.

When the sky is clouded the outgoing radiation is reduced. Geiger cites the following results of measurements of outgoing radiation, as percentages of the values for cloudless sky:

Cloudiness in tenths: 0, 1, 2, 3, 4, 5, 6, 7, 8, 9, 10

% Outgoing radiation: 100, 98, 95, 90, 85, 79, 73, 64, 52, 35, 15

Outgoing radiation is strongest in desert climates where it can be utilized as a source of energy for cooling buildings, as discussed in detail in Chapter 16.

1.3. Air Temperature

The rate of heating and cooling of the surface of the earth is the main factor determining the temperature of the air above it. The air is transparent to almost all solar radiation, which therefore has only an indirect effect on air temperature.

The air layer in direct contact with the warm ground is heated by conduction; this heat is transferred to the upper layers mainly by convection and with the turbulence and eddies in the air. Currents and winds bring large masses of air into contact with the earth's surface, to be warmed in this way.

At night and during winter the surface of the earth is usually colder than the air, on account of longwave radiation to the sky, and so the net heat exchange is reversed and air in contact with the ground is cooled.

The annual and diurnal patterns of air temperature thus depend on the variations in surface temperature. In this respect wide differences exist between land and water surfaces. Great bodies of water are affected more slowly than land masses under the same conditions of solar radiation. Therefore land surfaces are warmer in summer and colder in winter than sea surfaces on the same latitude. The air masses originating over these surfaces differ accordingly. The average temperature of air is higher in summer and lower in winter over land than over the sea.

A change in altitude also alters the temperature of the air. When a mass of air rises, as for instance when it is pushed up a mountain, it moves from a higher to a lower pressure region and so expands and is cooled. Conversely, when an air mass descends it is compressed and heated. These are known as adiabatic cooling and heating processes and the rate of temperature change is about 1 deg C per 100 metres in altitude (5·4 deg F per 1000 ft).

When water vapour condenses to form liquid droplets the latent heat evolved provides energy to heat the air or to reduce cooling. Therefore when condensation occurs in rising air, the rate of cooling is decreased for as long as the condensation continues. In the free atmosphere, air temperature decreases with altitude up to the stratosphere. The decrease, which is known as the "lapse rate", varies with the season and the time of day, but averages about 0·6 deg C per 100 metres (3·6 deg F per 1000 ft). During the day the lapse rate is greater near to the ground, owing to the conductive heating of the lower air layers in contact with the earth. The heated air expands, becomes less dense and tends to rise, making the lower air layer unstable and so constantly mixing with the upper layers.

During the night, especially when the sky is clear, the earth's surface cools appreciably more than does the air and so, near the ground, the lower air layers are colder than those above them. This results in a reversal of the normal vertical temperature gradient near the ground and the phenomenon is known as surface "inversion". As the colder, lower air layer is heavier than the warmer air above it, the air becomes stable under inversion conditions and all vertical movement is suppressed. The conditions promoting surface inversion are long nights, clear skies, dry air and the absence of wind.

An inversion can also be produced when masses of cold and warm air meet and the warm air is lifted above the cold air mass. This is a dynamic inversion.

The cold air near the ground tends to concentrate in low areas, such as valleys, and there the temperature may be several degrees lower than over higher ground.

Pressure differences over the earth cause the migration of air masses; air at a temperature acquired in one region may move to an area at a different temperature, altering the prevailing conditions. Thus a subtropical air mass moving towards the poles causes an elevation in temperature while a polar air mass reduces the temperature in the regions en route.

1.4. Air Pressure and Winds

The distribution and characteristics of the winds over a region are determined by several global and local factors. The principal determinants are the seasonal global distribution of air pressure, the rotation of the earth, the daily variations in heating and cooling of land and sea and the topography of the given region and its surroundings.

The pressure belts and regions

Over each hemisphere of the earth's surface there are belts and centres of high and of low atmospheric pressure. Some of these are permanent while others only exist for part of the year.

Two high-pressure belts surround the earth at the subtropical latitudes between 20° and 40° in the two hemispheres, and are shifted in summer towards the poles and in winter towards the equator. During the winter, both are continuous round the earth and the pressure is higher over the continents than over the oceans. In summer low-pressure centres (depressions) develop over the continents, interrupting the continuity of the belts. The polar regions are zones of permanent high pressure but at a lower pressure than in the subtropical belts.

The equatorial belt is the principal region of low pressure which is maintained throughout the year. In the summer of each hemisphere there is a shift towards higher latitudes, particularly over the great continents. Thus, in July–August the region covers mainly the northern tropics extending from North-East Africa to Central-East Asia, and its centre is in the Persian Gulf. In January–February the region covers mainly the southern tropics. Other low-pressure centres exist in the higher latitudes forming a belt in the southern hemisphere approximately over the Antarctic. In the northern hemisphere the distribution of the low-pressure areas is complicated by the presence of large land masses around the Arctic Ocean. Because of this, high- and low-pressure areas occur at about the same latitude and constantly move eastwards, so that any one place is subjected to successive periods of high and low air pressure.

The main cause of the pressure belts and centres is the uneven distribution of solar radiation over the earth and the resulting variation in surface heating. A large quantity of radiation is received by the equatorial region and here the air is heated above the level in adjacent regions. This air expands and is lifted upwards, leaving a belt of low pressure towards which air flows from the surrounding regions still at a higher pressure.

As the centre line of the maximum radiation zone in each hemisphere is shifted in summer towards the subtropics, the low pressure belt moves accordingly. The distribution of land masses and oceans in these latitudes determines the summer position of the maximum heating zone, especially in the northern hemisphere. There the highest temperatures are obtained over the land area of South-West Asia, shifting the centre of the zone to the Persian Gulf.

The air mass which is lifted to form the equatorial low-pressure belt divides in the upper atmosphere and flows towards the poles; it sinks back to earth between the latitudes 20° and 40° in winter, and in the 30–40° zone in summer according to the position of the sun. This elevates the air pressure in these regions, creating the subtropical high pressure zones. The polar high pressure regions result from the chilling of the lower air layers over the ice surface. The pressure difference between centres of high and low pressure also varies over the earth. According to Ashbel [1.1], the difference in winter between the low over southern Greenland and the high over eastern Russia is about 70 mm Hg while the low over the Mediterranean only differs from the high over Russia by 40 mm Hg.

Air flows from higher pressure to lower pressure zones. The permanent and semi-permanent regions of high pressure are sources of large masses of air which, because they remain for some time in a region under relatively constant conditions, acquire specific physical characteristics, considerably uniform within the mass, according to the nature of the surface on which they rest. The main regions of sufficient size and uniformity of conditions to generate such air masses are:

a. The polar regions (throughout the year)

b. The cold land masses of Asia, North Africa, Australia and North America (in winter)

c. The subtropical high pressure belt, particularly over the oceans (in summer).

The bodies of air may be therefore classified as "Polar" or "Tropical", and as "Continental" or "Maritime".

Air masses migrate from their high pressure sources towards the regions of low pressure. However, the flow is not in the direction of the greatest pressure gradient, at right angles to the lines of equal pressure (isobars), but is deflected by a phenomenon known as the Coriolis force, resulting from the rotation of the earth. For example, an air mass over the equator has the rotational velocity of the earth at this latitude, which is about 1670 km/h eastwards. When the air is set in motion due north this velocity is maintained, apart from a slight reduction by friction with the earth's surface. But as the rotational speed of the surface of the earth decreases with circumference towards the poles (at 30° latitude it is only 1120 km/h), the equatorial mass moves eastwards faster than the land beneath it, and this air appears to come from the south-west. Thus the original northerly direction undergoes an easterly deflection relative to the earth. This applies to all air masses moving northwards away from the equator. Similarly air moving towards the equator will undergo a relative westerly deflection.

Relative to the true air direction the deflection due to Coriolis force in the nothern hemisphere is to the right and in the southern hemisphere to the left. Thus, the pattern of divergence from high pressure centres is clockwise in the north and anticlockwise in the south; the convergence at low pressure centres follows the reverse pattern. The Coriolis force is zero at the equator and increases towards the poles; its magnitude is proportional to the sine of the latitude.

The wind systems

There are three global belts of winds in each hemisphere: the trade winds, the westerlies and the polar winds. In addition there are wind systems known as the monsoons which are the result of annual differences in heating of land and sea areas.

Local wind patterns occur over mountains and valleys and there are day and night breezes along shorelines [1.4].

The trade winds

The trade winds originate in the sub-tropical high pressure

regions of the two hemispheres and converge at the inter-tropical front forming the low-pressure equatorial belt. They flow to the south-west in the northern hemisphere and to the north-west in the southern hemisphere. The characteristics of the trade winds depend on the surface over which they travel. Over most of the oceanic surfaces the two air streams have a similar temperature and humidity so that only small disturbances are produced when they meet: here they travel with a constant direction and speed (15–35 km/h and up to 45 km/h). But over the Indian Ocean and the south-west Pacific the directions are reversed by the monsoons in the summer of each hemisphere. Complicated patterns and diversions are also obtained over land masses.

The westerlies

The westerlies also have their origin in the sub-tropical regions, but flow towards the sub-arctic low-pressure regions. Along the polar fronts the westerlies and the polar winds converge and because of the vast differences between the temperatures of the two air masses the fronts are very stormy. In the winter of the northern hemisphere the winds vary greatly in speed and direction, and form systems of travelling depressions. In summer, however, they are less variable and generally the air flow is to the north-east. In the southern hemisphere, which has much smaller land masses, the winds are more regular but here also the pattern at any one place is complicated by the travelling depressions.

The polar winds

The polar winds are formed by the cold air masses spreading out from the polar and arctic high-pressure regions. Their general direction is to the south-west in the northern hemisphere and north-west in the southern hemisphere.

The monsoon winds

The difference between the annual mean temperature patterns over land and sea produces the winter land winds and summer sea winds known as the monsoons. Their effect is greatest in the region of the Indian Ocean bounded by Australia, South Asia and East Africa. In this area the extremes of pressure are on the continents and air flows from the high pressure in one hemisphere to the low pressure in the other. In January the flow is from central Asia to Australia, in a south-west direction over southern Asia, and changes at the equator until a south-eastern direction is followed at the north-west coast of Australia. In June the flow is from Australia to the Indian Peninsula, in a north-west direction over Australia and north-east on reaching south Asia.

Land and sea breezes

During the day the air over land is heated more than that over sea surfaces on the same latitude. The warmer air rises and colder sea air flows inland. At night the process is reversed.

Winds generated in this way are known as breezes. As the temperature difference between land and sea is greater in the daytime than at night, the sea breeze overland is stronger than the land breeze to the sea. Breezes occur with greater strength and regularity where daily temperature patterns are regular, as in equatorial climatic regions. The distance of a place from the shore determines the time at which the sea breeze is felt there, this being later as the place is further from the sea. The breeze stops at about sunset and later at night the land breeze begins.

The land and sea breezes are modified by the global pressure and wind systems. For instance, when a depression covers the interior of a land mass in summer, air flow from the higher pressure over the sea by the western coast is facilitated and this coast may experience a strong sea breeze during the day; but at night the pressure overland is not increased sufficiently for more than a little air to move out to sea, so that any land breezes are very light.

Mountain and valley winds

In mountainous areas local thermal differences result in local wind patterns. The winds are shallow surface currents, directed up the mountain during the day and down at night, and are caused by the difference in temperature between air over the sun-lit slopes and the air at the same altitude over the valley. The air near to the mountain surface is heated more than the free atmosphere at the same height and so rises up. At night the process is reversed. In this way strong winds are generated in large mountain valleys, blowing up-valley in the daytime and down into the valley at night.

1.5. Atmospheric Humidity

The term atmospheric humidity refers to the water vapour content of the atmosphere. Water vapour enters the air by evaporation, primarily from the surfaces of the oceans but also from moist surfaces, vegetation and small water bodies. The vapour is carried and distributed over the earth's surface by the winds.

The air's capacity for water vapour increases progressively with its temperature, which is the principal determining factor. Therefore the vapour distribution over the earth is not uniform but is highest in the equatorial zones and decreases towards the poles, varying parallel with the pattern of annual solar radiation and temperature averages.

Table 1.III
Moisture potential capacity of air (after Ashbel)

Air temperature (°C)	Vapour pressure (mm Hg)	Absolute humidity (g/m³)	Specific humidity (g/kg)
−20	0·96	1·10	0·66
−10	2·15	2·38	1·64
0	4·58	4·85	3·77
5	6·54	6·81	5·41
10	9·21	9·42	7·53
15	12·79	12·85	10·46
20	17·54	17·32	14·35
25	23·76	23·05	19·51
30	31·82	30·40	26·23
35	42·18		
40	55·32		
45	71·79		
50	92·51		

The moisture content of the atmosphere can be expressed in several terms, such as the absolute humidity, specific humidity, vapour pressure and relative humidity. Absolute humidity is defined as the weight of water vapour per unit volume of the air (g/m³) and the specific humidity as the weight of water vapour per unit weight of air (g/kg). The vapour pressure of the air is the part of the whole atmospheric pressure that is due to the water vapour (mm Hg). When the air actually contains all the water vapour it can hold it is said to be saturated and its relative humidity is then 100%. When the actual vapour content is less than the potential content at the same temperature the relative humidity is less than 100%. Thus the relative humidity at any temperature is the ratio of the actual absolute humidity to the maximum moisture capacity of the air at that temperature (percent of the absolute saturation humidity).

Table 1.III gives the values of the vapour pressure (mm Hg), absolute humidity (g/m³) and specific humidity (g/kg) for saturated air at sea level (760 mm Hg), as functions of temperature [1.1].

From the physiological point of view, the vapour pressure of the air is the most convenient way by which to express the humidity conditions because the rate of evaporation from the body is proportional to the v.p. differences between the skin surface and the ambient air. On the other hand, the relative humidity affects the behaviour of many building materials and their rates of deterioration.

Both the vapour pressure and relative humidity vary greatly with the place and time. The vapour pressure ranges from very few mm Hg in the cold regions and desert to about 25 mm Hg and even over 30 mm Hg in very hot wet regions. In some mines, where wetting is used for dust suppression, it may be above 40 mm Hg.

The vapour pressure level is subject to wide seasonal variations and is usually higher in summer than in winter. Diurnal differences are small, although regions near the sea which experience diurnal alternations of sea and land breezes may have variations of a few mm Hg.

The reduction in vapour pressure with vertical height is faster than the reduction in air pressure so that the concentration of water vapour decreases with altitude and the vapour content of the upper air layers is lower than that nearer the ground. Any vertical mixing of the air therefore reduces the v.p. near the ground. As a result, the diurnal pattern of vapour pressure varies with the vertical air mixing.

Over land areas without sea breezes the vapour pressure reaches its highest level before noon; then strong convective currents start, causing vertical mixing and the v.p. near the ground is reduced. With the termination of these currents in the evening, the vapour pressure starts to rise again. Over water surfaces, and also in the rainy seasons over land, the diurnal pattern of vapour pressure follows that of the air temperature [1.1]. The greatest annual variations in the vapour pressure are found in regions under the influence of the monsoons; these receive hot humid air from the oceans and dry air from the inner continental areas.

The relative humidity may undergo wide variations even when the vapour pressure remains nearly constant. These are caused by the diurnal and annual changes in air temperature, which determine the potential moisture capacity of the air. Large diurnal variations in relative humidity are found mainly in the continental regions experiencing large diurnal temperature range. In such regions the relative humidity is very low in the early afternoon, when the temperature is maximum, while at night the air may be almost saturated.

1.6. Condensation and Precipitation

When air containing a given amount of water vapour is cooled, its moisture holding capacity is reduced, increasing the relative humidity until it becomes saturated. The temperature at which this air becomes saturated is known as the dew-point. The dew-point at a given atmospheric pressure depends only on the vapour pressure of the air. Any cooling below the dew-point causes the condensation of the vapour in excess of the air's capacity at the new lower dew-point.

Cooling of the air may be effected by three processes: contact with cooler surfaces, mixing with cooler air and expansion associated with rising air currents (adiabatic cooling). The first two processes result in dew and fog formation; the third is the one which can cause large-scale precipitation.

Dew and fog formation

Cooling by contact with colder surfaces is limited to the lower air layers. When condensation results it takes the form of dew on the cold surface. When the air not in direct contact with the cold surface is cooled below its dew-point, fog is formed. This cooling of the lower air layers can be caused by mixing with the lowest cold layer and by longwave radiation loss from the vapour molecules to the cooler ground. Fog can result also from the drainage of cold air into low-lying areas.

The conditions promoting the formation of fog are:

a. Cloudless sky, which promotes longwave radiation to outer space and cooling of the ground and the lower air layers

b. A temperature inversion near the ground, which prevents vertical mixing of the lower air with the upper layers

c. Absence of wind, which may also prevent heating of the lower air layer by vertical mixing.

Fog is thicker and more prevalent in valleys and topographical depressions where the colder, heavier air tends to collect. It frequently occurs in coastal regions with shore winds bringing moist air in contact with a colder land surface.

Precipitation

Large-scale cloud formation and precipitation result from adiabatic cooling of large air masses, and are affected greatly by the vertical stability of the air.

As air rises the pressure on it is reduced and it expands and cools. The energy required for the expansion is drawn from within the air mass, causing the cooling. The rate of cooling with ascent is constant at 10 deg C per 1000 metres (5·4 deg F per 1000 ft) as long as condensation does not take place, and is known as the "dry adiabatic rate". With the onset of condensation the heat liberated in the process reduces the cooling rate of the air mass. The retarded rate is known as the "wet adiabatic rate" and is not constant but depends on the air temperature. When the temperature is higher at the beginning of the condensation, more vapour is available for condensation and the rate is lower. At high temperatures the wet adiabatic rate is about 5·4 deg C per 1000 m (3·0 deg F per 1000 ft).

When the lapse rate within a mass of air is less than the wet adiabatic rate the air is absolutely stable; any air particle which rises is cooled adiabatically, thus becomes colder and more dense than the surroundings and sinks back to its original level.

If the lapse rate is between the wet and dry adiabatic rates, the air is in a state of conditional instability. When such an air mass is forced to rise (over mountains, etc.) it is cooled according to the higher dry adiabatic rate, and remains stable, as long as the altitude is below that at which condensation commences. But above the condensation level the air is cooled at the lower, wet adiabatic rate and at a certain point becomes warmer than the surroundings, and therefore unstable, continuing to rise without the original elevating force.

When the dry adiabatic rate is less than the lapse rate the air mass is absolutely unstable; any particle which rises (*e.g.* with a wind or through heating by sunlit ground) is cooled adiabatically to a temperature above the surrounding temperature, which varies according to the lapse rate. The particle therefore expands, becomes less dense and continues to rise.

A mass of rising air cools by expansion, eventually reaching its dew point. Then large scale condensation occurs, forming clouds composed of innumerable tiny water droplets and sometimes ice crystals. Heavier droplets begin to form as the air continues to rise and when they are large enough to fall and withstand the evaporative loss during the descent, then finally precipitation occurs.

Air masses which are made to rise for different reasons produce three main types of precipitation: convectional, orographic and convergent [1.5].

Convectional precipitation comes from ascending humid air masses, heated by contact with hot surfaces. The latent heat released when condensation begins reduces the rate of cooling with elevation and speeds up the ascent. This precipitation occurs mainly in tropical regions, during the afternoons of the hot season. It may also be caused by air masses of marine origin, advected by the winds towards land which is warmer in daytime than the sea surface. When a layer of warm air is covered by a mass of cold, dense air, the system is unstable and eventually overturning takes place. Then the warm moist air is lifted abruptly, expands, cools and releases its moisture as convectional precipitation.

Convectional rain usually falls in heavy showers of short duration. Orographic precipitation originates in air masses which are made to rise over mountain slopes by pressure gradients. As these approaching masses rise first over the stagnant air in front of the mountains, orographic rains may start before any abrupt rise in the land surface. The rainfall is greatest on the windward side of the mountain and diminishes beyond the ridge, resulting in more arid conditions there. In this way a mountain ridge may mark a sharp division between quite different climatic types.

Convergent precipitation occurs with the elevation of air in regions where air masses converge at low pressure zones or fronts. The rising air expands, cools and its moisture condenses to form clouds and then precipitates.

At the tropical front the two converging air streams have similar characteristics and their simultaneous ascent is rapid, resulting in showery rains. At the convergence front in the middle latitudes the two streams have different temperatures and the warmer air from the south-west rises above the colder air from the north-east. The slope of the ascent, and consequently the rate of elevation, is very small. The rain resulting from this slow ascent is gentle, widespread and of long duration [1.5].

Chapter 2

Elements of Heat Exchange between Man and his Thermal Environment

2.1. Outline of the Problem

The maintenance of thermal equilibrium between the human body and its environment is one of the primary requirements for health, well-being and comfort. It involves keeping the temperature of the core tissues of the body within a narrow range, regardless of the relatively wide variations in the external environment. The conditions under which such balance is achieved and the state of the body when it reaches equilibrium with the environment depend on the combined effect of many factors. Some of these are individual characteristics such as the activity, acclimatization, clothing, etc., of the subject and others are environmental factors, such as the air temperature, radiation, humidity and air motion.

The body produces energy from the food ingested by the process of metabolism at a rate which depends on its activity. When work is performed by the body only a small part of the energy is utilized for mechanical work and the rest is transformed into heat. This internal heat production should balance heat losses and gains to and from the environment, if stabilized inner body temperature is to be maintained. When this balance is not achieved, the temperature of the internal parts of the body rises or falls, as the heat loss is smaller or greater than the heat production, until stabilization is achieved at a new level or until the body collapses.

Heat exchange between the body and the environment takes place through convection and radiation exchanges with the ambient air and the surrounding surfaces, respectively. In addition, heat is lost from the body by the evaporation of sweat and water in the lungs. All these modes of heat exchange are governed by purely physical laws but several physiological mechanisms enable the body to regulate the rates of heat production and the methods of heat loss so that the equilibrium can be maintained. These mechanisms are

19

the rate and distribution of blood flow, the metabolic level and the rate of sweating, apart from the conscious adaptation of clothing to the environmental conditions. When the body is subjected to thermal stress, changes may occur in the levels of various physiological parameters, such as the skin temperature, body temperature, heart rate, sweat rate, etc., which serve to facilitate the achievement of thermal balance under the stress conditions and in extreme conditions reflect the inability of the body to fully achieve it.

The basic formula which describes the heat exchange between the body and the environment is:

$$M \pm R \pm C - E = Q$$

where M is the metabolic rate, R, C and E are the radiative, convective and evaporative heat exchanges respectively, and Q is the change in the heat content of the body, reflecting the variations in the average body temperature.

R, C and E are functions, on one hand, of the external environmental factors such as the temperature, velocity and vapour pressure of the air and the mean radiant temperature of the surroundings, and on the other hand of the temperature and vapour pressure of the skin. The quantities of radiation, convection and evaporation can be evaluated by the use of coefficients which are derived from various physiological and physical experiments, as will be discussed later on.

When the body is clothed the thermal exchange between it and the environment is modified by the properties of the clothing, which create a secondary environment to which most of the body is exposed. Although this secondary environment is affected by the external conditions, the exact nature of its dependence is complicated and not always known. For instance, a change in the external air motion will result in a change in the air flow underneath the clothing, but the relationship between the internal and external air flows is not necessarily linear. The pattern of this relationship will also be affected by other factors such as the properties of the clothing material and the design of the clothing, which may vary to a great extent.

A clearer understanding of the relationship between the factors determining heat exchange of the clothed body can be gained by dividing them into two groups: (a) the primary or independent factors, and (b) the secondary or dependent factors, as listed in Table 2.I.

Table 2.I

Factors affecting the heat exchange of the clothed body

Primary factors	Secondary factors
Metabolic rate	Clothing temperatures
Air temperature	Air motion beneath clothing
Mean radiant temperature	Skin temperature
Air motion	Sweat rate
Vapour pressure	Wetness of skin and clothing
Clothing type and materials fit	Cooling efficiency of sweating

Each one of the primary factors can vary independently of the others and usually these variations will cause changes in several of the secondary factors. For instance, a change in air velocity may affect air motion through and underneath the clothing, skin temperature, clothing temperatures, sweating, skin wetness and the cooling efficiency of sweating. In the present chapter the relationship between the body and the thermal environment will be analyzed from the point of view of the processes of heat exchange and the environmental factors involved. In subsequent chapters the physiological and sensory responses to thermal stress and the various methods of evaluation of the combined effect of the environmental factors (thermal indices) will be described.

2.2. Metabolic Heat Production

Metabolism is the process by which food matter combines in the body with oxygen and generates the energy required for the functions of various organs in the body, such as contraction of the muscles during work and the involuntary activity of the internal organs, blood circulation, breathing, internal secretion of glands and sweat formation, etc., and for building body tissues. Its rate is grossly proportional to the weight of the body. The level maintained at complete rest in a lying position is referred to as the basal metabolism, although the metabolic level is lowest during sleep.

When work is performed the metabolic rate is increased in order to provide the energy needed for the work. As the efficiency of the body as a "machine" is low, the amount of this energy produced by the body is much greater than the energy equivalent of the mechanical work performed and the excess is transformed into heat. The ratio of the mechanical work to the total additional energy produced by the body as a result of the activity is defined as the efficiency of the mechanical work. The efficiency depends on the type of activity and the training of the workers. It is lower for work done by the hands than for that done by the feet. Various sources [2.1, 2.2, 2.10] give different data about the efficiency of mechanical work, but an average of 20% seems to be suitable as a working value [2.8]. Muscular tension, even without movement, also increases the metabolic rate. Bruce [2.6] states that with complete relaxation the basal metabolism drops to about 20% below the standard level.

Table 2.II

Metabolic levels of various activities
(kcal/h (Btu/h))

Basal metabolism:	60–70 (240–280)
Sitting at rest:	90–100 (360–400)
Sedentary activity:	100–120 (400–480)
Walking on a level at 4 km/h:	210–270 (840–1080)
Walking on a level at 7 km/h:	300–400 (1200–1600)
Walking up 10% slope at 4 km/h:	340–480 (1360–1920)
Light industrial work:	150–300 (600–1200)
Moderate industrial work:	300–480 (1200–1600)
Heavy industrial work:	450–600 (1800–2400)
Very heavy work:	600–750 (2400–3000)

It is possible to compute the metabolic rate from measurements of the oxygen consumption of the body. Every litre of oxygen which is used in the metabolic process produces on average about 5 kilocalories, the exact amount being determined by the type of food oxidized. For a given level of activity the metabolic rate depends upon age, sex and the size and weight of the body. In order to eliminate variations due to the last two factors, the metabolism may be expressed per square metre of the surface area or per kg of the weight of the body. For an average man the values of 1·86 sq m (20 sq ft) for surface area or 70 kg weight are taken. Table 2.II gives some typical metabolic rates, average values from various sources, for adult men performing different activities, in kcal/h/man (in parentheses, in Btu/h/man).

2.3. Dry Heat Exchange by Convection and Longwave Radiation

When enclosed, the body exchanges heat with the ambient air by convection, and with the surrounding surfaces by longwave radiation. It may lose or gain heat by these channels depending on whether the environment is respectively colder or warmer than the body surface.

The convective heat exchange depends on the velocity of the ambient air. Customarily it is assumed to be proportional to the square root of the velocity although the exact relationship may depend on the clothing and a recent study [2.9] suggests that a power of 0·3 of the air velocity would be more applicable. Convection is assumed to be a linear function of the temperature difference between the air and the skin $(t_a - t_s)$ and radiation to be proportional to the difference between the fourth powers of the absolute temperatures of the surrounding surfaces and the skin $(T_w^4 - T_s^4)$. The skin temperature, however, is not constant but varies with changes in the environmental conditions; in cold conditions the skin temperature is higher than the air temperature while in hot conditions the gradient is reversed.

Exact determination of the convective and radiative heat exchanges under given conditions of air temperature, humidity, velocity, mean radiant temperature and clothing would require the estimation of the average skin temperature under these conditions; such estimation is possible using a suitable formula (see Section 3.4). But use can be made of the fact that at approximately 35°C (95°F) the average skin temperature equals the air temperature; below that level the skin temperature is higher than that of the air, and above it the skin temperature is the lower. For practical purposes, therefore, the convective and radiative heat exchanges can be computed as functions of the difference between 35°C (95°F) and the air and radiant temperatures respectively, by suitable adjustment of their coefficients.

The heat exchange of a clothed human body by convection and radiation depends on the clothing, as most of the heat exchange takes place at the external surface of the clothing and affects only indirectly the body itself.

For a man in an enclosed environment, where the temperature difference between the body and the surrounding surfaces is small, the heat exchange by radiation depends on the mean radiant temperature (M.R.T.) of the environment. The M.R.T. is the weighted average temperature of the surfaces surrounding the space, weighted according to the emissivities of the various surfaces (*see* Section 6.2) and the solid angle which they subtend at the subject. In practice the environment is very seldom homogeneous and in many cases there are great differences in the temperatures of the surfaces. Such conditions are found particularly in industrial buildings, but occur also in residential and office buildings heated by methods based on radiation or, in winter, near large glass areas. In these situations, therefore, the body may gain and lose radiant heat on different sides at the same time. Although the effect of such uneven heat exchange and the resulting skin temperatures on health and comfort is not fully known yet, the quantitative thermal exchange can be estimated by utilizing the concept of the M.R.T. Experimentally the M.R.T. of a given environment is estimated from measurements of the air velocity and the temperature of a Globe Thermometer. This instrument is an ordinary thermometer inserted inside a blackened copper sphere about 10–15 cm in diameter. When the Globe temperature (t_g or T_g) and the air velocity over it (v) are known, the M.R.T. of the environment can be computed according to either Bedford's or Belding's formula.

Bedford's formula [2.3] is (after simplification):

$$(\text{M.R.T.})^4 = T_g{}^4 + 1 \cdot 03 \times 10^{-8} \, V^{0 \cdot 5} \, (t_g - t_a)$$

where M.R.T. and T_g are given in absolute °F, t_g and t_a in °F and V in ft/min.

Belding's formula [2.5] is:

$$\text{M.R.T.} = t_g + 0 \cdot 24 \, V^{0 \cdot 5} \, (t_g - t_a)$$

where M.R.T., t_g and t_a are given in °C and V in m/sec.

For an unclothed body the general laws of convection and

radiation are valid and these two factors can be estimated separately, from measurements of average skin temperature, air temperature and velocity and the mean radiant temperature of the surrounding surfaces. However, the estimation is not accurate, because of the complicated geometry of the body and the large variations in surface temperature and wind speed over the body. The conditions are even more complicated for a clothed body. Here, there are three separate processes of heat exchange operating simultaneously: between the clothed parts of the body and the clothes, between the clothes and the environment and between the exposed parts of the body and the environment. The proportions of convection and radiation in each of these processes are different, as are the factors which have to be taken into account in the calculations. In considering the heat exchange between body and clothing, both the skin temperature and the temperature and velocity of the air between the skin and clothing (where the air is almost still), as well as the mean radiant temperature of the interior surface of the clothing, have to be taken into account. In the heat exchange between clothing and environment, the temperature of the external surface of the clothing (which is usually much closer to air temperature than that of the skin), the temperature and speed of the external air and the mean radiant temperature of the surrounding surfaces are involved. Similarly, suitable factors must be taken into account for the heat exchange between the exposed parts of the body and the environment.

In practice, it is almost impossible to estimate accurately the individual elements of heat exchange between the environment and the clothed body when the mean radiant temperature is close to air temperature, and separate measurements of the radiation and convection exchanges of a clothed body are largely unreliable. However, the total quantity of heat exchange by radiation and convection combined, or dry heat exchange (D) may be determined more simply and accurately. Dry heat exchange may be assumed to be a function of the environmental wind-speed and temperature (measured by means of a Globe Thermometer). The coefficients of dry heat exchange will vary with the type of clothing and may be determined experimentally from measurements of the weight loss at low humidity and constant activity, under different clothing conditions. If the level of humidity is low enough to eliminate its effect on the sweat rate, then the changes in weight loss reflect only the changes in the dry heat exchange.

When the body is inside an enclosure with surfaces differing appreciably in their temperature from that of the ambient air, or is exposed to solar radiation, it is subjected to radiant heat exchange beyond that encountered in a homogeneous environment. The additional radiant exchange depends on the clothing worn and the posture of the body with respect to the source of radiation. The radiant exchange under given conditions of clothing and posture can be assessed by observing the variations in the sweat rate, or evaporative rate, which are caused by variations in the mean radiant temperature of the enclosure, or in the intensity of solar radiation impinging on the body. This procedure is valid only under those conditions where all of the latent heat of vaporization is drawn from the body (100% sweating efficiency), as discussed in detail in the next section.

Several investigators have suggested formulae for the estimation of convective and radiative heat exchanges or, alternatively, for the combined dry heat exchange. Below are given for comparison one of each of these equations, expressed in the same system of units: heat exchanges (R, C and D) in kcal/h/man, air and radiant temperatures (t_a and t_g) in °C and air velocity (V) in m/sec.

Belding has suggested the following formulae for semi-nude men [2.5]:

$$R = 11 \ (t_w - 35)$$

(where $t_w = t_g + 0.24 \ V^{0.5} \ (t_g - t_a)$)

$$C = 1.0 \ V^{0.6} \ (t_a - 35)$$

For light clothing it was recommended that each of these coefficients be reduced by one-third.

Givoni and Berner-Nir [2.9] have suggested a procedure by which the combined dry heat exchange (D) by convection and radiation in a homogeneous environment can be computed, independently of the heat exchange with radiation sources at different temperatures from the air, according to the following formula:

$$D = \alpha V^{0.3} \ (t_a - 35)$$

where α is a coefficient depending on clothing as follows:

Semi-nude	= 15·8
Light summer clothing .	= 13·0
Industrial or military overall	= 11·6

Formulae for calculating the solar heat load, depending on clothing, posture, wind and the reflectivity of the terrain, are given in the section on the Index of Thermal Stress (*see* Section 5.6).

2.4. *Evaporative Heat Loss*

Every gram of water that is evaporated consumes in the process about 0·58 kcal (0·145 Btu), the latent heat of vaporization. When evaporation takes place in the lungs or in the pores of the skin all this heat is taken from the body. Thus the body can lose great quantities of heat even when the ambient air and mean radiant temperatures are above the skin temperature. Under certain conditions, however, the actual cooling obtained by the body as a result of evaporation of a given amount of sweat is not equal to the latent heat of the sweat, as part of the heat of vaporization may be taken from the ambient air and not from the body, so reducing the cooling efficiency of the evaporation process. The ratio of the heat removed from the body by evaporation to the potential cooling of the evaporation is defined as the physical efficiency of sweat evaporation. Of more significance from the physiological viewpoint is the ratio of the heat removed from the body to the potential cooling of the sweat secreted: the physiological efficiency of sweat secretion.

The cooling efficiency of sweat secretion and evaporation depends on the rate and place of the evaporation process. When the evaporation is rapid compared with the sweat secretion, it takes place on the skin surface or even inside its pores. In this case almost all of the latent heat of vaporization is drawn from the body, since conditions are far more favourable for heat flow by conduction from the skin to the external surface of the thin layer of liquid than for flow from the external air. In contrast, the formation of a thicker layer of liquid and sweat drops on the skin surface, especially on the body hair, builds up higher resistance to heat flow from the body to the surface of evaporation, and a certain quantity of heat may be drawn from the surrounding air, reducing the actual cooling received by the body.

In the latter case, if the quantity of sweat increases relative to its evaporation, some of the sweat is transferred to the clothing and evaporates there. In these circumstances, heat flow to the surface of evaporation is easier from the external air than from the skin surface and the cooling efficiency of the evaporation undergoes a considerable reduction.

The factor determining the rate and place of evaporation is the ratio of the amount of evaporated sweat (e) to the maximum evaporative capacity of the air (E_{max}), i.e. e/E_{max} [2.7]. As the ratio e/E_{max} increases, the surface of evaporation is removed further from the skin surface and the cooling efficiency decreases. Alternatively, it is possible to express the cooling efficiency of sweating as a function of the ratio between the overall heat stress operating on the body (metabolic heat production $\pm$ the heat exchange), which is equal to the required evaporative cooling (E), to the potential evaporative cooling of the environment (E_{max}). The evaporative potential depends on the clothing and on the levels of ambient vapour pressure and wind velocity. The lower the vapour pressure and the higher the air velocity, the greater the evaporative potential. Clothing reduces the air velocity and increases the humidity over the skin and thus reduces the evaporative cooling potential for the body. Although the total evaporation from the body-clothing combination may not be decreased, the reduced evaporation directly on the skin reduces the net cooling obtained by the body.

Several formulae have been suggested for the computation of the maximum evaporative capacity of the air (in kcal/h/man) as a function of the air velocity (in m/sec) and vapour pressure (in mm Hg). Two of these are given below.

The formulae suggested by Belding [2.5] according to clothing are:

$$\text{Semi-nude: } E_{max} = 2 \cdot 0 \ V^{0 \cdot 6} \ (42 - VP_a)$$
$$\text{Light clothing: } E_{max} = 1 \cdot 33 \ V^{0 \cdot 6} \ (42 - VP_a)$$

and that put forward by Givoni and Berner-Nir [2.9] is:

$$E_{max} = pV^{0 \cdot 3} \ (42 - VP_a)$$

where p is a coefficient related to the clothing as follows:

Semi-nude . . . . . . 31·6
Light summer clothing . . 20·5
Industrial and military overalls 13·0

It should be emphasized that E_{max} in the last formulae refers to the maximum body cooling obtainable from the evaporation and not to the sweat evaporated. Therefore the values are usually lower than those obtained from measurement of the total evaporation.

The cooling efficiency of sweating (f) can be computed according to the formula suggested by Givoni and Berner-Nir [2.9]:

$$f = e^{0·6 \ (E/E_{max} - 0·12)}$$

where e is the base of the natural logarithms and E is the total heat load $(M \pm C \pm R)$. Further discussion of this subject is given in the section on the Index of Thermal Stress (see Section 5.6).

Chapter 3

Physiological and Sensory Responses to Thermal Stress

Man's thermoregulation is a complex system of autonomic and voluntary responses, which govern the rate of heat loss from the body and, in some cases, the heat production as well. Although heat exchange at the body surface depends on the physical factors of temperature and vapour pressure differences between the skin and the environment, the body can control it by dynamic regulation of the various physiological systems and behavioural patterns.

Thermal stress is manifested in several physiological and sensory responses which reflect the strain imposed on the body to maintain thermal balance under stress conditions, or are caused by the discrepancy between the rates of heat production and heat loss. The main physiological responses are these: the circulatory regulation (vasomotor regulation and pulse rate), change in skin temperature and inner-body temperature and weight loss (sweat rate). The main sensory responses are the thermal sensation (feeling of warmth) and the feeling of skin wetness (sensible perspiration).

Although all these responses are affected by changes in the environmental conditions and rate of physical activity, they do not respond in the same way to the various changing factors. Some are more sensitive to internal heat stress (metabolic rate) and others to environmental stress; some are more affected by humidity and others by temperature, etc. In this chapter, the magnitude and pattern of change with both the duration and the severity of the exposure will be discussed. Where methods are available for the prediction of the expected level of a physiological parameter under given conditions of the thermal environment and metabolic rate they will be described.

PHYSIOLOGICAL RESPONSES

3.1. Circulatory Regulation

Introduction

Starting from the neutral point of comfortable conditions, the first physiological mechanism which is activated to adjust the rate of heat loss to variations in the external thermal environment is the regulation of the blood flow in the peripheral layer of the body, the subcutaneous layer. This system is the vasomotor regulation control.

Beneath the skin there is a network of fine blood vessels; the rate of blood flow in the peripheral layer is controlled by the size of these vessels. By means of the vasomotor regulation system, the body is able to dilate them (vaso-dilatation) or to constrict them (vaso-constriction) and in this way to augment or restrict the blood flow in the subcutaneous layer.

The blood, being composed mainly of water, has both a high heat capacity and a high thermal conductivity. Because of its high heat capacity, it may carry and transfer large quantities of heat through small changes in its temperature. Increased peripheral blood flow by vaso-dilation brings to the skin larger quantities of heat from the body core, while vaso-constriction reduces this heat transfer. Lee [3.14] has given the range of the total cutaneous blood flow to be from 0·16 litre/m^2/min for a man under vaso-constriction, to 2·2 litre/m^2/min under full vaso-dilatation. The thermal resistance of the subcutaneous layer also depends on its blood content. The subcutaneous tissue, being rich in fat, is a poor heat conductor; when the blood content of this layer is increased, its thermal conductivity is augmented greatly because of the high conductivity of the blood, and more heat can flow through it by conduction. Therefore, by means of the vasomotor regulation, both the resistance of the subcutaneous layer to heat flow across it by conduction and the rate of convective heat transfer through the blood from the body core to the skin can be controlled. Under exposure to mild heat stress the peripheral circulation is the primary mechanism involved in the maintenance of adequate heat flow from the body core to the skin, where it is dissipated to the environment.

The total heat flow (by convection and conduction) from the

body core to the skin, divided by the gradient between the body core temperature and the average skin temperature, is defined as the thermal conductance of the peripheral tissues. It is low under exposure to cold and high under exposure to heat.

When the body is exposed to a cold environment the reduced heat transfer from the body core to the surface due to the vaso-constriction causes a reduction in the skin temperature, especially at the extremities, and so the heat loss from the skin to the environment is reduced. The lower peripheral conductance under vaso-constriction enables the body to prevent excessive heat loss and a fall of the inner body temperature, in spite of the greater thermal gradient between the core and the skin resulting from the lower skin temperature. At the same time the lower skin temperature reduces heat flow from the skin to the external environment.

On the other hand, when the body is exposed to a hot environment, vaso-dilatation increases the convective heat transfer from the body core to the surface and raises the skin temperature. This increases the heat loss to the environment by convection and radiation. The higher conductance of the peripheral layer under vaso-dilatation enables the required heat flow from the body core to the skin to be maintained in spite of the smaller temperature difference.

The higher cutaneous blood flow causes compensatory adjustments in the circulation [3.14, 3.15]. The adjustments include:

a. A reduction in the blood flow to internal organs, such as the kidneys, which is achieved by vaso-constriction of the blood vessels of these organs.

b. An increase in the volume of the circulating blood, which occurs during exposure to heat. This adjustment is achieved by utilizing blood reservoirs in the body to increase and decrease the circulating volume according to the environmental conditions and the activity.

The increased blood flow through the skin is accompanied by a rise in the overall blood circulation, which is reflected by a higher heart rate. An increase in heart rate may be caused both by a higher environmental heat stress and by a higher metabolic rate, and thus is an indicator of the total demand on the circulatory system imposed by the work and heat load. When work is performed, the blood flow is increased mainly to supply the additional oxygen requirements of the muscles, but a further increase is necessary to augment the heat flow from the inner parts of the body to the skin. As well as responding to the metabolic and thermal factors, the heart rate is also sensitive to the emotional state of the individual.

Heart rate is one of the principal physiological control mechanisms enabling adjustment of the oxygen supply and heat loss to different, and variable, conditions of work, climate and clothing. It is also one of the main indicators of thermal and metabolic stress and may serve as a criterion for safe limits of work under heat stress and for the required frequency and duration of rest periods.

Heart rate response to various work levels and environmental heat stress has been studied in numerous experiments [3.6, 3.7, 3.9, 3.17, 3.18]. A predictive formula has been developed by Givoni [3.6] for the heart rate after 30 min of exposure to a constant condition, but this formula does not include any effects of clothing nor does it predict the pattern of heart rate with time during work or during recovery.

In a recent study by Givoni and Goldman a comprehensive dynamic (time function) formula has been developed for the heart rate response of reasonably fit, young men to the combined effects of the environmental conditions, the work load as expressed by the metabolic rate, and the thermal properties of the clothing [3.7c, 3.7d).

Prediction of heart rate

The prediction of the heart rate pattern proceeds in three stages:

i. In the first stage, a heart rate index, I_{HR}, is computed.
ii. Based on the heart rate index the final, equilibrium, heart rate is computed.
iii. Finally, the time pattern of the heart rate is computed for any sequence of work and rest periods, taking into account the corresponding environmental conditions.

The heart rate index

The heart rate index, I_{HR}, expresses the total load on the heart rate. It takes into account the metabolic rate, environmental conditions and clothing worn. The formula of I_{HR} is:

$$I_{HR} = 0 \cdot 4M + (2 \cdot 5/\text{clo})(T_a - 36) + 80 \exp(0 \cdot 0047(E_{req} - E_{max})). \quad (1)$$

where:

M = metabolic rate, watts

clo = thermal resistance of clothing, clo units

T_a = air temperature, °C

E_{req} = the total thermal load, by metabolism and environment;

$= M \pm (R+C)$, watts   (2)

$(R+C) = (11·6/\text{clo})(T_a-36)$; watts/°C-man   (3)

E_{max} = evaporative capacity of the environments

$= 25·5 (\text{im/clo})(44-P_a)$; watts/mm Hg-man   (4)

im/clo = evaporative coefficient of clothing

P_a = vapour pressure of the ambient air, mm Hg.

The final heart rate

The relationship between the heart rate index and the equilibrium heart rate HR_f involves two regions; up to a given limit the relationship is linear, while above this limit it is exponential.

In consequence, two predictive formulae have been developed for the equilibrium heart rate (HR_f) according to the computed range of I_{HR}; with I_{HR} below 225, a linear relationship between final heart rate and rectal temperature has been assumed, and for I_{HR} above 225 an exponential relationship. The predictive formulae thus derived are:

$$\text{for } 0 < I_{HR} < 225: \ HR_f = 65 + 0·35(I_{HR}-25) \qquad (5)$$

$$\text{for} \quad I_{HR} > 225: \ HR_f = 135 + 0·42$$
$$\times [1-\exp 0·01(-(I_{HR}-225))] \quad (6)$$

Should I_{HR} be lower than 25, which could occur if this model is used in cold environments, HR_f is assumed constant at 65 beats/min.

Time patterns of heart rate

The time pattern of elevation in heart rate upon exposure to metabolic and/or heat stress depends on the level of the total stress and whether the subjects are at rest or at work. Under work conditions, the greater the stress (i.e. the higher the equilibrium heart rate) the longer it takes to reach the final level. One feature of the change from sitting at rest to a work condition is the instantaneous initial elevation in the heart rate while the subject rises and anticipates work. Taking this feature into account, it was found possible to express the time pattern for heart rate during work ($HR_{t(w)}$) as:

$$HR_{t(w)} = 65 + (HR_f - 70) 1 - 0.8 \exp[-(6 - 0.03 (HR_f - 65)t)] \quad (7)$$

and the time pattern for heart rate at rest ($HR_{t(r)}$) is given by:

$$HR_{t(r)} = 65 + (HR_f - 65)(1 - e^{-3t}) \quad (8)$$

where:

HR_f = equilibrium heart rate given by equations (5) or (6)
65 = assumed heart rate (beats/min) at rest in comfortable conditions
t = time in hours.

The Time Pattern During Recovery: After cessation of work, heart rate decreases towards the equilibrium resting level appropriate to the given climatic and clothing conditions. The rate of decrease, however, is not constant but depends upon the total elevation of the heart rate above its resting level and also upon the cooling power of the environment (CP). The effect of the magnitude of heart rate elevation on the rate of its decline can be expressed by an exponential factor k, and the effect of the available cooling power by a factor b. The larger the cooling power (by convection and evaporation combined) the more rapid the decline in heart rate. Mathematically, this time pattern for heart rate during recovery, $HR_{t(rec)}$, can be expressed as:

$$HR_{t(rec)} = HR_w - (HR_w - HR_r) e^{-kbt} \quad (9)$$

where:

HR_w = heart rate at the end of the work period
HR_f = equilibrium heart rate for resting at the given climatic and clothing conditions, by formula 3 or 4
$k = 2 - 0.1 (HR_w - HR_r)$ (10)
$b = 2.0 + 12(1 - e^{-0.3CP})$ (11)
CP = index of the cooling power of the environment
$\quad = 0.27$ (im/clo) $(44 - P_a) + (0.174/clo)(36 - t_a) - 1.57$

$$(12)$$

Correspondence Between Predicted and Measured Heart Rates: The validity of the prediction model for the heart rate was examined by computing the time pattern of heart rate for a variety of combinations of environmental conditions, work level and clothing, which were investigated in experimental studies, and comparing the predicted patterns with those observed in the experiments.

Figure 3.1 (top left) [3.7c] shows the average heart rate of 24 subjects, walking for 100 min on a level treadmill at 1·56 m/s. The environmental conditions were: air temperature 49°C, R.H. 20%, air velocity 1·4 m/s and the subjects were clad only in shorts. The remaining parts of Fig. 3.1 show predicted and measured heart rate

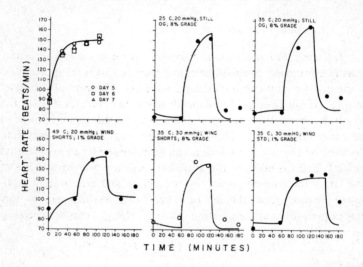

Fig. 3.1.

patterns from another study under a wide range of work, environmental and clothing conditions. The experiments included, in each 3 hour exposure, a rest period of 60 min, work of 30–90 min, and recovery for 30–90 min. The work consisted of walking on a treadmill at 1·34 m/s at 1% or 8% grade; clothing included shorts, standard fatigues (STD) or protective overgarments over the fatigues (OG); air temperature was 25, 35 òr 49°C, vapour pressures 10, 20 or 30 mm Hg and air velocity 0·7 or 4·0 m/s. It can be seen that there is good agreement between the predicted patterns and the measured values.

Figure 3.2 [3.7c] shows experiments where the work-rest pattern was more complicated. In one test, subjects dressed in a long-sleeved shirt and trouser fatigue uniform, worked for 50 min, rested 15 min and worked again for 50 min at 35°C with 70% R.H. and 0·7 m/s air motion. The work consisted of walking a 1·16 m/s on a level treadmill with 26 kg of load ($M = 350$ watts). The results during the

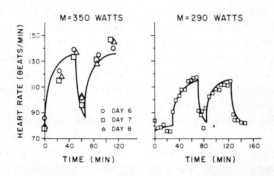

Fig. 3.2.

last 3 days of an 8 day acclimatization are shown in Fig. 3.2 (left). In a second test, 6 of these subjects sat under these same conditions for 30 min, walked (without load; $M = 290$ watts) for 40 min, rested for 15 min, walked again for 40 min and finally rested for 20 min. The results are presented in Fig. 3.2 (right). Again a good agreement for the entire time pattern is shown between predicted and the frequent measured values.

3.2. Sweating

The regulation of the evaporative cooling by sweating is the principal mechanism of thermal adjustment both in hot conditions, and when working in a comfortable environment.

Evaporation from the body takes place in two forms:
a. Passive water loss from the lungs and the skin
b. Active sweating by secretion of the sweat glands.

Passive water loss from the skin is a diffusion process and is caused by the vapour pressure difference between the body and the ambient air. Water loss from the lungs depends on the ambient vapour pressure and on the rate of breathing, which in turn depends mainly on the metabolic rate and oxygen requirements. The combined water loss by these two processes is termed "insensible perspiration". It is almost unaffected by the ambient temperature. When at rest a man evaporates about 40 g/h by these processes. Insensible perspiration cannot be considered as a regulating mechanism on exposure to external heat stress, although the evaporation in the lungs automatically increases in approximate proportion with the internal heat production. On the other hand, it decreases with the elevation of the ambient vapour pressure, in contradiction to the physiological requirements.

Active sweating starts when the dry heat loss by convection and radiation, plus the loss by insensible perspiration, falls below the rate of heat production. Sweat is secreted by special glands, the eccrine sweat glands, which lie deep in the skin and are distributed over almost the entire body; it is a very dilute solution, of over 99% water, the principal solute being sodium chloride. According to Leithead and Lind [3.15] the sweat glands, on subjection to heat stress, are activated by the sympathetic nerves. There are two control mechanisms: stimulus from the peripheral receptors for heat and that from the thermoregulation centre in the hypothalamus (in the brain).

A given peripheral stimulus will thus evoke a greater sweat secretion when the hypothalamus temperature is raised (for instance, as a result of physical activity). The sweat glands can be activated not only by heat and work, but also by psychological stimuli, especially those located on the palms of the hands and soles of the feet, the face and the chest.

For men working in the heat, the sweating rate may be about 1 litre per hour. For hard work in a very hot environment the sweat rate may reach about 2·5 l/h but such a rate can only be sustained for about half an hour [3.5]. Several investigators [3.22, 3.28] have observed a reduction in sweat rate after about two hours of exposure to work in the heat. The following maximal rates were observed by Wyndham [3.28] after each hour of exposure, in experiments lasting for five hours:

Hour of exposure	1st	2nd	3rd	4th	5th
Sweat rate (g/h)	1130	1130	870	600	485

In the experiments by Sargent *et al.* [3.22] hourly sweat rates were measured during six 1-hour periods of tread-mill marching. In one case the subjects drank freely and in a second case drinking was restricted. Their results are summarized below:

	Hour of exposure	1st	2nd	3rd	4th	5th	6th
S.R., (g/h)	Free drinking	420	680	680	600	550	610
	Restricted drinking	360	600	600	550	500	600

The greater the temperature of the skin or internal body, the more the sweat glands are stimulated to pour out their secretion.

The activity starts, under rest and light clothing conditions, when the air temperature is about 25°C. An increase in the metabolic rate lowers the temperature at which the sweat glands are activated. When the evaporative capacity of the air is high enough to evaporate the sweat in the pores of the skin, the skin remains dry and the increased sweating is not felt at all. In this way the sweat rate may reach quite high levels without being noticed, and can be detected only by weighing. During work in the heat great quantities of water are removed from the body by sweat secretion. This causes diminution of the circulating blood volume, which if not replaced by sufficient fluid intake will bring the body to a state of dehydration. The diminished blood volume may impair the heat transfer from the interior of the body to the skin, resulting in a sharp rise in body temperature. The rate of sweating is controlled by the need to prevent excessive rise in body temperature as far as possible and this occurs despite, or at the expense of, other body needs. Diminished urine formation and a highly concentrated urine results from the circulating fluid being deviated from the kidneys to the sweat glands. Dehydration is characterized by thirst, fatigue, giddiness and, in advanced stages, may even cause death [3.15]. Voluntary under-drinking under heat stress conditions leads to voluntary dehydration. Under special circumstances, such as in the case of young people who wanted to demonstrate their endurance during marches in the heat (in Israel) voluntary dehydration produces fatal results. Even thirst is not always strong enough to induce sufficient drinking, so that the need for education of the public on the need for ample drinking in the heat cannot be over-emphasized.

The loss of salts, if the diet does not contain enough of them, may cause depletion of extracellular sodium and result in heat cramps [3.16]. This possibility was considered a major danger until recent years and special salt tablets were given to soldiers and workers in hot environments. Recent studies by Sohar et al. [3.23] suggest, however, that in practice the hazards of salts depletion were over-estimated.

Another danger of high and prolonged sweating is the fatigue of the sweat glands, which may cause inadequate sweating even without dehydration.

Sweat rate (indicated by weight loss) can be used as a good criterion for the evaluation of the combined effect of heat and work in people who are acclimatized to work in the heat and are well hydrated. Even in this case its reliability as an index of the physiological strain is limited to conditions of moderate stress, associated with a weight loss of not more than about 1000 g/h during short exposures (up to 2 hours) and of an average of about 800 g/h for longer exposures. In more severe conditions the elevation of the sweat rate is rather small and not sufficient for the maintenance of thermal equilibrium, while the body temperature and pulse rate may rise to dangerous levels.

As the results obtained by Wyndham and those by Sargent et al., mentioned above, lead to contradictory conclusions on the change in sweat rate with exposure time, it seems that more research is needed to clarify the form of this pattern and its relation to metabolic and environmental conditions.

There are two methods available for computing the expected weight loss under exposure to different combinations of work, clothing and environmental conditions. The $P._4S.R.$ index [3.18] and the Index of Thermal Stress [3.6] give similar predictions, but the latter is applicable to a wider range of metabolic rates.

3.3. Inner Body Temperature Response to Work, Environmental Conditions and Clothing

While the blood circulation and sweating are active mechanisms of thermoregulation, the body temperature is a passive response to heat stress, mainly metabolic, and is determined on the one hand by the rate of heat production and on the other hand by the interplay between the rates of heat transfer from the body core to the skin, and from the skin to the environment. Normal body temperatures (measured as rectal and oral temperatures) at rest and in comfortable environments are relatively constant, when the rectal temperature is about 37°C (98·6°F) and oral temperature about 36·7°C (98·1°F). The body temperature varies during the day, having a minimum early in the morning and a maximum late in the evening. The diurnal range is about 0·6°C. Individual variations of $\pm 0\cdot 3$ deg C and more are not uncommon. During physical exertion the body temperature rises, as a result of the additional heat production in the working muscles, and stabilizes at a new, higher level, mainly dependent on the metabolic rate.

The effect of environmental conditions on rectal temperature has been the subject of many studies, which were summarized by Minard and Copman [3.19]. They concluded that, under mild environmental conditions and with a constant metabolic rate, the rectal temperature is not affected by changes in the environmental temperature. This they explained to be the result of the increase in sweat rate, which compensated the body fully for the additional environmental heat load. In hot conditions, however, rectal temperature was found in several investigations to be affected significantly by the environmental heat stress.

In a study by Robinson [3.21] of men working at a constant metabolic rate of 190 kcal/m² h, rectal temperature was elevated sharply with the increase of air temperature and humidity above 33°C, at 60% relative humidity, and above 38°C, at 30% R.H., while there was only a very slight response to environmental stress below this level. Experimental studies by Givoni and Berner-Nir [3.6] and an analysis of the results of Wyndham's [3.28] work, suggest that rectal temperature is always affected slightly by the environment, even under "comfortable" conditions, and that the relation between rectal temperature and the ambient conditions depends on the metabolic rate and the cooling efficiency of sweating.

Givoni and Goldman [3.7a, 3.7b, 3.7d] have developed a biophysical model which predicts the dynamic variations in the inner body temperature, as measured by the rectal temperature, as a function of the physical activity level (metabolic rate), the environmental conditions and the thermophysical properties of the clothing.

The model includes two basic components. The first is the equilibrium, "final", rectal temperature and the second is the dynamic pattern of approaching the equilibrium level.

Theoretically, for any combination of metabolic rate, environment and clothing, there must be some internal body temperature and corresponding skin temperature, which will allow elimination of the metabolic heat. In reality, of course, such temperature may be beyond the limit of human endurance, with collapse or death occurring before this theoretical equilibrium body temperature is attained. Even so, this theoretical equilibrium temperature will determine the rate of rise in the core temperature, and hence the tolerance time.

Factors affecting the "equilibrium" rectal temperature

The equilibrium rectal temperature depends on the metabolic heat production and the environmental heat load, which, in turn, depends on the heat exchange with the environment, as affected by the clothing properties.

In numerous studies it has been observed that rectal temperature rises with the metabolic rate and that this elevation was higher as the environmental temperature and humidity were higher. Therefore, it has been assumed that the effects on the equilibrium rectal temperature of all the factors enumerated in the theoretical analysis given above can be grouped into three components: (1) the direct effect of the metabolic heat production; (2) the direct effect of the environmental heat exchange; and (3) the effect of the total metabolic plus environmental heat load in relation to the evaporative capacity of the environment.

Metabolic heat load

The total energy production · is the source of internal heat generation. However, when the body produces net external work, *e.g.* when a weight is lifted, whether external load or the weight of the body itself, that part of the energy transformed into external work is not converted into heat, in accordance with the law of energy conservation. It is possible to directly convert the external work (in kg-m/min) into its heat equivalent (in watts). The difference gives the amount of metabolic energy ultimately transformed into heat. The external work W_{ex} (watts) performed while walking at a speed v (m/s), up grade G (%) for a total mass m_t (kg) is:

$$W_{ex} = 0·098\, m_t \times v \times G \qquad (13)$$

Therefore, the metabolic heat load is the total metabolic rate (M) minus the energy converted into external work in grade walking, or:

$$M_{net} = M - (0·098\, m_t \times v \times G) \qquad (14)$$

M can be computed for any given conditions of total mass of body weight, W, and load carried, L (in kg), speed of walking (v, in m/s) and grade (G, in %), according to the formula:

$$M = (W+L)\,[(2+1·5\,v^2)+0·3\,vG] \qquad (15)$$

The environmental heat load by convection and longwave radiation

The environmental heat load $(R+C)$ has been assumed to be proportional to the difference between the ambient temperature, T_a (in a homogeneous environment) and 36°C, which is approximately the crossover point between skin and air temperatures. It is inversely proportional to the total thermal resistance of the clothing system (clo); this depends on the clothing type and is a function of both subject motion and air speed. The formula used for the computation of the environmental heat exchange for an average man with a surface area of 1·8 m² is [3.7b]:

$$(R+C) = (11·6/\text{clo})\,(T_a - 36); \text{ W/°C-man} \qquad (16)$$

Required evaporative cooling: The required evaporative cooling (E_{req}), which of course equals the total heat load, is obtained by combining the two previous formulas ((15) and (16)), *i.e.*

$$E_{req} = (M_{net}) + (R+C) \qquad (17)$$

Evaporative capacity: The evaporative capacity of the environment has been assumed to be proportional to the difference between the vapour pressure of the air (P_a) and the vapour pressure of the skin, which is 44 mm Hg assuming a skin temperature of 36°C. It is also proportional to the permeability index of the clothing (im/clo), which depends on the clothing type and air speed. The evaporative capacity for an average man of 1·8 m^2 surface can be expressed by the formula:

$$E_{max} = 25·5 \, (im/clo) \, (44 - P_a); \; W/mm \; Hg\text{-}man \qquad (18)$$

The values of im/clo for different clothing types and various wind speeds were obtained from measurements on a static wetted copper manikin.

When the ambient vapour pressure is greater than 44 mm Hg then condensation occurs on the body surface. This latent heat of condensation is added to the total heat load.

The "effective" wind speed

When people are engaged in physical work, like walking, their movements produce an air flow, in addition to the ambient air speed. As a first approximation in view of the absence of quantitative information on this subject, it has been assumed in the model that the air flow produced by the movements of the body is proportional to the excess of the metabolic level above the resting level. Therefore, the effective air speed (V_{eff}) produced by work was estimated by computing a coefficient that would fit both the still air and wind conditions. The estimate obtained in this way is:

$$V_{eff} = V_{air} + 0·004 \, (M - 105); \; m/s \qquad (19)$$

The "effective" values of clo and im, for the various clothing systems, have been expressed as functions of corrected air speed.

The equilibrium body temperature

Using the effective air speed (V_{eff}) and the modified thermophysical properties of clothing, the coefficients of the predictive formula for the equilibrium rectal temperature have been estimated, yielding the formula:

$$T_{ref} = 36·75 + 0·004 \, (M - W_{ex}) + (0·025/clo) \, (T_a - 36)$$
$$+ 0·8 \exp [0·0047 \, (E_{req} - E_{max})] \quad (20)$$

The time pattern of the rectal temperature

Time Pattern at Rest Under Heat Stress Conditions: When climatic conditions are changed during rest, there is an appreciable time lag in the initiation of any detectable change in rectal temperature. The rate of change is slow at first, then accelerates and finally diminishes while approaching the new equilibrium level. It has been found that this complex pattern can be expressed by the following formula, which involves a double exponential:

$$\text{Resting } T_{re_t} = T_{re_0} + (\Delta T_{re})\,(0\cdot1)\exp\left[0\cdot4^{(t-0\cdot5)}\right] \qquad (21)$$

where:

T_{re_t} = rectal temperature at any time t

T_{re_0} = initial rectal temperature (°C)

ΔT_{re} = difference between the new final equilibrium rectal temperature (T_{re_t}) in the new environment and T_{re_0}

= time (h), with $t - 0\cdot5$ allowing 30 min for the initial lag in resting rectal temperature change.

Pattern of Elevation During Work: During work the following general equation could fit the patterns observed:

$$\text{working } T_{re_t} = T_{re_0} + \Delta T_{re}\left[1 - \exp\left(-k\,(t - t_d)\right)\right] \qquad (22)$$

where:

T_{re_t} = rectal temperature at any time t after beginning work (h), °C

k = time constant (°C/h) $\varepsilon\,2 - 0\cdot5\,(\Delta T_{re})$

t_d = time lag (h) for work induced rectal temperature change, $t_d = (58/m)$, h.

Recovery Time Pattern of Rectal Temperature After Work: During the recovery after work the metabolic rate is again relatively constant, about 105 W. The rate of recovery depends, however, on the level of rectal temperature reached by the end of work. In fact, because of the inertia of the body, rectal temperature may continue to rise during the initial phase of recovery. The time lag in the body cooling, as well as the time constant of the decline in rectal temperature, depends on the combined dry and evaporative effective cooling power for the environment–clothing combination during recovery (CP_{eff}). If the environmental heat load increases and the evaporative capacity is decreased, the time lag is longer and the time constant decreases. However, even if the skin is completely wet at the end of work, the relative importance of the evaporative capacity is smaller than that of the dry heat exchange, since the sweat rate decreases during the recovery period; thus, the actual evaporative cooling perhaps averages only 70% of the evaporative capacity. It is possible to describe the pattern of recovery by the formula:

$$\text{recovery } T_{re_t} = T_{re_w} - (T_{re_w} - T_{re_r}) [1 - \exp(-\alpha(t - t_{d_{rec}}))] \quad (23)$$

where:

T_{re_w} = rectal temperature at the beginning of decrease (°C) (note, not necessarily equal to T_{re} at the end of work; *see* below)

T_{re_r} = equilibrium resting rectal temperature (°C)

α = time constant of recovery

$t_{d_{rec}}$ = time lag of recovery.

Validation of the predictive formulas

To validate the prediction formulas, independent experimental series have been carried out, with a wider range of environmental and metabolic conditions. In addition, the experimental results from several previous studies were compared with the predicted results using the given metabolic environmental and clothing conditions, in accordance with the above formulas.

Figures 3.3 and 3.4 [3.7b] show some results from experiments comprising cycles of rest, work and recovery. In the experiments shown in Fig. 3.3 the total time was three hours with a rest of 60 min, work for 0·5, 1·0 or 1½ hours and recovery for the rest of the experimental time. The experiments were conducted under a variety of work, climate and clothing conditions. In the experiments shown in Fig. 3.4 two groups of subjects worked for 25 min, in hot, dry environments. The first group then recovered in the hot room while the second group recovered in a comfortable room.

It can be seen that even for such complex patterns of activity and environments the biophysical model can predict with reasonable accuracy the patterns of the changes in the rectal temperature.

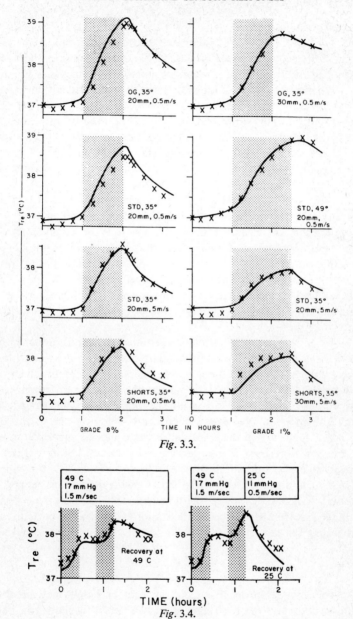

Fig. 3.3.

Fig. 3.4.

Discussion of the model

The need to have different mathematical expressions for rest, work and recovery arises from the different relationships between the stress factors and the physiological control mechanisms.

When a person at rest is exposed to a hot environment, the stress is external; the heat load has to overcome the thermal resistance of the clothing and the peripheral layers of the body before affecting the rectal temperature. In addition, the surface cooling obtained from sweat evaporation further delays the heating of the body core mass. As a result, the initial phase of the elevation in body temperature is both delayed in onset and begins at a slow rate.

When a person starts work, the main heat stress is internal; the rise in core temperature precedes the increase in the rate of heat flow from the core to the skin. Therefore, the elevation in rectal temperature occurs earlier and it proceeds more rapidly than it would under an equal external heat stress. In addition, the increase in sweat rate is gradual so that, at the beginning of the work, there is less evaporative cooling than at a later stage; consequently, the rate of temperature elevation is faster at the beginning of work, slowing down later on.

While the metabolic heat production decreases abruptly when work is stopped, during the initial part of the recovery period the sweat rate is still high; furthermore, the skin is superhydrated in comparison to what it would be under rest at the same environmental and clothing conditions. As a result, the rate of cooling of the body is high at this stage. However, subsequently the sweat rate declines below its high level at the cessation of work and the superhydration of the skin disappears. Thereafter, the body receives less evaporation and its rate of cooling declines.

As a result of these different situations in the various stages of the rest-work-recovery cycle, the time constants and time lags which characterize the time pattern of the response have had to be adjusted separately for each stage.

3.4. The Mean Skin Temperature

The skin temperature affects the heat exchange between the human body and the environment in two ways: by modifying the dry heat exchange through convection and radiation and by determining the evaporative capacity of the body under the ambient vapour pressure and wind conditions.

In contrast with the consistency of the internal body temperature, the temperature of the peripheral tissues may vary greatly within the range 15–42°C and evidently, for limited periods, without harmful consequences.

At any particular part of the body the skin temperature is determined by the local equilibrium conditions of heat flow from the body core to the skin and the heat loss from the skin to the environment.

The skin temperature over the body is not constant and consequently temperature gradients between the body core and the skin are different. The differences between the various parts of the skin are greatest in cold conditions, when the extremities and in particular the soles of the feet are the coldest areas, while the forehead and chest are the warmest; then the difference between the extreme points may be more than 10 deg C. As the environmental temperature rises the various parts of the skin are warmed, but at different rates, so that the skin temperature becomes more homogeneous. At about 32°C (90°F) the variation over the whole skin is less than 2 deg C (about 3·5 deg F). Because the skin temperature is not uniform it is customary to take measurements at several points, usually up to 16 points, and to compute the mean weighted skin temperature. The weighting is according to the relative sizes of the skin section represented by the points of measurement.

At environmental temperatures below the comfort zone the skin temperature may serve as an objective measure of the physiological and sensory cold stress. In these conditions it is a sensitive index, while the other physiological responses, such as sweat rate, pulse rate and rectal temperature, respond only slightly or do not respond at all to variations in the external temperature (except when the environmental temperature drops to such low level that the body cannot maintain thermal equilibrium).

Studies conducted at air temperatures in the comfort zone [3.8, 3.13] have demonstrated that the skin temperature is almost unaffected by humidity but depends mainly on the velocity and (dry bulb) temperature of the air. On the other hand, studies conducted at high temperatures have demonstrated the significance of wet bulb temperature [3.9]. This apparent contradiction is explained by the difference in skin wetness under the two conditions. In comfortable conditions, when the skin is dry, the rate of evaporative cooling is limited only by the rate of sweat secretion and not by the evaporative capacity of the air. Thus the skin temperature depends only on the dry cooling power of the environment and is not affected by the humidity. But under conditions of high temperature and humidity when the skin is completely wet, the rate of evaporation and the cooling derived from it depend only on the evaporative capacity of the air and not on the rate of sweat secretion. In this case the skin temperature is stabilized at a level which depends on the balance between heat supply from metabolism and the convective and radiative heat gain on one hand, and the heat loss through evaporation on the other hand, by a process similar to that determining the temperature of a wet bulb thermometer. In such circumstances the wet bulb temperature is the principal factor on which the skin temperature depends.

Increasing the air velocity brings the skin temperature closer to

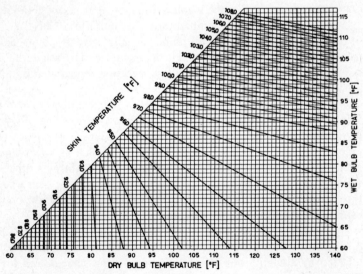

Fig. 3.5.   Chart for the estimation of average skin temperature at rest in still air.

the air temperature, compared with its value in still air. Exposure to radiation always elevates the skin temperature and radiative cooling decreases it.

These considerations were expressed in quantitative terms and a formula and nomograms have been developed [3.6] to enable the estimation of the mean skin temperature as a function of dry and wet bulb temperatures, air velocity and mean radiant temperature of the surroundings. The average skin temperature for people at rest and in still air can be determined from Fig. 3.5 according to the dry and wet bulb temperatures. For other conditions corrections can be applied.

The correction for an air velocity above 30 ft/min (15 cm/sec) is given by the formula:

$$\Delta t_{s(V)} = 0.282 \, (V-30)^{0.2} \, [(t_a - ST_s)^{0.2} - 0.51]$$

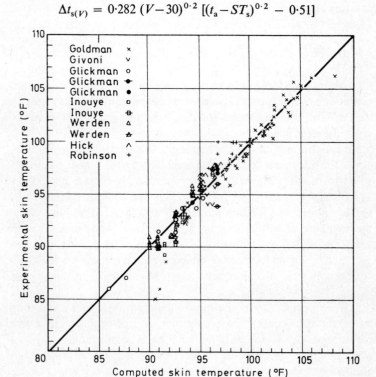

Fig. 3.6.   Correlation between observed skin temperatures and computed values.

where:

$t_{s(V)}$ = change in skin temperature from its still air value (°C);
ST_s = still air value of skin temperature (°C) (from nomogram);
t_a = air temperature (°C)
V = air velocity (ft/min).

When the mean radiant temperature is different from the air temperature, another correction should be applied using the formula:

$$\Delta t_{s(R)} = 0.057\ R$$

where R is the deviation of the M.R.T. from the air temperature (deg C). Figure 3.6 shows the correlation between the theoretical mean skin temperature, computed according to the nomogram and formulae, and that measured in many investigations. The ambient conditions ranged from 20° to 60°C.

3.5. Metabolic Response to Cold and Heat Exposure

At rest, the lowest metabolic rate occurs under comfortable conditions. When man is exposed to a cold environment his metabolic heat production is increased above the comfort level. With light cold stress the electrical activity in the muscle fibres increases (cold muscle tone) and this may elevate the metabolic heat production to 30–100% above the rate under comfortable conditions [3.10]. Under severe cold stress involuntary shivering occurs and metabolic rate may rise to 2–3 times the comfort level [3.10]. This elevation in metabolism is highest in men who are unacclimatized to cold. After acclimatization the metabolic elevation is lower, but still remains above the comfort level. Davis [3.3] has summarized various studies dealing with cold acclimatization and gives the following information on metabolic changes observed during exposure to cold conditions in summer and winter.

In September, when the natural cold acclimatization is a minimum, the heat production on the first day of exposure to a temperature of 13.5°C was 64% higher than in comfortable conditions. During 31 days of repeated exposure the metabolic rate decreased gradually to values only 30–40% above the comfort level.

In March, when the natural cold acclimatization is a maximum, the initial metabolic rate under exposure to 11·8°C was 30–40 % above the base level and so remained throughout the experimental period of 31 days. Bruce [3.1] quotes results of studies which have shown that the basal metabolic rate is relatively constant in the temperature range 20–39°C (68–102°F) in still air. Below 20°C an increase in metabolic rate occurs on account of higher muscular tension and at still lower temperatures there is a greater increase caused by involuntary shivering. At environmental temperatures above 30°C, the increased body temperature stimulated the oxidation rate in the tissues, which gives an elevation in basal metabolic rate. An elevation of the metabolism by 25–30 % on sudden exposure to severe heat stress is mentioned for unacclimatized men, but acclimatization greatly reduces this response.

Consolazio, Johnson and Pecora [3.2] also state that in extreme heat a given task causes a higher metabolic rate than the same task in a moderate environment.

In an experimental field study Consolazio compared metabolic rates during various activities and during the rest periods afterwards, under three environmental conditions: cool shade, hot shade and hot sun. He found that the metabolic rate increased by 4·0–19·4 % in hot sun and 2·2–14·2 % in hot shade when compared with the rate in cool shade. In another laboratory study where light, moderate and heavy activities were performed in air temperatures of 21·2°, 29·4° and 37·8°C, Consolazio found a consistent increase in the metabolic rate with increasing temperature. An increase of about 11 % was found for all activities on changing from 21·2° to 37·8°C. He attributes the higher metabolism to a combination of the increased blood transport, sweat gland activity and higher metabolism due to the higher temperature of the tissues.

SUBJECTIVE SENSORY RESPONSES

In contrast with the physiological responses, which may be measured objectively, the determination of the subjective sensory responses depends on the self-evaluation of a man exposed to a given environment. This evaluation is not unequivocal but varies with different individuals, and also with the same individual at different times.

Thermal comfort can be defined in a negative sense, as the absence of irritation and discomfort due to heat or cold, or in a positive sense, as a state involving pleasantness. The range of conditions in which thermal comfort is experienced is called the comfort zone. Although it is defined as a subjective assessment of the environmental conditions, the limits of the zone have a physiological basis. Physiologically the comfort zone is the range of conditions under which the thermoregulatory mechanisms of the body are in a state of minimal activity.

Thermal comfort should not be confused with thermal balance. The latter, while essential for comfort, can also be achieved under conditions of discomfort, through the activation of thermoregulatory mechanisms.

Maintaining thermal comfort does not imply that the indoor thermal conditions should be kept constantly at a precise level. The thermoregulatory systems are capable of achieving comfort within a given zone of conditions. In addition, some slight fluctuations in the indoor conditions, such as temperature and particularly air velocity, are beneficial as they prevent a monotonous feeling and have an invigorating effect. Such fluctuations are important for increasing the effectiveness of the thermoregulatory mechanisms, in particular the vasomotor system and the sensitivity of the thermoreceptors of the nervous system. Therefore the thermal requirement could be specified in terms of average values, with the acceptance of some variations and fluctuations.

Usually it is possible to determine more or less accurately the conditions of pleasantness and comfort. It is more difficult to evaluate the degree of discomfort. But experience has shown that such an evaluation is possible, although it requires some training and in particular a clear definition of the symptoms accompanying the different levels of response. In practice it is necessary to have a scale which expresses the different levels of the response in numerical values, with detailed specifications of the symptoms or subjective criteria for each level. The numerical presentation of these levels enables the responses to be analysed mathematically. Experience has shown that the repeatability of the subjective responses is not necessarily lower than that of the physiological responses. In many situations, especially when dealing with thermal conditions in buildings, the subjective attitude may be of even more significance than some objective physiological measurements.

The subjective evaluation of the thermal environment is included in two main responses: thermal sensation and sensible perspiration (skin wetness).

3.6. Thermal Sensation

The perception of environmental warmth or cold is a result of neural activity originating in nerve endings which act as thermoreceptors. There are specific thermoreceptors for warmth and for cold. In the comfort zone their activity is minimal and the central nervous system is stimulated at the lowest level. Under cold exposure the cold receptors are more active giving the sensation of cold and similarly under exposure to heat, the warmth receptors stimulate a feeling of warmth.

The experimental studies by Houghten, Yaglou and others [3.12] in which the subjective perception of the thermal environment was first investigated, employed direct and instantaneous comparison between two thermal environments. In one room the conditions were kept constant, while in another at a different temperature the humidity and air velocity were changed until the subjects felt the same thermal sensation on passing between the two rooms. The instantaneous "comparative" approach was adopted because with this procedure it is possible to perceive very small variations in the thermal conditions, while after several minutes of exposure to a given environment the body becomes "adjusted" and it is more difficult to remember the previous sensation. This procedure was based on the assumption that the difference between the two environments reflected by the first impressions would also be felt after longer exposures to each environment.

It has since been found that this assumption was not correct. According to Yaglou [3.28], when a man moves from humid conditions to a drier environment the moisture absorbed and adsorbed in his clothes and on his skin evaporates rapidly, giving an instantaneous cooling which disappears after some time. On the other hand, in the passing from a dry environment to a more humid one, the heat liberated in the process of moisture adsorption and absorption on the skin surface and the clothes causes an instantaneous heating effect, which also disappears after some time.

As a result of these phenomena, the thermal effect of humidity is much greater during a change than during a longer stay in a given environment, and consequently instantaneous impressions are not suitable as a method of research on the thermal sensation.

Nevertheless, the thermal sensation is relatively a rapid response, and after about 15 minutes of exposure it reaches the equilibrium state.

The thermal sensation can be graded according to the severity of the sensation of cold or warmth. In many environmental studies the following scale has been used:

0 — Unbearably cold	5 — Slightly warm
1 — Very cold	6 — Warm
2 — Cold	7 — Hot
3 — Cool	8 — Very hot
4 — Comfortable	9 — Unbearably hot

Experience has shown that a person can distinguish not only between the various levels but also determine intermediate levels such as 4·2 (not entirely comfortable but definitely not slightly warm) or 4·7 (less than slightly warm but definitely not comfortable) or 4·5 (somewhere in between).

Every individual will have his own scale for evaluating his feelings, but the consistency of his own evaluation is good. Therefore, in comparing results obtained with different people or groups, it is of more significance to evaluate the relative effect of changes in the different factors than to have an absolute evaluation of a given condition.

Stevens and Stevens [3.24] have studied the thermal tactile sensation by having their subjects touch an aluminium cylinder at various constant temperatures and stating their subjective feeling in relation to a standard stimulus. They found that the subjective relative tactile perception of warmth could be expressed by the formula:

$$W = K(t - 32 \cdot 5)^{1 \cdot 6}$$

where W is the subjective warmth, t is the temperature stimulus and $32 \cdot 5°C$ is the threshold temperature for warmth. The subjective perception of cold can be expressed by:

$$C = K(31 - t)$$

where $31°C$ is the tactile threshold temperature for cold.

Their formulae show that the subjective feeling of warmth grows progressively with deviation above the warmth threshold, while the subjective feeling of cold grows linearly with deviation below the cold threshold. The correlation between the sensation caused by touching a surface and that caused by an exposure to a hot or cold environment has not been examined, so that direct inference from this study to environmental problems is questionable.

3.7. Sensible Perspiration (Skin Wetness)

While thermal sensation exists in both cold and hot conditions, the sensible perspiration response is only applicable in conditions on the warm side of the comfort zone and in specific combinations of temperature, humidity, air velocity and metabolic rate. This response has clearly defined limits: the lower limit when the skin is entirely dry, and the upper limit when the whole of the body and clothing are soaked and dripping with sweat. Between these two limits there are intermediate levels which may also be defined quite clearly.

The sensible perspiration is closely associated with the wetted area of the skin. When the evaporative capacity of the air is much greater than the rate of sweat secretion the sweat evaporates as it emerges from the skin pores, without forming a liquid layer on the surface. Under such conditions the wetted area of the skin is minimal and the skin is felt as "dry". When the rate of sweating increases, or the evaporative capacity of the air decreases, the drops of sweat spread on the surface between the pores before evaporation, forming a greater area for contact with the ambient air. As a result the skin is felt as "moist", although the moisture is not visible to the eye. When the ratio between the sweat secretion and the evaporative capacity increases further the process is accelerated and the skin is covered with a liquid layer and felt as "wet". Finally, most of the sweat is unable to evaporate on the skin, soaking into the clothes and dripping from the body.

The various levels of skin wetness can be felt relatively accurately and as a result the spread of this response in experimental studies is smaller than that of thermal sensation.

The scale used by the author for subjective evaluation of the sensible perspiration in various physiological studies is:

0 — Forehead and body dry
1 — Skin clammy but moisture invisible
2 — Moisture visible
3 — Forehead or body wet (sweat covering the surface, formation of drops)
4 — Clothing partially wet
5 — Clothing almost completely wet
6 — Clothing soaked, sweat dripping off.

It has been found [3.5] that the wetness of the skin does not always correlate with the sweat rate and thermal sensation. This is because a given thermal stress, indicated by thermal sensation or sweat rate, could be the result either of body heating by convection under conditions of high temperature, low humidity and strong wind, or of a reduction in the cooling efficiency of sweating at a lower temperature in still air with a higher humidity. In both cases, the thermal stress expressed by sweat rate or by thermal sensation may be the same. However, in the first conditions sweat can evaporate very rapidly and the skin is dry, while in the second conditions the same amount of sweat evaporates slowly and the skin is moist giving a different evaluation of sensible perspiration. It has been found [3.5] that the sensible perspiration (S.P.) can be expressed as a function of the ratio of the heat load (E) to the evaporative capacity of the environment (E_{max}). It can be predicted by the formula:

$$S.P. = -0.3 + 5\,(E/E_{max}).$$

For details of the computation of E and E_{max} see the section on the Index of Thermal Stress (see Section 5.6).

Compared with the thermal sensation, the sensible perspiration is sensitive in particular to humidity and air velocity, and is always elevated by increase in humidity and reduced by increase in air velocity. It is less affected by air temperature as an elevation in it causes simultaneous increase in sweat rate and in the evaporative capacity of the air, which partially cancel each other from the point of view of skin wetness.

The sensible perspiration may also rise with the duration of the exposure. Therefore it may be used as a criterion for comparing different climatic conditions only when the exposure time is constant. In many cases more than an hour is required for reaching equilibrium.

Chapter 4

The Biophysical Effects of the Environmental Factors

In this chapter, the effects of metabolic rate and environmental factors on the physiological and sensory responses, and in particular the interactions between the effects of the various factors, will be discussed in detail. The factors involved are these: the physical work load (metabolic heat production), air temperature, humidity and velocity, mean radiant temperature (longwave radiation), solar radiation and clothing.

4.1. Air and Mean Radiant Temperatures (Homogeneous Environment)

As mentioned previously (*see* Section 2.3), the ambient air temperature and the mean radiant temperature of a homogeneous environment affect the "dry" heat exchange of the body by convection and radiation. The rate of this heat exchange depends on the air velocity and on the clothing.

Under constant conditions of vapour pressure and air velocity the body responds to a rise in the environmental temperature mainly with an elevation of the skin temperature and sweat rate. The rate of elevation is dependent on the humidity level and air velocity. Subjectively, the change in ambient temperature alters the feeling of warmth (thermal sensation). When the humidity level is high and the air velocity low, the feeling of skin wetness (sensible perspiration) also increases with the environmental temperature, but under conditions of low humidity and high air velocity the skin may remain dry even at high temperatures (despite the increase in sweat rate).

The quantitative effect of changes in the air temperature on the sweat rate of men at rest, under conditions of low humidity, can be estimated from the formula [4.4]:

$$\Delta S = \alpha V^{0.3} (t_a - 35)$$

where ΔS is the change in sweat rate (g/h), V is the air velocity (m/sec) and α is a coefficient corresponding to the clothing as follows:

Clothing	α
Semi-nude (shorts or bathing suit only)	26·9
Short trousers + short-sleeved shirt	22·0
Long trousers + long-sleeved shirt (or overall)	19·7

Pulse rate and rectal temperature are slightly altered by a rise in the environmental temperature under low heat stress, but may be greatly affected when the maintenance of thermal balance by evaporative cooling approaches its limit.

The primary physiological response to a drop in the environmental temperature below the comfort zone is the contraction of the peripheral blood capillaries, which reduces the flow of blood to the skin. This effects a reduction in the skin temperature, particularly of the hands and feet, and an increase in the tone of the muscles (indicated by their electrical activity) which elevates the metabolic heat production. The higher tone reduces the working efficiency of the muscles and so a task performed under cold conditions requires a greater effort than under comfortable conditions [4.5]. The evaporative weight loss remains constant at about 30 g/h and the pulse rate and inner body temperature are almost unaffected by the lower ambient temperature.

At rest under conditions of severe cold, active involuntary shivering increases the metabolic heat production to 2–3 times the comfort level. According to Goromossov [4.5], the physiological effects of convective and radiative heat exchanges are not the same. He holds that the human skin is selectively transparent to near infra-red and far infra-red radiations; the skin has a high absorptivity to shorter waves but is partially transparent to the longer waves. Therefore, radiant heat from hot surfaces is absorbed by the outer skin, but of the longer wave heat lost by the body, a significant fraction is emitted directly from the subcutaneous tissues such as the blood vessels and muscles. Consequently, convective heat exchange, which takes place only at the surface of the skin, and radiative exchange involving also the deeper tissues, should produce different effects. He refers to experiments in which the trunk temperature was significantly lower during radiative cooling than during convective cooling of the same magnitude.

However, a recent study by Mitchell *et al.* [4.10] has suggested that the absorptivity of the skin is very nearly 100% for the wavelength range 3–20 microns (*i.e.* including the range covered by Goromossov). From this the conclusion has been drawn that all the radiation lost by the body must be emitted from the outermost skin layer, in which case heat loss by convection and radiation would have the same effect. Goromossov also maintains that radiative cooling, when the air temperature is higher than the radiant temperatures of the surrounding surfaces, may irritate the body as the warmer air inhaled inhibits the thermoregulatory reactions.

It is evident that more research is needed to clarify this question of different thermal (and perhaps biological) effects of heat exchanges by conduction and radiation.

4.2. Physiological and Sensory Effects of Variations in the Mean Radiant Temperature (M.R.T.)

Several studies have been made of the effect of deviations in M.R.T. from air temperature on a number of physiological and sensory responses.

The effect of elevation in M.R.T. on the heart rate and rectal temperature of resting subjects wearing Navy regulation clothing has been studied by Humphreys *et al.* [4.7]. On average, an increase of 40 deg F (22 deg C) in the M.R.T. above the air temperature caused an elevation of about 0·6 deg C in rectal temperature and 15 beats per minute in the pulse rate.

Macpherson and his colleagues [4.9] have studied the effect of M.R.T. elevation on physiological responses of men clad only in shorts. An increase in M.R.T. of 1 deg C elevated the sweat rate by 11 g/h, the rectal temperature by 0·065 deg C. These values are averages of the results obtained under different conditions of air temperature (90° and 120°F), vapour pressure (16·5 and 27·0 mm Hg) and air velocity (0·5 and 1·75 m/sec). The effects of the radiation, however, differed widely under the various conditions mentioned. In particular the effect of M.R.T. elevation was more marked at the higher air temperature.

The effect of variations in M.R.T. on the thermal sensation of subjects wearing normal winter clothing has been studied by Houghten *et al.* [4.6]. They found that, on average, a change of one degree in the M.R.T. was equivalent to a change of about 0·5 degree in the Effective Temperature, or about 0·75 degree in the air temperature.

4.3. Humidity

The humidity of the air does not directly affect the heat load operating on the body, but it determines the evaporative capacity of the air and hence the cooling efficiency of sweating. In extremely hot conditions the humidity level determines the limits of the endurance time by restricting the total evaporation.

The humidity of the air may be expressed in various ways: in terms of the relative humidity, absolute humidity, specific humidity, or vapour pressure. The evaporative capacity of the air is determined by the difference between the vapour pressures of the skin and the ambient air. The vapour pressure of the skin depends on its temperature and ranges from about 37 mm Hg under comfortable conditions (corresponding to a skin temperature of 33°C), to 42 mm Hg in moderate heat (skin at 35°C) and to 47 mm Hg in severe heat (skin at 37°C). In most circumstances, 42 mm Hg is a suitable working value. Thus in warm, damp conditions the vapour pressure gives the most useful expression of humidity conditions, from the physiological point of view, because it is directly related to the potential evaporation from the body.

Expressing the humidity in terms of relative humidity may be misleading. For example, an r.h. of 100% at an air temperature of 25°C (77°F) corresponds to a v.p. of 24 mm Hg while the skin v.p. is about 37 mm Hg (and its temperature 33°C). The air in contact with the skin is heated to 31–32°C and its r.h. lowered accordingly allowing evaporation to take place. But an r.h. of only 50% when the air temperature is 50°C (122°F) corresponds to a v.p. of 46 mm Hg, or approximately the v.p. of the skin, which is at a lower temperature than that of the air (37°C). Under such conditions evaporation from the skin is impossible.

The effect of the air vapour pressure is closely related to the wetness of the skin. As long as the skin is dry, the rate of sweat secretion and evaporation depends only on the metabolic heat production and the dry heat exchange; the sweat is evaporated in the pores of the skin as it is secreted and variations in the humidity of the air do not affect the human body at all. When the ratio of the rate of sweat production to the evaporative capacity of the air reaches a value where the sweat cannot all be evaporated as it emerges from the pores of the skin, a liquid layer is formed around the pores and the area of wet skin increases. In this way the required evaporation can be achieved in spite of the reduced vapour pressure difference. Up to a certain level of humidity all the evaporation takes place on the surface of the skin, and the cooling efficiency remains almost 100%. At the limiting level the evaporation rate still equals the sweat secretion but subjective discomfort is caused by the feeling of moist skin.

At higher levels of humidity a greater area of the skin is covered with sweat and the thickness of the liquid layer is increased; part of the sweat is transferred to the hairs and is absorbed into the clothing. Even at this stage all the sweat secreted is evaporated, but part of it is evaporated at some distance from the skin. This means that part of the heat for the evaporation process is taken from the surrounding air and not from the skin, and consequently the cooling efficiency of the evaporation is reduced. As a result, the body has to secrete and evaporate more sweat than that equivalent to the required cooling. Under severe environmental conditions the humidity level may determine whether thermal balance is possible at all and, if not, will determine the endurance time of the subjects. Under such conditions small changes in the humidity may greatly affect the sweat rate, pulse rate, rectal temperature and endurance time.

The boundaries of these thermal regions determining the effect of humidity depend on the overall requirements for evaporative cooling and also on the velocity of the air and the clothing.

At air temperatures in the range 20–25°C (68–77°F) approximately, the humidity level does not affect the physiological and sensory responses, and variations in relative humidity between 30% and 85% are almost imperceptible. Only when the air is almost saturated are feelings of clamminess and dampness noticeable [4.8].

At temperatures above 25°C the influence of humidity on the responses becomes gradually more apparent, especially the effects on the skin wetness, skin temperature and, at higher temperatures, the sweat rate. The rectal temperature and heart rate also respond to changes in humidity but at higher temperatures and vapour pressures than those mentioned above.

An increase in the air velocity counterbalances the effect of humidity and therefore the lower limit of physiological and sensory response to humidity elevation is raised as the air velocity increases.

In a hot, dry climate, a low humidity may cause unpleasantness because of excessive dryness of the lips and the mucous membranes of the upper respiratory tract. According to Goromossov [4.5] it also weakens the filtering action of the upper respiratory tract with respect to microflora and dust.

According to Sulzberger [4.13], when the ambient levels of heat and humidity are high the outer skin layers cannot maintain an adequate rate of transfer of water from the internal body to the environment. As a result the skin swells and becomes soggy, while the orifices and pores are narrowed or occluded. The soggy membrane is a good culture medium for micro-organisms which may lead to certain skin diseases.

On the other hand, when the air is very dry, a hard, horny layer will form with cracks and fissures in the skin, causing irritation and various skin disturbances.

The effect of humidity under cold conditions is the subject of controversy. There are authors who believe that a high humidity at low temperatures is detrimental to health and causes subjective discomfort but others have found no effects of humidity under such conditions. The author's personal opinion is that a humid, cold environment may cause subjective discomfort and increase the possibility of contracting various diseases. It seems that the methods of experimental research which proved so successful in the study of heat stress phenomena are unsuitable for investigating this problem, which may be one of long term effect, and new methods, including observations of much longer duration, might be more successful in clarifying the question.

4.4. Air Velocity

Air velocity affects the human body in two different ways. Firstly it determines the convective heat exchange of the body and secondly it affects the evaporative capacity of the air and consequently the cooling efficiency of sweating. The effects of air velocity and air temperature on the convective heat exchange are interrelated, as the convection is a function of the product of some power of the velocity and the temperature difference between the skin and the

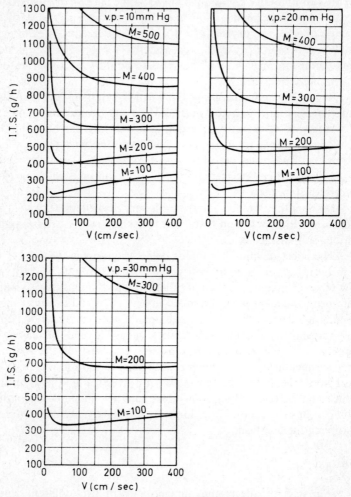

Fig. 4.1.   Optimum air velocities at 40°C at different metabolic rates (kcal/h) and humidity levels.

air. The effect of air velocity on the evaporative capacity is inter-related with the effect of humidity, as an increase in air velocity raises the evaporative capacity and thus may offset the effect of a high humidity.

When the air temperature is below skin temperature the two effects of air velocity operate in the same direction. Thus an increase in air velocity always produces a cooling effect, which increases as the air temperature is lowered. When the air temperature is above the skin temperature, however, the two effects of air velocity work in opposite directions. On one hand, increase in air velocity causes higher convective heat exchange and warms the body, but on the other hand an increase in air velocity increases the evaporative capacity and hence the cooling efficiency.

When the skin is wet and the cooling efficiency of sweating is below 100%, an increase in air velocity affects the sweating efficiency more than it does the convective heating. The net result is a cooling, which is reflected by a reduction in the sweat rate. At the same time, the higher velocity reduces the subjective discomfort due to wet skin. But this effect of air velocity only continues until the skin is dry. A further increase in air velocity does not effect the cooling efficiency of sweating although its convective heating effect continues.

Therefore at high air temperatures there is an optimum value of the air velocity, at which the air motion produces the highest cooling. Reduction of the velocity below this level causes discomfort and heating, by reduced efficiency of sweating, and increasing it beyond this level causes heating by convection. This optimum velocity is not constant but depends on the temperature, humidity, metabolic level and clothing. This is illustrated in Fig. 4.1 which shows the optimum air velocities at 40°C (104°F) at vapour pressures of 10,20,30 mm Hg and metabolic rates of 100–500 kcal/h, for subjects dressed in light summer clothing. These values were computed according to the Index of Thermal Stress (*see* Section 5.6).

In most cases the recommended air velocity at high temperatures is about 50% more than that inferred from the physiological con-siderations of the lowest heat load. This is to compensate for the subjective discomfort associated with moist skin. The small addi-tional heat load (which is demonstrated by a higher sweat rate) is counteracted by the reduction in subjective discomfort.

4.5. Clothing

Clothing forms a barrier to the convective and radiative heat exchange between the body and its environment and interferes with the process of sweat evaporation. It also reduces the sensitivity of the body to variations in air temperature and velocity. At air temperatures below 35°C (95°F) the effect is always to reduce the rate of "dry" heat loss from the body and so produce a heating effect. At air temperatures above 35°C the effect of the clothes is more complicated. On the one hand they reduce the "dry" heat gain from the environment but on the other hand increase the humidity and reduce the air velocity over the skin, resulting in a reduction of the cooling obtained from sweat evaporation. It does not mean that the total evaporation is reduced by the clothing; in most cases it is actually increased, but part of the evaporation then takes place from the clothing and not from the skin; so the cooling efficiency of the evaporation is reduced. The net result of the two opposing effects depends on the metabolic rate, humidity and air motion.

The thermal resistance (insulation) provided by the clothing depends not only on the resistance of the fabrics, but also on the stiffness and fit of the garments. Therefore this resistance must be computed from direct measurements of the dry heat exchange of subjects wearing the clothes. The unit of thermal resistance is the "clo" which is taken to be the thermal resistance of standard American indoor clothing. In physical terms the clo is equivalent to 0.18 deg C h m^2/kcal (0.88 deg F h ft^2/Btu).

When a man is exposed to solar radiation his clothing reduces the radiant heat gain. At rest and in conditions of low humidity this always reduces the overall heat load. But the cooling efficiency of sweating is also reduced and when the humidity is high and the evaporation restricted, or under working conditions when the sweat rate is increased, this may have a greater physiological effect than the lower heat gain, in which case the net result is an increase in the heat stress.

The relation between the physical activity and the effect of clothing has been demonstrated in several experimental studies.

Robinson and Turrel [4.12] found that, when subjects were exposed to solar radiation, clothing brought about a reduction of

200 g/h in the sweat rate of resting men, had no significant effect with subjects working at a medium rate (300 kcal/h) and caused an increase of about 200 g/h with men working hard (700 kcal/h).

Givoni and Berner-Nir [4.4] found that the sweat rate of subjects wearing light summer clothing was lower than that of semi-nude subjects but that the difference was much greater at a medium working rate (128 g/h) than at rest (28 g/h). But the restriction on evaporation imposed by the clothing depends on the humidity level. In a very dry climate, such as that in the desert, adequate evaporation can be maintained even when clothes are worn, in which case the protection provided against solar heat gain outweighs the effect of reduction in evaporative capacity, both at rest and when working. Thus Adolph and his associates [4.1], in their study in the desert, observed sweat rate reductions due to clothing of 250 g/h in resting subjects and 350 g/h in walking subjects.

The colour of the clothing apparently has little effect on the protection from solar radiation which it affords. In a study by Breckenridge and Pratt [4.2], exposure to solar radiation caused an increase in sweat rate which varied only slightly if the clothing was white, khaki or green (but with black clothing an appreciably higher heat stress was observed). This lack of variation may be explained by the higher transmittance of radiation through white fabrics than through coloured fabrics; inward reflection from the threads balances the effect of the higher outward reflection.

The interaction between the effects of wind speed and clothing is dependent on the air permeability of the clothes. For impermeable clothing, such as protective Arctic garments with an external wind-proof layer, the wind speed affects only the surface coefficient of the clothing system and does not alter the thermal resistance of the fabrics. On the other hand, when the clothing system is permeable to wind, either through the fabrics or between the body and the clothes, an increase in air velocity reduces the thermal resistance of the actual materials. Therefore the coefficient of dry heat exchange, as a function of the clothing, depends on the permeability of the system. For impermeable clothes Burton's formula [4.3] may be used:

$$\frac{(R+C)}{(t_s - t_a)} = \frac{22\cdot 8}{I_c + I_a}$$

$(R+C)$ is the dry heat exchange in Btu/h, $(t_a - t_s)$ is the temperature difference between the air and the skin. I_c and I_a are the insulations of the clothing and the external air layer respectively, in clo units. The value of I_a depends on the air velocity as follows:

V (m/sec)	0·15	0·25	0·5	1·0	1·5	2·0	2·5	3·0	5·0
V (ft/min)	30	50	100	200	300	400	500	600	1000
I_a (clo)	0·85	0·70	0·54	0·455	0·35	0·31	0·28	0·26	0·20

For permeable (light and medium) clothing, the coefficient of dry heat exchange can be computed according to the formula by Givoni and Berner-Nir [4.4] as given in Section 5.6.

4.6. Solar Radiation

Solar radiation has both thermal and biological effects on man. Biologically the body is affected by the ultra-violet (u.v.) portion of solar spectrum while the thermal effect is due to the visible and infra-red rays. The narrow band between 0·288 and 0·313 micron is

Table 4.I

Effect of solar radiation on elevation of sweat rate
(g/h) in relation to clothing and work

Activity	Semi-nude	Clothed	Difference
Sitting	324	132	192
Working	240	176	64
Average	282	154	128

the only effective part of the u.v. spectrum. This radiation has an anti-rachitis effect and causes tanning and sunburn (erythem) of white skin. Tanning is the result of an accumulation of the pigment melanine in the upper layer of the skin.

The thermal effect of solar radiation depends on the body's posture with respect to the sun, clothing, reflectivity of the surrounding terrain and wind velocity.

Clothing intercepts the solar rays at some distance from the skin, and part of the heat is dissipated into the environment. The proportion dissipated depends on the material and colour of the clothing and also on the air velocity. Interaction between the effects of solar radiation, metabolic rate and clothing is demonstrated by the experimental results shown in Table 4.I.

It can be seen that in the study the average weight loss due to exposure to solar radiation was greater in semi-nude than in clothed subjects. Semi-nude subjects showed a lower response at work than when sitting, but when clothed this effect was reversed.

The area of the body exposed to solar radiation is greater in the standing than the sitting position, but this is modified by the specific effect of a hat on the actual exposed area. When the solar altitude is high the hat may intercept a great part of the solar beam. An experimental study [4.4] has demonstrated that, at least around the 30° latitudes, the intensity of direct radiation falling on semi-nude men (with only a hat and bathing suit) sitting with their backs to the sun is greater than that falling on standing or walking men. This is explained by the high altitude angle of the sun during most of the daytime hours in summer and the shielding effect of the hat which is greater in the sitting than the upright position. This is illustrated by Table 4.II which shows the increase in weight loss due to exposure to solar radiation, obtained in experiments in the sitting and walking positions, according to the wind conditions.

Table 4.II

Effect of posture on increase in weight loss
(g/h) due to solar radiation

Wind speed (m/sec)	Sitting	Walking
1	341	259
2·5	306	220

It has been estimated from the experiments that the amount of direct radiation falling on semi-nude men (wearing hats) in a standing position is about 70% of that falling on men sitting with their back to the sun. This figure is applicable in summer months at latitudes between 35° north and south and for the hours between 9 a.m. and 3 p.m.

On the other hand, the amount of radiation reflected from the surroundings (see below) is about 50% lower for sitting than for upright men.

The albedo (reflectivity) of the terrain determines the amount of shortwave solar radiation reflected to the body from the surroundings and, through its effect on ground temperature, the longwave radiant heat emitted by the terrain. The first process is directly proportional and the second is inversely proportional to the albedo of the terrain.

The amount of the reflected and emitted radiation from the ground impinging on a standing man can be estimated by the formulae:

$$I_R = 0{\cdot}35 \, rI_H \quad \text{and} \quad I_R = 0{\cdot}30 \, rI_N$$

where I_R, I_H and I_N are the reflected, horizontal and normal radiations, respectively, and r is the reflectivity of the surroundings.

For surroundings with high albedo, such as a bright sand desert, the reflected radiation is about 15% and for surroundings with very low albedo such as forest or a lawn, it is about 4% of the normal radiation. For a snow cover it may be above 25%.

Table 4.III

Increase in weight loss due to solar radiation
(g/h) in relation to clothing and wind speed [4.4]

Wind velocity	Semi-nude	Light summer clothing
1 m/sec	300	191
2·5 m/sec	263	122
Difference	37	69

Wind speed reduces the heat gain due to solar radiation and the magnitude of this effect depends on the clothing. Their interaction can be explained by the effect of wind speed on the surface coefficient of the body-clothing system, which determines the fraction of the absorbed radiation dissipated into the ambient air. Even for a nude body a higher wind velocity increases the fraction of absorbed radiation which is lost to the external environment, but for a clothed body this effect is further increased. The interaction between the effects of solar radiation, clothing and wind velocity is illustrated in the previous table which shows the average increase in weight loss due to solar radiation (average of rest and work) according to the clothing and wind conditions (Table 4.III).

The reduction in the solar heat load due to wind diminished quickly as the wind speed increased and was estimated to be proportional to the power 0·2 of the velocity ($V^{0·2}$).

The formula by which the solar heat load (R) can be computed according to the factors discussed above is:

$$R = I_N K_{pe} K_{cl} [1 - a (V^{0·2} - 0·88)].$$

The values of K_{pe}, K_{cl} and a are given in the section on the Index of Thermal Stress (5.6).

4.7. Metabolic Heat Production

As mentioned in Section 3.5, the metabolic heat production is mainly proportional to the extent of physical activity, although it is somewhat influenced by the environmental conditions and increases with thermal stress (either cold or heat stress). The physiological effects of elevation in the metabolic heat production depend, however, upon the total thermal stress.

With an increase in the metabolic rate, more oxygen is required by the working muscles and higher quantities of heat have to be transferred from the body-core to the skin and dissipated into the external environment. Therefore, the primary physiological responses to the elevated heat production are an increase in the rate of blood flow and an elevation in the temperature of the inner-body, where heat is produced. Sweat secretion also increases, in order to remove the extra heat brought to the skin. But while the sweating is a response only to the thermal stimulus, the heart rate responds to both the oxygen and thermal balance requirements and the thermal stimulus. Thus, while a given amount of heat stress from either metabolic or environmental sources results in approximately the same sweat rate response, a given metabolic stress causes a much greater increase in the heart rate than the same environmental heat load.

The inner body temperature also rises more in response to a metabolic heat load, by which it is directly affected, than to the indirect influence of an environmental heat gain. The latter primarily causes an elevation in skin temperature, which reduces the temperature gradient between the body core and the skin. This is moderated partly by the increased cutaneous blood flow and the consequent increase in peripheral conductance (*see* Section 3.1) and partly by a restoration of the thermal gradient due to elevation of the inner body temperature.

Summarizing, it may be seen that the relative sensitivities to metabolic heat production and to environmental stress differ for the physiological responses; heart rate and inner body temperature are more sensitive to metabolic stress, the sweat rate responses are approximately equal, while skin temperature responds more to environmental heat loads.

Chapter 5

The Thermal Indices

5.1. Introduction

It has long been recognized that it is impossible to express human responses to the thermal environment as functions of a single environmental factor such as temperature, humidity, air velocity, etc., as these affect the human body simultaneously, and the influence of any one depends on the levels of the other factors.

It is therefore necessary to evaluate the combined effect of environmental factors on the physiological and sensory responses of the body and to express any combination of them in terms of a single parameter. Thus all the factors are combined into a single formula, known as a thermal index.

Many attempts have been made to develop thermal indices by reference to different physiological and sensory responses. At first the purpose of the indices was limited to the estimation of the combined effect of air temperature, humidity and air velocity on the subjective thermal sensation (or comfort) of men at rest, or engaged in sedentary activity. In time, the importance of radiant temperature was realized, particularly in factories but also in residential buildings. Later still, the effects of metabolic rate, clothing and finally solar radiation were also taken into account. As a result of this effort, a large number of thermal indices were developed. While the first indices were concerned mainly with thermal sensation, the more recent ones aim at estimating physiological responses to the combined effect of the climatic factors and work, and in particular the response of the sweat rate.

The various indices differ in their basic approach to the problem, in the units used as the basis for expressing the combined effect of the various factors, in the range of conditions of their application and in the relative importance attributed to each of the factors and their mutual interdependence.

The thermal indices which will be described and discussed in the following chapter are:

   a. Effective Temperature (E.T.)
   b. Resultant Temperature (R.T.)
   c. Predicted 4-hour Sweat Rate (P.$_4$S.R.)
   d. Heat Stress Index (H.S.I.)
   e. Index of Thermal Stress (I.T.S.).

5.2. The "Effective Temperature" Index (E.T.) (Fig. 5.1)

Description of the Index

The Effective Temperature index was developed in 1923–1925 at the research laboratory of the American Society of Heating and Air-Conditioning Engineers, by Houghten, Yaglou and Miller [5.11]. The factors it includes are: air temperature, humidity and air velocity. Two scales were developed, for semi-nude men and for people clad in summer clothing. The human response used as a criterion for determining the effects of these factors was the instantaneous thermal sensation experienced upon entering a given environment. In the experiments from which this index was developed the subjects walked to and fro between two rooms under different combinations of environmental factors, and the conditions in one room were adjusted so that the subjects felt the same thermal sensation when passing from one room to the other. The unit, or basis, of the E.T. index is the temperature of saturated "still" air with average velocity 12 cm/sec (25 ft/min). Any combination of air temperature, humidity and air velocity having a given value of the E.T. is supposed to produce the same thermal sensation; this is equal to that experienced in saturated still air at the same temperature as the value of the index.

The Effective Temperature index is in a form from which its value can be determined for any combination of dry and wet bulb temperatures and air velocity. Two nomograms were developed: one for people stripped to the waist and the other for people with customary indoor clothing.

The formulae from which these nomograms were constructed

were not published. The original E.T. index did not include the effect of radiant heat; it is possible, however, to take this factor into account by substituting the Globe Thermometer temperature (t_g) for

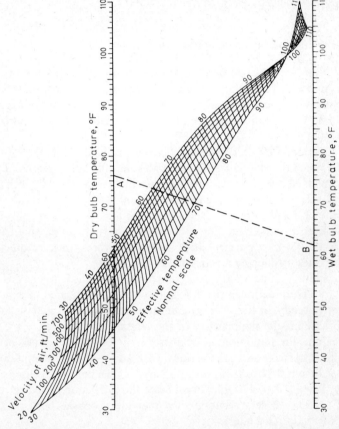

Fig. 5.1. Chart of the Effective Temperature Index. (Reprinted by kind permission from *ASHRAE Handbook of Fundamentals*—1967.)

air temperature, so including the mean radiant temperature of the environment.

Smith [5.18] has developed a modification to the E.T. index, by which the sweat rate can be predicted as a function of the E.T. index at different metabolic rates. He has prepared a suitable nomogram for this purpose. The range of conditions covered by the E.T. is:

Air temperature : 1–43°C (30–110°F)
Wet bulb temperature: 1–43°C (30–110°F)
Air velocity: 10–350 cm/sec (20/700 ft/min).

Examination and Evaluation of the E.T. Index

Numerous studies were carried out in which the validity of the E.T. index for predicting the degree of comfort, and in particular the adequacy of the weight given by it to each of the environmental factors, were examined. Several of these studies are summarized below.

Yaglou [5.20], one of the participants in the development of the E.T., noted that the index overestimates the effect of humidity. This he explained to be a result of the experimental method upon which the index was based; in passing from hot-dry air to a cooler but moister air the skin and clothing adsorbs moisture and the heat of adsorption gives a transient feeling of warmth. Similarly, on passing from cool–moist air to warmer, drier air the absorbed moisture quickly evaporates, producing a transient cooling effect.

Smith [5.18] carried out a comprehensive statistical analysis of the correlation between the E.T. and sweat rate measured in experimental studies in the U.K. Quadratic regression was used to take into account the nonlinearity of the relationship between the E.T. index and the physiological responses (*see* Section 5.7). The coefficients of correlation in the various work and clothing combinations ranged from 0·79 to 0·86, with the range of the confidence limits at 95% from 170 to 370 g/h. In all cases the prediction based on the E.T. index was less accurate than that given on the basis of the $P._4S.R.$ index (*see* later).

Glickman and co-workers [5.8] examined the validity of the E.T. index by observing the sensory and physiological response to pairs of conditions with the same E.T. value, but one with a relative humidity of 30% and the other at 80%. Air temperatures were adjusted accordingly. Their results showed overestimation of the effect of humidity under cool and comfortable conditions.

Koch, Jennings and Humphreys [5.13] examined the E.T. by

observing the conditions which produced the same thermal sensation at four relative humidities (30, 50, 70 and 90%) and various air temperatures. Their results also indicate appreciable overestimation of humidity effect.

Smith [5.18], in summarizing several studies made in the USA and the UK during the war on the validity of the E.T., mainly on its application to working men, mentions three main shortcomings: that it does not make allowance for the deleterious effects of low air speeds in hot and humid conditions, that at high air temperatures it exaggerates the stress imposed by air speeds of about 100 to 300 ft/min and that in hot environments it *underestimates* the effect of humidity.

Givoni [5.6] examined the weight attributed by the E.T. index to the influence of air velocity and humidity on thermal sensation and weight loss. His results indicated that the weight given to air velocity, below an E.T. value of 32°C, was in agreement with the physiological and sensory responses, while above this limit there was a discrepancy between the experimental results and the prediction of the index. At high temperatures the increase in air velocity produced a greater heating effect than was assumed from the E.T. index. With regard to humidity, the results confirmed previous findings about the overestimation of its effect.

One of the characteristic features of the E.T. index is the non-linearity of the relationship between the index values and the physiological responses. As the value of the index increases, unit rise produces greater physiological effect, as explained later (*see* Section 5.7).

It may be stated in conclusion that, while the E.T. index is still the most widely used, its validity has not been confirmed by examination in the experimental studies. Its employment in the comparison of different environments, or in the choice of alternatives for building design and air conditioning, may in some cases lead to erroneous conclusions.

5.3. The "Resultant Temperature" Index (R.T.) (Fig. 5.2)

Description of the Index

The Resultant Temperature (R.T.) index was developed by A. Missenard [5.17] in France. Its development was motivated by an

assumption that a firmer basis for a thermal index would be formed
by experiments in which thermal equilibrium was achieved between
body and environment, so that the effects of humidity and wind under

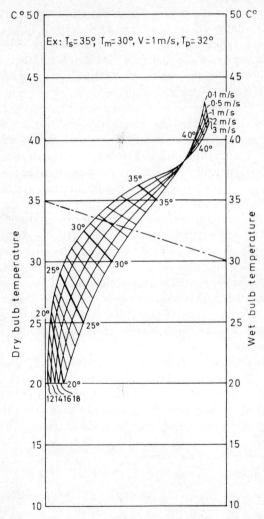

Fig. 5.2. Chart of the Resultant Temperature Index. (Reprinted by kind
permission of the author, from *Chaleur et Industrie*, July–August 1948.)

these conditions could be found. Thus a duration of exposure greater than was used in the experiments·for the Effective Temperature index was required. The experiments on which the R.T. was based were conducted with about six subjects in a psychrometric chamber. This index is identical in structure with the E.T.; from the experimental results two nomograms were plotted for clothed and unclothed subjects.

The range of climatic factors covered by the R.T. are:

Air temperature: 20–45°C (68–120°F)
Wet bulb temperature: 18–40°C (64–104°F)
Wind speed: Still air, up to 3 m/sec (600 ft/min).

Examination of the Resultant Temperature

Examination of the suitability of the R.T. index for prediction of the expected weight loss and thermal sensation under given climatic conditions was carried out by Givoni [5.6], for rest conditions only, as the index was not intended for application to working conditions. It was found that above the index value of 30°C, the relative weight attributed by the R.T. index to air temperature and humidity was in agreement with the results of the physiological experiments. In the range examined below 30°C there was slight overestimation of the effect of humidity, with respect to both sweat rate and thermal sensation. Investigating the effect of air velocity, it was found that in its higher range the index underestimated the cooling effect of air motion, while in its lower range the effect of wind was overestimated. As this index is also based on saturated air temperature, its relationship with the physiological responses is non-linear, as is the E.T. index.

Although the basis and form of the Effective Temperature and the Resultant Temperature indices are similar, the latter is in much better agreement with the observed physiological responses.

5.4. The Predicted Four Hours Sweat Rate ($P._4S.R.$) (Fig. 5.3)

Description of the Index

The $P._4S.R.$ index [5.16] was developed during World War II at the Royal Naval Research Establishment in England by McArdle and colleagues. The index takes into account metabolic level and two types of clothing, in addition to the climatic factors. The unit selected for the comparsion of combinations of climatic factors, metabolic levels and clothing is the sweat rate resulting from a 4-hour exposure to the given conditions. This index is thus directly based on a physiological response which is highly sensitive to variations in thermal environment and physical activity in the range which it covers. The experiments used as basis for the index were carried out over 4-hour periods under different combinations of climatic factors, under rest conditions (metabolic level, 54 $kcal/m^2/h$) and at rest and work alternately (average metabolic level 111 $kcal/m^2/h$).

The range of conditions covered by the index is:

Globe temperature (or air temperature in a homogeneous environment) (t_g): 27–54°C
Wet bulb temperature (W.B.T.): 16–36°C
Wind speed: 5–250 cm/sec
Metabolic level: 54–200 $kcal/m^2/h$
Clothing: shorts only, or overalls/shorts.

The P.$_4$S.R. index is in the form of a nomogram, the basic P.$_4$S.R. which can be obtained directly from data of the dry and wet bulb temperatures and air velocity. The first step in using the P.$_4$S.R. index is the determination of the Basic 4 h Sweat Rate (B.$_4$S.R.) from the nomogram. This corresponds to the Predicted 4 h Sweat Rate in litres (P.$_4$S.R.) for people sitting clad in shorts in a homogeneous environment.

If either the M.R.T., metabolic rate or clothing deviate from these basic conditions, two corrections to the B.$_4$S.R. are applied. The first is a series of corrections in the wet bulb temperature, to obtain the Corrected B.$_4$S.R. as follows:

a. When the M.R.T. differs from the D.B.T. (and as a result the t_g differs from the D.B.T.) the W.B.T. is corrected by addition of 0·4 $(t_g - D.B.T.)$ deg F.

b. When the metabolic rate exceeds the resting level (54 $kcal/m^2/$h), the W.B.T. is corrected by the addition of a value obtained from an insert given in the basic nomogram. Thus, for a metabolic rate of 100 $kcal/m^2/h$ a further 4 deg F is added to the W.B.T.

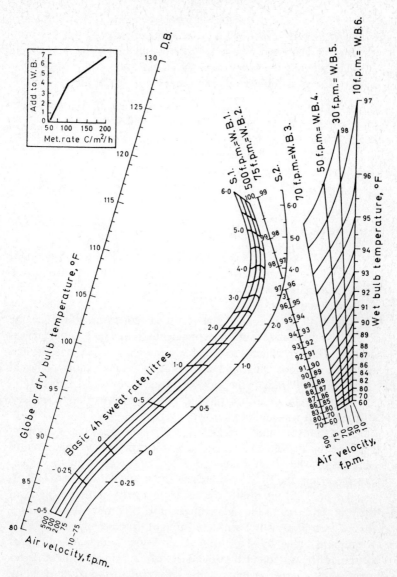

Fig. 5.3. Chart of the P.4S.R. Index. (Reprinted by kind permission of Medical Research Council and Royal Naval Personnel Research Committee from RNP 47/391, England—1947.)

c. If the weight of the clothing is above 600 g, 1·0 deg F is added to the W.B.T. for every 300 g increase in clothing weight. For overalls over shorts (total weight 1140 g) a value of 1·8 deg F is added.

The second step which gives the $P._4S.R.$ also comprises a series of corrections as follows (all quantities expressed in litres):

a. Men working in shorts at metabolic rate M (kcal/m^2/h):
$P._4S.R. = $ Corrected $B._4S.R. + 0·014 (M-54)$.

b. Men sitting in overalls over shorts:
$P._4S.R. = $ Corrected $B._4S.R. + 0·25$.

c. Men working in overalls over shorts:
$P._4S.R. = $ Corrected $B._4S.R. + 0·25 + 0·02 (M-54)$.

Examination of the $P._4S.R.$

Several studies have examined the validity of the $P._4S.R.$ index for the prediction of weight loss at rest and during manual work, and of thermal sensation at rest and during sedentary activity, under various climatic conditions.

Smith [5.18] examined the statistical correlation between the $P._4S.R.$ and the results of the experiments from which the index was derived. The experiments included rest and work as well as nude and clothed conditions. He found a variation in the regression coefficient from 0·87 to 0·95, and in the 95 % confidence limit from 160 to 350 g/h.

The correlation at rest was higher than with working men, and with shorts it was higher than with overalls.

Macpherson and colleagues [5.15] examined the agreement between the $P._4S.R.$ and several series of experiments conducted in Singapore. They have found good agreement between the values expected from the $P._4S.R.$ index and the measured ones.

Givoni [5.6] has studied the correlation between the $P._4S.R.$ and thermal sensation in the index range up to 1·2 (above this range the thermal sensation is not sensitive enough). In particular the relative weight attributed by the index to air velocity and humidity was examined. It was found that the effect of air velocity was in agreement with the experimental results. The effect attributed to humidity was found to be a little smaller than that observed in the experiments.

In conclusion it seems that the P.$_4$S.R. index enables reliable estimation of the overall thermal stress, manifested in the sweat rate and, within a given range of thermal sensation, under a variety of metabolic, climatic and clothing conditions.

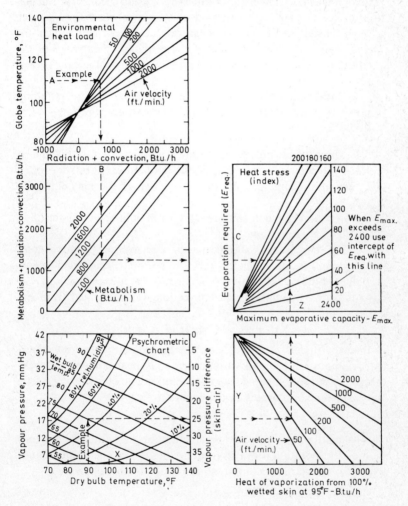

Fig. 5.4. Charts of the Heat Stress Index. (Reprinted by kind permission from *ASHRAE Handbook of Fundamentals*—1967.)

5.5. The Heat Stress Index (H.S.I.) (Fig. 5.4)

Description of the Index

The Heat Stress Index (H.S.I.) was developed by Belding and Hatch [5.3] at the University of Pittsburgh, using theoretical calculations of the external heat stress acting on a man exposed to a given thermal environment, of the heat produced by metabolism for various degrees of activity, and of the evaporative capacity of the environment. The index was based on several physiological assumptions:

a. Total heat stress acting on the body (metabolism $\pm$ radiation $\pm$ convection) equals the requirement for sweat evaporation

$$(E_{req} = M \pm R \pm C).$$

b. The physiological strain imposed on the body by a given heat stress is determined by the ratio of the required evaporative cooling (E_{req}) to the maximum evaporative capacity of the air (E_{max}), i.e. E_{req}/E_{max}.

c. Constant skin temperature (35°C) is maintained when the body is subjected to heat stress.

d. The maximum sweating capacity of an average person over an 8-hour period is approximately one litre per hour, calculated to give a cooling value of 2400 Btu/h (600 kcal/h). Heat exchange with the environment by radiation and convection was calculated from the basic formula:

$$M \pm R \pm C \pm H - E = 0.$$

In the experiments used as a basis for this index, the metabolic level (M), evaporation (E) and variation in body heat content (H) were measured and the combined sum of radiation and convection ($R+C$) was determined according to the equation:

$$R \pm C = M \pm H - E.$$

This calculation was based on the assumption that all the latent heat of sweat evaporation is drawn from the body. The coefficients found from these experiments and used as a basis for the index are:

Radiation : $R = 22\,(t_w - t_s)$
Convection: $C = 2\,V^{0.5}\,(t_a - t_s)$
Maximum evaporation: $E_{max} = 10\,V^{0.4}\,(P_s - P_a)$

where:

R, C, E, in Btu/h per (average) person
V = wind speed (ft/min)
t_w = mean radiant temperature (°F)
t_s = skin temperature (°F)
t_a = air temperature (°F)
P_s = skin vapour pressure (mm Hg)
P_a = air vapour pressure (mm Hg).

From the algebraic sum of metabolic level, radiation and convection, the evaporation required for thermal equilibrium is calculated. The maximum evaporative capacity of the air (E_{max}) is calculated from the wind speed and the difference between the air and skin vapour pressures at 42 mm Hg (at a temperature of approximately 35°C, when the skin is entirely covered with sweat).

The numerical value of the index, which represents the heat stress acting on the body, is found from the higher value obtained using the following formulae:

$$1. \text{ Heat stress} = \frac{\text{Required evaporation}}{\text{Maximum evaporative capacity}} \times 100$$

$$2. \text{ Heat stress} = \frac{\text{Required evaporation}}{2400} \times 100$$

(2400 is the theoretical cooling value, in Btu, of the evaporation of 1·0 litre of sweat).

A suitable nomogram was plotted (Fig. 5.4) so that the Heat Stress Index could be obtained for different conditions of air and radiant temperature, wind speed, humidity and metabolic level. The numerical values lie between 0 and 200. The value zero represents the absence of heat stress (approximately the comfort region) and 100 the upper limit for thermal equilibrium. The region of the body heating is between 100 and 200.

The range of conditions covered by the index is:

Dry bulb (or Globe) temperature: 21- 49°C (70- 140°F)
Vapour pressure: 3- 42 mm Hg
Air velocity: 0·25- 10·0 m/sec (50- 2000 ft/min)
Metabolic rate: 100- 500 kcal/h (400–2000 Btu/h).

Examination of the H.S.I.

The accuracy of prediction by the H.S.I. of weight loss at rest and during manual work, and of thermal sensation at rest and with sedentary activity, has been examined by Givoni [5.6] under various climatic conditions.

Figure 5.5 shows the sweat rate measurements from various studies against the Heat Stress Index values calculated for the experimental conditions under which the measurements were made. The results are marked separately for the different levels of humidity, wind speed and work.

Figure 5.5 shows separation of the two work levels. The sweat rate, measured for conditions of physical work, was higher than for conditions of rest and office work. For example, at a Heat Stress Index value of 150 the range of sweat rates measured under work conditions was approximately 400 to 1180 g/h, while under rest conditions, for the same Heat Stress value, it was approximately 200 to 800 g/h. Hence, it may be suggested that the effect attributed by the Heat Stress Index to metabolic rate was lower than that observed in the sweat rate measurements.

Separation is also observed for the different levels of wind speed. For a given value of Heat Stress Index, the sweat rate measured was lowest in still air (10–35 cm/sec).

Measurements taken in light wind (35–125 cm/sec) were higher, and those in medium and strong winds (125–400 cm/sec) were the highest. Hence, it may be suggested that the Heat Stress Index overestimates the cooling effect of wind.

For the humidity effect there is also a separation of the results obtained at different levels. The sweat rate measured at high humidity was lower than at low humidity for given air speed and Heat Stress Index values. Thus it seems that the index overestimates the warming effect of humidity. Examination of the index with respect to thermal sensation yielded similar conclusions.

It seems to the author that in spite of the great theoretical importance of the Heat Stress Index, permitting isolation of the different factors resulting in a given heat stress, and which actually served as a basis for the development of a new index by the author, it is doubtful whether it could be regarded as adequate for quantitative evaluation of the severity of thermal stress.

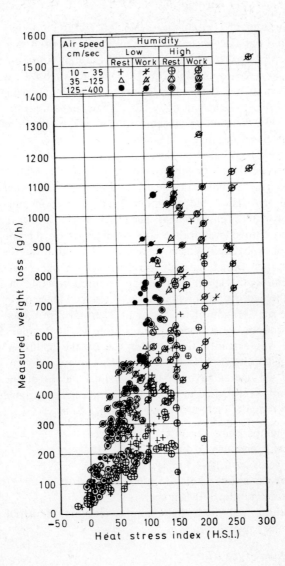

Fig. 5.5.   Correlation between observed weight loss and predictions of the Heat Stress Index.

5.6. The Index of Thermal Stress (I.T.S.)

The index of Thermal Stress [5.5, 5.6, 5.7] is a biophysical model describing the mechanisms of heat exchange between the body and the environment, from which the total thermal stress on the body (metabolic + environmental) can be computed. Above the comfort zone the sweat rate required to maintain thermal equilibrium can also be found, as long as the body can remain in equilibrium (with an elevated but constant rectal temperature). Below the comfort zone the index has a negative value indicating cold stress.

The I.T.S. is based on the assumption that, within the range of conditions where it is possible to maintain thermal equilibrium, sweat is secreted at a sufficient rate to achieve the evaporative cooling required to balance the metabolic heat production and the heat exchange with the environment. The relation between sweat secretion and the required evaporative cooling depends on the cooling efficiency of sweating. Where there is a reduction in the cooling efficiency of sweating, the body secretes sweat at a higher rate than that equivalent to the latent heat of the required cooling, in order to obtain the necessary cooling in spite of reduced efficiency.

The first version of the Index of Thermal Stress was intended only for indoor use and one type of clothing (light summer clothing). Later it was extended for outdoor use by the inclusion of solar radiation among its factors; it now also covers different types of clothing. At the same time, the numerical values of the various coefficients were revised in the light of additional experimental data.

The range of factors covered by the I.T.S. is:

Air temperature: 20–50°C
Vapour pressure: 5–40 mm Hg
Air velocity: $0 \cdot 10$–$3 \cdot 5$ m/sec
Solar radiation: whole range 600 kcal/h
Metabolic rate: 100–600 kcal/h
Clothing: semi-nude, light summer clothing, industrial or military overalls.

The Formula of the I.T.S.

The general formula of the Index of Thermal Stress (I.T.S.) is:

$$S = [(M-W) \pm C \pm R] \,(1/f)$$

where:

S = required sweat rate, in equivalent kcal/h
M = metabolic rate, kcal/h
W = metabolic energy transformed into mechanical work, kcal/h
C = convective heat exchange, kcal/h
R = radiant heat exchange, kcal/h
f = cooling efficiency of sweating, dimensionless.

The metabolic heat production $(M-W)$

The metabolic heat production is the difference between the metabolic rate (M) and the energy transformed into mechanical work (W). Investigators have found various different values for the mechanical work efficiency. In the I.T.S. an efficiency of 20% of the energy produced above the rest level (100 kcal/h) has been adopted. Hence the metabolic heat production is computed according to the formula:

$$M - W = M - 0.2 (M-100).$$

The convective heat exchange (C)

The convective heat exchange (C), or the dry heat exchange (D) in a homogeneous environment, is computed according to the formula:

$$C = \alpha V^{0.3} (t_a - 35)$$

where C is expressed in kcal/h, α is a coefficient depending on clothing, V is the air velocity in m/sec and t_a is air temperature in °C. The values of α for different types of clothing are given in Table 5.I.

Table 5.I
Clothing coefficients of the I.T.S.

Clothing	α	Coefficient K_{cl}	a	p
Semi-nude: bathing suit and hat	15·8	1·0	0·35	31·6
Light summer clothing: underwear, short sleeved cotton shirt, long cotton trousers, hat	13·0	0·5	0·52	20·5
Military overalls over shorts	11·6	0·4	0·52	13·0

The radiant heat exchange (R)

Longwave radiation

The I.T.S. does not as yet separately cover the factor of longwave radiation. It is tentatively suggested to adopt the procedure used by Belding and Hatch for the Heat Stress Index [5.3] and by substituting the Globe temperature (t_g) for the air temperature (t_a) in the equation of the convective heat exchange, to compute the combined radiative and convective heat exchange (C') for indoor exposure or to outdoor exposure in the shade.

Solar radiation

The radiant heat load due to solar radiation (R) is computed according to the formula:

$$R = I_N K_{pe} K_{cl} [1 - a (V^{0.2} - 0.88)]$$

where:

R = solar radiation heat load, kcal/h
I_N = normal solar intensity, kcal/h
K_{pe} = coefficient depending on posture and terrain
K_{cl}, a = coefficients depending on clothing
V = wind speed, m/sec.

The values of K_{pe} for different postures and terrains and of K_{cl} and a for types of clothing are given in Tables 5.II and 5.I.

Table 5.II

Combined solar load coefficient for posture and terrain

Posture	Terrain	K_{pe}
Sitting with back to sun	Desert	0·386
	Forest	0·379
Standing with back to sun	Desert	0·306
	Forest	0·266

The cooling efficiency of sweating (f)

The cooling efficiency of sweating (f) is the ratio between the cooling produced by the evaporation of sweat (E) to the latent heat of the sweat secreted (S), *i.e.* the ratio E/S.

As mentioned before (*see* Section 2.4), it has been found that the sweating cooling efficiency depends on the rate and place of the evaporation process which in turn depend on the ratio between the

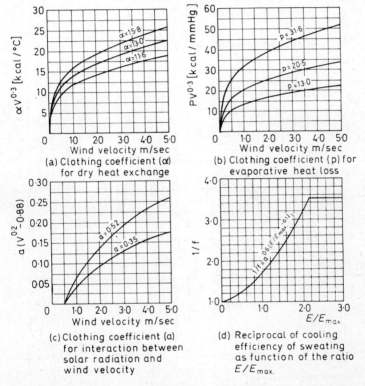

Fig. 5.6. Charts to determine coefficients of the Index of Thermal Stress.

total heat load (which equals the required evaporation cooling E), and the evaporative capacity of the air E_{max}, *i.e.*, on the ratio E/E_{max}.

In practice, the significant factor is the reciprocal of the sweat cooling efficiency $1/f$, the coefficient by which the numerical value of the required evaporative cooling is multiplied to give the required sweat rate. $1/f$ is computed according to the formula:

$$1/f = e^{0.6(E/E_{max} - 0.12)}$$

where $E = (M - W) \pm C \pm R$, kcal/h

and $E_{max} = pV^{0.3}(42 - VP_a)$, kcal/h

and where:

    p = coefficient depending on clothing

    V = air velocity, m/sec.

    42 = vapour pressure of the skin at 35°C, mm Hg

    VP_a = vapour pressure of the air, mm Hg.

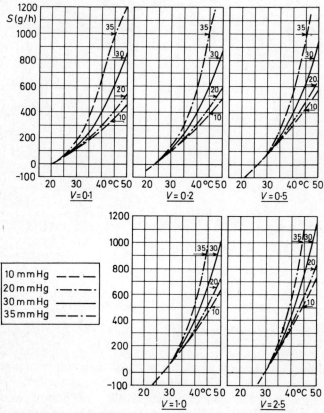

Fig. 5.7.   Expected weight loss of subjects at rest under different environmental conditions. Metabolic rate 100 kcal/h. Light summer clothing.

The lower limit of $1/f$ is $1 \cdot 0$ and is maintained as long as the ratio E/E_{max} is below $0 \cdot 12$. The upper limit of $1/f$ is $3 \cdot 5$ and is achieved when E/E_{max} reaches $2 \cdot 15$ and over.

The values of p for different types of clothing are given in Table 5.I.

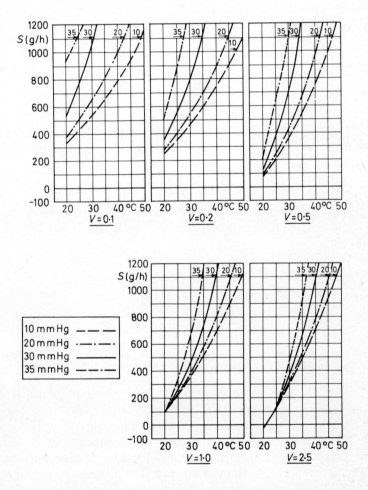

Fig. 5.8. Expected weight loss of subjects at medium work under different environmental conditions. Metabolic rate 300 kcal/h. Light summer clothing.

The Detailed Formula of the I.T.S.

The detailed general formula of the I.T.S. becomes:

$$S = [M - 0.2\,(m-100) \pm \alpha V^{0.3}\,(t_a-35) + I_N K_{pc} K_{cl}\,(1-a\,(V^{0.2}-0.88))]\,e^{0.6(E/E_{max}-0.12)}.$$

The constituent formulae for the various components have been given in the preceding paragraphs.

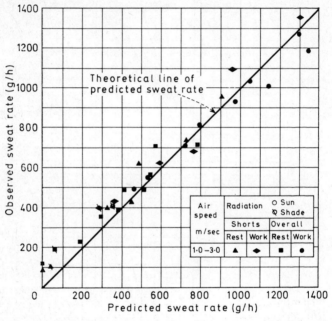

Fig. 5.9. Combined field study measurements of sweat rates under exposure to solar radiation, and their correlation with the Index of Thermal Stress.

To facilitate the computation of the index, nomograms were prepared to determine $\alpha V^{0.3}$, $pV^{0.3}$ and $a\,(V^{0.2}-0.88)$ as functions of V and $1/f$ as a function of E/E_{max} (Fig. 5.6).

The various coefficients related to the formula are summarized in Tables 5.II and 5.I. Figures 5.7 and 5.8 show the expected sweat rate as a function of temperature and vapour pressure, under two conditions of activity (rest and medium work) and four levels of air velocity. These figures refer to subjects clad in light summer clothing.

Experimental Examination of the I.T.S.

The validity of the I.T.S. has been examined by comparison between weight losses measured in several experimental studies and the values computed from the I.Ṫ.S. for the same environmental and metabolic conditions. Two experimental series, with the participation of the author [5.6, 5.7] and five studies by other investigators, Macpherson *et al.* [5.15], Dunham *et al.* [5.4], Kraning *et al.* [5.14], Henschel [5.10] and Gosselin [5.9], are summarized below.

The investigations were divided into three groups, according to the principal factor which they examined: outdoor exposure to solar radiation, controlled climatological factors and variations in the metabolic rate.

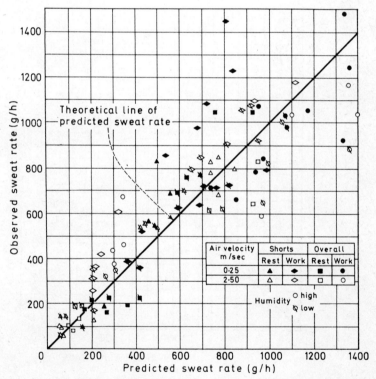

Fig. 5.10. Combined observations of sweat rate under controlled environmental conditions, and their correlation with the Index of Thermal Stress.

Figure 5.9 shows combined results of the field studies on solar radiation exposure: Givoni and Berner [5.7], Henschel [5.10] and Gosselin [5.9]. The data are marked according to the exposure to solar radiation, clothing and metabolic rates. It can be seen that the results of the three investigations fit a common regression line.

Figure 5.10 shows the combined results of studies in controlled environmental conditions: Givoni and Berner [5.7], Dunham et al. [5.4] and Macpherson et al. [5.15].

To emphasize the effect of air velocity, only the extreme values (still air and 2·5–4·0 m/sec) are given in this Figure.

The clothing, air velocity and metabolic rates are indicated with

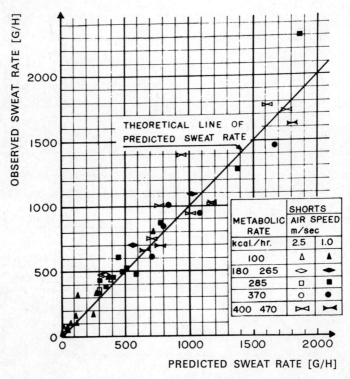

Fig. 5.11.   Combined observations of sweat rate at different metabolic rates and their correlation with the Index of Thermal Stress.

the data. The spread of results is greater than for the outdoor experiments, but the average fits the predicted line.

Figure 5.11 shows the combined results of investigations with several metabolic rates by Givoni [5.6] and Kraning *et al.* [5.14]. The results are marked according to the metabolic rates and air velocity. It can be seen that the results of both investigations form a common regression line close to the line predicted by the I.T.S. formula.

Summarizing, it seems possible to conclude that the Index of Thermal Stress provides an analytical method to determine the combined effect of metabolic rate, environmental conditions and clothing on physiological strain, manifested by sweat rate. In addition, the component formulae enable evaluation of the quantitative and relative effects of each single factor.

The upper limit of application of the index to prediction of the expected sweat rate is defined by the environmental and metabolic conditions yielding either a sweat rate of 1200 g/h or an E/E_{max} ratio of 2·2, when the cooling efficiency of sweating drops to about 0·285. The lower limit is set by an air temperature of 20°C.

5.7. *Analytical Comparison of the Various Thermal Indices*

In this section comparison is made between thermal indices and particularly between their units, experimental bases, range of applicability and the relative weights attributed to the effects of air temperature, humidity and air motion.

5.7.1. THE INDEX UNITS.—The unit of Effective Temperature and the Resultant Temperature indices is the temperature of still saturated air, in common with several other indices not examined in this review, such as the Operative Temperature, Equivalent Warmth and the Equatorial Comfort indices.

The unit of the P.$_4$S.R. and the Index of Thermal Stress is the expected sweat rate under given environmental and metabolic conditions, and that of the Heat Stress Index is the ratio of the evaporative cooling required by the body to the maximum evaporative capacity of the air (E/E_{max}). The choice of units has determined some of the properties of the indices. Saturated air temperature is inherently a factor of inconsistent physiological significance, because an increase in the temperature of saturated air is accompanied by an elevation of the vapour pressure. Moreover, the physiological effect of vapour pressure is not linear but progressive, increasing with the vapour pressure. Consequently, when the saturated air temperature is used as a unit the relationship between the index and the physiological and sensory responses is also non-linear. For example, varying the Effective Temperature from 25° to 27°C has little effect, while an increase from 35° to 37°C makes the difference between conditions tolerable for several hours and conditions which may result in heat stroke after only a short time. In these circumstances there is no possibility of evaluating directly the difference between two climatic conditions differing in their Effective Temperature, Resultant Temperature or the value of any other index based on the same unit. It is also impossible to evaluate directly the physiological effect of changes in air motion and humidity, expressed by changes in the value of the index, since this also depends on the existing index level when these changes take place.

The expected sweat rate seems to be a suitable basis for the assessment of stress imposed by a given environment or combination of work and heat load, for the whole range between the comfort zone and the limit of thermal equilibrium. Thus the indices using it as a base have direct physiological significance. These indices, however, do not give reliable predictions of discomfort due to skin wetness and care should be taken if they are used to evaluate conditions of high humidity and low air velocity, when skin wetness results in a primary sensory stress.

The E/E_{max} ratio, in spite of its significance in relation to the cooling efficiency of sweating and skin wetness, has not proved adequate for predicting either physiological responses or thermal sensation.

5.7.2. THE RANGE OF APPLICABILITY OF THE INDICES.—In comparing ranges of the thermal indices, a distinction should be drawn between the range of conditions covered and the zone in which physiological significance is retained.

Table 5.III summarizes the nominal range of environmental factors covered by each of the indices.

Table 5.III
Range of the indices

Index	Metabolic rate (kcal/h)	D.B.T. (°C)	W.B.T. (°C)	Air velocity (m/sec)
Effective Temperature	Rest only	1–43	1–43	0·10– 3·5
Resultant Temperature	Rest only	18–45	18–45	0·10– 3·0
P.₄S.R.	100–350	27–55	15–36	0·05– 2·5
Heat Stress Index	100–500	27–60	15–35	0·25–10·0
Index of Thermal Stress	100–600	20–55	15–35	0·10– 3·5

In summarizing the reliability of the thermal indices, inferred from the correlation observed between their predictions and experimental results of the physiological examinations carried out, the following conclusions are suggested:

Effective Temperature: Of all the indices reviewed, the E.T. index appears to be the least reliable in predicting the expected physiological and sensory responses, both in comfortable conditions and under heat stress.

Resultant Temperature: The reliability of the R.T. index is satisfactory in predicting responses of people at rest or engaged in sedentary activity.

P.₄S.R.: The reliability of the P.₄S.R. index is satisfactory under light to medium heat stress conditions for people at rest or engaged in light to medium work. Under severe heat stress it is still reliable in predicting the sweat rate, but this response alone is not so important, and so under these conditions the index is less satisfactory for predicting physiological strain.

Heat Stress Index: The H.S.I. is suitable for analysing the relative contribution of the various factors resulting in thermal stress, but is not suitable for predicting quantitative physiological responses to the stress.

Index of Thermal Stress: The I.T.S. is suitable for analysing the individual contributions of metabolic and environmental factors and for prediction of the physiological strain imposed on resting and working people. It is reliable in the range of conditions between comfort and severe stress, provided that thermal equilibrium can be maintained (stabilized rectal temperature and pulse rate). Beyond this limit the index does not apply.

Chapter 6

The Thermophysical Properties of Building Materials

Heat transfer in buildings may take place in four ways, by conduction, convection, radiation and evaporation (or condensation). Conduction is the flow of heat through a material by transfer from warmer to colder molecules in contact with each other. By convection, heat is transferred with the flow of molecules from one place to another with a change in their heat content. Radiation is the transfer of heat through space by electromagnetic waves. Evaporation and condensation involve changes of state (from liquid to gas and vice versa), which processes absorb or evolve heat.

During the process of flow the heat may change its mode of transfer. Thus solar energy reaches a wall in the form of radiation, is absorbed at the external surfaces and flows across the wall material by conduction. If the wall contains an air space, the heat flows across it by convection and radiation, continues its flow by conduction and is finally transferred to the indoor air by convection and to the other internal surfaces by radiation.

When the addition or loss of heat is associated with a change in temperature, it is known as sensible heat and when accompanied by a change of state is referred to as latent heat.

The properties of materials which affect the rate of heat transfer in and out of a building, and consequently the indoor thermal conditions and comfort of the occupants, are:

Thermal conductivity, resistance and transmittance
Surface characteristics with respect to radiation – absorptivity, reflectivity and emissivity
Surface convective coefficient
Heat capacity
Transparency to radiation of different wavelengths (*see* Chapter 12).

6.1. Thermal Conductivity, Resistance and Transmittance

Thermal conductivity is the property of a material which determines the heat flow in unit time by conduction through unit thickness of a unit area of the material, across a unit temperature gradient. It is expressed in the English system by k, in Btu/h ft^2 deg F/ft, and in the metric system by λ, in kcal/h m^2 deg C/m. It is assumed that the temperatures on either side of the material, and the distribution of temperature throughout the material, are uniform and constant with time (steady state conditions).

The reciprocal of the thermal conductivity ($1/k$ or $1/\lambda$) is the thermal resistivity of the material. Both conductivity and resistivity are independent of the size and thickness of the building elements.

The actual heat flow across a given building element (wall or roof) depends not only on the thermal conductivity of the material, but also on the thickness (d) of the element. The greater the thickness, the lower will be the rate of heat flow. Therefore the thermal resistance (r) of the element (*i.e.* its resistance to heat flow) is defined by:

$$r = \frac{d}{\lambda} \left(r = \frac{d}{k} \right)$$

Similarly, the thermal conductance of the element (c) is given by:

$$c = \frac{\lambda}{d} \left(c = \frac{k}{d} \right)$$

The flow of heat under steady state conditions across a wall element of surface area A and thickness d, built of a material having a given value of λ and subjected to a temperature gradient of $t_2 - t_1$, is then given by the formula:

$$q_{s-s} = A \frac{\lambda}{d} (t_2 - t_1)$$

where q_{s-s} is the rate of heat flow from the warmer to the colder surface in kcal/h (Btu/h).

In calculating the rate of heat flow between the indoor and outdoor air, the thermal resistance of air layers adjacent to the surfaces must also be taken into account. A film of still air forms on any surface, its thickness decreasing as the velocity of the adjacent air increases. As the thermal conductivity of air is very low, and consequently its resistivity high, the air film attached to a surface gives an appreciable resistance to heat flow across that surface. The reciprocal of the resistance of the air film is known as the surface coefficient, denoted by h_i for internal and h_e for external surfaces (see Section 6.3). This coefficient thus determines the heat flow from the surface to the ambient air for unit area, unit temperature gradient and unit time, and is expressed in kcal/h m^2 deg C (Btu/h ft^2 deg F).

When computing the rate of heat flow between indoor and outdoor air, the thermal resistances of both surfaces (i.e. the reciprocals of their surface coefficients) must be added to the thermal resistance of the wall itself. Thus the overall thermal resistance of a single layer wall to the heat flow (R) between the air on either side is given by:

$$R = 1/h_i + d/\lambda + 1/h_e$$

$$(\text{or } R = 1/h_i + d/k + 1/h_e).$$

The reciprocal of this thermal resistance is termed the thermal transmittance. This determines the rate of heat flow through a given building component and is denoted by K in the metric system, and in the English system by U. Thus $K = 1/R$ $(U = 1/R)$. The rate of heat flow (q) per unit area from internal to external air, under steady state conditions, can then be calculated from the formula:

$$q = K(t_i - t_o), \text{ kcal/h m}^2 \text{ deg C}$$

$$(\text{or } q = U(t_i - t_o), \text{ Btu/h ft}^2 \text{ deg F}),$$

where t_i and t_o are respectively the indoor and outdoor air temperatures.

When the wall is composed of several layers differing in thickness and conductivity, the overall thermal resistance of the composite wall is the sum of the separate resistances of the layers. Thus the overall resistance of a three-layer wall is:

$$R = 1/h_i + d_1/\lambda_1 + d_2/\lambda_2 + d_3/\lambda_3 + 1/h_e,$$

and the overall transmittance is:

$$K \text{ (or } U) = 1/R = \frac{1}{1/h_i + d_1/\lambda_1 + d_2/\lambda_2 + d_3/\lambda_3 + 1/h_e}$$

To give a numerical example in the metric system, the thermal transmittance of a concrete wall plastered on both sides is computed as follows. The thickness of the wall is 20·0 cm, of the external plaster 2·0 cm and of the internal plaster 1·0 cm; the thermal conductivity of the concrete is given as 1·2, of the external plaster as 0·8 and of the internal plaster as 0·6 kcal/m² h deg C; the external and internal surface coefficients are assumed to be 18 and 7 respectively. The overall thermal resistance is then given by:

$$R = 1/7 + 0·02/0·8 + 0·2/1·2 + 0·01/0·6 + 1/18 = 0·408$$

and the thermal transmittance by:

$$K = 1/0·408 = 2·45 \text{ kcal/m}^2 \text{ h deg C.}$$

6.2. Surface Characteristics with Respect to Radiation

The external surface of any opaque material has three properties determining behaviour with respect to radiant heat exchange, namely its absorptivity, reflectivity and emissivity.

Radiation impinging on an opaque surface may be absorbed or reflected, being fully absorbed by a perfectly black surface and fully reflected by a perfect reflector. Most surfaces, however, absorb only part of the incident radiation, reflecting the remainder. If the absorptivity is denoted by a and the reflectivity by r, then

$$r = 1 - a.$$

The emissivity (ε) is the relative power of a material to emit radiant energy. For any specific wavelength, absorptivity and emissivity are numerically equal, i.e. $a = \varepsilon$, but both may vary for different wavelengths.

Every surface emits radiation with a spectral distribution and intensity dependent on its temperature; radiation emitted by surfaces at ordinary temperatures is in the far infra-red range of the spectrum (peak intensity about 10 microns). The total intensity of radiation emitted by a body is:

$$q_r = 4\cdot9 \; \varepsilon \; (T/100)^4$$

where q_r is given in kcal/m^2 h and T is the absolute temperature in °K. In the English system,

$$q_r = 0\cdot173 \; \varepsilon \; (T/100)^4$$

where q_r is in Btu/ft^2 h and T is the absolute temperature, degrees Rankine (the absolute temperature in the Fahrenheit scale).

The emissivity of a perfectly black surface is 1·0; for other surfaces values range from 0·05 for some highly polished metals, to about 0·95 for ordinary building materials.

Radiation is absorbed selectively, according to the wavelengths incident on the surface. Thus a fresh whitewash has an absorptivity of about 0·12 for shortwave solar radiation (peak intensity 0·4 μ) but the absorptivity for longwave radiation from other surfaces at ordinary temperatures (peak intensity 10 μ) is about 0·95. Consequently this surface also has an emissivity of 0·95 for long wavelengths, and is a good radiator, readily losing heat to colder surfaces; but at the same time it is a good reflector for solar radiation. On the other hand, a polished metal has a very low absorptivity and emissivity for both shortwave and longwave radiations. Therefore, while being a good reflector of radiation, it is a poor radiator and can hardly lose its own heat by radiative cooling.

The colour of a surface gives a good indication of its absorptivity for solar radiation. The absorptivity decreases and the reflectivity increases with lightness of colour. But colour does not indicate the behaviour of a surface with respect to longer wave radiation. Thus, black and white paints have very different absorptivities for solar radiation and a black surface becomes much more heated on exposure to the sun. But the longwave emissivities of the two colours are equal and are therefore cooled equally at night by radiation to the sky.

Every surface absorbs and emits radiation simultaneously. The radiant heat exchange between two parallel surfaces depends on the effective emissivity (E) of both, given by the equation:

$$E = \frac{1}{1/\varepsilon_1 + 1/\varepsilon_2 - 1}.$$

The net radiant heat exchange per unit area (q_r) between two such surfaces is then given by the equations:

$$q_r = 4 \cdot 9E\left[(T_2/100)^4 - (T_1/100)^4\right] \text{ in the metric system}$$

and $q_r = 0 \cdot 173E\left[(T_2/100)^4 - (T_1/100)^4\right]$ in the British system.

Table 6.I gives typical values of shortwave absorptivity and longwave emissivity for various surface types and colours.

Table 6.I

Absorptivities and emissivities of various surfaces

Material or colour	Shortwave absorptivity	Longwave emissivity
Aluminium foil, bright	0·05	0·05
Aluminium foil, oxidized	0·15	0·12
Galvanized steel, bright	0·25	0·25
Aluminium paint	0·50	0·50
Whitewash, new	0·12	0·90
White oil paint	0·20	0·90
Grey colour, light	0·40	0·90
Grey colour, dark	0·70	0·90
Green colour, light	0·40	0·90
Green colour, dark	0·70	0·90
Ordinary black colour	0·85	0·90

6.3. The Surface Coefficient

As mentioned before, the surface coefficient determines the rate of heat exchange between the surface and the surrounding air, and the radiation exchange with other surfaces, or the sky. Thus the surface coefficient comprises two factors, involving the radiative and convective exchanges. The radiative coefficient is mainly dependent on the surface emissivity, and also to some degree on the mean temperature of the surfaces exchanging radiation. The convective coefficient depends primarily on the velocity of the air near the surface.

Approximate values of the coefficient of radiant heat exchange (H_r) for a black surface are given by Dreyfus [6.3].

Mean temperature (deg C)	20	30	40	50
H_r (kcal/m² h deg C)	5·0	5·4	6·0	7·0

For a surface with an emissivity ε the coefficient h_r is given by the product,

$$h_r = \varepsilon H_r$$

The convective heat transfer at the surface can be subdivided into two components: the thermal convection and the forced convection. Thermal convection is due to temperature differences between surface and surrounding air and depends on the magnitude of the temperature difference and on the position of the surface.

Dreyfus [6.3] gives the following values for the thermal convection coefficient for vertical surfaces, according to the temperature difference with the air.

Temperature difference (deg C)	2	10	30
Thermal convection coefficient (kcal/m² h deg C)	2	3	4

For an upper horizontal surface (roof), when the heat flow is upwards, these values have to be multiplied by a factor of 1·33, and for a horizontal lower face (ceiling) by a factor of 0·67. The forced convection is the dominant factor in cases where the surface is exposed to the effect of wind. It is primarily dependent on the wind speed near the surface and on the surface roughness. To give an average value Dreyfus [6.3] suggests this formula for estimating the convective coefficient h_c, in the presence of wind:

$$h_c = 3 \cdot 6 V$$

where h_c is expressed in kcal/m² h deg C and V in m/sec.

The actual surface coefficient is the sum of the radiative and convective coefficients and is denoted by h, or by h_i for internal and h_e for external surfaces.

When the windows are closed, the indoor air is almost still and the mean temperature is generally about 20–25°C. In these conditions, h_r is 5 metric units and the convective coefficient determined by thermal effect is about 2, so that the overall surface coefficient is:

$$h_i = 5 + 2 = 7 \text{ kcal/m}^2 \text{ h deg C } (1 \cdot 47 \text{ Btu/ft}^2 \text{ h deg F}).$$

When windows are open and the room space cross-ventilated, the indoor air velocity may be about 1 m/sec. Then the surface coefficient is:

$$h_i = 5 + 2 + 3\cdot6 \times 1 = 10\cdot6 \text{ kcal/m}^2 \text{ h deg C (2 Btu/ft}^2 \text{ h deg F).}$$

For an external surface with a greater difference in temperature from the adjacent air, the thermal convective coefficient is about 5·0 and, with a light wind of about 2m/sec, the surface coefficient is:

$$h_e = 5 + 5 + 2 \times 3\cdot6 = 17\cdot2 \text{ kcal/m}^2 \text{ h deg C (3·4 Btu/ft}^2 \text{ h deg F).}$$

With a higher wind speed of about 7 m/sec, this coefficient becomes:

$$h_e = 5 + 5 + 7 \times 3\cdot6 = 35\cdot2 \text{ kcal/m}^2 \text{ h deg C (7 Btu/ft}^2 \text{ h deg F).}$$

In practice, different values have to be used under summer and winter conditions. In winter, windows are closed and the calculation of maximum heat loss is of principal interest, occurring when the wind speed is high. Under such conditions, the internal coefficient should be about 7 metric units (1·4 English units) and the external one about 30 (6·0). In summer, windows are opened, and of main importance is the estimation of maximum solar heating, encountered at low air velocities. In these conditions a suitable internal coefficient would be about 13 (2·6), with an external coefficient of about 18 (3·6) units.

All the values quoted above refer to surfaces of average roughness. On increasing the roughness, contact is improved between surface and air and the surface coefficient increases. For very smooth surfaces, such as glass, the surface coefficient is about 30% lower, and for very rough surfaces 30% higher than the average values given before.

6.4. Thermal Conductance of Air Spaces

In many cases, building components include internal air spaces. Such air spaces provide a resistance to heat flow which depends on their thickness and on the characteristics of the enclosing surfaces. Heat transfer across an air space takes place by radiation from the warmer to the colder surface, by conduction across the still air layer on both surfaces and by convection currents in the enclosed air.

The radiant component depends on the effective emissivity of the surfaces involved, as discussed earlier (*see* Section 6.2) and is not affected by the direction of heat flow or its distance (*i.e.* depth of the space). As mentioned before, the emissivity of the average building material is about 0·90. The effective emissivity of an air space enclosed by such materials is:

$$E = \frac{1}{\dfrac{1}{0·9} + \dfrac{1}{0·9} - 1} = \frac{1}{1·22} \simeq 0·82$$

If one surface of the air space is covered by a reflective foil then:

$$E = \frac{1}{\dfrac{1}{0·05} + \dfrac{1}{0·9} - 1} = \frac{1}{20·11} \simeq 0·05$$

and if both surfaces bordering the space are covered by foil, the effective emissivity falls to 0·03.

Heat exchange by conduction across the air films and by convection in the air depends on the position (vertical or horizontal) of the space and its width, and on the direction of heat flow (upwards, downwards or horizontal), because these affect the stability of the air

Table 6.II

Conductance of air spaces

Position and direction of heat flow	Reflecting material on one side	Ordinary materials on both sides
Vertical, both directions	2·4 (0·48)*	5·0 (1·0)*
Horizontal, upwards	2·7 (0·55)*	5·3 (1·06)*
Horizontal, downwards	1·2 (0·24)*	4·0 (0·8)*

* Equivalent British units.

layers adjacent to the surfaces. When the space is horizontal and the lower enclosing surface warmer than the upper surface (heat flow upwards), the air in contact with the lower face is warmed, becomes less dense and rises through the air space, carrying heat from lower to upper surface. Under these conditions thermal convection obtains its highest value.

On the other hand, when the air space is horizontal but the upper surface is the warmer (heat flow downwards), the warm air in contact with this surface is less dense and the colder air near the lower surface more dense than the rest of the air in the space. This arrangement is therefore stable, thermal convective currents are inhibited and motionless layers of appreciable thickness created. Here the thermal convection is a minimum.

When the air space is vertical an intermediate position with respect to convective heat flow is achieved.

Values for the thermal conductance of air spaces, according to their positions, widths and effective emissivities, are given in Reference 6.1. For vertical and horizontal unventilated air spaces the approximate values shown in Table 6.II, averages of figures from different sources, may be used. The figures are given in kcal/m^2 h deg C, in parentheses in Btu/ft^2 h deg F.

It may be seen that by lining one surface with a reflective material its thermal resistance is increased two- or threefold. This is particularly useful for upper boundaries of horizontal air spaces where dust accumulation is minimal; lining the lower surface is much less effective because in time the reflective power is greatly reduced by dust.

For vertical air spaces, higher resistance is obtained by fixing the reflective layer in the middle of the space. In this case two additional surfaces, both reflective, are provided and the air attached to them adds to the overall thermal resistance of the air space.

6.5. Heat Capacity

The term heat capacity of a wall or roof refers to the amount of heat required to elevate the temperature of a unit volume of the wall, or unit area of the surface, by one degree. In the first case it is referred to as the volumetric heat capacity of the material (C_V) and in the second as the heat capacity of the wall (C_W).

The unit of C_V is kcal/m^3 and of C_W is kcal/m^2. The first term is used in the description of a material and the second in the description of building components.

Materials are heated differently by the same quantity of heat, according to the product of their specific heat and density. Values for several different materials are given in Table 6.III [6.3].

The heat capacities of materials are only significant when thermal conditions are fluctuating. Under conditions approaching a steady state, as when there is a great difference between the outdoor

Table 6.III

Thermophysical properties of various building materials
(after Dreyfus [6.3] and others)

Material (dry state)	Conductivity λ	Specific weight ζ	Specific heat c	Diffusivity $\dfrac{\lambda}{\zeta c}$	$\lambda \rho c$
	$\dfrac{kcal}{m\ h\ deg\ C}$	$\dfrac{kg}{m^3}$	$\dfrac{kcal}{kg\ deg\ C}$	$\dfrac{m^2}{h}$	
Ordinary concrete	1·1	2·300	0·24	20	620
Mortar	0·6	1·800	0·24	13	260
Lightweight concrete	0·27	600	0·25	18	40
Bricks	0·70	1·800	0·22	18	280
Wood	0·11	500	0·34	6·5	19
	0·17	800	0·34	5·5	46
Insulating wood fibres	0·038	230	0·35	4·8	3·1
	0·17	800	0·34	5·5	40
Felt of mineral wool	0·05	450	0·19	5·9	4·3
Expanded polystyrene	0·03	50	0·4	15	0·6

temperature and the indoor (kept nearly constant by heating or air-conditioning), the heat capacity has little effect on internal thermal conditions. The heat flow and temperature distribution depend in this case mainly on the thermal transmittance of the building envelope and on the amount of heating. But under fluctuating conditions, when the structure is heated and cooled periodically as a result of variations in outdoor temperature and solar radiation, or intermittent heating, the heat capacity has a decisive effect in determining indoor thermal conditions.

Of the two components of the heat capacity, *i.e.* specific heat and density, the range of the first is very small. Among building materials the highest specific heats are those of wood and plastics (0·4–0·5 according to the water content) and the lowest is that of steel (0·11) so that the entire range is relatively about 1 to 4·5. In contrast, the density range is very wide. The relative density of air (which can be considered as a "building material" in the form of air spaces) is about 0·00115 while that of dense concrete is 2·4, *i.e.* a range about 1 to 2000. Even if the density of light expanded polystyrene (0·02) is taken as the lowest among the materials in use, the range is 1 to 120. As a result the heat capacity of a wall, or of the structure as a whole, is closely related to its weight.

6.6. *Combinations of the Basic Thermophysical Properties*

The thermal conductivity and heat capacity of the materials, as well as the thickness of the building components and the order of the layers in composite constructions, can be combined in several ways, each of which is of importance under certain conditions.

Thermal diffusivity

The first derived property of a material is the thermal diffusivity (α), which is defined as the ratio between the thermal conductivity (λ) and the volumetric heat capacity, or:

$$\alpha = \frac{\lambda}{\rho c} = \frac{\lambda}{C_V}$$

where ρ is the density, c is the specific heat and C_V is the volumetric heat capacity.

The thermal diffusivity is a property of the material and not of the component. It is used mainly in theoretical computations of heat flow and temperature patterns under periodic conditions (*see* Section 7.5.).

Thermal resistance–capacity product (*time constant*)

The product of the thermal resistance and heat capacity, RC_W, is a property of the building component. It has a dimension of time:

$$RC_W = (d)\,(d \times h \times \deg C/kcal)\,(kcal/d^2 \times \deg C) = h$$

and therefore may be termed the time constant of the component.

Mathematically the time constant is equal to the square of the thickness divided by the thermal diffusivity:

$$RC_W = (d/\lambda)\,(d\rho c) = d^2/\lambda/\rho c = d^2/\alpha.$$

The time constant of a wall affects the relationship between the outdoor and indoor conditions when the external factors (air temperature and solar radiation) are only directly operating on the external surfaces. Under such conditions the time constant determines the amplitude of indoor temperature under a given average amplitude of the external surface temperatures, as well as affecting the time lag between the outdoor and indoor maxima (*see* Section 7.5).

Thermal conductivity–capacity product
The product of the thermal conductivity and volumetric heat capacity, $\lambda \rho c$, greatly affects the indoor conditions under the influence of factors operating within the building, such as solar radiation penetrating through the windows, air temperature and velocity in a ventilated space, internal sources of, for example, heating, cooling, intermittent heating, etc.

6.7. The Equivalent Resistance–Capacity Product (RC) of Multi-layer Elements

In multi-layer walls the combined effect of thermal resistance and heat capacity depends not only on the overall thermal transmittance and heat capacity but also on the specific order of the various layers, which may differ in their thickness and thermophysical properties.

Several methods were developed to take into account the order of the layers and to compute what may be termed the equivalent thermal resistance–capacity product, *i.e.* the equivalent *RC*, of multi-layer building components. Of these methods, three will be described in some detail: those of Mackey and Wright, of Roux, Richards and van Straaten, and of Raychaudhury and Chaudhury.

a. The method of Mackey and Wright [6.4]
Mackey and Wright rearranged the basic components of the *RC* product in the following form:

$$R \times C = (L/k)(L\rho c) = (k\rho c)(L/k)^2$$

where: L is the thickness, c the specific heat, ρ the density and k the thermal conductivity.

For a multi-layer building component the equivalent values of $K\rho c$ and L/K are computed according to the following formulae (after Dreyfus [6.3]):

Equivalent $L/K = A$ and equivalent $k\rho c = B$. A and B are computed as follows:

$$A = \left(\frac{L}{\lambda}\right)_i + \left(\frac{L}{\lambda}\right)_{m_1} + \left(\frac{L}{\lambda}\right)_{m_2} \cdots + \left(\frac{L}{\lambda}\right)_e$$

$$B = \frac{1 \cdot 1}{A}\left[\sum \left(\frac{L}{\lambda}\right)(K\rho c) - \left(\frac{K}{L}\right)_e (K\rho c)_e\right] + \frac{K\rho c_e}{A}\left[\left(\frac{L}{\lambda}\right)_e - 0 \cdot 1 \left(\frac{L}{\lambda}\right)_i - 0 \cdot 1 \left(\frac{L}{\lambda}\right)_{m_1} \cdots \text{etc.}\right].$$

The indices i, m_1, m_2 ... and e represent the innermost, intermediate and external layers, respectively.

When the second term in the computation of B is negative it is "neglected". The value of $A^2 B$, when A and B are computed according to these formulae, is the equivalent RC of the multi-layer building component.

As an example of the procedure of computation, the equivalent RC is computed for a wall with the structure given in Table 6.IV. In order to utilise the equations developed by Mackey and Wright or

Table 6.IV

Computation of the equivalent RC for a particular wall
according to Mackey and Wright [6.4]

Layer	ρ (lb/ft³)	L (ft)	k $\left(\dfrac{\text{Btu}}{\text{ft}^2\,\text{h deg F}}\right)$	ρc	$k\rho c$	$L/k = n$	$(L/k)(k\rho c)$
Ext. plaster	110	0·05	0·7	24	16·8	0·07	1·18
Bricks	100	0·37	0·6	22	13·2	0·62	8·18
Air space	—	—	—	—	—	1·00	—
Concrete	150	0·50	1·1	33	36·3	0·45	16·33
Int. plaster	100	0·05	0·6	22	13·2	0·08	1·06
						2·22	26·75

the tables based on them (see Section 7.5) all parameters are expressed in British units.

From Table 6.IV the following values are obtained:

Equiv. $L/K = A = 2\cdot22$

Equiv. $k\rho c = B = \dfrac{1\cdot1}{2\cdot22}\,(26\cdot75 - 1\cdot18)\ +$

$$\dfrac{16\cdot8}{2\cdot22}\,0\cdot07\ -\ 0\cdot1\,(26\cdot75 - 1\cdot06).$$

The second term of B is negative and neglected. Therefore $B = 12\cdot75$. The equivalent RC is then:

Equiv. $RC = A^2 B = 2\cdot22^2 \times 12\cdot75 = 62\cdot84$ hours.

b. The thermal time constant (Raychaudhury and Chaudhury)

The concept of the thermal time constant was suggested by Bruckmayer [6.2] and further developed by Raychaudhury and Chaudhury [6.5]. It expresses the equivalent diffusivity of multilayer structures. It is defined as the Q/U ratio for the structure where Q is the heat stored in the material and U is the heat transmitted.

Mathematically, the Q/U ratio of the multilayer structure is defined as the sum of the individual Q/U values of the separate layers, i.e.:

$$Q/U = \sum Q_i/U$$

where:

$Q_1/U = (R_{s0} + l_1/2k_1)\,(l\rho c)_1$
$Q_2/U = (R_{s0} + l_1/k_1 + l_2/2k_2)\,(l\rho c)_2$
$Q_i/U = (R_{s0} + l_1/k_1 + \ldots l_i/2k_1)\,(l\rho c)_i$

where R_{s0} is the thickness of the external surface, l_i, k_i and ρc_i are respectively the thickness, thermal conductivity and volumetric heat capacity of the ith layer; the Q/U ratio has a dimension of time and is given in hours.

Raychaudhury and Chaudhury [6.5] have found that for multilayer construction both the thermal damping and the time lag of the internal temperature wave are functions of the Q/U ratio. Thermal

Table 6.V

Computation of the Thermal Time Constant

Layer	ρ	L	k	ρc	$l\rho c$	L/k $= r$	Mid-layer accum.	Fractional T.T.C.	Accum. T.T.C.
Ext. surface	—	—	—	—	—	0·20	—	—	—
Ext. plaster	110	0·05	0·7	24	1·20	0·07	0·235	0·3	0·3
Bricks	100	0·37	0·6	22	8·14	0·62	0·58	4·7	5·0
Air space	—	—	—	—	—	1·00	1·39	—	—
Concrete	150	0·50	1·1	33	16·50	0·45	2·115	34·9	39·9
Int. plaster	100	0·05	0·6	22	11·00	0·08	2·38	26·2	66·1

damping is taken to be the ratio of the difference between the external and internal ranges of temperature to the external range.

Analysis of the experimental results of Raychaudhury and Chaudhury shows, however, that the relationship between Q/U and thermal damping is not constant but varies with the components (walls, roofs or complete buildings).

A sample computation of the thermal time constant for the wall specified in Table 6.IV is demonstrated in Table 6.V. The Q/U values

Table 6.VI

Q/U values of walls and roofs [6.5]; order of layers
given from the exterior inward

Component	Description	Q/U
Wall	1½ in plaster, 9 in brickwork, 1½ in plaster	18·2
Wall	½ in plaster, 4½ in brickwork, ½ in plaster	6·7
Wall	½ in plaster, 4½ in brickwork, 2 in air space, 4½ in brickwork, ½ in plaster	25·2
Wall	1 in plaster over wire mesh, 1 in expanded plastic, 4½ in brickwork, ½ in plaster	50·2
Wall	½ in plaster, 4½ in brickwork, 1 in expanded plastic, 1 in plaster over wire mesh	17·1
Roof	½ in plaster, 6½ in reinforced concrete, ½ in plaster	10·7
Roof	½ in cement concrete, 2 in vermiculite concrete, 4½ in reinforced concrete	55·2

of different types of walls and roofs, as calculated by Raychaudhury and Chaudhury, are given in Table 6.VI.

c. The R × C product

In South Africa, Roux, Richards and van Straaten used the ratio C/U of the heat capacity of the whole structure per unit external surface area (C) to the overall heat transmission coefficient (U) as an indication of the effective diffusivity of the building and as a criterion by which to evaluate its thermal performance under non-steady heat flow conditions.

The factor C is computed according to the formula:

$$C = S \left(\frac{A_e W_e + A_i W_i}{A_e} \right)$$

where S is the specific heat of the wall materials (about 0·22 for ordinary materials), A_e and A_i are the total surface areas and W_e and W_i are the weights per unit surface area of the external and internal walls respectively. U is the weighted average heat transmission coefficient, computed in the conventional way, as discussed previously (*see* Section 6.1).

van Straaten [6.7] gives the computed C/U values for houses of different construction as presented in Table 6.VII.

Table 6.VII
RC Values for houses of different construction

External walls	Internal walls	C/U
Corrugated galvanized steel on metal frame	—	0·3
4 in solid breeze blocks	4 in solid breeze blocks	19
4½ in brick	4½ in brick	27
6 in no-fines stone concrete	4 in no-fines stone concrete	37
9 in hollow breeze block	4 in solid breeze block	44
11 in cavity brick	4½ in brick	70

Chapter 7

The Thermal Effect of Building Materials

7.1. General Discussion

The envelope of a building separates the indoor space from the external environment and in this way modifies or prevents the direct effect of climatic variables such as outdoor air temperature, humidity, wind, solar radiation, rain, snow, etc. This envelope is usually composed of two types of material, opaque and transparent, although translucent materials are sometimes included.

The quantitative effect of the envelope depends on its thickness and thermophysical properties. The materials within the internal space, such as floors, partitions and even furniture, also modify the indoor temperatures by affecting the heat capacity of the structure as a whole and the rate of absorption of heat generated or penetrating within the building.

When the windows of a building are open, there is a flow of outdoor air through the indoor space, but even when the windows are closed they offer a very low resistance to heat flow and air can infiltrate through the cracks around them. Through transparent and translucent materials (glass and plastics) and through open windows, solar radiation can penetrate and heat the building from the inside. Thus large quantities of heat may enter and leave the building, by-passing the modifying influence of the rest of the envelope. The external temperature and humidity conditions may then affect the inside directly, although the quantatitive effect of air flow is also dependent on the properties of the materials.

When the indoor thermal conditions are not controlled by mechanical means ("natural" conditions), the materials affect the temperatures of both the indoor air and surfaces and thus have a very pronounced effect on the occupants' comfort. Even when control is used, in the form of heating or air-conditioning for instance, the thermophysical properties of the materials used determine the amount of heating or cooling which is provided (the capacity of the heating or air-conditioning plant) and also the temperature of the internal surfaces (radiant temperature). Therefore, even in these circumstances, the materials have an effect on the comfort of the occupants, as well as on the economical efficiency of the control systems.

Before discussing the quantitative aspects of the thermal effect of building materials, a schematic description is given to show the heat flow and temperature patterns in a building exposed to a given series of climatic conditions.

Outdoor temperature and solar radiation follow diurnal and annual cyclic patterns; the range of variation depends on the geographic location, as discussed in Chapter 1.

The indoor thermal conditions in buildings without mechanical control follow this pattern, but in a modified form which depends on the details of design and construction.

The principal modifications are changes in the amplitude of variation and in the timing of the maximum and minimum temperatures. To illustrate the relation between outdoor and indoor temperatures, a typical daily pattern is here described and analysed.

Before sunrise, both the outdoor air and the external surfaces of the building envelope are at their minimum temperatures. After sunrise the outdoor air temperature increases, reaching its maximum in the early afternoon (about 2–4 p.m.). The rate of this rise depends to a great extent on the distance from the sea. In coastal regions, especially where the wind blows from the sea during the day, the rate of temperature rise is small and the daily amplitude is about 4–7 deg C (7–12.5 deg F). In inland regions it may be as much as 15–20 deg C (27–36 deg F) or more.

The rise in the outdoor air temperature causes heat flow to the external surfaces of the building envelope, raising their temperatures. This effect is almost identical for all the surfaces, regardless of their position. At the same time solar radiation, whether it is direct, diffused from the sky or reflected from neighbouring surfaces, impinges on the building. Part of the radiation is reflected but the rest is absorbed by the surface, further elevating its temperature to a level above that of the air. The position of the surface determines the intensity of incident solar radiation, resulting in different temperature patterns for the roof and each of the walls. The magnitude of the temperature elevation is proportional to the absorptivity coefficient of the surface in question (*see* Chapter 6).

The process of heat flow through a wall from the external surface at an elevated temperature may be visualized by considering the building envelope divided into several layers. The heat flow into each layer causes an elevation of its temperature and the heat used for this is stored in the layer; the excess heat is subsequently transferred to the next, colder layer. Thus each layer receives less heat and is subject to a smaller temperature rise than the layer externally adjacent to it. As a result of this heat storage within the structure of the envelope, less heat reaches the innermost layer than crosses the outermost one, and its temperature elevations are smaller.

After the external surface reaches its maximum temperature and starts to cool, the process is reversed. First, the heat accumulated in the wall flows in two directions, inwards and outwards, and later the entire flow is outwards. Then the process may be visualized as a successive cooling of the various layers.

In this way any plane of the wall undergoes wave-like cycles of heating and cooling. The amplitude of the internal wave is smaller than that to which the external surface is subjected and the internal maximum and minimum temperatures are delayed. The ratio of the internal to the external amplitude depends on the thermophysical properties and thickness of the structure. As the thickness and heat capacity of the walls increase and the thermal conductivity of the materials decreases, the amplitude of the internal wave diminishes (smaller amplitude ratio) and the timing of the maxima and minima is more retarded (greater time lag).

The combined effect of thermal conductivity and heat capacity of homogeneous walls is expressed by the thermal diffusivity of the material (α/pc) and of composite walls by the equivalent RC or Thermal Time constant described in the preceding chapter. The quantitative dependence of amplitude ratio and time lag on the properties is discussed later.

The process described above does not take into account those factors affecting the internal air and surface temperatures without the modification of the walls. Such factors exist, however, and include ventilation of the building, solar radiation penetrating through the windows and heat generated within the building. Ventilation brings the outdoor air into direct and immediate contact with the indoor air and surfaces, possibly at different temperatures. Solar radiation entering through glazed areas is either reflected from the floor to the internal surfaces, or is absorbed in the floor, elevating its temperature and subsequently heating the indoor air and other surfaces. Various processes of habitation such as cooking, washing, use of electrical equipment, etc., liberate heat inside the building.

All these factors affect the internal temperature directly, by-passing the modifying effect of the walls and roof. The quantitative effect of these factors also depends on the thermophysical properties of the materials, but combined differently from when the climatic factors operate on the external surfaces. Here, the main property of the material affecting its response to internal heating (or cooling) is the product of the thermal conductivity and volumetric heat capacity ($\lambda \rho c$) particularly that of the internal wall layers. When this product is high, as it is for concrete, the walls can absorb heat from internal sources more quickly and with a lower resultant temperature elevation. On the other hand, when the value of $\lambda \rho c$ is low, for insulating materials for instance, the internal surfaces are heated more readily.

The value of $\lambda \rho c$ also determines the relation between the indoor air and surface temperatures, especially when the building is venti-lated. With high $\lambda \rho c$ values there might be an appreciable difference between these because the air temperature in a ventilated building approaches that outside, while the surface temperatures may be kept at a much higher level by the heat flow from within the walls. With low values of $\lambda \rho c$ the rate of heat flow from inside the wall is reduced and the quantity of stored heat is small, and thus surface temperatures closely follow that of the indoor air.

In a similar manner, the $\lambda \rho c$ value determines the pattern of indoor air temperatures when the heating and cooling are inter-mittent. Buildings of materials with high values of $\lambda \rho c$ are warmed slowly when the heating system is turned on, but cool slowly after it is closed down; the reverse is true when $\lambda \rho c$ is low.

7.2. Parameters of the Pattern of Indoor Temperature from a Bioclimatological Viewpoint

The pattern of indoor temperatures may be expressed using several parameters, the choice of which depends on their significance from the viewpoint of the occupants' comfort in different climatic conditions.

a. The ratio between the temperature amplitudes of the internal and external surfaces (decrement factor) and the time lag between their maxima and minima

These parameters express the thermal properties of the walls from the physical point of view and may be given direct, although not simple, mathematical analysis; they are employed in most theoretical works. However, they may have only limited application as guides for selecting building materials according to the human requirements under differing climatic conditions. For example, walls with a low amplitude ratio (high decrement factor) will have a reduced maximum temperature in the day but an elevated minimum at night, with a possibly detrimental effect on sleep.

In addition, the parameters are applicable only when the ventilation conditions are constant throughout the day and night, and the building is assumed to be closed at all times. When ventilation is used selectively, for example during the evening and night only, the minimum and maximum temperatures are affected differently and both the decrement factor and time lag deviate from the computed values. Furthermore, conclusions based on these parameters may sometimes be misleading. Thus in hot dry regions it is assumed that the smaller the decrement factor (smaller internal amplitude) the more satisfactory the building. But night ventilation, mainly effecting a reduction in the minimum temperature, increases the internal amplitude and consequently reduces the decrement factor, while greatly improving the thermal performance of the building.

Therefore the decrement factor alone is not an adequate criterion for the choice of materials in such a situation. This parameter has a further drawback in that it does not relate closely to temperature patterns too divergent from symmetrical standard, such as those occurring in eastern walls.

b. The ratio between the integrals of the temperature/time functions of the internal and external surfaces (area under curves of temperature pattern)

As with the amplitude ratio this parameter is concerned with physical characteristics of the walls and may be given the same mathematical analysis. The ratio may be obtained by integration of the respective computed temperature/time functions, or graphically from observed temperature curves.

It has some advantage over the amplitude ratio because it is less sensitive to deviations in the external surface temperature and hence identical walls of different orientations will vary less in their ratios of temperature × time "areas" than in their amplitude ratios. Physiologically, the limitations of the two parameters are similar.

c. The difference between the maximum external and internal air temperatures

When selecting building materials according to human thermal requirements, this is the principal factor to consider in regions of low humidity with temperatures high during the day and low at night (arid zones). Here the windows can comfortably be kept closed during the day, enabling a suitable choice of materials to effect a reduction in the indoor maximum, and may be left open at night to reduce the indoor minimum.

This parameter can be predicted by certain formulae derived experimentally for specific ventilation patterns, according to the thermophysical properties of the materials, as well as by inference from the values derived from the decrement factors. It is greatly influenced by the external colours and thus takes into account the combined effect of the materials' properties and colour.

To provide sufficient information to evaluate the thermal performance of a building, this parameter should be supplemented with a consideration of the time lag between the respective maxima, which may also be predicted from empirical formulae.

d. Difference between minimum indoor and outdoor air temperatures

This parameter can be dealt with in the same way as the maximum temperature deviation. It is of importance in humid regions with warm windless nights, particularly when the daytime conditions are, in contrast, more windy and of moderate temperatures, as in many coastal regions.

In such regions it is of most significance to consider the minimum indoor temperature when the windows of the building are open during the night.

7.3. Effect of Thermal Resistance on Indoor Temperatures

The effect of the thermal resistance of a structure on the internal climate depends to a great extent on the presence or absence of artificial conditioning. Thus the two situations, where thermal control is mechanical (by heating, cooling, air-conditioning) and where the indoor conditions are determined only by interplay between the structural and environmental factors, are discussed here individually.

7.3.1. EFFECT IN WINTER AND IN AIR-CONDITIONED BUILDINGS.— In winter, when buildings are heated, the thermal resistance of the external walls determines their internal surface temperature and the rate of fuel consumption (when constant indoor air temperature is maintained), or the indoor air temperature (when heating appliances with constant output are used).

To some extent, further heating may compensate for a low thermal resistance, but in such a situation the gradient between the indoor air and the colder internal surfaces of the external walls increases until a limit is reached where condensation may take place (see Chapter 9). In addition, higher air temperatures are required to compensate the body for higher radiant heat loss to the cool surrounding surfaces.

As the average indoor-outdoor temperature difference in winter is usually large in comparison with the daily fluctuations, the heat flow in continuously heated buildings approaches a steady state and the thermal resistance is the principal, although not single, factor affecting internal conditions (see Chapter 16). When the heating is intermittent, other factors such as the heat capacity (see Section 7.4) assume greater significance.

In buildings air-conditioned in summer, the effect of thermal resistance is similar to that in winter, although the direction of the indoor-outdoor temperature difference is not always constant and may reverse at night. Because this difference is usually small compared with the diurnal fluctuations in summer, the relative importance of thermal resistance in determining the internal conditions is smaller, and that of heat capacity greater than in winter.

The size of the heating or cooling system in any building depends on the overall rate of heat flow, which is given by the product of the global coefficient of heat exchange (*see* Chapter 16) and the internal-external temperature difference. The global coefficient of heat exchange comprises three main parts: (a) heat flow across the opaque envelope (walls, floor and roof), (b) heat flow through the glazed areas, and (c) heat flow via air infiltration (through cracks around windows, etc.). The relative effect of thermal resistance of the walls depends on the relative weight of the first component of global heat exchange. On average this may comprise about 40–60 per cent of the total coefficient.

The difference between the internal air and surface temperatures of a given wall (Δt_i) depends on the product of the indoor–outdoor temperature difference (Δt) and the overall coefficient of thermal transmittance (U or K) (*see* Chapter 6) and on the internal surface coefficient (h_i). It may be estimated from the formula:

$$\Delta t_i = \frac{K\Delta t}{h_i} = \frac{K\Delta t}{7} \text{ (deg C).}$$

When a surface temperature drops below the dew-point of the interior air, condensation forms on the surface. Increasing the thermal resistance of the wall lowers the risk of condensation, by reducing the extent to which its internal surface is cooled. In regions where the humidity is high in winter, this consideration may be the main criterion for determining the required thermal resistance.

This subject is given further discussion in connection with design principles in cold regions (*see* Chapter 16) and the specific problem of condensation is dealt with in the chapter on wetness (*see* Chapter 9).

7.3.2. EFFECT WITHOUT AIR-CONDITIONING IN RELATION TO THE LOCATION OF RESISTANCE AND THE EXTERNAL COLOUR.—In summer, and in buildings without air-conditioning, increasing the thermal resistance of a wall or roof reduces the heat flow from external surfaces into the building during the day and out of it at night. The effect of the increased resistance on the internal temperatures depends on the location of the insulating layer and on the colour of the external surfaces.

When the additional insulation is given in the form of a special layer of insulating material it is more effective, in damping the heating effect of solar radiation absorbed in the outer surface and of steep rises in outdoor air temperature, when attached to the external side of the wall than when placed on its internal side. Therefore the maximum internal temperature is lower and the minimum higher with external rather than internal insulation.

The thermal effect of insulation layer location is illustrated by results of experiments at the Building Research Station in Haifa [7.4], in which the reduction in the maximum internal surface temperatures of grey coloured panels made of 5 cm concrete, brought about by the addition of 0·5 and 5·0 cm thick layers of expanded polystyrene, was measured with the insulation placed internally and externally. With these layers placed internally, the maxima were reduced by 3·2 and 13·3 deg C and with external insulation the respective reductions were 7·5 and 15·5 deg C. Thus the relative effect of location of the insulation is greater as the insulation is thinner.

Another characteristic of internal insulation is that it reduces the absorption rate of heat generated within the building and of heat penetrating through the windows in the form of solar radiation or hot outdoor air. This point is discussed in more detail later on (Section 7.6).

When the external surface is dark, its temperature is appreciably elevated above that of the outdoor air and the resulting heat flow tends to raise the internal surface temperature. Under such conditions an increase in the thermal resistance reduces the heat flow across the wall and generally lowers the internal temperatures. This effect is not linearly related to the thermal resistance, but is roughly proportional to its logarithm. Starting with walls or roofs of very low resistance, additional insulation causes an appreciable reduction in the daytime temperatures, while slightly elevating those at night. But above a resistance of about 2 m^2 h deg C/kcal, further increase shows very little effect on the internal surface temperature. This figure only applies where the corresponding heat capacity is negligible, as with curtain walls for example [7.4, 7.5].

The effect of thermal resistance on the internal temperature of black coloured horizontal sandwich panels is shown in Fig. 7.1. One whitewashed panel was also included for comparison. The results were obtained in experiments carried out at the Building Research Station in Haifa [7.4]. All panels were of 2·0 cm asbestos-cement. One

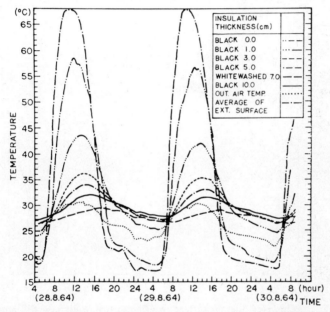

Fig. 7.1. Patterns of internal surface temperatures of externally black-painted sandwich panels made of asbestos-cement and expanded polystyrene.

of them was without any insulation and to the underside of the rest were affixed 1, 3, 5, 7 and 10 cm of expanded polystyrene. In this way the increase in thermal resistance was achieved almost without simultaneous increase in the heat capacity of the panels.

On the other hand the effect of thermal resistance when the external colour is white is quite different, in particular in regions where the outdoor temperature amplitude is small. Here the temperatures of the external surfaces are close to the level of the outdoor air and heat flow across the building envelope is much smaller. The thermal resistance of the walls or roof therefore has only a slight effect on the daytime temperature and may elevate the minimum temperatures more than reduce the maxima [7.4, 7.5].

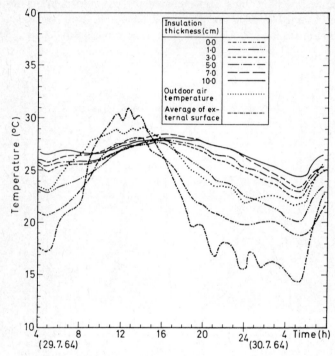

Fig. 7.2.   Pattern of internal surface temperatures of whitewashed sandwich panels made of asbestos-cement and expanded polystyrene.

This is illustrated in results of measurements at the Building Research Station in Haifa in mid-summer, shown in Fig. 7.2, where the internal surface temperatures of whitewashed sandwich panels with different thickness of insulation were observed.

In spite of the high solar intensity the maximum temperatures were below the outdoor air maximum, regardless of insulation thickness, but the minimum temperature was higher as the insulation thickness was made greater.

Only in regions with appreciable daily amplitude, of the order 10 deg C (18 deg F) and more, where the humidity is low enough to allow comfort without ventilation, is there a significant improvement in the indoor conditions when the thermal resistance of externally white walls is increased beyond about 0·5 m² h deg C/kcal.

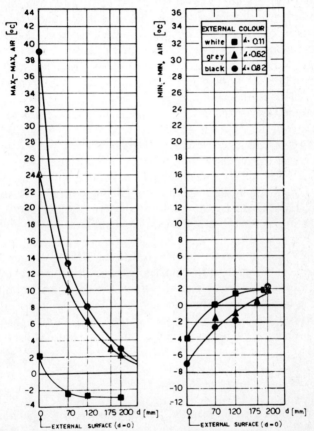

Fig. 7.3.   Differences between maximum and minimum internal surface temperatures and corresponding air temperatures as function of insulation thickness of light horizontal panels.

The interaction between the effects of thermal resistance and external colour is further illustrated in Fig. 7.3, which shows the elevation above the outdoor maximum of internal surface temperatures of lightweight horizontal panels, externally black, grey or white as a function of insulation thickness.

It may be seen that with a black external colour the addition of 1 cm of insulation to the uninsulated panel reduced the maximum internal temperature by about 15 deg C (27 deg F). The successive additions of 2 cm of insulation (to totals of 3 and 5 cm) caused further reductions of about 7 and 2·3 deg C respectively, and another 5 cm (total 10 cm) effected a further reduction of only 1·7 deg C. On the other hand, when the external colour was white, the maximum temperatures of all the panels were almost the same, irrespective of the insulation. The minimum temperature (elevation above outdoor minimum) rose as the thickness of insulation was increased, under all external colours.

In summarizing the effect of the thermal resistance produced by addition of thermal insulation to walls of low heat capacity, it may be concluded that, in a warm climate and under natural indoor conditions without artificial heating or cooling, there is an optimal thermal resistance determined by the external colour and existing ventilation. An increase beyond this optimal level produces little or no improvement on indoor conditions of comfort.

The adjustment of thermal resistance alone to improve the internal conditions in warm climates, without further control through adaptation of the heat capacity, is limited to regions where the outdoor maximum temperature does not rise above about 30°C (86°F). This is because, with lightweight structures of low heat capacity, the possible reductions in daytime indoor temperatures are rather limited.

7.4. Heat Capacity and Thickness of Walls

As mentioned in Section 7.1, the exterior of the building envelope is alternately heated during the day and cooled at night. The temperature range of an external surface depends mainly on its colour and orientation.

Part of the heat absorbed during the day warms the mass of the walls and roof and only the remainder passes to the interior. The ratio between the heat absorbed and that stored in the materials depends mainly on the heat capacity of the envelope, i.e. on the product of its weight and specific heat. Thus, under periodic variations in outdoor conditions and with given conditions of temperature difference and thermal resistance, heat flow into a building decreases as the heat capacity of its structure increases.

At night the heat stored in a structure of high heat capacity is released, reducing the rate of heat flow from the interior to a level below that anticipated for the existing temperature difference, from considerations of the thermal resistance alone. In this way the heat capacity moderates the rates of heat flow in and out of the building interior, and hence the indoor temperature fluctuations. In addition, it causes a delay in the timing of the heating and cooling periods of the temperature and heat flow cycle (time lag effect).

During the winter, and particularly in cold regions where the whole temperature range of external surfaces is below the level of the heated interior, the heat capacity only smooths over the fluctuations in the rate of heat loss without affecting the direction and average magnitude of the thermal gradient. Thus, with high heat capacity, the outdoor daily averages are of more significance than the extreme conditions. But, during the summer, and in warm regions, the external surface temperatures are above the internal level during the day and below it at night. Here, in addition to its quantitative damping effect on heat exchange, the heat capacity may also have a qualitative influence on the direction of flow.

A construction of high heat capacity thus enables a considerable degree of control of the internal thermal conditions in regions with a large diurnal temperature range and intense solar radiation. It is possible to regulate temperature fluctuations, not only those due to the heating patterns of external surfaces exposed to solar radiation and the outdoor air, but also those resulting from heat penetrating through windows with solar radiation and air infiltration or generated within the building by cooking, etc.

Therefore a large structural heat capacity can be a great advantage, particularly in arid or semi-arid inland regions where solar radiation is intense and the diurnal temperatures cover a wide range. On the other hand, such buildings cool slowly at night and have appreciably higher nocturnal temperatures than low heat capacity structures. A high capacity is therefore unsuitable in regions where thermal discomfort is mainly experienced at night, as in many humid coastal areas.

As mentioned before, the heat capacity per unit surface area of a structure is the product of the density, thickness and specific heat of its components. But the thermal effect of changing the density of the material is quite different from that of increase in thickness, even when resulting in the same change in heat capacity. The specific heats of standard inorganic materials are confined to a very small range (about 0·22–0·4 cal/g deg C) and thus heat capacity is almost entirely regulated by the weight of the structure. Any increase in heat capacity achieved by higher density is accompanied by a decrease in the thermal conductivity, thus reducing the thermal resistance. The replacement of heavyweight with lighter materials of higher thermal resistance, with no change in wall thickness, reduces the heat capacity and is therefore only moderately effective in improving the thermal conditions in summer. When the wall thickness is increased to raise the heat capacity, the overall thermal resistance increases also almost proportionally and thus the thermal effect is much greater.

According to the theoretical formulae given below (Section 7.5) the internal temperature amplitude varies as an exponential function of the thickness of the wall, and consequently the maximum temperature should decrease, and the minimum increase exponentially with increase in thickness. In practice, the quantitative effect of thickness on both the indoor surface and air temperatures also depends on the ventilation and external colour.

An illustration of the effect of thickness of lightweight concrete slabs in relation to their external colour, on the deviation of the maximum and minimum temperatures from the corresponding air temperatures, is shown in Fig. 7.4. These are the average results obtained in an experimental series (Section 7.5) in which the external and internal surface temperatures of Ytong panels, with thickness varying from 7 to 20 cm, have been measured.

It can be seen that with dark external colours the maximum internal temperatures were reduced exponentially as the thickness increased, but with white external colour the thickness did not affect the indoor maximum. The minimum temperatures, on the other hand, were elevated with increasing thickness regardless of the external colour.

These results agree well with those obtained with sandwiched panels of expanded polystyrene (*see* Sub-section 7.3.2).

The effect of thickness of lightweight concrete vertical walls was also observed in this study. Some of the results are summarized in Table 7.I, which gives results of measurements of the maxima and

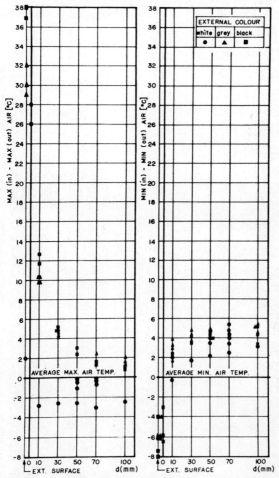

Fig. 7.4. Differences between maximum and minimum internal surface temperature and corresponding air temperatures as function of thickness of Ytong horizontal panels.

Table 7.I

Maximum and minimum temperature* and amplitude ratio** of lightweight concrete walls

	External colour	Ventilation conditions	12 cm				17 cm				22 cm			
			Δt_{max}	Δt_{min}	$\Delta t_{(i)}$	$\dfrac{\Delta t_{(i)}}{\Delta t_{(o)}}$	Δt_{max}	Δt_{min}	$\Delta t_{(i)}$	$\dfrac{\Delta t_{(i)}}{\Delta t_{(o)}}$	Δt_{max}	Δt_{min}	$\Delta t_{(i)}$	$\dfrac{\Delta t_{(i)}}{\Delta t_{(o)}}$
Indoor air temperature	Grey	Closed	6·2	1·9	10·5	1·64	4·6	3·7	7·1	1·11	3·6	5·3	4·6	0·72
	Grey	Ventilated	0·9	0·5	7·7	1·15	0·3	1·0	6·5	0·97	0·4	1·5	6·0	0·90
	White	Closed	−2·6	2·5	4·3	0·46	−3·1	3·6	2·7	0·29	−3·6	4·3	1·5	0·16
	White	Ventilated	−0·9	−0·4	5·1	0·91	−1·1	−0·1	4·7	0·84	−0·9	0·3	4·6	0·82
indoor surface temperature	Grey	Closed	10·4	0·0	16·2	0·46	6·4	3·0	9·6	0·30	4·4	4·5	6·1	0·20
	Grey	Ventilated	6·0	1·0	11·7	0·33	4·5	2·6	8·6	0·27	3·5	4·8	5·4	0·18
	White	Closed	−2·7	0·7	6·0	0·56	—	—	—	—	−4·1	2·1	3·2	0·34
	White	Ventilated	−0·8	−0·7	5·5	0·64	—	—	—	—	−2·1	0·4	3·9	0·56

* Maximum and minimum temperatures are expressed as deviations from the corresponding air temperature.

** The amplitude ratio of indoor air is based on outdoor air, and that of the internal surface on the external surface temperature.

minima of the internal air and surfaces, and the amplitude ratio of lightweight concrete walls of different thicknesses, computed on the basis of observed external surface and air temperatures (Section 7.5).

It can be seen from the Table that when the external colour is dark and the interior unventilated, the effect of thickness on the internal temperatures is exponential, *i.e.* in accordance with the theoretical predictions from the formula. When ventilation is used the effect of thickness on air temperature is very slight, while the surface temperature is still influenced. In the unventilated building with a white exterior, the exponential trend still holds, although the magnitude of the effect is small. But with white external colour and ventilation the internal temperatures were virtually unaffected by wall thickness.

This may be explained as follows. In practice the temperatures within ventilated buildings are determined by the combination of effect of two factors: heat flow across the walls, and outdoor air entering the space. When the external colour is light, the effect of ventilation is dominant and marks the influence of wall thickness. On the other hand, when the exterior is dark, the possible heat flow across the walls is increased greatly, so that the effect of thickness on temperatures is much more noticeable.

7.5. *Prediction of the Indoor Temperature Characteristics*

Several methods, both theoretical and experimental, have been developed to predict the characteristics of internal temperatures of interest for heat flow calculations or from the point of view of human comfort.

Most of the theoretical methods are based on the analysis of external heat load pattern (air temperature and solar radiation) into a series of superimposed waves of sinusoidal patterns (fundamental waves and harmonies, Fourier analysis). The internal air temperature pattern is then considered as a corresponding series of similar waves with reduced amplitudes and a phase delay. The ratio between the amplitudes of the external and corresponding internal waves (decrement factor) and the phase difference between the waves (time lag) are then computed as functions of the thickness, thermal conductivity and heat capacity of the materials.

The relationship between the internal and external waves depends on the period of the whole cycle. The period of the fundamental wave is 24 hours, that of the first harmonic $24/2 = 12$ hours, of the second harmonic $24/3 = 8$ hours, etc. The decrement factor and time lag increase with the wall thickness (L) and the volumetric heat capacity (ρc), and decrease with thermal conductivity (k) and the period of the cycle (T).

The experimental predictive methods are based on internal temperature measurements under natural conditions, in buildings or models constructed of different materials. These attempt to relate statistically the patterns of internal temperature to the various characteristics of the building materials.

One theoretical and two experimenal methods are described below.

a. Theoretical method: Mackey and Wright

Mackey and Wright [7.7] developed formulae and nomograms to determine the decrement factor and time lag under natural external conditions, as functions of the thermal diffusivity (α) and thickness (L) of the building components, and of the cycle period (T). Their method is applicable to homogeneous and to multi-layer walls. The indoor air temperature is assumed to be constant (as it is in air-conditioned buildings).

The first stage of this method is the computation of the sol-air temperature (*see* Chapter 10) operating on the external surface, according to the solar radiation incident on the wall, the absorptivity and the pattern of outdoor air temperature. The difference between the maximum and minimum sol-air temperatures for the given wall is the external amplitude (θ_o). The internal surface temperature is assumed to follow a cycle of amplitude θ_i which is related to the external amplitude by the decrement factor (λ).

i.e. $$\theta_i = \lambda\theta_o.$$

The timing of the internal maximum is delayed by φ, the time lag. The equations given by Mackey and Wright for λ and φ, as quoted by Dreyfus [7.1] are

$$\lambda = e^{-L\sqrt{\frac{\pi}{\alpha T}}}$$

$$\varphi = \frac{1}{2} L \sqrt{\frac{T}{\pi\alpha}}$$

and for the fundamental wave ($T = 24$ hours). This gives:

$$\lambda = e^{-0.362L\sqrt{\frac{\pi}{\alpha T}}}$$

$$\varphi = 1.38L \sqrt{\frac{1}{\alpha}}$$

Nomograms were prepared to determine the fundamental decrement factor and time lag from the computed values of the equivalent Kpc and K/L (reciprocal of the equivalent thermal resistance L/K, see Chapter 6). The conditions assumed, for application of the nomograms, are these:

Film coefficient of outdoor air = 4·0 Btu/h ft² deg F
Film coefficient of indoor air = 1·65 Btu/h ft² deg F
Indoor air temperature constant
Sol-air temperature periodic.

Table 7.II

Decrement factor as a function of K/L and Kpc
(after Mackey and Wright)

Kpc \ K/L	1000	500	200	100	50	30	20	10	5	3	2	1	0·5
10,000	0·62	0·51	0·28	0·33	0·07	0·04	0·02	—	—	—	—	—	—
5,000	0·68	0·62	0·45	0·40	0·14	0·08	0·05	—	—	—	—	—	—
2,000	—	0·69	0·62	0·50	0·32	0·20	0·13	0·06	—	—	—	—	—
1,000	—	—	0·69	0·61	0·48	0·35	0·26	0·14	0·04	—	—	—	—
500	—	—	—	0·61	0·62	0·61	0·42	0·23	0·10	0·03	—	—	—
300	—	—	—	—	0·65	0·63	0·52	0·35	0·16	0·07	0·02	—	—
200	—	—	—	—	0·68	0·65	0·60	0·45	0·24	0·11	0·05	—	—
100	—	—	—	—	—	0·66	0·63	0·55	0·38	0·23	0·12	0·02	—
50	—	—	—	—	—	—	—	0·60	0·49	0·36	0·23	0·06	—
20	—	—	—	—	—	—	—	—	0·55	0·46	0·37	0·16	0·02
10	—	—	—	—	—	—	—	—	—	0·49	0·41	0·26	0·08
5	—	—	—	—	—	—	—	—	—	—	0·43	0·30	0·14

Table 7.II was derived from the formulae and gives the variations in fundamental decrement factor with K/L and Kpc.

With the composite wall described previously (*see* Section 6.7) as an example and taking $L/K = 2\cdot22$, $Kpc = 12\cdot75$ and $K/L = 0\cdot45$, the approximate value of the fundamental decrement factor obtained from the Table (by interpolation and extrapolation) is $0\cdot05$.

*Table 7.*III

Decrement factor and time lag for different walls and roofs (after Dreyfus)

Component	Composition (from exterior to interior)		Decrement factor	Time lag
Roof	Rockwool	4 cm	0·046	11h 50m
	Concrete	10 cm		
Roof	Concrete	10 cm	0·45	3h
	Rockwool	4 cm		
Wall	Plaster	15 cm		
	Concrete	10 cm		
	Air space		0·073	10h
	Concrete	10 cm		
	Plaster	15 cm		
Wall	Plaster	1·5 cm		
	Hollow concrete blocks	10 cm		
	Air space		0·056	10h 50m
	Hollow concrete blocks	10 cm		
	Plaster	1·5 cm		
Wall	Plaster	1·5 cm		
	Hollow bricks	10 cm		
	Air space		0·10	8h 45m
	Hollow bricks	10 cm		
	Plaster	1·5 cm		
Wall	Concrete	15 cm		
	Ventilated air space		0·073	10h
	Concrete	15 cm		

Table 7.III gives values of the decrement factor and time lag for various types of homogeneous and composite walls and roofs, computed by Dreyfus [7.1] according to the formulae of Mackey and Wright. It may be seen that in a wall (or roof) composed of a heavy- and a lightweight insulating layer, such as concrete with mineral

wool or expanded polystyrene, the location of the insulation has a pronounced effect on the decrement factor. Thus for a composition of 10 cm concrete and 4 cm mineral wool, the placement of the insulation as an external layer results in a decrement factor of only 0·046, while when it is placed as an internal layer the factor is 0·45.

b. Experimental methods

For standard building materials, such as bricks, concrete, stone, etc., the indoor temperature is closely related to the thickness of the walls and internal partitions. It has also been observed that, in any region, maximum outdoor temperatures vary more in summer than the minima, and thus the daily outdoor amplitude is to some extent related to the maximum. These relationships have been used to derive experimental formulae for prediction of the indoor maximum temperature, expressed as the reduction in indoor below outdoor maximum, as a function of the average weight of the building per unit external surface area. These formulae assume a minimal ventilation effect and are therefore only applicable to dry regions.

In Australia, Drysdale [7.2, 7.3] suggested the formula:

$$t_{max(i)} = t_{max(o)} - 0·009W\,[t_{max(o)} - 68]\;°F,$$

where W is the average weight per unit area of the external walls (lb/ft^2). This formula assumes that the building is single-storeyed with a standard roof, as is common in Australia.

In India, Raychaudhury and Chaudhury [7.8] suggest this formula:

$$t_{max(i)} = t_{max(o)} - 0·004W\,[t_{max(o)} - 60]\;°F,$$

where W in this case is the average weight of the whole structure, including roof, internal and external walls, per unit area of the whole external surface (lb/ft^2).

7.6. Effect of Materials on Internal Heating

When heat enters directly or is generated within a building, by heating, lighting, sunlight penetration, etc., the indoor temperatures rise immediately without the time lag characteristic of heat flow through the walls and roof.

The temperature elevation depends on the rate of heat absorption into materials surrounding the heated space.

The quantitative effect of various materials on the elevation of indoor air and surface temperatures has been studied experimentally at the Building Research Station, Haifa [7.6]. The testing set-up comprised four identical models of external dimensions 115 cm × 153 cm and internal height 157 cm built of lightweight, 15 cm thick

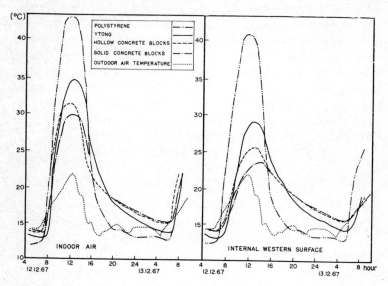

Fig. 7.5. Diurnal patterns of indoor temperatures in models subjected to penetration of solar radiation.

concrete walls whitewashed externally. One wall contained a window of glass area 66 cm × 101 cm. Internal walls were built inside the identical external walls so that the internal dimensions of the internal space remained constant.

The materials were different in each model and included 5 cm expanded polystyrene beyond an air space of 3 cm, and 7 cm blocks of lightweight concrete (Ytong), ordinary concrete and hollow concrete, beyond an air space of 1 cm.

The windows all faced south and were shaded by green internal venetion blinds, so that heating was caused primarily by penetration of solar radiation.

Figure 7.5 shows typical diurnal patterns of the indoor air and average internal surface temperatures when the models were without ventilation.

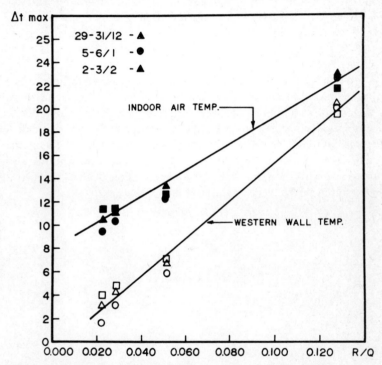

Fig. 7.6.   Correlation between elevation of indoor maxima above outdoor maximum temperature, as function of the R/Q values.

It can be seen that while the elevations above outdoor air maximum of indoor air and surface maxima, in the model with the expanded polystyrene, were about 19 and 21 deg C, the respective elevations with the Ytong walls were about 7 and 13 deg C with the hollow concrete blocks 4 and 10 deg C and with the full concrete blocks 2 and 8 deg C. The night temperatures were in the opposite order: lowest with the polystyrene and highest with the concrete internal walls.

It can be seen from these results that when there is a significant internal heating the response depends greatly on the thermophysical properties of the materials but the effect of thermal resistance is in the opposite direction from its effect when the heat load operates on the external walls from the outside. High thermal resistance and low heat capacity cause rapid heating and cooling, and vice versa.

The combined effect of thermal resistance (R) and heat capacity (Q) on the response to internal sources of heating can be expressed by the R/Q ratio.

Figure 7.6 shows the correlation between measured elevations of the indoor air and internal surface of western wall maxima above the outdoor air maximum, as a function of the R/Q value of the various models. It can be seen that the elevation of the indoor maxima increases almost linearly as the R/Q value increases, and that the differences between the indoor air and surface temperatures also increased with the ratio, indicating a diminution of the rate of heat absorption in the walls as the R/Q increases.

Chapter 8

The Thermal Effect of Roof Types and Ceiling Heights

The roof is the building component most exposed to the climatic elements. The impact of solar radiation on clear days in summer, the loss of heat by longwave radiation during the night and winter, the rain and snow, all affect the roof more than any other part of the structure. In cold regions and seasons, its effect on the indoor climate is in one direction: it serves as a major potential route of a heat loss which is quantitatively dependent on its thermal resistance. It also presents some specific problems in connection with condensation.

Under warm ambient conditions, the indoor temperature is affected by the roof, to an extent dependent on certain details. In hot countries it is popularly believed that the roof is the main heating element of a house. This is so in the majority of cases but only because the roof is incorrectly designed. As discussed later, it may be designed to avoid this effect.

The external surface of the roof is often subject to the largest temperature fluctuations, depending on its type and external colour. In this respect, roofs may be divided into two main categories: (a) solid homogeneous or composite heavyweight roofs, and (b) lightweight roofs of a single layer, or of two layers (roof and ceiling) separated by an air space. These two groups are discussed below individually.

Closely related to the thermal performance of roofs is the problem of ceiling height influence on indoor climate and on the comfort of the occupants. This is discussed at the end of the chapter.

8.1. Heavyweight Solid Roofs

Heavyweight solid roofs are usually flat, although they may occasionally be inclined. Generally built of concrete, they have relatively high heat capacities. Transference of absorbed heat from

145

the external surface of the roof can only be effected by conduction through the mass of the roof to the ceiling surface, unless an air space is included in the structure of a composite heavyweight roof. Therefore the principal determining factors of the thermal characteristics of solid roofs are their external colour, thermal resistance and heat capacity.

a. External colour

The nature and colour of the external surface determine the amount of solar radiation absorbed in the roof structure during the day, the amount of longwave radiative heat loss into space at night, and consequently the pattern of external surface temperature and internal heat exchange with the roof.

In air-conditioned structures, to a very great extent this determines the cooling load due to the roof area. In unconditioned buildings, external colour is the main determining factor for the ceiling temperature pattern and consequently for the occupants' comfort.

An illustration of the effect of colour on the external surface

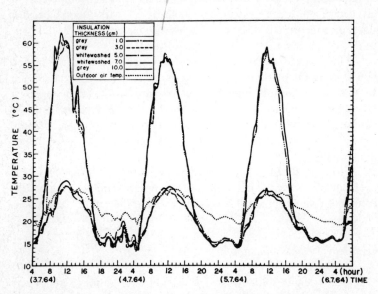

Fig. 8.1. Pattern of external surface temperatures of grey and whitewashed panels made of expanded polystyrene sandwiched between asbestos-cement sheets.

temperature of horizontal roofs is given in Fig. 8.1, which shows results of measurements carried out in Israel in summer time on lightweight horizontal panels [8.5]. The external colours were grey and whitewashed. It can be seen that with a dark exterior the surface temperature was elevated up to 32 deg C (57 deg F) above the maximum air temperature, while the corresponding increase for whitewashed surfaces was only about 1 deg C (about 2 deg F). At night the surface temperatures were invariably below the outdoor air level, on account of longwave radiant heat loss to the sky. The average surface temperature of the whitewashed roofs was appreciably lower than the ambient outdoor level.

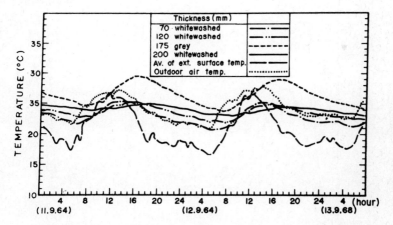

Fig. 8.2a.   Internal surface temperatures of horizontal panels of Ytong. White-washed and grey external colour.

The effect of external colour on ceiling temperature is of course related to the thermal resistance and heat capacity of the roof structure. As the thickness, thermal resistance and capacity of the roof increase, the differences in maximum ceiling temperatures caused by the external colours are reduced, although a significant difference remains in the average temperatures. This is illustrated in Fig. 8.2, which shows results of ceiling temperature measurements [8.6] taken with models of lightweight concrete roofs of thickness 7, 12, 17.5 and 20 cm. It may be seen that the differences between the ceiling temperatures of the black and whitewashed roofs were much greater for the 7 cm thick roof than for that 20 cm thick.

Variation in the external colour of solid flat roofs is also reflected in the air temperatures beneath the ceiling and in the habitation zone. An experimental study [8.4] showed that differences,

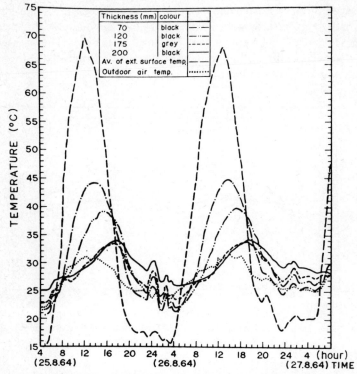

Thickness (mm)	colour	
70	black	— · —
120	black	— · · —
175	grey	— — —
200	black	————
Av. of ext. surface temp.		— —
Outdoor air temp.		········

Fig. 8.2b. Internal surface temperatures of horizontal panels of Ytong. Black and grey external colour.

up to about 3 deg C (5·4 deg F) for the air layer 10 cm (4 in) below the ceiling and up to 1 deg C (2 deg F) for the layer 1·2 m (4 ft) above the floor, existed between the temperatures in houses with grey and whitewashed concrete roofs. This is illustrated in Fig. 8.3, which shows that the temperatures of ceilings under grey roofs were higher than those of the upper air layer, indicating a heat flow from the roof into the house. On the other hand, ceiling temperatures in houses with whitewashed roofs were below the upper air level during most of the day, implying a flow of heat from the room into the roof. In this instance the roof acted as a cooling element for the building. This interesting phenomenon arises because the average external surface temperature of the whitewashed roofs is lower than the outdoor air average.

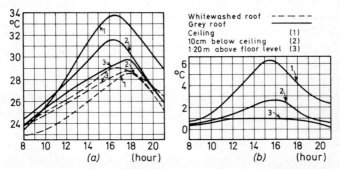

Fig. 8.3a.   Effect of flat roof colour on indoor temperatures.

Fig. 8.3b.   Differences between grey and white roofs.

b. Thickness and thermal resistance

The effects of thickness and thermal resistance of solid flat roofs on the indoor climate are interrelated with the external colour effect and depend on the diurnal variations in outdoor air temperature. In comparison with the fluctuations in external surface temperature, those of the internal surfaces are moderated by the roof structure, and the regulating effect increases with thickness and thermal resistance (*see* Sub-section 7.3.2).

The influence of several thermal insulation types on ceiling temperatures was studied by Neumann *et al.* [8.2, 8.12] in Israel. They compared the temperatures over the ceiling of a reinforced concrete roof 8 cm thick, divided by beams into twenty equal bays, each 2.4 m (8 ft) square. The windows were open in the hall below.

Tests were made on various methods of protecting the roof against excessive heating:

a.   Reflection of solar radiation by whitewashing.

b.   Increase in thermal resistance by layers of such insulating materials as sea shells, vermiculite-concrete, burnt clay blocks, etc.

    c. Shading provided by wooden boards placed $2\frac{1}{2}$ cm (1 in) above the roof surface.

    d. Combinations of these methods.

Temperatures over the underside of the roof were measured by thermocouples in the middle of each bay. Table 8.I summarizes the methods of protection and the test results. Each numerical value constitutes the mean of 5 days' measurements.

From this study it was concluded that all the roof protection systems had a very similar effect on the maximum ceiling temperature, reducing it by about 5 deg C below that of the unprotected section.

With regard to the minimum, whitewashing proved to be more efficient, permitting the ceiling to cool down as much as the unprotected area, whereas the insulting materials reduced the cooling rate at night, raising the minimum.

Comparing the effects on maximum temperatures of whitewashing the red burnt blocks and the uninsulated roof, it appears that colour has a much smaller influence as the thermal resistance of the roof increases. Whitewashing the insulated roof reduced the maximum by as little as 1 deg C, compared with 5 deg C reduction with the unprotected roof.

The effect of the insulation layer was not proportional to its thickness but diminished progressively as extra insulation was added. Thus with the layers of seashell insulation, it can be seen that the 6 cm layer reduced the maximum temperature by 5 deg C but 12 cm caused a reduction of 6 deg C; doubling the thickness of the insulation increased its effect by only one-fifth.

In regions where the diurnal range of outdoor air temperature is small, of the order of 5–8 deg C (9–15 deg F), while the maximum ceiling temperatures of whitewashed roofs are almost unaffected, the minima increase with the thickness and thermal resistance of the roofs. This results in a corresponding elevation of the average temperatures of such roofs.

Therefore in warm regions, if the daytime outdoor temperatures are not much above the comfort zone (not exceeding about 32°C, 90°F), there is no advantage of great thickness and thermal resistance

Table 8.I

Temperatures on the underside of the roof [8.2]

Means of thermal protection	The temperature in °C at the hour							Difference $t_{max} - t_{min}$
	6·00	8·00	10·00	12·00	14·00	16·00	18·00	
Not protected	21·4	23·4	27·7	30·3	29·7	28·8	27·8	8·9
Ytong blocks 20 cm high 2½ cm apart	22·7	23·5	24·6	25·9	26·0	25·9	25·6	3·3
Ytong blocks 20 cm high closely arranged	23·3	23·4	24·8	25·9	25·9	25·9	25·5	2·6
Burnt-clay hollow blocks 2 cm apart	22·9	23·6	25·0	26·3	26·3	26·0	25·8	3·4
Burnt-clay hollow blocks 2 cm apart, white-washed	23·0	23·6	24·5	25·8	25·9	25·8	25·7	2·9
Hollow concrete blocks 20 cm high, 2½ cm apart	23·2	23·9	25·1	26·1	26·3	26·0	26·1	3·1
Layer of sea-shells, 6 cm thick	23·1	23·6	24·7	26·1	26·1	26·1	26·2	3·1
Layer of sea-shells, 12 cm thick	23·1	23·6	24·2	25·5	25·7	25·7	25·6	2·6
Covering of wooden boards, whitewashed	23·1	23·5	24·8	25·9	26·2	26·3	26·1	3·2
Sand lime bricks 2 cm apart	23·0	23·4	25·4	26·7	26·4	26·5	26·1	3·7
Layer of vermiculite-concrete 10 cm thick	23·5	24·0	24·8	25·9	25·7	25·8	25·7	2·4
Sand lime bricks, closely arranged	23·3	23·7	24·2	25·8	25·8	26·1	26·1	2·8
Whitewash	21·9	22·6	23·8	25·7	26·1	26·1	25·8	4·2

in summer, although some minimum resistance is required for winter comfort.

The effect of thickness and insulation is very different when the external colour is dark. As the external temperature of a dark surface is much higher than the outdoor and indoor temperatures, the daytime ceiling temperature and heat flow from the roof into the house are determined by the thermal resistance of the roof.

In regions where the diurnal range is wide and air temperatures rise above 33°C (91°F), thermal insulation is useful even with white-washed roofs, to reduce heat flow due to the outdoor–indoor temperature gradient. The required amount of insulation is related to the external colour.

c. Location of insulating layers

Particularly when the external colour is dark, the location of insulation in a composite concrete roof affects both its efficiency in ensuring comfort in summer, and its durability. When the insulation layer is placed above the structural concrete layer it greatly reduces the amount of heat penetrating to this layer during the day. The reduced amount which penetrates is absorbed in the sizeable mass of concrete and the resulting elevation in temperature is small. On the other hand, when the insulating layer is placed below the concrete layer the latter absorbs great quantities of heat. As the thermal resistance of the concrete is low, the underside temperature of this layer closely follows the external surface pattern. Thus the upper surface of the insulation layer is at a much higher temperature than that of the indoor air. Despite the thermal resistance provided by the insulating material, enough heat flows through to raise considerably the inner surface temperature, as the heat capacity of the insulation is very low and additional resistance below it is provided by the attached film of still air. Therefore the ceiling temperatures and maximum heat flow to the interior are higher than when the insulating layer is external.

Thermal insulation placed above the structural roof and below a dark coloured waterproofing layer allows this upper layer to be overheated, by preventing heat loss from its lower surface. This causes swelling and blistering of the asphalt, and evaporation of its volatile oils [8.15]. If the insulating material is vapour permeable, like mineral wool or foamed concrete, the vapour accumulates above it and beneath the waterproofing material. The moisture condenses at night and evaporates during the day; pressure builds up and bubbles may form, tearing the waterproofing membrane loose from the slab below [8.17]. For this reason a light external colour is essential in warm regions even when the roof is well insulated.

In cold regions, such as Norway, it is recommended [8.8] that no roofs should be without insulation over heated rooms, and that the insulation layer should be located above the concrete slab, but with provisions for ventilation and removal of water vapour between the insulation and the upper waterproofing layer.

d. Cooling by evaporation

Evaporative cooling may be used to prevent heating of the roof, using either stationary water ponds above the roof, or by spraying. Sutton [8.15] reports experiments in which the surface temperature of a lightweight wooden roof deck was reduced from 150°F to 100°F by water spraying, and to 108°F and 103°F by water pools 2 in and 6 in deep respectively.

With a combination of a white water-resistance external surface and water spraying it is possible to reduce the external surface temperature well below the outdoor level. Similar results can also be obtained by combining evaporative cooling methods with shading of the roof.

Cooling by spraying can be applied not only to flat but also to pitched roofs. From the practical point of view this method suffers many drawbacks: evaporative cooling is most effective in arid conditions, but such regions usually have restricted and costly water supplies; water ponds may provide a breeding ground for mosquitoes, etc.

8.2. Lightweight Roofs

Lightweight roofs may be a single layer or comprise two layers, roof and ceiling, separated by an air space. Standard roofing materials are tiles (clay or cement), asbestos-cement, galvanized steel, and aluminium sheets; ceiling materials include plaster on expanded metal, fibreboards and gypsum sheets. Of the heat from solar radiation absorbed by the outer roof layer, part is lost to the surroundings by convection and radiation and the remainder is transferred to the ceiling, primarily by radiation.

The factors which may influence the thermal performance of double roofs are:

a. The material and colour of the external roof

b. The ventilation conditions in the intermediate space

c. The thermal resistance of the two layers.

Single layer roofs are discussed at the end of this section.

a. External colour

As with the solid flat roof, the external colour determines the amount of solar radiation absorbed in this layer of the double light-weight roof. However, there are some differences in the effect of this factor with double roofs. As the roof layer is very thin, the temperature of the underside closely follows that of the external surface and is correspondingly affected by the external colour. But the air space between the roof and ceiling acts as an insulation and moderates the quantitative effect of external colour on the ceiling temperature and indoor climate; the moderating influence depends on the conditions in this roof space. With cement tiled roofs and plastered ceilings it was found in an experimental study [8.3] that whitewashing the tiles reduced the daytime ceiling temperature by about 3 deg C (5·4 deg F).

b. Ventilation of the space beneath a pitched roof

There is a distinct difference in function between the ventilation of the occupied building space and that of the attic space. In the former case ventilation has a direct physiological effect on the occupants while in the second its effect is indirect, through influence on ceiling temperature and heat flow across the ceiling.

The temperature and air exchange rate in the attic space, and hence the thermal effect of ventilation by special openings, fittings or by mechanical means, depend greatly on the materials and colour of the roof. Ordinary materials used in pitched roofs, such as cement or burnt-clay tiles and sheets of asbestos-cement, are usually of dark colour and absorb most of the incident solar radiation by which they are heated to a temperature much above the outdoor level. Sheets of metals, such as galvanized steel or aluminium, have low emissivities when new and lose a great part of their reflectivity in ageing (*see* Chapter 6) and thus are also appreciably heated.

Part of the heat from absorbed solar radiation is lost again by convection to the ambient air, some is re-radiated to space, and the rest is transferred through the roof materials to elevate the temperature of the underside of the roof. Since pitched roofs are composed of thin layers, and have a high thermal conductivity, this elevation is considerable. The heat from the underside is transferred from the roof to the ceiling by convection and longwave radiation. Even if the underside temperature remains unchanged, ventilation of the attic space may have a direct effect on the convective heat transfer, and radiative heat flow is indirectly affected if the roof temperature is altered.

Even in the absence of express ventilation of the attic space there may be an appreciable air flow across it, particularly if air can infiltrate through gaps between roof tiles. This air flow is reduced if the roofing used is in sheets, of metal or asbestos-cement for instance.

Ventilation of the attic space using special openings or devices becomes increasingly effective, in preventing excessive heating of the ceiling, as the roof covering is darker, better sealed, thinner and of higher thermal conductivity. When these conditions are reversed, the effective cooling due to special ventilation may be negligible.

Two full-scale experimental studies, one in Israel [8.2] and the other in South Africa [8.17] demonstrated the relationship between roofing materials and the effect of roof-space ventilation.

The study in Israel was conducted in the semi-arid area of Beer-Sheba; the roofs were composed of red cement tiles and the ceilings of plastered expanded metal mesh. Openings to provide ventilation to the roof-space were 17 cm high along two long walls of the building and 7 cm high on both sides below the top tile course, and circular apertures 15 cm in diameter were placed in the gables. Observations were made when all the apertures were closed and when they were open. Temperatures were measured at the following points: undersurface of tiles, centre of attic space, upper surface of ceiling, inside the rooms (120 cm above the floor).

In the unventilated buildings the temperature of the under-surface of the tiles was about 14 deg C above that of the outdoor air, that of the air in the attic was about 2–3 deg C above, at the upper and lower surfaces of the ceiling 1–2 deg C above and the air temperature in the room about 2–3 deg C below the outdoor air level. It was found that roof-space ventilation affected temperatures in the following way:

(i) The temperature of the undersurface of the tiles was reduced by about 1 deg C before noon and by about 2 deg C in the afternoon when the wind velocity was a maximum

(ii) The attic space air temperature was reduced by about 1 deg C

(iii) The temperatures of both the under and upper surfaces of the ceiling were reduced by about 0·5 deg C

(iv) The effect on the internal air was within the range of experimental error and could not be determined.

In the same study it was found that, even without attic ventilation, when the roof tiles were whitewashed both the undersurface of the tiles and the air in the space below it were only heated by 3–4 deg C, while the surfaces of the ceiling were about 2 deg C below the outdoor air level. So it appeared that ventilation of the attic had not even a potential cooling capacity.

In South Africa the effect was studied of natural and mechanical ventilation of the space beneath a pitched roof with corrugated galvanized steel covering and a ceiling constructed of asbestos-cement bonds. It was found that the attic air temperature was lowered during the day by up to 14 deg F by natural ventilation and by up to 19 deg F with mechanical ventilation. The indoor air was cooled during the day by 1–2 deg F under natural conditions, and by 1½–3 deg F with mechanical ventilation. Ventilation reduced ceiling temperatures by about 4–6 deg F. At night the temperatures in the ventilated attic were slightly higher.

The difference between the results of the two studies is explained by the roof coverings. The temperature of air below a roof covered with corrugated galvanized sheeting rises considerably above the outdoor level owing to the relative imperviousness of the roof surface. On the other hand, ventilation through the gaps in a tiled roof prevents the air in the attic from being heated to such an extent, even when apertures are not specifically provided for this purpose.

c. Effect of insulation of double lightweight roofs

In South Africa, Lotz and Richards [8.11] studied the effect of roof insulation on ceiling and air temperatures in full-scale heavyweight brick houses with galvanized corrugated iron roofs and ceilings of ¼ in plasterboard. The control building had no insulation and the others were provided with insulation of several types: a reflective metal foil fixed to the underside of the roof beams, loose-filled mineral wool 2, 4 and 6 in thick, and exfoliated vermiculite 1 and 2 in thick, laid directly on the ceiling. Their results are summarized in Table 8.II.

Table 8.II

Effect of ceiling insulation on indoor temperatures (deg F)
(after Lotz and Richards [8.11])

Type of insulation	Reflec-tive	Vermiculite		Mineral wool		
		1 in	2 in	2 in	4 in	6 in
Max. ceiling temperature	−12·8	−8·1	−10·2	−10·5	−15·5	−16·1
Max. air temperature	− 2·9	−1·5	− 2·2	− 2·2	− 3·7	− 3·4
Min. air temperature	0	+0·1	+ 0·1	+ 0·1	− 0·3	+ 0·3

It may be seen that the effect of bulk insulation increased with its thickness, but that this increase varied exponentially: 1 in produced about one-half the effect of 6 in and very little difference was observed between 6 in and 4 in. The reflective insulation was equivalent to a thickness of about 3 in of mineral wool.

The addition of insulation slightly elevated the minimum temperature but the effect was much smaller than on the maximum temperature.

Lotz [8.10] studied the effect of location of reflective insulation in the attic space on dust accumulation and the efficacy of the reflective insulation. He found that reflective insulation laid directly on the ceiling became covered with dust and its emissivity increased rather quickly, with a resulting decrease in the insulation efficacy. When the foil was fixed 1 in above the ceiling the rate of dust accumulation on its lower surface was much smaller and consequently it retained its reflective quality much better and longer.

d. Single-layer lightweight roofs

This type of roof is usually made of corrugated sheets of asbestos-cement, aluminium or galvanized steel, without additional ceiling materials, and is generally provided in the lowest priced housing. In the absence of the screening effect of a ceiling, the indoor climate is directly affected by fluctuations in the underside temperatures of the roofing. Therefore the thermal effect of these roofs during the day depends almost entirely on the external finish of the sheets, although to some degree the ventilation of the interior is important.

When the external colour of a single layer roof is white, heating by solar radiation is almost prevented, while longwave radiation to the sky is fully utilized. Under such conditions the indoor temperature barely exceeds, and may even be below, that of the outdoor air during the day, while at night it approaches, or may fall below, the outdoor minimum. The average indoor temperature may therefore be considerably below the external average. Provided that whitewashing can be frequently renewed, these conditions are quite satisfactory in warm regions.

On the other hand, when the exterior is dark, the underside temperature of the roof may be over 30 deg C above the outdoor level, causing appreciable radiant heat load on the occupants, in addition to the elevation of the indoor air temperature. This may subject the occupants of such a building to severe heat stress and discomfort.

Van Straaten [8.16] quotes results of a study in South Africa in which temperatures of galvanized steel roofs were measured under different external colours. When unpainted, the roof was at 140°F, when black it was at 158°F, and the temperature was reduced to 146°, 123°, 119° and 111°F by red, aluminium, cream and white exterior colours.

During the night, particularly in clear conditions, the ceiling temperature of these roofs falls to a much lower level than with double or heavyweight roofs. This may cause both discomfort to the occupants and condensation of water vapour within the building and even of the atmospheric water vapour. This may occur in winter as well as in summer, and for metal roofs causes rapid deterioration by corrosion.

8.3. Influence of Ceiling Height on Indoor Thermal Conditions

The effect of reduced ceiling height on indoor comfort in hot regions has aroused scientific interest in many countries, for several reasons:

a. A desire to economise without adversely affecting the comfort of the occupants. Reduced ceiling height permits economy in materials (walls, partitions, plastering, staircases, etc.) and labour, and consequently a reduction in construction cost.

b. The increasing use of prefabricated components has led to a search for simpler methods of production and assembly. Reduction of ceiling height may facilitate the design of full-height elements, thus lowering the costs of the elements and of their erection.

c. Certain trends in modern architecture advocate lower ceiling heights for residential buildings, with a view to creating the impression of larger size and providing a more intimate atmosphere.

d. In multi-storey buildings, the number of storeys can be increased by lowering the ceiling heights, without affecting ventilation conditions or the need for increased spacing of the buildings (which is a function of block height). This provides the possibility of reduction in site development cost per dwelling unit.

Systematic studies of this problem were undertaken in Australia, England, India, South Africa, U.S.A. and Israel. The results of these studies will be summarized in this chapter.

In Australia, Lee [8.9] computed the radiation received by a person in a standing position from ceilings of different heights, temperatures and areas.

Some data for a 3 m wide ceiling are given in Table 8.III.

In order to evaluate the significance of these figures, one must

Table 8.III

Radiation from ceiling at different temperatures, kcal/h (Btu/h)
(after Lee [8.9])

Ceiling height (m)	Ceiling Temperature			
	35°C (95°F)	40·5°C (105°F)	46·1°C (115°F)	51·7°C (125°F)
2·40	5·7 (23)	17·7 (71)	30·2 (121)	44 (176)
3·60	3·7 (15)	11·7 (47)	20·2 (81)	29 (116)
Difference due to 1·20 m reduction	2 (8)	6 (24)	10 (40)	15 (60)

consider that light activity in a sitting position produces approximately 100 kcal/h (400 Btu/h).

At a ceiling temperature of 35°C (95°F), a 1·20 m reduction in height results in a radiation load increased by 2 kcal/h (8 Btu/h) or a 2% increase in the overall cooling requirements of the body, and thus has little significance, if any.

In England, Crowdan [8.1] made a comparison of temperature and air-change measurements in rooms identical in all respects except height. Ceiling heights were 2·40, and 2·10 m respectively. The tests took place during the winter. Observations were also conducted on the subjective responses of occupants. In addition, an opinion survey was taken in apartments with lower ceiling height (2·25 m) than is usual in England (2·40 m). The conclusion was that there is no adverse effect, either climatologically or psychologically, in a reduction from 2·40 to 2·24 or even to 2·10 m. Ninety per cent of the occupants of the lower-ceilinged apartments told the interviewers that the height seemed appropriate to them, and a large majority did not notice that the height was lower than usual.

In India an experimental study was conducted [8.7] in which indoor air and Globe temperatures were measured in four experimental units 3 × 2·5 m (12 × 10 ft) with a verandah to the west. The units were identical except for their heights which were 2·40, 2·70, 3·00 and 3·30 m (8, 9, 10 and 11 ft).

The results of this study showed that raising the ceiling height above 2·70 m (9 ft) had no significant thermal advantage, irrespective of ventilation conditions and seasonal variations. The differences between the 2·70 m (9 ft) unit and the higher units were always less than 0·25 deg C (0·5 deg F). Consistently higher maximum temperatures (of the order of $\frac{1}{2}$–1 deg C (1–2 deg F)) were found within the lowest unit of 2·40 m (8 ft) than in the rest. However, no pronounced increased radiation (measured by Globe Thermometers) was found in the lowest unit, even under the severest conditions.

In South Africa, Richards [8.13] made a theoretical analysis of the factors affecting the determination of ceiling height. It also included an experimental section on the thermal effect of changes in ceiling height on the subjective responses of occupants. In the theoretical analysis, the following significant factors for the determination of ceiling height were isolated:

a. Adequate overhead clearance in standing position. As a result of anatomical studies, it was concluded that a height of 2·30 m is sufficient from this point of view.

b. Psychological considerations. The conclusion was that persons accustomed to higher-ceilinged apartments will undergo an initial period of psychological discomfort, after which they become adjusted to the new environment.

c. Lighting. The determining factor in natural lighting is the design of the windows which is not affected by ceiling height. Lighting fixtures, however, should be adjusted to the smaller height. The installation of indirect lighting, as well as of elaborate chandeliers, is more complicated in lower rooms.

d. Acoustics. The opinion of the Acoustical Division of the National Physical Laboratory of South Africa was quoted, according to which it is unlikely that lowering the ceiling from 2·70 to 2·25 m would have any significant adverse effect.

e. Ventilation. Indoor air motion is governed by the design of the openings only, irrespective of ceiling height. Hence lowering the ceiling does not affect ventilation conditions.

The study included an experiment on the effect of reduction in height from 2·70 m to 2·25 m carried out with twelve subjects, male and female. The subjects were blindfolded and required to report whether they felt any change in radiation, from ceilings heated to 45°C, at room temperature of 30°C. No significant correlation was found between the responses and change in height.

As a result of this analysis and experimentation, a minimum ceiling height of 2·25 m was recommended for Africans, and 2·30 m for the taller white population.

In the U.S.A., at a nation-wide Woman's Congress [8.8] on apartment design, the question of ceiling height was also discussed. An overwhelming majority stated that the customary ceiling height in the U.S.A. (2·40 m) is adequate, although a small number preferred a slightly higher living room ceiling (2·55 m).

In Israel, two experimental studies on the thermal effect of ceiling height were conducted, in two climatic regions [8.3, 8.14].

Measurements of indoor temperatures were taken in full-scale houses of different ceiling heights, ranging from 2·30 m to 3·00 m. In both studies, identical results were obtained, which may be summarized as follows:

a. Differences in air temperature between rooms with ceiling heights of 2·50, 2·80 and 3·00 m varied by less than 0·5 deg C., *i.e.* insignificantly from the physiological viewpoint. These variations did not specifically favour either high or low ceilings.

b. In multi-storey buildings, reduced ceiling height in all except the upper storey results in reduced indoor air temperature.

c. The effect of reduced ceiling height in top-storey rooms depends on the type of roof. In houses with whitewashed r.c. roofs (12 cm thick), air temperature in the lower rooms was approximately 0·5 deg C lower than in the higher ones, while in houses with pitched roofs, covered with red cement tiles, it was approximately 0·5 deg C higher.

When measurements were conducted with closed windows (permitting the maximum possible effect of ceiling height) it was established that differences in thermal conditions between low- and high-ceilinged buildings, even those with pitched roofs, were physiologically insignificant, and when the windows were open even this slight difference vanished.

From all the above studies it can be concluded that, in hot regions, rooms with low ceilings (about 2·50 m) are not thermally inferior to higher ceilinged rooms (up to 3·30 m).

Chapter 9

Wetness in Buildings

9.1. Introduction

Wetness in buildings constitutes a potential hazard to health and comfort and a source of aesthetic and material damage.

Damp walls may increase the frequency and severity of various ailments, for instance chills and rheumatism [9.5]. The thermal resistance of external walls is reduced by water content and this lowers the internal surface temperatures, increases the likelihood of condensation and causes thermal discomfort and higher heating expenses. The aesthetic damages include efflorescence of soluble salts on the surfaces of porous walls, changes of colour and paint staining and peeling. Wet walls may also provide ground for, and encourage, fungus attack and unpleasant odours. Damages to materials involve dimensional changes (warping) and rotting of wood, metal corrosion, softening of gypsum or lime plaster, disintegration of the bonding in laminated panels, etc.

The present chapter analyses the conditions and mechanisms resulting in wetness, the classification of wall types with respect to wetness characteristics, methods of preventing wetness, and specific problems related to prefabrication.

Wetness in buildings is a possible result of several factors, including:

    a. Penetration of rain water through the walls and roof

    b. Penetration of rain water through window cracks

    c. Condensation on internal surfaces of water vapour generated in the building

    d. Migration of water at ground level through the floor and up the walls.

9.2. Rain Penetration

Water penetration to the internal surface of a building element may be activated in various ways, among them capillary action, wind pressure, gravity, diffusion, absorption and with temperature differential. The first two are of the most quantitative importance and these are given further analysis in detail. For clarity of presentation it is convenient to discuss two extreme conditions: that in which a wall without cracks activates capillary suction and, secondly, where an impervious wall contains cracks; in practice these two factors are present together in various degrees.

Birkeland [9.2] gave the following analyses of mechanisms involved in the two extreme cases.

Capillary suction in a wall without cracks

When rain water strikes the external surface of a porous wall it is absorbed by capillary suction. If the rate of water incidence on the external surface is less than the potential absorption rate, the actual absorption depends only on the intensity of rain, as all the water is absorbed. If the rate of absorption is the smaller, a film of water forms on the surface and the excess runs down the wall without penetrating it. Thus low intensity rains of long duration may cause more water to reach the internal surface than intense but short-lasting rains.

When water initially hits a wall, absorption is a maximum, decreasing with the duration of the rain. With renewal of showers after a break the initial rate is resumed, which means that short intermissions in the rain do not noticeably affect the rate of absorption. When rain continues for long periods without any breaks, which could allow absorbed moisture to evaporate, the water accumulates in the wall throughout the rainy period. After the material is saturated, any additional rain or wind pressure may result in damp appearing on the internal surface.

Wind pressure effecting water penetration through cracks

The effective wind force causing water to penetrate through cracks depends on the width of the latter.

Capillary suction is active in cracks from several hundredths of a mm to about one mm width, the effect decreasing with increasing width. Wind force begins to affect water penetration when the width is about 0·01 mm, and the result increases with width until, for a 0·1 mm crack exposed to high wind, the capillary and wind forces are approximately equal. At 0·5 mm and above, the capillary force is very small in comparison with the dominant wind force.

Wind pressure is particularly effective when a film of running water forms over the wall, bridging the cracks. The external air pressure on the water over a crack is greater than that from inside the crack and the wind pushes the water into the space; the film is then formed again and the cycle repeats itself.

A combination of the effects of gravity and wind pressure results in the water penetrating along an oblique path. In horizontal cracks, water may rise to a height of several cm in this way.

Relative importance of the different factors

Unlike the extreme cases described above, rain penetration in practice results from combined effects of the several factors mentioned in Section 9.1, the relative importance of each factor varying for different wall types.

In walls of sand-lime brick, or in masonry walls of concrete blocks, etc., bonded by mortar and unplastered, the method of water penetration depends on the structure of the pores of the material. When there are numerous very small capillary pores, as in sand-lime and clay bricks, the capillary force dominates, but the larger interconnected pores found in some concrete blocks are more susceptible to water forced in by wind pressure.

However, the joints between the blocks are not impervious, on account firstly of the porosity of the mortar and secondly of cracks resulting from deformation by expansion, shrinkage, humidity and temperature variations, etc. These cracks may show considerable size variation, but they are usually too wide for capillary action to be significant, and therefore wind pressure exerts the dominant force. The considerable size of this penetration is demonstrated by the majority of cases in which the internal surfaces of externally unplastered walls becomes damp, where wetness first appears at the joints in the walls. In walls of high quality pre-cast concrete, water penetration is almost entirely through the panel joints.

When surfaces are painted or plastered, water absorption depends to a great extent on the quality and absorptivity of this outer layer. In many instances penetration occurs through cracks in the plaster but whether infiltration continues to the internal surfaces is determined by the characteristics of the wall itself. A combination of mechanisms may exist here, as when wind pressure causes water to penetrate the plaster layer and capillary suction transfers it across the wall.

The most extensive and intensive period of water penetration into building structures occurs during rainstorm seasons, where intense rains are combined with high winds, and the walls most severely affected are those directly exposed to these winds.

9.3. Condensation

Although condensation phenomena were discussed in Chapter 1, a short review will be given here before proceeding to specific problems encountered in buildings.

Air at any particular temperature has only a limited capacity for water vapour; the vapour required to saturate the air (saturation limit) increases with temperature. Table 9.I gives the saturation limit in g/m^3 for air temperatures from 5° to 22°C at standard atmospheric pressure (at sea level, 760 mm Hg).

Table 9.I

Saturation vapour content as a function of air temperature

Air temp. °C	5	6	7	8	9	10	11	12	13
Vapour g/m^3	6·8	7·2	7·7	8·2	8·8	9·4	10·0	10·7	11·4

Air temp. °C	14	15	16	17	18	19	20	21	22
Vapour g/m^3	12·0	12·8	13·6	14·5	15·3	16·3	17·3	18·3	19·3

The relative humidity is 100% when the air is saturated; below saturation point the r.h. is approximately given by the ratio of the existing vapour pressure to the saturation vapour pressure. When a mass of unsaturated air is cooled, a temperature is eventually reached at which its vapour content is sufficient to saturate the air mass. This temperature is known as the dew-point of the air for the given vapour content. Further cooling below the dew-point lowers the saturation limit and the excess vapour condenses into water.

For example, air at 18°C has a potential capacity of 15 g/m³ for water vapour; the relative humidity is 80% if the actual vapour content is only 12 g/m³. But this amount of vapour is enough to saturate air at 14°C, which is therefore the dew-point of the given air. Any cooling below 14°C will result in condensation.

Surface condensation

When unsaturated air comes into contact with a surface at a temperature below its dew-point, the air in direct contact with the surface quickly becomes saturated and the excess vapour condenses on the surface. As a result, the partial pressure of the vapour near the surface falls below the average level in the room and the pressure difference thus created causes a flow of vapour towards the area of condensation. This does not mean that the vapour pressure in the room stabilizes at the saturation level for the temperature of the cold surface, but that a dynamic equilibrium is established between the rates of vapour generation and of vapour dissipation through surface condensation and continuous air exchange in the room.

Water vapour is continuously generated in an occupied building, by breathing, perspiration, cooking, laundering, and other habitation processes, and flueless heating devices such as gas or kerosine heaters also produce an appreciable amount of vapour. The rate of production in these ways is not constant but rises in bursts when they are in process. The vapour evolved is usually adsorbed and absorbed into all suitable internal surfaces to be re-released at a slower rate into the air. When the internal surfaces are non-absorptive the indoor vapour pressure level follows the fluctuations in vapour production. In a survey in Israel [9.5] fluctuations in vapour pressure of up to 7 mm Hg were found in overcrowded prefabricated (non-absorptive) buildings.

The actual rate of surface condensation is found to be smaller than anticipated from consideration of the water vapour level and surface temperature [9.7]. This happens for two reasons:

a. As a result of the condensation the vapour level falls in the region of the surface and continuation of the condensation process is limited by the rate at which vapour is transferred to this area from the main volume of the air.

b. Condensation of vapour releases latent heat (0·6 kcal/g) which raises the surface temperature above the pre-condensation level. This rise in temperature (Δt) depends on the condensation rate (q) and can be found from the following relationship:

$$\Delta t = \frac{0 \cdot 6q}{h_i}$$

$$= \frac{0 \cdot 6q}{7} = 0 \cdot 085q$$

where h_i is the internal surface coefficient, taken as 7 in the metric system.

The condensation does not necessarily occur in the room where vapour is generated, but more often in that in which the surface temperatures are lowest.

The kitchen and bathroom are principal areas of water vapour production, and it is difficult to prevent some condensation in these rooms, but the vapour expands and spreads to other rooms so that the v.p. tends to equalize throughout an apartment and condensation takes place in those rooms where the surface temperatures are sufficiently low. Condensation often occurs behind beds and chests, etc., where the wall is insulated from heating by the indoor air.

Condensation within the walls

As the level of water vapour inside a building is always higher than that outdoors, if a wall is permeable there is an internal to external flow of vapour through it, and a vapour pressure gradient exists across the wall. In winter, when the windows are usually closed and the outdoor temperatures lower than those indoors, there is also a temperature gradient across the wall, which could result in the vapour pressure at a certain depth within the wall being higher than the saturation level for the temperature at the same depth. Under such conditions condensation occurs within the wall, water accumulates and the wall becomes wet from inside.

Water condensation on the internal surface may also be absorbed into the wall to further increase its wetness.

Vapour is also absorbed into the wall at temperatures above the dew point, as a result of a phenomenon termed capillary condensation. At the dew point temperature, a layer of condensed liquid lines the surfaces of pores within the wall. At relative humidities below 100% a certain amount of vapour condenses in the pores, because of the molecular attraction between the vapour and wall material; the tendency of this water to evaporate is inhibited by the capillary tension exerted on it by the pore surface. Some equilibrium water content is established, corresponding to the pore size, with which the tension varies inversely, and the relative humidity, with which the evaporative tendency varies inversely.

At a constant relative humidity, the wetness is also affected by temperature, elevation of which causes slight increase in wetness. The effect of humidity is not linear but progressive: near the saturation level small increase in humidity results in a sharp rise in the water content of the wall material.

Factors affecting condensation

The principal factors affecting the occurrence and extent of condensation in a building are the indoor vapour pressure level, the temperature and absorptivity of the internal surfaces, and the vapour transmission of the walls.

The relationship between the indoor and outdoor vapour pressures depends on the ventilation conditions; as the indoor level is the higher in unairconditioned buildings, ventilation must always reduce this level and consequently the likelihood of condensation. As the outdoor air temperature in winter is lower than the interior level, a maximum limit is placed on the ventilation rate by the minimum permissible indoor temperature. It is particularly important to avoid concentrated currents of cold air near the inlets, which cause uncomfortable draughts.

The internal surface temperatures depend on the quantity of heating, on the indoor and outdoor temperatures and on the thermal resistance of the external walls. In winter, when heating is used extensively, the temperature of the internal surfaces of the external walls is usually lower than that of the indoor air.

When heat flow reaches a steady state the difference between these surface and air temperatures (Δt_i) is given by:

$$\Delta t_i = \frac{K}{h_i}(t_i - t_e)$$

$$= \frac{K}{7}(t_i - t_e)$$

where K is the overall heat transfer coefficient of the wall, t_i and t_e are the internal and external air temperatures and h_i is the surface coefficient, taken to be 7.

All units are in the metric system (*see* Chapter 6).

The thermal resistance of the wall is, as mentioned before (*see* Section 6.1), the reciprocal of its overall coefficient of heat transfer (or thermal transmittance), but for considerations of condensation the determining factor is not the average resistance but the value at the coldest part of the wall. When a building element of adequate thermal resistance contains sections of lower resistance, for instance concrete beams or columns included in a brick wall, condensation takes place initially on these sections which are known as cold bridges or thermal bridges.

Effect of cold bridges on the internal surface temperatures

The internal surface temperature at any point on a wall containing a cold bridge is not determined entirely by the resistance at that point. There will be a lateral heat flow towards the bridge from adjacent parts of the wall and consequently the temperatures at the cold bridge are somewhat higher, and close to it somewhat lower, than would be computed from the above formula.

The ratio (ρ) of the air–surface temperature difference at the cold bridge to that at a point at some distance from it remains independent of the indoor and outdoor temperatures and is expressed by [9.7]:

$$\rho = \frac{(t_i - \theta_i) \text{ at the cold bridge}}{(t_i - \theta_i) \text{ far from the bridge}}$$

where t_i and θ_i are respectively the internal air and surface temperatures. The value of ρ at the point of greatest air–surface temperature difference (ρ_{max}) is defined as the coefficient of heterogeneity of the internal surface. In France [9.7] maximum permissible limits for the heterogeneity coefficient were determined according to the prevailing climatic conditions; 1·5 in northern and central France, and 2·0 in the southern regions, were found permissible. For high quality walls this limit is reduced to 1·2.

Table 9.II

Heterogeneity coefficients for a concrete column inside a brick wall, covered by bricks on the interior [9.7]

Column width (cm)	Width of the covering (cm)									
	1	2	3	4	5	6	7	8	9	10
10	2·0	1·8	1·6	1·5	1·3	—	—	—	—	—
15	2·1	1·9	1·8	1·6	1·5	1·4	1·4	1·3	—	—
20	2·1	2·0	1·8	1·7	1·6	1·5	1·5	1·4	1·4	—
25	2·2	2·0	1·9	1·8	1·7	1·6	1·6	1·5	1·4	1·4

The relationship between the heterogeneity coefficient and the width of the thermal bridge was also investigated in France [9.7] where it was found that insulating the column, particularly on the external surface, reduced the coefficient. The quantitative relationship between insulation thickness and the coefficient for concrete columns of different widths, brick-insulated on the inner side and incorporated in a brick wall, is given in Table 9.II.

Table 9.III

Heterogeneity coefficients for prefabricated concrete wall with internal lightweight insulation (after [9.7])

Width of cold bridge (cm)	Thickness of internal leaf (cm)								
	4	6	8	10	12	14	16	18	20
5	2·4	2·0	1·8	1·7	1·6	1·5	—	—	—
10	—	2·8	2·4	2·2	2·1	2·0	1·9	1·8	1·7
15	—	—	—	2·8	2·6	2·4	2·2	2·1	2·0
20	—	—	—	—	—	2·7	2·5	2·3	2·2

External insulation, using foamed plastics for instance, is inefficient unless the width of this material is much greater than that of the column; otherwise heat may be drawn from within the wall into the column, by-passing the insulation. Three times the column width is recommended for the insulation, *i.e.* extending the width of the column to both sides of it. For maximum efficiency, this is also recommended for internal insulation.

The heterogeneity coefficient permissible in prefabricated walls with internal insulation increases with the width of the cold bridge and decreases with the thickness of the internal layer of concrete. Table 9.III gives recommended limits [9.7] for the coefficient, in walls with lightweight internal insulation, as a function of the thickness of the internal leaf.

9.4. Classification of Wall Types

According to characteristics with respect to wetness, walls may be classified into several groups. The types of primary importance are these: breathing massive walls, cavity walls, impervious walls.

a. Breathing massive walls

The materials comprising breathing massive walls include bricks, standard and lightweight concretes, and concrete blocks. These are porous to water and vapour and absorb appreciable quantities of water when exposed to rain and when vapour condenses on the internal surface or within the wall. Evaporation of this water usually takes place from the external surface, although when the indoor vapour pressure falls below that of the internal surface the evaporation may also take place from here. To enable preferential evaporation to the outdoor air, the wall should be more permeable in this direction, and in particular the exterior layer should be porous. But this is contrary to the requirements for preventing rain water absorption, and it is therefore difficult to achieve satisfactory conditions with this type of wall in cold regions with intense rains. Possible solutions include treating the surface to render it water repellent or covering it with sheets (of asbestos-cement or plastics, for example) which protect the surface from rain but do not prevent the evaporation process. This last, while very effective, considerably alters the architectural appearance of the wall, although satisfactory solutions may be developed.

Conventional solid masonry walls do not provide sufficient rain protection unless the material and workmanship are of very high quality, the thickness considerable and the permeability low. External rendering of good quality is usually required to rain-proof these walls. This is particularly true of hollow concrete masonry walls, as was demonstrated in a study in Australia [9.1], where experiments showed that capillary cracks in the mortar joints, resulting from volume changes, caused these walls to leak. Even high quality concrete blocks were unable to provide sufficient rain protection without further treatment for water repellence.

b. Masonry cavity walls

Cavity walls comprise an exterior and an interior leaf enclosing an air space. When no connection is made between the two leaves, the air space interrupts capillary action and the path of water entering through cracks and thus prevents the direct and continuous penetration of rain water from the outer to the inner leaf. But if masonry tiers connect the two leaves, these may form bridges for water penetration, reducing the effectiveness of the cavity in this respect.

Wind blowing against the wall during rain builds up a pressure gradient across the external layer, forcing water towards the cavity, a process greatly facilitated by cracks in the material. Water seeping from the internal face of this layer then flows down the surface and, unless drainage is provided, accumulates and causes severe dampness problems at floor level. Weep holes, as well as providing an outlet for this water, allow the pressure on the two sides of the external leaf to equalise to a certain extent, reducing the overall rate of rain penetration.

Ventilation of the air space enables water vapour from the inner leaf to be removed without further transfer through the external layer. It is, therefore, possible to use an entirely impervious external surface without affecting the vapour removal, and condensation within the wall is avoided. However, when ventilation is used the temperature of the air space may fall almost to the outdoor level and, if the inner layer is of low thermal resistance, excessive heat loss in cold regions could lower internal surface temperatures below the limit for condensation. Thus it is preferable for the ventilation rate to be kept at the minimum level for vapour removal.

Filling the cavity with insulating materials (*e.g.* expanded polystyrene) which neither absorb nor transfer water, improves the thermal resistance of the wall without reducing resistance to rain [9.2]. But the insulating layer should either be free from joints altogether, or with water-tight joints.

The thermal effectiveness of cavity walls is greater when the internal leaf is the thicker and the outer leaf functions only as a protective layer. In this way the main mass of the wall is kept dry and is protected from water, solar radiation and extremes of heat and cold. The air space can then be well ventilated, to remove any incidental wetness.

Summarizing and correlating the interrelated factors mentioned here, it may be said that the most efficient wall preventing both rain penetration and condensation, would comprise an inner leaf of "breathing" material sufficiently thick to provide adequate thermal resistance and covered with sheeting of an impervious material placed beyond an air space provided with drainage and good ventilation. In these conditions, condensation will occur on the inner surface of the exterior layer, which causes no damage.

c. Impervious walls

By definition, an impervious wall contains a layer impervious to water, whether in liquid or vapour form. When this layer is external it is impossible to prevent condensation within the wall and evaporation into the indoor air is only possible when the indoor vapour pressure falls below that of the wall. If cracks or small holes are present in the outer water-repellent layer, rain water may penetrate the layer but drying to the outer air is still prevented, so that water steadily accumulates in the wall.

In certain cases where the vapour pressure of the interior is very high, on account of overcrowding, for instance, the whole wall may become saturated.

When the impervious layer is internal, condensation occurs on the interior surface, but if this surface is covered with an absorptive layer such as plaster a certain amount of condensation can be absorbed during periods of high vapour production without causing visible wetness.

If the external layer is not entirely impervious, an equilibrium is established which depends on the interplay between the permeability to water vapour tending to migrate from the interior outwards and the capillary forces which suck the rain water penetrating the external surface.

d. Waterproof coatings

When the absorbancy of the rendering, or of the wall itself, is too high, it is possible to coat the surface with a waterproof substance such as paraffin, treated cement paint or a silicone.

A comparative study by Soroka [9.9] demonstrated that wide differences exist between the various products of a similar type. In general it may be said that silicone-based coatings were more effective than cement or paraffin products. Silicones, however, while reducing water absorption into the wall, allow water to penetrate if the coating cracks and greatly retard evaporation, so that any water trapped in the wall has no external outlet [9.2].

Elastic coatings are based on rubber or rubber-like materials. As long as the elasticity of such a coating is sufficient to withstand forces which cause the main body of the wall to crack, these materials are suitable for application to walls containing cracks. But elastic materials also prevent outward flow of water vapour and if the wall is wet before the coating is applied, or becomes wet from condensation, drying is prevented. Therefore these coatings should only be applied to cracked walls subject to dynamic expansion and contraction, when no other waterproofing method is available.

9.5. Wetness Problems Specific to Prefabrication

Prefabricated walls are usually made of high quality materials and the manufacturing processes are under good control. It is therefore unlikely that rain penetration would occur through these walls, especially if an impervious insulating layer is used. However, there is a risk of water penetration through the joints between prefabricated elements and of condensation on cold bridges. The possibility of condensation is increased if the internal partitions are of dense prefabricated concrete, smoothly finished and unplastered. Here the absorption capacity of the internal surfaces is reduced and vapour pressures are correspondingly higher.

9.5.1. RAIN PENETRATION THROUGH JOINTS.—The mechanism of rain penetration through joints, and the methods suitable to prevent it, depend on the type of joint. The joints used in prefabricated panels fall into three main categories:

    a.　Monolithic non-elastic closed joints made of mortar.

    b.　Closed monolithic elastic joints made of elastic, rubber-like materials.

    c.　Open joints where rain penetration is prevented by the profilation of the joints and by equalization of the air pressure inside and outside them.

In practice, several features of different types may be combined to achieve more effective rain protection.

Because the width of the cracks in prefabricated panel joints is usually in a millimetre range, the primary mechanism of rain penetration is effected by the air pressure gradient across the joint, which is caused by the wind.

The water-tight qualitites of the different types of joints are discussed below.

Monolithic non-elastic closed joints

    The joining of panels by applying mortar to the space between them (sometimes into special grooves) was the first method to be used in prefabricated construction. This type of joint can only be waterproofed if the mortar does not crack, but in practice cracks always appear. Initially cracking is caused by shrinkage and later cracks are the result of thermal movement and differential setting. Thermal movement particularly is the cause of cracks in the vertical points. The width (ΔL) of the crack forming between panels of width L, under a temperature difference of T and coefficient of expansion α, is given by:

$$\Delta L = \alpha L T.$$

The value of α for concrete is about 10^{-5} per deg C, and for lightweight concrete even larger, and thus a summer-winter temperature difference of 40 deg C on panels of width 4 m would be expected to produce cracks between the panels of 1·6 mm. In practice the temperature difference is often much greater, especially in cold regions, and cracks of 2–3 mm and more (from the combined effect of initial shrinkage, thermal movement and differential setting) are not uncommon.

As these cracks sometimes do not appear until several years after the building is completed and occupied, water penetration through the cracks and the appearance of damp on the internal surfaces at the joints are subject to the same delay.

It may be inferred that this type of joint is not recommended, except for use in arid climates.

Monolithic elastic closed joints

These joints are made of elastic, rubber-like materials, such as butyl-rubber or polysulphide, which stick to the edges of the panels. When correctly constructed they may remain waterproof as long as the sealing materials retain their elasticity and adherence to the panels, but experience has not yet been long enough for the long-term weathering properties and life-expectancy of the materials to be stated with confidence.

In general it may be said that the elastic materials are adversely affected by exposure to the climatic elements, in particular to ultra-violet radiation.

The results of field studies in Israel, where ultra-violet light is intense, suggest that virtually every material tested deteriorated after a few years. At the present stage it is therefore recommended that the elastic seals be protected by a covering of opaque tape or metal or, when the seal is recessed into the joint, by a special mortar over a separating tape.

If closed joints are to be used in cold regions, they have the advantage that the inner parts of the joints are protected from direct contact with cold air, which reduces the risk of condensation at the edges of the panels.

Open joints (Fig. 9.1)

Open joints are so called because the external side of the horizontal joint is open to the exterior and the vertical joint includes an air space (decompression space) connected with the outdoor air.

At the horizontal joint the lower panel contains an upstand about 5 cm high and the upper panel has an apron of the same height. The two components are separated by a gap of about 2 cm to prevent capillary action.

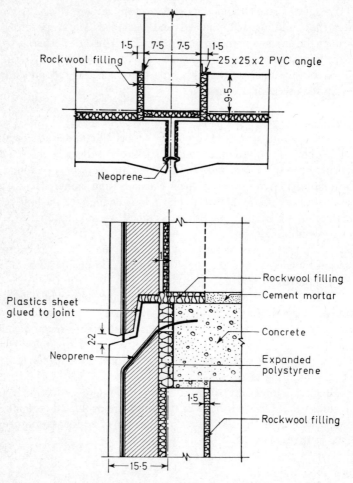

Fig. 9.1.   An example of an open prefabricated joint (dimensions in cm).
(By kind permission of Modul Beton, Israel.)

The penetration of water through the horizontal joint is therefore prevented by gravity. The height of the upstand and apron should suffice to withstand the dynamic pressure exerted by wind and air-tightness is achieved by sealing the joint above and behind the upstand.

In the vertical open joint direct penetration of wind-driven rain is prevented by a rain bar which at the same time allows the air pressure to equalise outside and inside the ventilated decompression space, eliminating the capillary suction and pressure differential which would otherwise force water into the joint.

The effectiveness of an open joint depends mainly on its specific design, and some features developed to improve water-tightness are noted below [9.6]:

a. Minimum width for vertical joint about 1 cm, and for horizontal about 1·5 cm, to prevent capillary suction and formation of film of rain water

b. Minimum height of upstand in horizontal joint about 5 cm

c. Provision of drainage in vertical joint, for any water penetration beyond the rain bar, achieved most efficiently by oblique grooves beyond the decompression space to which the water is directed

d. Outward drainage of the decompression space at the base of the panel, space located in front of the horizontal upstand of the panel below

e. Vertical grooves or projections near the vertical joint to help prevent penetration of rain driven by an oblique wind, particularly useful when the total thickness of the wall is less than 20 cm— adequate depth is very important for an effective open joint.

An example of an open joint is shown in Fig. 9.1.

9.5.2. CONDENSATION PROBLEMS IN PREFABRICATED BUILDINGS.— For several reasons the problems of condensation may be more acute in prefabricated structures than in standard buildings.

a. Prefabricated concrete is denser than concrete cast *in situ*, and is therefore a better heat conductor. Places where heat flow through concrete is uninterrupted by thermal insulation, as along the edges of many prefabricated panels, are thermal bridges on which condensation may take place.

b. If open joints are used, cold air penetrates the depth of the joint, which may already be a thermal bridge, further cooling the internal surface temperatures at this point.

c. The internal surfaces in many prefabricated buildings are very smooth and of low absorptivity. At times when water vapour production is very high, this vapour is not absorbed by the surrounding surfaces and the vapour pressure reaches a much higher level than under similar conditions in a building with standard plastered walls.

d. Even a small quantity of condensation, which would be absorbed easily into plastered walls, produces patches of damp on the non-absorptive prefabricated surfaces.

A field study in Jerusalem [9.5] showed that wetness was more severe in prefabricated structures than in conventional buildings with similar conditions of occupation.

It is recommended therefore that requirements for thermal insulation and local exhaust ventilation of kitchens and bathrooms should be more rigid for prefabricated than for conventional constructions.

Chapter 10

Sun Motion and Control of Incident Solar Radiation

PROFESSOR MURRAY MILNE

*UCLA School of Architecture and Urban Planning,
Los Angeles, California 90024, U.S.A.*

10.1. Introduction

Sunlight falling on a building raises indoor temperatures in two different ways. When incident solar radiation (or insolation) falls on the external envelope of a building the energy that is absorbed increases surface temperatures, which in turn causes heat to be conducted inward through the walls and roof. But when solar radiation falls on a window, almost all of the energy passes directly through the glass into the interior where it becomes trapped by a process called the greenhouse effect. Direct radiation falling on and through the transparent surfaces on a building contributes disproportionate amounts of energy to the building's heat balance. During cold weather this insolation is a valuable free source of heat, but when interior temperatures are above the comfort range, it only adds to the occupant's discomfort, and more expensive kinds of energy must be used to "pump" it back outdoors.

10.2. Solar Radiation

Energy radiated from the sun falling on the earth is reflected and transmitted innumerable times before it is finally absorbed. A great deal of solar radiation is scattered and absorbed by dust, water droplets and aerosols in the earth's atmosphere. All opaque building materials absorb some proportion of the insolation and reflect away the rest. Transparent materials not only absorb and reflect, but also transmit insolation. A very simple equation expresses the relationship

181

between the proportions of energy that are absorbed (a), reflected (r) and transmitted (t):

$$a + r + t = 1 \cdot 0.$$

For opaque materials this means simply that all energy must either be absorbed or reflected.

All building materials emit or re-radiate some proportion of energy that is absorbed. A material's emissitivity (e) is the same as its absorptivity (a) if both values are taken for energy at the same frequency. However, when energy is absorbed by any material, its frequency is slowed slightly. This means that radiation absorbed at one frequency will have to be emitted at another. In fact, the values of a building material's absorptivity, reflectivity and transmissivity are inevitably different for different frequencies of radiation (*see* Table 6.I). For example, this means that a material with high absorptivity at high frequencies and low emissivity at low frequencies would become an energy trap. Other interesting materials are glass and whitewash whose selective frequency-dependent properties are immensely valuable in the design of solar collectors, or surfaces that reject insolation (*see* Sections 6.2 and 12.2).

Absorbed radiation

The most effective way the designer can control the amount of heat reaching the interior of a building is to give careful consideration to the way the external envelope either absorbs or reflects solar radiation. Surfaces with low absorptivity to shortwave radiation which reflect off most of the sun's heat and light (*see* Table 6.I) usually are smooth, light coloured surfaces; in fact whitewash is one of the most effective reflectors of solar radiation. On the other hand, if the designer wanted to capture and absorb the sun's heat, very dark, dull surfaces would be better; surfaces covered with lamp black are among the most effective solar energy absorbers. The amount of energy absorbed (I_a) is the product of the incident solar radiation (I_i) times the absorptivity of the surface (a);

$$I_a = a I_i.$$

This relationship holds for angles of incidence up to about 45°, but beyond this the amount of energy absorbed decreases progressively as the incoming solar radiation becomes more parallel to the wall.

Transmitted radiation

The solar radiation falling on transparent or translucent surfaces that is not transmitted, must be either reflected or absorbed. Of the energy that is absorbed by a glass or plastic window, roughly half is radiated and convected back out to the exterior. Thus half of the absorbed energy plus all of the transmitted energy ends up on the inside of the building (*see* Fig. 10.1). Less solar energy is transmitted

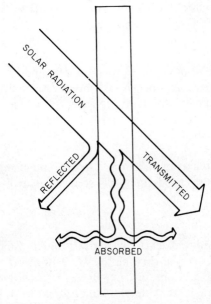

Fig. 10.1.   All incident solar radiation is either transmitted, reflected or absorbed.

directly into the building if the designer uses glass with a high reflectivity and high absorptivity. But if the designer wants to collect as much solar energy as possible, glass with high transmissivity and low absorptivity should be used. Optically transparent glass must have two smooth shiny surfaces and so a certain amount of energy will always be reflected, but to achieve much greater reflectivity, metallized coatings are applied (*see* Section 12.2).

Even more precise control of the thermal performance of windows is possible by using various types of shading devices. They are most effective when installed outside the glass, but they can also be hung inside and can be either fixed or movable. Curtain, draperies and venetian blinds are the most common examples of interior sun control devices (see Section 12.3). External sun control devices are discussed later in this chapter.

The effectiveness of various window treatments is measured in terms of the shading factor: the ratio of the total solar heat gain of the combination of glass plus shade compared to common window glass alone. Adjustable exterior louvres consistently provide the lowest shading factors (see Table 12.III).

Insolation

The total solar radiation (insolation) falling on a surface can be divided into three components: (I_D) direct radiation from the sun, (I_d) diffused radiation from the sky hemisphere and (I_R) reflected radiation from the ground and nearby buildings:

$$I = I_D + I_d + I_R.$$

Because of differences in direction, intensity and changes over time, different design strategies must be used to control each type of radiation.

Direct radiation

Solar radiation reaches the earth's outer atmosphere at a constant rate of 1·94 cal/cm^2/min or 429·2 Btu/h/ft^2. This value is known as the Solar Constant ($I°$). But as it penetrates the earth's atmosphere, some of the direct radiation is diffused, scattered and absorbed. If the sun is directly overhead and if the atmosphere is perfectly clear, the intensity of direct solar radiation will be decreased as a function of the atmospheric extinction coefficient (E), the value of which ranges from 0·07 in dry winter months to 0·21 in more humid summer months. As the sun moves lower in the sky, the distance solar radiation must travel through the air mass of the atmosphere increases as a function of the solar altitude (A). When the altitude of the sun is 30° the radiation must travel through an air mass equal to twice the thickness of the atmosphere. At altitudes of 20° and 15° the sun's radiation must travel the equivalent of three and four normal trips through the atmosphere. Thus the number of air masses is equal to the reciprocal of the sine of the altitude angle. The intensity of radiation directly normal to the earth's surface on a clear day can be computed by:

$$I_{DN} = I°/\exp{(E/\sin A)}.$$

Because the daily and yearly motion of the sun around a building is perfectly predictable, it is possible to design precise means of controlling the amount of direct solar radiation that falls on walls and roof, and penetrates through the windows. The amount of direct radiation falling on a surface is equal to the direct normal radiation corrected for the angle of incidence (θ) of the surface:

$$I_D = I_{DN} \cos \theta.$$

If the surface is a wall or other vertical plane the angle of incidence is computed as a function of the sun's altitude angle (A) and its bearing angle relative to the wall (b):

$$\cos \theta = \cos A \cos b.$$

If the direct radiation is falling on a roof or other horizontal surface, the angle of incidence is simply the complement of the altitude angle ($\theta = 90° - A$).

$$I_{DH} = I_{DN} \sin A.$$

Diffused radiation

The amount of diffused radiation contributed by the total sky vault is usually about one tenth of total radiation, but higher percentages apply when the sun is lower in the sky or when small amounts of haze or dust are present in the atmosphere. Diffused radiation is not distributed uniformly over the sky vault, but tends to be more concentrated around the sun and near the horizon.

For the sake of simplicity, an acceptable approximation of the diffused radiation incident on a horizontal surface (I_{dH}), is a function of direct normal radiation (I_{DN}) and the atmospheric extinction coefficient (E). On a clear day the constant of proportionality (k) ranges from about 0·05 (at $E = 0·07$) to about 0·15 (at $E = 0·20$), and so 0·12 is a good average.

$$I_{dH} = kI_{DN}.$$

On more overcast days, the amount of diffused radiation increases and the amount of direct radiation is reduced proportionately. Table 10.I gives approximate values of k for various sky conditions.

Table 10.I

Diffused radiation on a horizontal surface. (*Based on M. R. Sharma and R. S. Pal,* Solar Energy, *Vol. IX, No. 4, Oct.–Dec. 1965, pp. 183–192.*)

Sky condition	Ratio of actual direct to maximum direct radiation	Ratio of diffused to maximum direct radiation
Clear	1·00	0·12
Clear, slightly hazy	0·80	0·25
Hazy	0·60	0·35
Overcast	0·40	0·55

Reflected radiation

The intensity of reflected radiation is a function of the average reflectivity or albedo ($\bar{r}$) of all nearby surfaces. Therefore, changing the physical properties is the easiest way to control the amounts of reflected radiation. This may mean changing their colour, texture or orientation, or may even mean changing the type of material of which a surface is composed, for example planting vegetation on adjacent ground surfaces.

The amount of radiation reflected in all directions from the ground onto a wall is difficult to determine precisely because of the complex geometric calculations needed to arrive at an accurately weighted average reflectivity ($\bar{r}$). However, if the total radiation falling on a horizontal surface (I_{TH}) is known, and if average reflectivity can be estimated, then the following formula will suffice for calculating the radiation reflected onto a vertical surface (I_{RV}):

$$I_{RV} = \frac{(\bar{r}.I_{TH})}{2}$$

This equation assumes that all reflected radiation is perfectly diffused, or reflected equally in every direction. Therefore a vertical surface, regardless of the direction it faces, "sees" only one-half of the radiation reflected from a horizontal surface.

In all but the most severe environments, part of the ground surface is covered with shadows, sometimes cast by objects as small as blades of grass or grains of sand. Therefore the proportion of the horizontal surface that is in shadow should be considered when estimating average reflectivity.

Table 10.II

Percentage of incident solar radiation diffusely reflected
(Summarized from Weast [10.13])

Material	Estimated average reflectivity (%)
Dark forest, green fields	3–8%
Buildings, wet sand, rock	8–15%
Asphalt, dry bare ground	15–25%
Bricks, dry grass, desert, salt flats	25–40%

10.3. Apparent Sun Motion

In order to design buildings which precisely respond to direct radiation, the designer must be able to quickly and easily establish the sun's position for any time of the day and any day of the year. The key is in knowing how to make the mental leap from the astronomer's sun-centred point of view to the architect's earth-centred point of view (*see* Fig. 10.2). Since Copernicus, everyone understands that the earth revolves around the sun once every year, that it rotates about its own axis once every 24 hours, and that the earth's axis is not perpendicular but is tipped 23°27′ to the plane in which it orbits the sun (an angle which appears repeatedly in the explanation of apparent sun motion).

The designer needs to only understand these three facts in order to describe the apparent motion of the sun about a fixed earth. Because earth–sun relationships are purely relative, the designer is perfectly correct in thinking of the earth as standing still while the sun moves through the sky from horizon to horizon.

The northern hemisphere is used in all the following explanations of apparent sun motion, but sun motion is symmetrical about the equator, and so whatever happens in the northern hemisphere will be repeated in the southern hemisphere six months later.

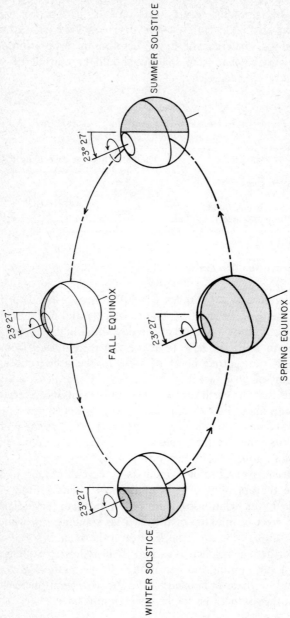

Fig. 10.2.   The earth's axis is tilted at a constant angle in space as it revolves around the sun.

Summer and winter solstice

The change in seasons is explained by the fact that as the earth orbits the sun, its axis always remains tipped in the same direction, pointing toward Polaris, the distant "North" Star. This means that at one point in the orbit the axis leans away from the sun, and at the opposite point, half a year later, the axis is tipped toward the sun. These times are known as the winter solstice and summer solstice.

The term solstice literally means the place where the sun stands still. An earth-bound observer would notice that on each successive day prior to the summer solstice, the sun's path gradually climbs higher and higher in the sky, but on the solstice it stops, and then it begins to fall. The winter solstice marks the stopping or turning point as the sun's daily path drops lower in the sky. In the northern hemisphere the summer solstice occurs on June 21 or 22 (accounting for leap years) and it marks the longest day of the year. The winter solstice occurs on December 21 or 22 and is the shortest day of the year. For convenience we will simply use the twenty-first day of each month as the temporal reference point.

The sun at noon on the summer solstice stands directly overhead at the Northern Tropic, and on the winter solstice it stands directly overhead at the Southern Tropic. The tropics are located at 23°27′ north and south latitudes respectively. Because the earth's axis is tilted towards the sun during the spring and summer, more than half of the northern hemisphere is in sunlight. In fact, on the region of the globe inside the Arctic Circle the sun never sets on the summer solstice. The Arctic Circle is exactly 23°27′ below the north pole, which means that it lies at 66°33′ north latitude. On the summer solstice a person living at this latitude could awake at midnight to watch the sun swing around to the north, dip down to barely touch the horizon, then begin to climb again into the eastern sky.

The most curious circumstances occur at the north pole, where for six months the sun circles around the horizon day after day without setting. It actually is following a gradually rising spiral until reaching its maximum altitude of 23°27′ on the summer solstice. During the other six months of the year the north pole is in darkness.

When it is the summer solstice in the northern hemisphere, it is the winter solstice in the southern hemisphere, and all these phenomena are exactly reversed.

Equinox

At a point in the earth's orbit halfway between the summer and winter solstice, the earth's axis is perpendicular to the incoming sun rays (*see* Fig. 10.2). Here the sun stands directly over the equator and everywhere on the globe the days and nights are exactly twelve hours long (except at the poles). Equinox literally means the time when the length of the days equal the nights. The vernal (spring) equinox occurs about 21 March, and the autumnal (fall) equinox occurs at about 21 September.

Measuring the sun's position

To an observer standing anywhere on the earth, the sun appears to sweep broad arcs through the sky. At any instant, the observer can establish the location of the sun by measuring the angle of its altitude (A) above the horizon, and the angle of its bearing (B) relative to true south. For centuries, mariners have made these same measurements using sextant and compass, and with the aid of the ship's clock and a book of tables they were able to establish their location on the high seas. But because buildings do not move from place to place, the designer's task is much easier. Knowing the latitude (L), the designer can easily approximate the sun's altitude and bearing on any day of the year.

An observer watching the sun's motion very carefully for a full year, would see that the sun actually follows a long continuous spiral. An imaginary line drawn between the sun and the observer's location on earth would trace out huge flat cones with the observer standing at the vertex. In the winter the observer would see the cone of revolution as concave downward toward the south, and in the summer the cone is concave upward to the north, while on the equinox the cone is flattened out into a disc. The axis of these cones is exactly parallel to the earth's axis (*see* Fig. 10.3).

Time

Solar noon is the instant when the sun is exactly south (or north) of the observer. Due to eccentricities in the earth's orbit, the correspondence between solar noon and clock time changes slightly over the year, but this can be ignored as it is seldom of any significance in the design of buildings.

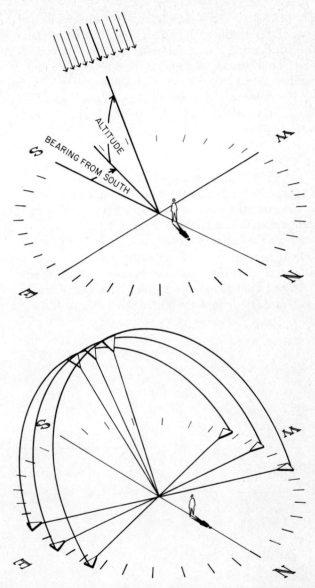

Fig. 10.3.   An observer can measure the sun's altitude and bearing angle relative to due south. Throughout the year the noon altitude angles differ by 46°54′.

The hour angle (H) is a measure of the sun's motion relative to solar noon. It is measured in degrees on a plane perpendicular to the earth's axis. Because it takes 24 hours for the earth to spin through 360°, each hour sees 15° of longitude pass beneath the sun. A simple computation shows that the earth spins one quarter of a degree per minute. For reference the prime meridian (0° longitude) is established as running through the Old Royal Observatory at Greenwich, England.

Noon altitude angles

The sun's altitude is easiest to compute at solar noon where it is exactly due south (or due north). This calculation is greatly simplified by assuming that the sun's rays are parallel everywhere on the earth. This assumption is justified because the sun is at such an immense distance from the earth and is so much larger in diameter.

On the equinox the sun's altitude at solar noon is easiest to compute because the sun stands directly overhead at the equator and sits exactly on the horizon at the poles. This means that its altitude angle will equal 90° minus the latitude (*see* Fig. 10.4).

$$A = 90° - L.$$

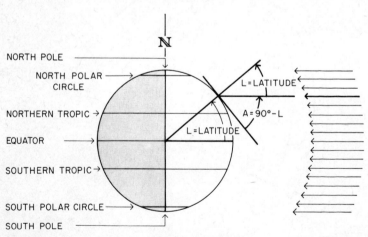

Fig. 10.4.   On the equinox the sun's altitude at solar noon at any place on earth is equal to 90° minus the latitude.

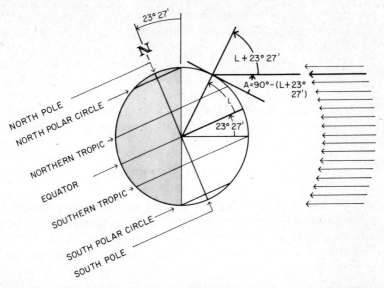

Fig. 10.5.   On the winter solstice the sun's altitude at solar noon is 23°27′ less than on the equinox.

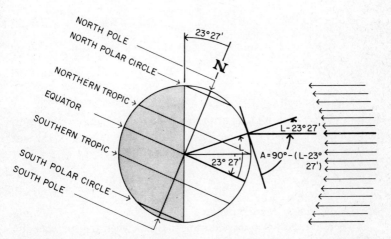

Fig. 10.6.   On the summer solstice the sun's altitude at solar noon is 23°27′ greater than on the equinox.

On the winter solstice, the earth's axis is tipped $23°27'$ away from the sun and so all the noon altitude angles must be reduced by $23°27'$ (see Fig. 10.5):

$$A = 90° - L - 23°27'.$$

At the summer solstice the earth's axis is tipped $23°27'$ toward the sun and so the altitude angles at solar noon are simply increased by $23°27'$ (see Fig. 10.6):

$$A = 90° - L + 23°27'.$$

From these three examples it can be concluded that the altitude of the sun at solar noon, on any day of the year, equals the equinox altitude corrected plus or minus for the declination (d) of the earth's axis. The value of the declination angle is negative in the fall and

Table 10.III

Approximate declination angles on the 21st day of each month

Approximate declination of earth's axis	Positive declination		Negative declination	
	Spring	Summer	Fall	Winter
0°	March 21		Sept. 21	
11°20′	April 21	Aug. 21	Oct. 21	Feb. 21
20°10′	May 21	July 21	Nov. 21	Jan. 21
23°27′		June 21		Dec. 21

winter when the earth's axis tips away from the sun, and in the spring and summer it is positive (see Table 10.III). The altitude of the sun at solar noon can be expressed:

$$A = 90° - L \pm d.$$

Sunrise and sunset bearing angles

There are only two days during the year when the sun sets due west. On all other days the bearing of sunset is either to the south or north of due west; during the winter the sun rises in the southeast and sets in the southwest, but in summertime it rises in the northeast and sets in the northwest.

At the equator the bearing angle of sunsets during different seasons always occurs along the horizon somewhere between the extremes of 23°27′ north or south of due west. At higher latitudes the seasonal deviation of the sunset bearing angle increases gradually until at the Polar Circle the bearings of sunset on the summer and winter solstices are 90° north and south of due west. This means that in the summer a curious thing happens: the sun sets in the north and it rises in the north. However, recall that this is exactly the situation

Table 10.IV

Seasonal deviation of the bearing of sunrise and sunset measured from due east and due west on the summer and winter solstice

Latitude	Summer and winter solstice Bearing from E or W	Altitude
0°	±23°27′	0°
10°	±24°	0°
20°	±25°	0°
30°	±27°	0°
40°	±31°	0°
50°	±39°	0°
60°	±53°	0°
66°33′	±90°	0°

described earlier when on midsummer's night the sun dips down to the north to touch the horizon, at midnight, then begins to rise again toward the east. The sun's motion seems equally bizarre on the winter solstice at the Polar Circle: at noon the darkness is broken with a faint glow in the south, slowly half of the sun appears above the horizon, it pauses then slowly sinks out of sight again. Imagine the dilemma a designer faces here; at one time or another during the year the sun will rise or set on all four sides of the buildings built at this latitude. It is not surprising that architects in countries near the Polar Circle have learned to site buildings and to design elevations which capture as much low angle sun as possible during the brief moments of winter daylight, but respond to the fact that sunlight approaches from every direction during the summer.

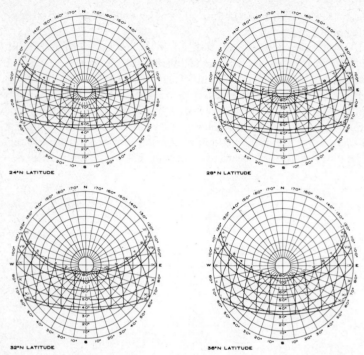

24°N LATITUDE   28°N LATITUDE

32°N LATITUDE   36°N LATITUDE

Fig. 10.7. Sun charts give bearing and altitude angles for every time of day and every month (indicated by Roman Numerals I through XII). (Reprinted, by permission, from Ramsey/Sleeper, *Architectural Graphic Standards*, 6th ed., pp. 70–71. Copyright ©1970 by John Wiley & Sons, Inc.)

General equation of sun motion

The data in the tables and sun charts in this chapter are sufficient for the design of sun control devices on buildings, but for the reader interested in the exact trigonometric relations of apparent sun motion, the following general equations for altitude (A) and bearing (B) are given in terms of latitude (L), hour angle (H) and declination (d):

$$\sin A = \sin L \sin d + \cos L \cos d \cos H$$
$$\sin B = \sin H \cos d \sec A$$

At the sunset the equation of bearing simplifies to the following:

$$\cos B = \sin d \sec L \ (A = 0°).$$

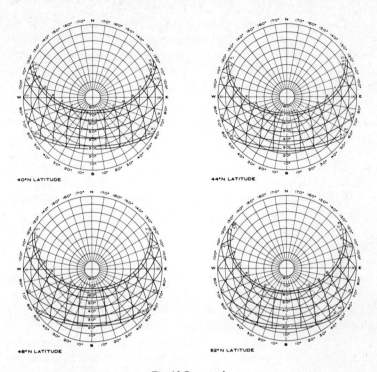

40°N LATITUDE

44°N LATITUDE

48°N LATITUDE

52°N LATITUDE

Fig. 10.7—contd.

10.4. Sun Path Diagrams

The designer will find that general information about the sun's bearing and altitude can be most easily obtained from Sun Charts, while specific information about the shadows cast by a particular object is easiest to obtain using the "Flagpole" Shadow Paths.

Sun charts

Laid out in polar coordinates, a sun chart is prepared individually for each latitude. This is a circular diagram from which the altitude and bearing of the sun can be read directly for any date and time (*see* Fig. 10.7).

The observer is assumed to be at the centre of the chart, and the compass bearings are marked on the circumference of the diagram, representing the horizon. The altitude of the sun is measured by equally spaced concentric circles with the value of the angles indicated on a line along the north-south axis. Curved lines running from east to west represent the daily path of the sun for every month. These curves are crossed by the hour lines, representing the true solar time. The intersection between the curve for a certain month and an hour line establishes the sun's position at that time, from which the bearing and altitude can be read directly. The bearings angles of sunrise and sunset are shown by the intersection of a daily sun path curve and the horizon circle, and their respective times can be found from the relative positions of the hour lines.

"Flagpole" shadow paths

An easy way to understand how sunlight moves across a horizontal plane in relation to a fixed point in space, is to plot the shadows cast by the top of a flagpole. This involves fixing the flagpole's location and height, then laying out the bearing and altitude angles for each hour of the day on the equinox, and summer and winter solstice (*see* Fig. 10.8). Notice that the shadow paths asymptotically approach the sunrise and sunset bearings and are symmetrical on either side of noon. These three curves will be most useful to the designer if the height of the flagpole was chosen to represent the height of a familiar object or a building under study.

A freehand approximation of the flagpole shadow paths can be drawn easily without referring to the sun charts or tables. The first step is to find the altitude angles (A) at solar noon on the equinox and on the summer and winter solstice (remember that $A = 90° - L \pm d$). To find the length of the shadow from the base of the flagpole, simply lay out the noon altitude angles on an elevation of the flagpole. Then lay out the sunrise and sunset bearings for the same three times of the year, and using them as asymptotes, draw a smooth symmetrical curve through each noon shadow which approaches but never intersects the sunrise and sunset asymptotes.

Notice that at the instant of sunrise the shadow of the top of the flagpole will be cast westward toward infinity, but a moment later, as the sun rises above the horizon, the shadow will begin moving

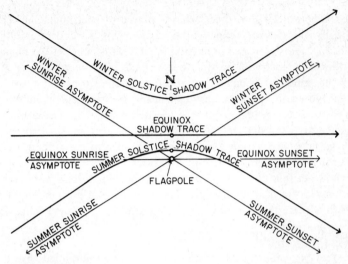

Fig. 10.8.   The shadows cast by a point in space (*i.e.*, the top of a flagpole) are delimited by the sunrise and sunset asymptotes (by John S. Fisher).

rapidly across ground plane, heading in towards the flagpole. This is especially evident when looking at the shadow traces on the summer and winter solstice, but notice that the equinox "curve" is a special case. It appears to be a straight line running exactly east and west through the noon shadow, parallel to the sunrise and sunset asymptotes. In fact if they were drawn at a much larger scale (where the earth's spherical curvature would be in evidence) these parallel lines would clearly begin to approach each other, and would eventually meet at infinity (in spherical geometry parallel lines may intersect).

Understanding sun path diagrams

The behaviour of the equinox shadow path is just another example of how the immense differences between the distances encountered in astronomy and in architecture seem to cause strange and inconsistent things to happen. What we know about the sun-centred universe does not seem to agree with what we experience every day: we seem to be living on an infinitely large plane with the sun spiralling around it, yet we "know" we are on a tiny spinning tilted sphere a huge distance from a source of heat and light. The difficulty the designer experiences when trying to understand the sun's apparent motion, is in making mental leaps between the planar rectilinear geometry of the kind that we experience here on the earth, and the spherical geometry of the type that astronomers use. In planar geometry parallel lines can never meet (except at infinity), but in spherical geometry there is no such restriction. The earth we perceive as being flat, yet we "know" it is a very small sector of a very large sphere. To give an approximate idea of the differences in scale, if the sun were the size of a basketball, then the earth would be no larger than the head of a pin, and they would be separated by the length of a basketball court. This may help to explain why it is safe to assume that the sun's rays are parallel everywhere on earth.

Using the "flagpole"

Plotting sun/shadow patterns is greatly simplified by the assumption that the sun's rays are parallel; this means that shadows cast by rectilinear objects will always be made up of parallelograms. For example, after locating one corner of the sunlight falling through

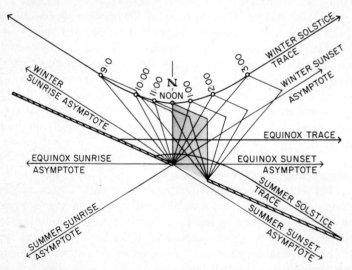

Fig. 10.9. The corner of the sunlight pattern follows the "flagpole" shadow trace.

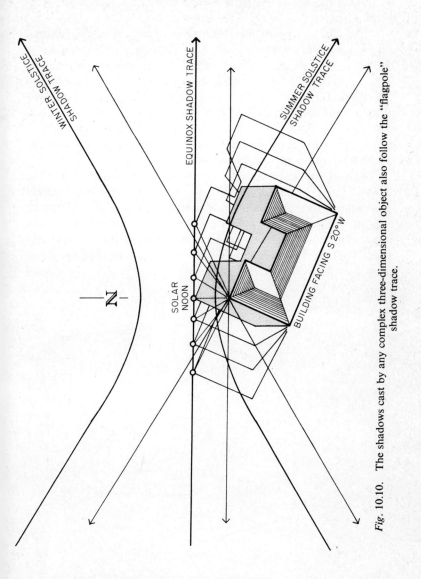

Fig. 10.10.   The shadows cast by any complex three-dimensional object also follow the "flagpole" shadow trace.

a window, the rest of the pattern is an easily constructed parallelogram.

The easiest way to find the reference corner of the sunlight parallelogram, is simply to overlay the flagpole plot. Regardless of the orientation of the window, align the plan view of the flagpole with a corner of the window and orient solar noon due north (*see* Fig. 10.9). This means that without reconstructing the bearings and altitude angles, the complete sequence of hourly and annual sun patterns can be plotted. The most important thing to remember is that the tip of the flagpole must exactly match the height and location of the reference corner of the window.

It is of course possible to use the same technique to plot the shadows cast by buildings or sun shades or any other three-dimensional object no matter how complex (*see* Fig. 10.10). In fact, any sun/shadow pattern falling on the floor or the ground or any horizontal plane can be drawn immediately using the appropriately scaled flagpole plot. In fact the designer will probably find that a few

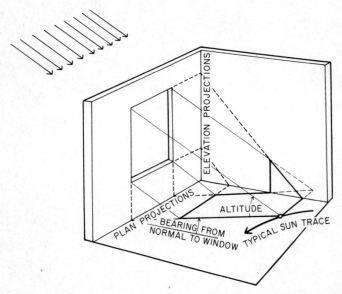

Fig. 10.11.   Shadows cast on vertical surfaces can be found by projection from the horizontal.

flagpole plots kept on hand for different height objects at his latitude, will prove very useful.

Shadows falling on walls and other vertical planes

By projection from the standard horizontal plane flagpole sun path diagrams, it is possible to construct the sun/shadow patterns falling on walls or other vertical planes (*see* Fig. 10.11). Occasionally however, it is helpful to have a more direct means of finding the shadows cast on a vertical plane.

A good metaphor here is to imagine the shadows cast by a nail in a wall (*see* Fig. 10.12). And in fact this can be easily done by finding the same information as in the flagpole plot: the three noon altitudes and the six sunrise and sunset bearings. All the same issues repeat exactly, except that solar noon altitude angles are plotted on a

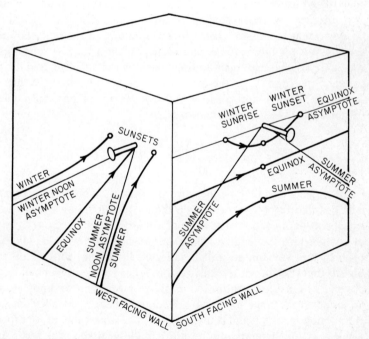

Fig. 10.12.   The shadows cast by the head of a nail show the sun's motion relative to a vertical surface.

vertical rather than horizontal surface, and the sunrise/sunset asymptote is replaced by an analogous asymptote, which is the altitude angle cast by the nail just as the sun's bearing is parallel to the wall. For instance for a south facing wall, the summer sun will rise to the north of due east and will be high in the sky before the rays of sunlight first fall parallel to the wall, casting the shadow of the head of the nail downward towards infinity. Thus, on a south facing wall the "sunrise" asymptote is the altitude angle of the summer sun when its bearing is due east. Another symmetrically opposite asymptote angle occurs at sunset as the sun swings toward the north of due west. Notice that in the winter when the sun rises south of due east, the sunrise and sunset shadows fall directly on the wall and so no asymptotes come into play. As always the equinox shadow will appear to follow a straight line.

For east and west facing walls, shadow path diagrams can be constructed using the same set of rules (*see* Fig. 10.12). Readers who are intrigued by the geometry of sun motion may have already observed that the curves traced by the shadows of the nailhead on the wall are the intersections of a vertical plane with a set of cones which are aligned with their vertices touching the nailhead, and their common axis parallel to the earth's axis. Notice also that the intersection of a horizontal plane with the same set of opposed conic sections gives the flagpole shadow trace.

10.5. Sun Control Devices

Knowing exactly how the sun will strike a building means that it is possible to precisely calculate the length of the overhang of a sun shade, depth of a fin, the angle of a solar collector, the placement of a courtyard, the length of the shadows cast by nearby buildings, or even the way sunsets will be affected by distant hills or other objects that rise above the local horizon. It has been said that building designers in previous cultures knew much more than we know now about how to turn the sun to our advantage. The reason of discussing sun motion in such detail is to give today's designers the information needed to understand how to use a building's physical form to control solar energy.

Fins and overhangs

The pioneering work on the development of simple design methods for sun control was done by the Olgyay brothers at Princeton University. They pointed out that there are only two basic types of sun controls: vertical shading elements called fins, and horizontal shading elements called overhangs. The effect each will have on the window can be easily plotted as a shading mask (*see* Fig. 10.13). By convention, the reference point on the window is usually located at the bottom centre of the glass area. The shading mask simply shows the angle between the reference point and the edge of the fin or the overhang. The shading effect of fins or any vertical edge that cast shadows is indicated by radial lines emanating from the reference point; these represent the sun's bearing angles. The shading effect of an overhang or any horizontal edge is indicated as a semi-circular

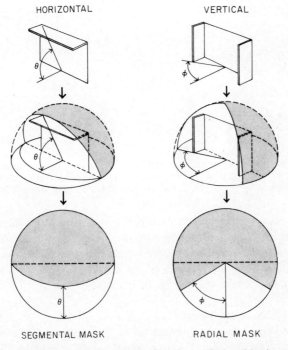

Fig. 10.13.   Shading masks show the shadows by vertical and horizontal edges.

segment showing the vertical angle in the plane normal to the reference point. The shading mask does not restrict the size of the sun control devices; a small overhang close to the window has the same performance as a larger fin farther away.

It is important to notice that the performance of both fins and overhangs can be specified completely in terms of horizontal or

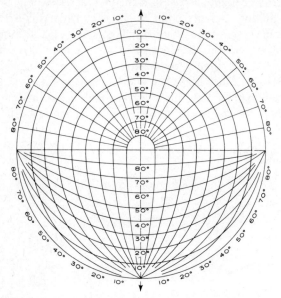

Fig. 10.14. The shading mask protractor is to be overlaid on the sun charts (Fig. 10.7). (Reprinted, by permission, from Ramsey/Sleeper, *Architectural Graphic Standards*, 6th ed., p. 74. Copyright © 1970 by John Wiley & Sons, Inc.)

vertical angles from the reference point; this means that the shading mask is independent of the orientation of the window, or its latitude. Therefore a shading mask protractor can be used as an overlay on the sun chart for any latitude and it can be rotated for a window facing in any direction (*see* Fig. 10.14).

Design of sun control devices

Designing shading devices is a straightforward matter of marking on the sun chart the times and dates when shading is desired, then overlaying the shading mask protractor oriented to match the window, and simply reading off the angles of fins and overhangs that will achieve the desired performance.

An example of showing how to design sun controls is given in Fig. 10.15. The grey area on the sun chart indicates the times during

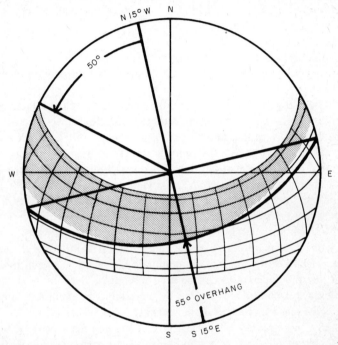

Fig. 10.15.   An example with the needed shading shown on the sun chart and the shading mask protractor overlaid establishing cutoff angles for the design of sun control devices. (Reprinted, by permission, from Ramsey/Sleeper, *Architectural Graphic Standards*, 6th ed., p. 76. Copyright © 1970 by John Wiley & Sons, Inc.)

the year when shading is desired. The building's orientation was selected by rotating the shadow mask overlay which shows that on windows facing S 15°E, a 55° overhang is needed, while on windows facing N 15°W, a 60° fin is required. There are many different ways the building could be designed to meet these requirements. Highly effective sun control devices can be made up of fins and overhangs of any size or shape. At the smallest scale they may be made up of tiny louvres assembled into a window screen. At larger scale the fins and overhangs may become important architectural elements in the design of the facade. A more subtle approach integrates horizontal and vertical shading elements into the form of the building itself using pilasters, balconies, peristyles, brisesoleil, zigzag facades plus cantilevered masses and all kinds of structural elements.

Form and orientation

Shading devices can be designed in innumerable forms, but there are a few basic rules of thumb that apply to different orientations.

Overhangs and other horizontal elements are most effective in shading south facing elevations. In the hot climates of the lower latitudes long verandas and roof overhangs work well, as do movable horizontal louvres. At the mid latitudes, longer overhangs are required on south elevations, creating possibilities for using pergolas with slatted trelliswork or even movable canvas awnings. At the highest latitudes horizontal elements on southern windows begin to encroach significantly into the field of view: ranks of louvres hung from solid horizontal overhangs may drop down almost to the horizon. Fortunately at high latitudes natural ventilation through operable windows will usually eliminate overheating, which means that internal sun shades can be used to control glare. Note that all these devices can be represented by the same type of shading mask.

Fins and other vertical elements are most successful in shading easterly and westerly elevations. Radial shading masks can be used to represent pilasters, free standing fins, and even movable vertical louvres. However, in extremely hot low latitude climates, sun control problems are so severe that east and west elevations are usually left completely windowless.

Eggcrate type sun control devices are represented by superimposing the shadow masks of both the horizontal and vertical elements. Either element may be fixed or movable, and either may be angled sideways or downwards to provide more precise control. Eggcrate shading devices can be designed at any size, ranging from the delicate deeply pierced masonry screens of India, to the huge floor-height elements used on highrise buildings. Of course the small deeply recessed windows used in extremely hot arid climates have the same type of shading mask.

Special responses to sun motion

By superimposing the shading masks which indicate the behaviour of a given form for various times of the year, it is sometimes possible to design extremely precise responses to the sun's motion. For instance, to completely shade a south facing window on

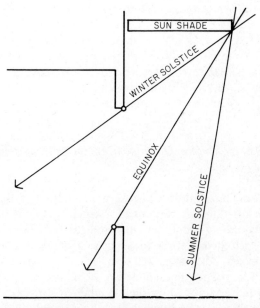

Fig. 10.16.   An example of a sun control device designed to eliminate all sun in the spring and summer, and yet to admit the maximum on the winter solstice.

the equinox, and expose it completely to solar radiation in the winter, the equinox noon altitude is projected up from the reference point, and the winter noon altitude is projected from the top of the window, and the point where they intersect establishes precisely the overhang that is needed (*see* Fig. 10.16). Note that the difference between the two shadow masks indicates the intermediate period of partial sunlight.

Of course plant materials have always been used to shade buildings. Deciduous trees are the most responsive shading devices; providing maximum shade during the height of summer, then obligingly dropping their leaves when maximum insolation is needed during the cold winter months. Plant materials are also extremely effective in shading windows from extremely low altitude sun. For example dense, heavily leafed upright materials, planted at a distance from a west facing window, not only provide a delightful view but also control late afternoon heat loads. Of course, free standing architectural elements can perform the same function. Siting buildings to mutually shade each other is a strategy long used by urban designers and in part explains why residential streets inevitably run east and west in cities with warm climates (such as the midwestern United States). However in colder or more overcast regions (such as the British Isles) "Sun Rights" laws have been written prohibiting a building from excessively shading its neighbours.

10.6. Effect of Surface Orientation on Intensity of Incident Solar Radiation

There are huge variations between the amounts of solar radiation falling on the different surfaces of a building. Figure 10.17 shows graphically the variations in solar radiation intensity on vertical surfaces orientated towards the eight semi-cardinal directions, and on a horizontal surface, as well as on a surface which always faces the sun. This particular example was computed for 32°N latitude, but other latitudes will show slightly different patterns.

From this example it may be seen that a southern wall receives much more radiation in December than in June. Southeastern and southwestern walls also receive a higher level of radiation in the winter, but the annual variations are smaller than for southern surfaces. Notice that at this latitude, the time of maximum intensity on a southeastern and southwestern wall shifts by about one hour closer to noon in the summer. The radiation on western and eastern walls is approximately constant, regardless of season. The northern wall receives direct radiation only between March 21 and September 23, during the early morning and late afternoon hours. Horizontal surfaces (roofs) receive the highest solar radiation in summer, but between November and January they receive less than the south wall and less than even southeast or southwest walls. It should be noted that a roof receives no reflected radiation, unless it is close to high ground or to a taller structure.

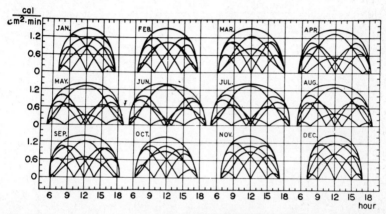

Fig. 10.17.   Variations in solar intensity on surfaces with different orientations.
(By permission from Ashbel.)

Solar collector orientation

Solar collectors used for heating buildings rarely are designed to move or track the sun. Inevitably they are permanently mounted at a fixed orientation which will receive the maximum amount of insolation during the coldest months of the year. Thus at latitudes above the Northern Tropic, they are oriented due south and are tilted back to be perpendicular to the average altitude of the noon sun. This means that on the equinox the angle of tilt should equal the latitude, and on the winter solstice it should equal the latitude plus 23°27′. Although researchers differ, the average value most often chosen for mounting fixed solar collectors is latitude plus 10° (*see* Fig. 10.18).

When reflecting surfaces are placed adjacent to the collector, other orientations may be used, but the designer is advised to confirm the configuration by plotting ray diagrams for direct and reflected radiation during the critical months of the year. For architectural reasons it may sometimes be necessary to attach collectors to walls, roofs or other non-optimum orientations, in which case it may be necessary to increase the area of the collector in proportion to the secant of the deviation from the optimum collector angle.

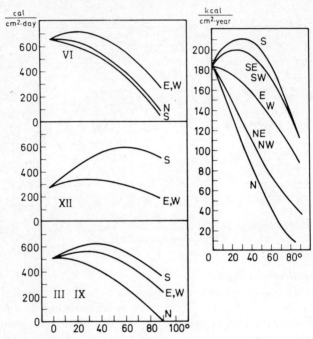

Fig. 10.18.   Variations in solar radiation intensity on sloping surfaces with different orientation. (By permission from Ashbel.)

When solar energy from a fixed collector is needed all year long, it can be shown that a south facing surface tilted at an angle equal to the local latitude will receive the maximum total radiation. A detailed discussion of heating and cooling of buildings is given in Chapter 18.

For the reader intrigued by the geometry of collector design, for a tilt angle (T), the angle of incidence θ of the solar beam with the normal to the surface is given by:

$$\cos \theta = \sin (L - T) \sin d + \cos (L - T) \cos d \cos H$$

Chapter 11

Orientation and its Effect on Indoor Climate

11.1. Introduction

The orientation of a room is the direction faced by its external elevations. The problem of building orientation is one related primarily to long blocks, where the row or rows of rooms share either one or two common external walls. The orientation of such a building is the direction faced by these facades, *i.e.* the direction perpendicular to the axis of the block. In a square, or almost square, apartment or house, each of the rooms has a different orientation and the orientation of the whole building should as far as possible be in accordance with the different requirements for these rooms.

The choice of orientation is subject to many considerations, including the view in different directions, the position of the building in relation to roads nearby, the topography of the site, the location of sources of noise, and the nature of the climate. This last is the aspect with which this chapter is concerned.

Building orientation affects the indoor climate in two respects, by its regulation of the influence of two distinct climatic factors:

a. Solar radiation and its heating effect on walls and rooms facing different directions

b. Ventilation problems associated with the relation between the direction of the prevailing winds and the orientation of the building.

Considerations of these two factors may lead to contradictory orientation requirements. Thus in a hot country one orientation may provide the required lower temperatures, while another could result in higher indoor air velocities. The final choice in such a situation should be based on evaluation of the quantitative physiological advantage of each factor, which is also determined by the ambient air temperature and humidity levels.

In analysing the effects of orientation, however, it is more convenient to approach these factors separately and then to find the optimum solution for any particular situation. As will be seen later, it is possible to adjust the design of a building to modify the effects of orientation on both temperatures and ventilation conditions.

11.2. Combined Effect of Solar Radiation and Ambient Air Conditions—the Sol-air Temperature

The combined thermal effect of solar radiation is expressed in the sol-air temperature, a concept introduced by Mackey and Wright.

The sol-air temperature includes three component temperatures: the first is that of the outdoor air; the second represents the fraction of solar radiation absorbed by the surface on which it is incident. The third represents the long-wave radiant heat exchange with the environment.

To give a thermal definition, the sol-air temperature for the surface of a given structural element is a theoretical external air temperature which, in the absence of radiant heat exchange, would produce the same thermal effects on the element as the existing combination of incident radiation and ambient air conditions. That is, it would produce the same external surface temperature, heat flow into and across the element, and internal temperatures.

The general formula of the sol-air temperature is:

$$t_{sa} = t_a + \frac{aI}{h_o} + (t_r - t_a)\frac{h_r}{h_o}$$

t_{sa} = sol-air temperature
a = absorptivity of the external surface
I = intensity of total incident solar radiation on the surface
h_o = overall external surface coefficient
t_r = mean radiant temperature of the surroundings
h_r = external radiative surface coefficient.

I is the sum of the direct, diffused and reflected radiation falling on the surface in its particular orientation, and is computed according to the procedures described above. a depends on the external colour and typical values are given in Table 11.I [11.1, 11.2, 11.6]. The magnitude of h_o depends on the air velocity near the surface and a value of 19 kcal/m²/h (4·0 Btu/ft²/h) is adopted for design purposes by the ASHRAE [11.1] Guide, while in France a value of 18 units (3·6) is recommended. The nature of the environment determines t_r, which can be estimated by computing the expected average ground and "sky" temperatures. The value of h_r increases with the average temperature of the external surface and the surroundings (*see* Section 6.3); for average temperatures of 25°C and 55°C (77° and 113°F), h_r is 5·15 and 7·87 (1·05 and 1·61 in British units) [11.2].

Table 11.I

Absorption coefficients of various colours (per cent)

New whitewashed surface	10–15
White oil paint	20–30
White marble	40–50
Medium grey	60–70
Bricks, concrete	70–75
Glossy black	80–85
Matt black	90–95

Using the full formula to compute the sol-air temperature is a complex procedure as the prior estimation of t_r and h_r is required. Therefore a simplified form is generally employed:

$$t_{sa} = t_a + \alpha I/h_o.$$

The derivation of the sol-air concept was presented by Dreyfus as follows [11.2]. Consider a wall of absorptivity a, exposed to solar radiation I, an outdoor air temperature of t_a and surroundings of mean radiant temperature t_r. The external surface temperature of this wall will attain a certain level t_s, which will vary slowly with time. The conditions of thermal equilibrium for the wall can be expressed:

$$aI + h_c (t_a - t_s) + h_r (t_r - t_s) = -\lambda \frac{\Delta t_s}{\Delta x} \qquad \text{(i)}$$

λ = thermal conductivity of the material

h_c = convective coefficient

h_r = radiative coefficient

Δt_s = temperature difference between external surface and a plane at distance Δx from it, assumed very small.

$\dfrac{\Delta t_s}{\Delta x}$ therefore represents the rate of heat flow into the wall from the external surface. The longwave radiant heat exchange $h_r\,(t_r - t_s)$ can be rewritten in the form:

$$h_r\,(t_r - t_s) = h_r\,(t_r - t_a) + h_r\,(t_a - t_s) \tag{ii}$$

and equation (i) then becomes:

$$aI + (t_a - t_s)\,(h_r + h_c) + (t_r - t_a)\,h_r = -\lambda\frac{\Delta t_s}{\Delta x}. \tag{iii}$$

But $(h_r + h_c)$ is the overall external surface coefficient (h_o), and dividing equation (iii) through by h_o yields, on rearranging:

$$(t_a - t_s) + \frac{aI}{h_o} + (t_r - t_a)\frac{h_r}{h_o} = -\frac{\lambda}{h_o}\cdot\frac{\Delta t_s}{\Delta x}. \tag{iv}$$

Now, theoretically, if the wall is exposed to the temperature t_{sa}, by definition the same external surface temperature and heat flow into the wall will result. The thermal equilibrium under these conditions is expressed:

$$h_o\,(t_{sa} - t_s) = -\lambda\frac{\Delta t_s}{\Delta x} \tag{v}$$

or

$$(t_{sa} - t_s) = -\frac{\lambda}{h_o}\cdot\frac{\Delta t_s}{\Delta x} \tag{vi}$$

and hence:

$$(t_{sa} - t_s) = (t_a - t_s) + \frac{aI}{h_o} + (t_r - t_a)\frac{h_r}{h_o} \tag{vii}$$

and thus the equation of the sol-air temperature is obtained:

$$t_{sa} = t_a + \frac{aI}{h_o} + (t_r - t_a)\frac{h_r}{h_o}.$$

11.3. Effect of Orientation on External Surface Temperatures

The temperature of an external surface not only affects the internal thermal conditions, but has also an important influence on the thermal expansion and contraction of the building element, and consequently on its durability and weathering capacity. In certain cases, for instance where bituminous or plastics waterproofing materials are considered for use, the maximum surface temperature anticipated may be a factor determining the choice of the material at all.

The intensity of incident radiation on surfaces in different orientations was discussed in the previous chapter (*see* Section 10.6). The quantitative effect of this radiation, however, depends primarily on the external colour, and to a certain extent on the air speed close to the surface. The thermal effect of any intensity of radiation varies inversely with the lightness of colour and the air velocity.

The external surface temperature depends on both the ambient air temperature and the incidence of solar radiation. The former is almost independent of orientation, and the quantitative effect of variations in wind speed over the walls and roof is not very great. When accuracy is required in calculations, the expected air velocity should be determined precisely, but for general surface temperature estimations, an average value is adequate.

In the absence of solar radiation, the temperature patterns of wall surfaces in any orientation are more or less parallel to that of the outdoor air and the roof temperature may be several degrees below the outdoor level, as heat is lost by longwave radiation. But on exposure to solar radiation, whether direct, diffused or reflected, the temperatures of these surfaces rise in proportion to the quantity of this radiation absorbed. When the colour of the surface is light, absorptivity is low and the ambient air temperature has a greater thermal effect than the incident radiation, whereas with dark external colours the influence of irradiation is the more dominant. The heat flow into the wall, determined by the thermophysical properties of its materials, has an obvious effect on the external temperature of the surface.

The effects of all these factors on the surface temperatures of walls and roofs, particularly those of lightweight curtain walls, were made the subject of an experimental study at the B.R.S. in Haifa [11.3, 4, 5], the results of which are summarized below.

11.3.1. INTERACTION BETWEEN THE EFFECTS OF ORIENTATION AND EXTERNAL COLOUR.—Figures 11.1 and 11.2 show external surface

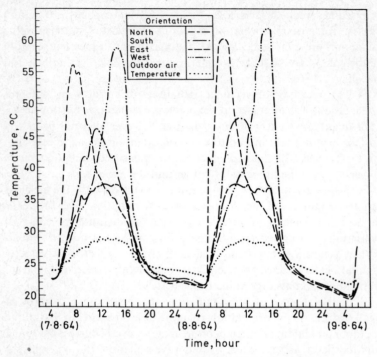

Fig. 11.1.   External surface temperatures of grey walls with different orientations.

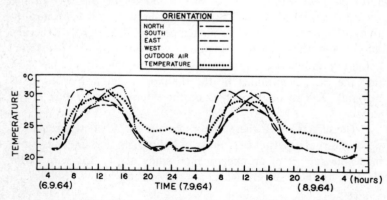

Fig. 11.2.   External surface temperatures of white coloured walls with different orientations.

temperatures of lightweight curtain walls facing the four cardinal directions, measured for two external colours, grey and white. Comparison of these Figures indicates that between the orientation and colour there was considerable interaction of effect. Differences of up to 23 deg C were observed in the temperatures of grey walls in different orientations, while for whitewashed walls deviations were all less than 3 deg C.

This demonstrates that discussion of the thermal effect of orientation is meaningless unless reference is made to the external colour (absorptivity) of the surfaces in question. It is also clear that considerable control on the effect of irradiation is possible through choice of colour.

11.3.2. APPROXIMATE ESTIMATIONS OF EXTERNAL SURFACE TEMPERATURE.—From the results of the same study, empirical formulae have been developed to enable prediction of the exterior temperature (t_s) of lightweight insulated walls and roofs.

For a horizontal surface:

$$t_s = t_a + \frac{aI}{12} - 5$$

and for a vertical surface:

$$t_s = t_a + \frac{aI}{12} - 2$$

where t_a is the outdoor air temperature, a the absorptivity of the surface which depends on the colour, and I the intensity of incident radiation.

The form of these expressions resembles that of the sol-air temperature (*see* Section 11.2) but differs from it in two respects. The value 12 has been substituted for 18 for the surface coefficient. This is because 18 corresponds to a relatively high wind speed, justifiable for calculations of heating requirements, but something of an overestimate when the expected maximum temperatures are the main consideration. The second difference is that constant values have been assumed for the loss in temperature due to longwave radiation to the sky: 5 and 2 deg C for horizontal and vertical surfaces respectively. However, this phenomenon should not be neglected if accurate

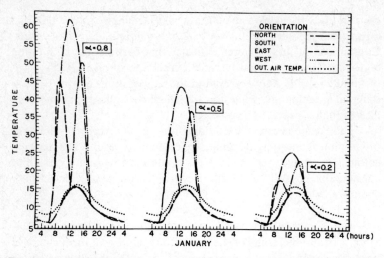

Fig. 11.3.   Computed external surface temperatures in January of walls of different orientations and external colours (absorptivities).

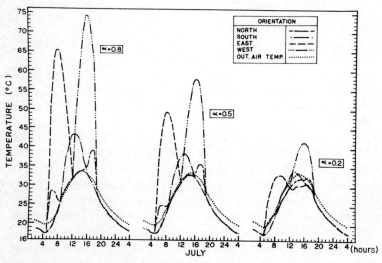

Fig. 11.4.   Computed external surface temperatures in July of walls of different orientation and external colour.

calculations are required, when the drop in temperature should be computed according to the ambient vapour pressure and cloudiness. Figures 11.3 and 11.4 show external surface temperatures of walls facing the different orientations and of various colours (absorptivities), computed according to this formula for the conditions prevailing on clear days in January and July in the semi-arid zone of the Negev in Israel [11.4].

11.4. Effect of Orientation on Internal Temperatures

The magnitude of the thermal effect of wall orientation on the interior is dependent on many design and construction characteristics, and in practice this may vary from a negligible to a very significant factor. Analysis of the problem is perhaps best presented by specifying the conditions under which the effect is insignificant, and on this basis to consider the factors contributing to increase in influence.

To provide a starting point, one may consider a building with rooms facing several directions, externally white and located in a built-up area of structures of similar colour; the thermal resistance is medium to high and the windows are effectively shaded. In such surroundings, even the walls shaded from the sun receive a high intensity of radiation reflected from surfaces nearby. Because of the low absorptivity of all the surfaces, temperatures will closely follow the outdoor air pattern, showing little variation with orientation. Such differences which do exist are further diminished by the insulation properties of the structural materials, and the internal surface temperatures will be virtually uniform. The shaded windows prevent direct penetration of solar energy into the building but allow the rooms to be ventilated by a flow of external air, irrespective of orientation. Thus under these conditions the temperatures within all the rooms follow a pattern determined by that of the outdoor air, the structural heat capacity and the thermal resistance of the building materials, and are affected very little by the orientation of the individual rooms.

If, instead of white, the exterior of the walls is dark, the external temperature pattern varies according to the irradiation of the surface, a factor determined by its orientation, as described in the preceding section. The magnitude of the temperature elevation above the ambient level also depends on the wind direction. For instance, in an area where the prevailing winds are westerly, the elevation above the outdoor level of the surface temperature of an eastern wall in the morning will be above that of a west-facing wall in the afternoon, although the intensity of irradiation is almost the same in the two cases.

The influence of orientation on external temperatures in turn affects the heat flow through the wall and the internal surface temperatures. Quantitatively, the pattern and amplitude of temperature elevation depends on the heat capacity and resistance of the walls, following the external fluctuations more closely as the capacity and resistance are reduced, and less influenced by orientation when these, particularly the resistance, are high.

To illustrate the interdependence of the effects of orientation, external colour and wall thickness, Fig. 11.5 shows internal surface temperature patterns measured on lightweight concrete walls facing the four cardinal directions; the walls were lightweight concrete (Ytong) of two thicknesses (10 cm and 20 cm), externally painted grey and white.

It will be seen that with a white exterior the internal temperatures fluctuated above the average outdoor level, but the extent of fluctuation was greater with the thinner walls. Only slight differences in pattern were observed between the orientations; the maximum differences between the warmest (east or west) and the coolest (north) walls were again larger for the thinner than for the thicker walls (less than 1 deg C (2 deg F) as compared with 1·5 deg C (3 deg F)).

When the external colour was grey, however, temperature differences between the orientations and thicknesses of the walls were much more marked. For the 10 cm walls the minima were all somewhat below the average outdoor temperature, while the range of maxima was about 4·5 deg C (8 deg F), and the widest difference at any instant was about 7 deg C (13 deg F). Increasing the thickness to 20 cm effectively moderated these variations. The range of minimum temperatures was about 2·5 deg C (4·5 deg F), the range of

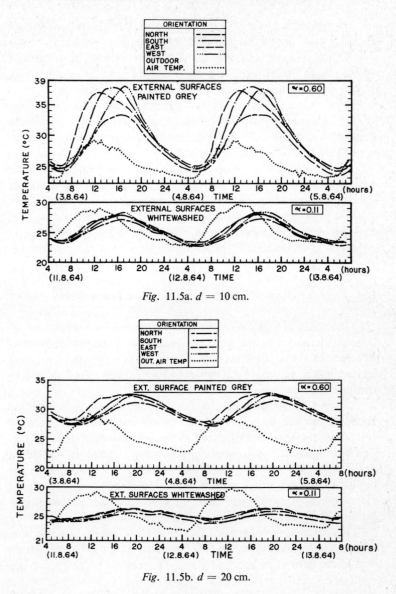

Fig. 11.5a. *d* = 10 cm.

Fig. 11.5b. *d* = 20 cm.

Fig. 11.5a, b. Internal surface temperatures of walls of different orientation, thickness and external colour.

maxima about 1·3 deg C (2 deg F) and the greatest difference observed was about 2·7 deg C (5 deg F).

Although there is an effective similarity between the effects of whitewashing and of increasing the thermal resistance and capacity, in that both reduce the differential effects of orientation, a basic difference exists in mechanism and a practical qualitative difference in effect between the two methods. Whitewashing, by reducing the absorptivity of the wall surfaces, minimises the quantity of solar radiation effective in heating the building and thus reduces both the maximum and minimum temperatures. On the other hand, increasing the resistance and heat capacity of the structure moderated the internal heating effect of the elevated external surface temperature and, while the internal maxima are lowered, the minima are raised. For this reason whitewashing is preferable in hot countries, and insulation is recommended primarily for regions with cold winters.

11.5. Effect of Window Orientation on Internal Temperatures

The effect of window orientation on the indoor temperatures is largely determined by the ventilation conditions and the degree and efficiency of the window shading. The latter is a subject of the next chapter and at present it will suffice to state whether shading devices used are effective or not.

When shading is not effective, solar radiation enters through the windows and directly heats the building interior, the temperatures of which will obviously be influenced by the orientation of the windows. The heating effect of solar energy penetrating a glazed wall or closed unshaded windows is magnified, as the energy is transformed in the building into heat which cannot be dissipated by convection to the exterior or by longwave radiation, to which the glass is opaque (*see* Section 12.2).

The quantitative thermal effect of window orientation has been studied experimentally at the B.R.S. in Haifa [11.5], under different ventilation and shading conditions. The results of this study are summarized here.

The experimental set-up comprised four identical models of 15 cm thick Ytong (lightweight concrete), the front wall of which contained a window and the rear wall a smaller opening with an insulated shutter-board; the four models were orientated so that the window of each faced one of the four cardinal directions. Results are given according to the shading (none, internal, external) and the ventilation (none, cross-ventilated), some in detail and the remainder only with respect to the outdoor–indoor differences in maxima.

Figure 11.6 gives air temperatures within unventilated models with unshaded windows. Before sunrise the thermal conditions in all the models were approximately the same, but during the day the temperature patterns reflected differences in the irradiation of the differently orientated windows. Immediately after sunrise, the model with the eastern window showed a steep rise in temperature, 13 deg C in four hours, compared with 5 deg C outdoors during the same period. The indoor maximum was about 6 deg C above that outside. In the west-window model the temperature rise was moderate until noon, but on exposure to direct radiation in the afternoon this rise

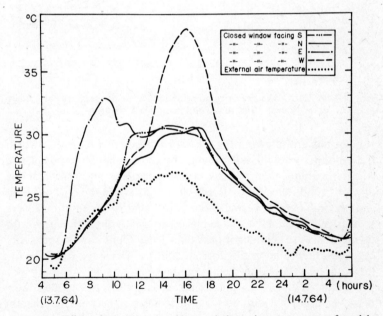

Fig. 11.6. Effect of window orientation on indoor air temperatures of models, unventilated and without shading.

accelerated and a maximum of about 11 deg C above the outdoor level was registered. The heating patterns were similar in the models with southern and northern windows, except that around midday the temperature was slightly higher in the south-facing model. The maxima were about 3·5 deg C above that outside.

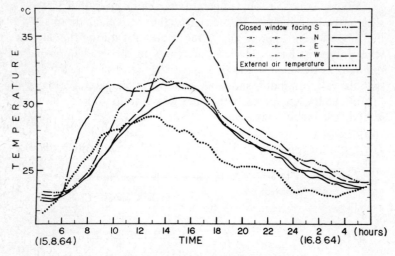

Fig. 11.7. Effect of window orientation on indoor air temperatures of models, unventilated and with internal dark shading.

Results are shown in Fig. 11.7 for unventilated models in which the windows were internally shaded by green venetian blinds. There is a noticeable similarity between these patterns and those for the previous conditions, but both the elevations above the outdoor level and the differences between the four window orientations were smaller. When the blinds were placed externally the differences with orientation were very slight (less than 1 deg C) as can be seen from Fig. 11.8. Before noon the internal temperatures were a little below the outdoor level and in the afternoon slightly higher.

Figure 11.9 shows the trends taken when the models were cross-ventilated but without shading. Differences between the different window orientations were relatively small. During the periods without direct irradiation the indoor temperatures in all the models were

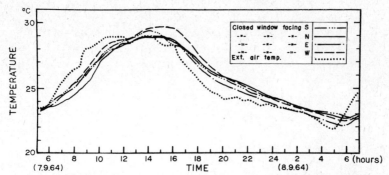

Fig. 11.8.   Effect of window orientation on indoor air temperatures of models, unventilated and with low ventilation rate and external dark shading.

similar and close to the outdoor temperature. When radiation entered the window of each model the air temperature rose slightly above the level in the other models, the maximum differences being 1·5 deg C.

Table 11.II summarizes the deviations of the indoor from the outdoor maxima under all the test conditions of the study. The variations with orientation could provide an approximate criterion for evaluating the effect of this factor. These variations are, of course, subject to seasonal fluctuation, but may nevertheless indicate the trend and order of magnitude of the effect of window orientation.

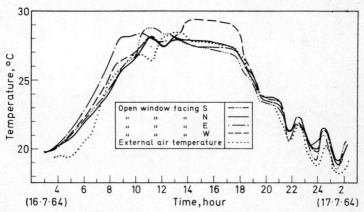

Fig. 11.9.   Effect of window orientation on indoor air temperatures of models with cross-ventilation and windows unshaded.

Table 11.II

Differences between indoor and outdoor maxima (deg C)

Shading variant	Ventilation variant	Orientation					Average east–west	Average north–south
		East	West	North	South			
None	Window and opening closed	5·9	11·3	3·5	3·5	8·6	3·5
	Window open, opening with slot	0·0	0·9	−0·4	0·4	0·45	0·45
	Window closed, opening open	4·0	7·7	2·2	5·7	5·85	3·95
External Dark	Window and opening closed	0·0	0·5	−0·3	0·0	−0·15	0·25
	Window open opening with slot	0·3	0·45	0·25	0·65	0·45	0·38
External Light	Window and opening closed	−0·3	0·3	−0·3	−0·1	0·0	−0·05
	Window open, opening with slot	0·1	0·3	−0·2	0·0	0·2	−0·1
Internal Dark	Window and opening closed	2·6	8·0	1·6	3·0	5·3	2·3
Internal Light	Window and opening closed	1·7	6·5	0·6	1·5	4·1	1·05

From all the results of the study, it can be concluded that both the shading and the ventilation of rooms influence the importance of window orientation in determining the indoor temperatures. In ventilated buildings with effectively shaded windows the internal temperatures are virtually independent of orientation. If the shading is absent or ineffective, but the rooms are ventilated, small variations occur in the air temperature with the window orientation, but obviously the internal surfaces exposed to the penetrating radiation will be heated. When there is no shading and no provision for ventilation (*e.g.* with glazed walls or fixed windows) the differences in solar heating due to orientation are maximal and both the temperature patterns and levels show wide variations. Under intermediate conditions such as those quoted above, the influence of window orientation is evident, but to a lesser degree.

In practice, the quantitative effect of solar radiation penetrating through the windows depends on the thermal properties of the structural materials, particularly those of the internal layers. With lightweight walls of low conductivity the internal temperatures will be higher than with high heat capacity heavyweight walls, which may absorb appreciable quantities of heat without significant increase in temperature. For this reason the lightweight structures may be more susceptible in the effect of window orientation than similar heavyweight buildings (*see* Chapter 7).

11.6. Effect of Orientation on Ventilation

The numerous factors affecting ventilation conditions are the subject of a more detailed discussion in Chapter 15, but for comprehensive consideration of the problems of orientation the relevant conclusions will be reviewed here.

Window orientation with respect to the prevailing wind direction is likely to have a considerable influence on the ventilation of the interior. The principal requirement for satisfactory ventilation is the provision of openings on both the windward and the leeward sides of a building, a necessity confirmed by laboratory and field studies. Observations in full-scale buildings, made in Israel, showed that if there is only one opening, or if two openings are located on leeward sides of the building, the average indoor air velocity is very low; in the former case the velocity is almost independent of the wind direction, and is approximately 10 to 15 % of the external wind speed. When the openings are placed on both windward and leeward sides, it was observed that the average velocity is much greater, ranging from 30 to 50 % of the external speed, depending on the inlet and outlet sizes and on the relation between the wind direction and the axis between inlet and outlet. When the wind is parallel to this axis the air flows straight through the room, ventilating only a limited section, in which the air velocity is high. On the other hand, if the wind has to change direction within the room, a larger volume is affected by the air flow and the average velocities are higher.

Thus it is apparently unnecessary to orientate the main facades of a long building so that wind enters perpendicular to the windows. For instance, with a due westerly wind, good ventilation can be obtained with the inlet facades facing from south-west to north-west, provided that outlets are available.

It should just be noted here that it is possible to induce cross-ventilation in rooms with only a single exterior wall, to which the wind is oblique at an angle of up to 60°, by providing each of the windows in that wall with a vertical projection (*see* Section 15.4).

In general, though, it can be stated that with the provision of both leeward- and windward-facing openings good cross-ventilation can be ensured with a wide range of orientations with respect to the wind. If this condition is not satisfied, poor ventilation will result, regardless of orientation.

11.7. General Summary of the Effect of Orientation

The studies discussed above have demonstrated that the effect of the orientation of a room on the climate within is determined by interaction of many factors in the design and construction of the building.

With adequately insulated walls of light external colour, and effectively shaded windows, internal temperature differentiation with orientation may be negligible. Under such conditions, the indoor climate is to a greater extent dependent on ventilation and therefore orientation is more important with respect to winds than in relation to the patterns of solar irradiation. This is particularly so in humid regions, where the primary physiological comfort requirement is for air motion. Even here the inlet wall need not face directly into the prevailing wind; winds incident to the wall at up to 45° can provide satisfactory ventilation, giving a possible 90° range of orientation.

If, however, the exterior of the wall is dark, and if large glazed areas are not effectively shaded, orientation may have a profound effect on the conditions. interior Thus in areas where ambient temperature has greater physiological influence than ventilation (*e.g.* where the humidity is low), orientation with respect to the sun is an important consideration for human comfort. Under these circumstances a north-south orientation of the main facades is preferable to one east-west.

For long building blocks these conclusions are applicable directly. But even in this case the building has two principal facades and when the depth of the building is such that two rooms are designed across its depth, with or without a hall in between, it is possible to place rooms with different functions on each facade.

When dealing with a building nearly square on its plan, the term orientation is applicable in effect not to the building as a whole but to its different rooms. In every case, the relative advantages and disadvantages of a given orientation for each of the individual rooms in the apartment, *e.g.* living room, bedroom, children's room, etc., have to be weighted. In most cases there are specific considerations for various rooms. For example, sun is required more in the morning in bedrooms and children's rooms; for bathrooms and W.C.s the leeward side of the building is more desirable.

In other cases daylighting considerations are involved and may assume even a primary role, such as in class-rooms, drawing rooms, etc. All these considerations depend to a great extent on the prevailing climatic conditions, so that the functional and thermal considerations should be analysed in each case.

Chapter 12

Thermal Effect of Windows and Efficiency of Shading Devices

12.1. The Problems

One of the characteristics of modern architecture is the widespread use of glazing in the building facades. This, and the increasing use of lightweight structures, has caused considerable changes in the relationship between interior and ambient climates and the problem of overheating has become a major concern even in temperate and cold countries.

The thermal effect of a glazed wall section is dependent on the shading provided and the spectral properties of the glass. In this chapter several factors related to the thermal effects of windows are analysed, a general discussion of the qualitative principles involved being followed by a summarized account of certain quantitative experimental studies.

The characterizing property of transparent materials such as the glasses and certain plastics is the ability to transmit radiant energy directly; this mainly involves the visible wavelength range, although infra-red radiation may on occasions be transmitted.

On impinging on a transparent or translucent surface, radiant energy is divided into three components: a part is reflected, having no thermal effect on the material; a further component is absorbed by the material, subsequently to be dissipated to either side by convection and longwave radiation; the third component is directly transmitted through the material. The relative proportions of the three components are determined by the angle of incidence with the surface and the spectral properties of the glass. From the combined viewpoints of illumination and heating, the principal distinctions between types of transparent materials are their different relative transmittances and ranges of transmitted wavelengths.

The proportion of energy directly transmitted through a transparent material, as mentioned before, depends on the angle of incidence of the incoming radiation, decreasing when this angle is over 45°. Over 60° the percentage of radiation reflected at the external surface increases, and a sharp progressive reduction in the transmitted component results. Absorbed radiation is almost independent of the angle of incidence.

The thermal effect of transparent building materials can be considered from two points of view; the actual heat gain of the interior space is important for calculations of cooling load in airconditioned buildings, while the resulting indoor temperatures are of more significance to comfort in rooms without mechanical forms of heat control.

Shading the glass affects the quantity of incident radiation and hence modifies both the heat flow to the interior and the indoor temperatures. The quantitative modification depends on the location of the shading with respect to the glass, whether internal or external. When shading intercepts radiation outside the glass, part is reflected outwards, part reflected inwards and the remainder is absorbed, elevating the temperature of the shade. Heat flows, therefore, by convection and radiation from the shade; heat removed by convection with the wind barely affects the glass, and the transparent materials are opaque to the longwave range of radiation. Thus only a small fraction of the incident radiation penetrates externally shaded glazed areas.

When the shading is internal, in the form of venetian blinds or roller shades for instance, solar radiation is transmitted through the glass before interception. The radiation absorbed into the shading material is re-released to the interior and almost all of this heat remains within the space as the opaqueness of the glass prevents longwave radiative heat dissipation. Only the radiation reflected outwards from the shading at the original wavelengths is transmitted in part to the exterior (some is reflected back by the glass and absorbed) and has no internal heating effect. The effectiveness of internal shading is therefore determined by its reflectivity (colour), and on the whole is much less than that of external shades.

The functional requirements for solar control differ widely with regional climates and, within each region, with seasonal climatic variations. This problem is further complicated because of the different yearly patterns of temperature and solar radiation. While the intensity of solar radiation (in the nothern hemisphere) has its maximum on June 22nd and 'its minimum on December 22nd, the temperature yearly wave is delayed on account of the heat capacity of the earth's surface and reaches its maximum in July–August and its minimum in January–February. Therefore when the sun is excluded in the hot late summer by some fixed arrangement it will be excluded too in the cool spring, so that some compromise is required in this case.

Different types of buildings and even various rooms in a home may have different requirements for sunlight. A sociological study in the Netherlands by Bitter and van Ierland [12.3] has shown that for the kitchen and bedrooms there is clear preference to have sunlight in the morning while in the living-room more people prefer it in the afternoon. Most housewives interviewed thought that if they would have to choose between sunlight in bedrooms or in the living room, they would prefer the second alternative.

In cold climates, the main problem is to ensure some minimum amount of solar radiation for lighting and heating. In tropical regions the main problem is to prevent overheating due to solar radiation, while in temperate and sub-tropical areas both problems, of ensuring radiation in winter and preventing overheating in summer, exist although with different relative importance.

Further analysis of the problems and data related to the effect of windows and shading devices on indoor conditions is presented in the book by Olgyay, "Solar Control and Shading Devices" [12.11], in a special issue of the Architects' Journal [12.1] and in the Proceedings of the C.I.E. Conference on "Sunlight in Buildings" [12.9], and the interested reader is referred to them.

12.2. Thermal Properties of Glass

The unique property of glass, and some transparent plastics, which is responsible for their specific thermal effect, is the differential transparency to shortwave and longwave radiation. While transmitting most of the radiation in the range 0·4–2·5 microns, which approximately coincides with the range of the solar spectrum, glass is completely opaque to radiation of longer wavelength, around 10 microns.

Thus glass transmits radiation in a selective manner, permitting solar radiation to penetrate into the building to be absorbed by the internal surfaces and objects and to elevate their temperature. But the heated surfaces emit radiation at peak intensity with a wavelength of about 10 microns and this radiation cannot be transmitted outwards through the glass owing to its opaqueness to this wavelength.

By this process, known as the "greenhouse" effect, a glass surface exposed to the sun causes an elevation of the internal temperatures beyond that which would be obtained by penetration of solar radiation through open windows, even when the effect of ventilation is taken into account.

The solar spectrum can be broadly divided into two fractions: light (wavelength 0·4–0·7 micron) and heat (wavelength above 0·7 micron). It should be realised that light is ultimately converted also into heat.

The function of all window glasses is to admit daylight into the building, but inherently they also transmit heat. The absolute and relative transmittances of light and heat differ for different glasses. Glasses used in buildings can thus be divided into several types, according to their spectral transmission, absorption and reflection characteristics, the main types being clear, heat absorbing, heat reflecting and grey or coloured glasses. In practice, all types of glasses absorb and reflect solar radiation, but heat-absorbing glasses absorb, and heat-reflecting glasses reflect, infra-red radiation to a greater extent than ordinary clear glass. Grey and coloured (anti-glare) glasses absorb more of the visible part of the solar spectrum and may be grey or coloured, according to the fraction of the visible light mostly absorbed.

Heat-absorbing glass is characterized by the high absorption of the infra-red portion of the solar spectrum, while transmitting most of the visible light. The increased selective infra-red absorption is due to a higher content of iron oxide among the ingredients of the glass. In consequence of the absorption the temperature of the glass is elevated significantly above the outdoor air level.

Solar heat gain through heat-absorbing glass comprises two

parts: the first is the direct transmission of visible shortwave and infra-red radiation and the second is the inward heat flow by convection and longwave radiation from the heated glass surface.

Heat-reflecting glasses are obtained by depositing very fine, semi-transparent metallic coatings on the surface of the glass, which reflects selectively a greater proportion of the infra-red radiation. As the coating is sensitive to mechanical damage, reflecting glasses require protection either by double glazing with an air space or by lamination.

The ratio of the total transmitted heat to the transmitted light thus differs for the different types of glass and is lowest for heat-reflecting and highest for grey (anti-glare) glasses.

The spectral characteristics of the glass surface can be modified also by the application of coatings to ordinary clear glass. According to Petherbridge [12.12], such coatings absorb mostly in the visible part of the solar spectrum and thus reduce the light more than the heat.

Solar absorbance of any specific glass is determined by the product of its absorption coefficient and its thickness. Reflectance depends greatly on the angle of incidence of the sun-rays upon the glass (the angle between the rays and the normal to the glass plane); it is lowest when the rays are perpendicular to the glass surface and

Table 12.I

Heat gain through various types of glasses, per cent of radiation at normal incidence (Average values from various sources
[12.8, 12.11, 12.12, 12.15])

Type of glass	Direct transmission	Due to absorbed radiation	Total
Clear glass	74	9	83
Window glass	85	3	88
Light heat-absorbing glass	20	25	45
Grey glass	30	30	60
Lacquered glass	38	17	55

increases when the rays become more oblique. The increase in reflectance is small when the angle of incidence is between 0° (normal) and about 60° but then the reflection increases sharply and progressively with further increase in the incidence angle.

Table 12.I summarizes typical values of heat gain through various types of glasses, divided into the portion directly transmitted through the glass and that resulting from the radiation absorbed in the glass. The figures given are averages of those given by various sources, and refer to the case when the sun's rays impinge on the glass at angles from the normal to 45°. For lower angles, the increases in the portion of the reflected radiation should be taken into account.

12.3. Functions and Types of Shading Devices

Windows may have a profound effect on the indoor thermal conditions. Heat gain through a sunlit glass area is many times higher than through an equal area of ordinary wall, and its effect is felt almost immediately, without any appreciable time lag. This is particularly the case when the building is built of lightweight materials. In experiments conducted in South Africa by van Straaten [12.14], the maximum heat flow through a western glass wall was 152 Btu/ft^2 h, while the corresponding rate for a lightweight wall poorly insulated ($U = 0.4$) was about 18 units, for a better insulated light wall ($U = 0.2$) it was 11, and for a 9-inch brick wall ($U = 0.4$), 10 Btu/ft^2 h.

But when shading devices are applied in combination with the glass they can modify the thermal effect of windows to a very great extent. Another way of controlling the thermal effect of windows, although to a lesser degree than is possible by shading, is by the use of special glasses or glass treatments, as discussed in the previous section.

Shading devices can be applied either externally, internally or between double glazing. They may be fixed, adjustable or retractable and of a variety of architectural shapes and geometrical configurations. Internal shading devices include venetian blinds, roller blinds, curtains, etc. Usually they are retractable, i.e. can be lifted, rolled or drawn back from the window, but some are only adjustable in their angle. External shading devices include shutters, awnings, overhangs and a variety of louvres: vertical, horizontal and a combination of both (egg-crate). Shading between double glazing includes venetian blinds, pleated paper and roller shades. Usually they are adjustable or retractable from the inside.

Shading devices may perform a variety of functions: controlling heat gain either constantly or selectively (eliminating the sun in overheated periods, admitting it in underheated periods). They may affect daylight, glare, view and ventilation. The relative importance of these factors varies under different climatic conditions and in various situations. Thus in houses, direct penetration of sunshine may be welcomed in winter and undesirable in summer while in classrooms it may be disturbing regardless of the climatic conditions. Sometimes requirements may be contradicting, *e.g.* good lighting for seeing and prevention of overheating, but in many cases solutions can be found which fulfil seemingly contradictory requirements.

Adjustable and retractable shading devices can be adjusted to fulfil the changing requirements at will, but fixed devices exert their effect in a predetermined fashion, depending on the interplay between their geometrical configuration, orientation and the diurnal and annual patterns of the sun movement. To adjust this effect to the functional requirement, it is necessary to take into account all these considerations when designing the details of the shading devices.

12.4. *Efficiency of Adjustable Shadings*

The geometrical configuration of adjustable shading devices (whether horizontal or vertical, their width to spacing ratio, etc.) does not affect their shading efficiency as they always can be turned so as to cut off the sun's rays. Nevertheless, the efficiency of adjustable shadings is variable and depends on their position with respect to the glass and on their colour, as well as on the ventilation conditions.

In the studies on the efficiency of adjustable shadings two approaches have been used. The first one was the computation or measurement of the "shading factor", which is the ratio of the heat entering the window-shading combination to that entering an unshaded window. The second approach was to determine the thermal effect of the shading by comparing actual indoor temperatures obtained with different types of shadings with those obtained without shading. Results obtained by the first approach are summarized in the present paragraph while those obtained by the second approach will be summarized in a following one.

The solar heat gain through glass-shading combinations can be divided into three components:

a. The part transmitted through the glass-shading combination after reflection between the slats (q_{tsg})

b. The part absorbed in the glass (q_{ag}), of which about $\frac{1}{3}$ is transferred to the interior.

c. The part absorbed in the shade material, which in the case of internal shading is almost fully dissipated subsequently into the interior and added to the heat gain, and in the case of external shading is almost fully dissipated to the outdoor, and only about 5% of it enters indoors.

Table 12.II

Partitional heat gain (kcal/h m²) through different types of shading and the corresponding shade factors (%)

	a		q_{tsg}	$\frac{1}{3}q_{ag}$	q_{ag}	q_{in}	q_{in} (%)	q_{in} (%) experimental
Internal	30°	0·2	63·78	23·64	81·90	169·32	42·8%	—
		0·4	50·16	21·90	151·86	223·92	56·6%	54%
		0·6	21·12	19·62	218·94	259·23	65·6%	—
	45°	0·2	44·76	23·64	88·92	157·32	39·3%	40%
		0·4	30·90	22·20	150·18	203·28	51·4%	51%
		0·6	9·92	20·24	214·92	245·08	62·0%	61%
External	30°	0·2	63·78	1·38	5·04	70·20	17·8%	—
		0·4	49·92	9·06	0·96	59·94	15·2%	—
		0·6	21·12	0·36	13·38	34·86	8·9%	—
	45°	0·2	44·76	5·16	0·84	50·76	12·9%	—
		0·4	30·90	0·59	9·01	40·50	10·2%	11%
		0·6	9·924	0·038	21·59	31·89	8·1%	—

Impinging radiation = 395 kcal/h m²
q_{in} = total solar heat gain.

When the geometrical configuration is such that not all of the sun-rays are intercepted by the shading, a fourth component has to be included, namely the part penetrating between the slats.

As an illustration of the relative importance of each component, and the total solar heat gain through various glass-shading combinations, the partitional solar heat gain through a window facing south-west, on July 21 at 2 p.m. in Israel, has been computed [12.3]. The variables are: shading location (internal and external) slats angle (30° and 45°) and slat reflectivity (0·2, 0·4 and 0·6). The results are shown in Table 12.II, where experimental results were included also for comparison.

Shade factors of various types of shading

Shade factors of various types of internal and external adjustable shading devices were computed or measured in several research institutions.

Table 12.III summarizes some of the results obtained in these studies. It gives the shade factors of various shading devices, depending on their location in relation to the glass and their colour (expressed in terms of reflectivity).

From Table 12.III several conclusions can be drawn:

a. External devices are much more efficient than internal ones.

b. The difference in efficiency between external and internal devices increases as the colour of the shades is darker.

c. For external devices, the efficiency increases as the colour is darker.

d. For internal devices, the efficiency increases as the colour is lighter.

e. With efficient shading, such as external shutters, it is possible to eliminate more than 90% of the heating effect of solar radiation.

f. With inefficient shading, such as dark-coloured internal devices, about 75–80% of the solar radiation impinging on the window may be expected to enter the building.

The increased efficiency of external shading when the colour is darker exists only when the windows are closed. With open windows the effect of colour of the shading depends to a great extent on their orientation with regard to the wind direction. For instance, when the

Table 12.III

Shading factors of various glass-shading combinations
(percent of heat gain through unshaded ordinary glass)

Shading absorptivity	Data						
	Combination of glass and						
	Internal shading slats at 45°	Internal shading slats at 45°	Internal shading slats at 45°	External shading slats at 45°	External shading slats at 45°	Roller shade	Cloth curtain
	Computed (*)	Measured (**)	Measured (**)	Computed (*)	Measured (**)	Measured (**)	Measured (**)
0·2	40·3	40	—	12·8	—	—	White 38·2
0·4	51	51·0	White cream 56	10·2	10	White cream 41·0	—
0·6	62·0	61	Average colour 65	8·05	—	Average colour 62·0	—
0·8	—	71	Dark colour 75	—	—	Dark colour 81·0	Dark colour 64·0
1·0	83	Black 80	—	5·0	—	—	—

(*) = Computations based on conditions in Israel, on July 21st at 2 p.m.
(**) = Measured at the ASHRAE Research Laboratory, Cleveland, U.S.A.

wind in the afternoon blows from the west, and the windows are open, dark-coloured shading devices of a western window may heat the entering air when it flows over them. When the shading devices are of large capacity, such as concrete sunbreaks, their heating effect may continue long after sunset. Dark shading devices on the leeward of the building have a much smaller heating effect as the air passing over them flows away from the building.

12.5. Evaluation of the Performance of Fixed Shading Devices

Fixed shading devices, by definition, cannot be adjusted according to the variations in sun position, or the functional requirements which may vary from season to season and even in different hours of the day. Therefore the relationship between the geometrical configuration of a given shading at a given orientation and the annual and diurnal patterns of the sun determine the effectiveness of that device in preventing solar radiation from penetrating behind the shading at times when it is undesirable.

An evaluation of the expected performance of a planned shading type and its geometrical characteristics, prior to actual construction, is thus essential for satisfactory thermal performance of the building.

Several methods exist for such examination. One of them is to construct a model and to test it under artificial or natural irradiation conditions. Such techniques are described in detail in the literature [12.2, 12.11] and will not be reviewed here. Several graphical methods will be discussed below.

Sunlight patches

When the solar azimuth and altitude for a given location and time are known, either from tables or by using the solar charts and shadow angle protractors relevant to the given geographical latitude (*see* Section 10.4), the patch produced on the floor by sunlight penetrating through a window can be determined graphically. The plan of the room should have the north marked accurately on it. Then the azimuth of the sun is marked on the drawing with reference to one of the corners of the window and thus the direction and side limits of the sun patch on the floor, bounded by the vertical sides of the window, can be drawn directly, as shown in Fig. 12.6. The next step is to draw the shadows cast by the top and bottom edges of the window, or by the edge of an overhang in front of the window. These can be obtained by marking the altitude of the sun on the vertical cross-section through the window at a plane parallel to the sun direction. The relevant segments are marked on the shadow lines of the vertical sides of the window already obtained. The shadows are cast by the top and bottom edges (or by an overhang). The area formed by the two pairs of parallel lines defines the patch of the sun on the floor.

When a sun patch obtained in this way extends beyond the boundaries of the floor area of the room it means that the sun-rays impinge on the inner walls of the room.

When sun patches are required for different hours or months, the process can be simplified by utilizing only the cross-section perpendicular to the window. The solar altitude angle is then drawn on it. The distance from the outer edge of the window top or overhang to the point where the solar beam strikes the floor is then marked along the azimuth lines. The method is illustrated in Fig. 12.6.

Masks of shading devices

A shading mask is a projection on a horizontal plane of the sections of the sky which are obscured by any object from an observer standing at the centre of the diagram. When a shading device is placed in front of a window it shows those parts of the sky from which direct sunshine cannot impinge on the window.

Any object of regular geometrical lines has a characteristic shading mask, which represents the section of the sky which it will obscure. Horizontal lines of the shading device will be shown as segmental lines and their distance at the centre from the baseline diameter is given by the projection of the solar altitude angle on the plane of the diagram. When they are parallel to the wall they appear as segmental lines based on the diameter representing the wall. Perpendicular horizontal lines appear as segments based on the diameter perpendicular to the wall. The segments representing oblique horizontal lines are based on a diameter rotated at the same angle as the oblique lines. Vertical lines are shown as radial lines diverging from the centre of the diagram.

Thus horizontal shading devices will have a shading mask in the form of segmental lines, vertical devices a form of radial lines and an egg-crate type a combination of both types of lines.

The form of the shading mask is determined only by the angular relations and is independent of the actual sizes. Thus a deep overhang forming an angle of 45° with the window sill, and a set of small horizontal louvres having the same angle between their depth and spacing, will have the same shading mask.

Figure 12.7 shows typical masks of various types of shading devices. When the mask of a given shading device is used in conjunction with a sun-path diagram (*see* Section 10.4) drawn to the same scale, it is possible to determine the times when the sun will either strike the window or be intercepted by the shading.

The method of Olgyay and Olgyay

Olgyay and Olgyay [12.11] have suggested a method by which the design and examination of shading devices are carried out in four steps.

In the first step, the times when shading is needed (overheated period) is determined. According to their suggestion, provisions for shading are required at any time when *outdoor air temperature* exceeds 70°F, in regions with latitude of 40° approximately. For every 5° latitude change towards the equator the limiting temperature should be elevated by 0·75 deg F.

In the second step, the position of the sun, when shading is needed, is determined by using a sun-path diagram (*see* Section 10.4). The overheated period is marked on the sun-path diagram. This is done by constructing a table of average temperature for every hour in every month, thus obtaining the times of the overheated period. The boundary lines of the overheated period can then be transferred to the sun-path diagram.

In the third step, the type and position of the shading device is determined. The "shading mask" of a given shading device is plotted on a protractor, having the same scale as the sun-path diagram (*see* Section 10.4).

In the fourth step, the dimensions of the shading devices are determined so as to interrupt the sun during the overheated period and to let it in during the underheated period.

The efficiency of various types of fixed shading devices

Givoni and Hoffman [12.5] have analysed the efficiency of various types of fixed shading devices in different orientations by computing:

a. The daily pattern of the intensity of solar radiation falling on an unprotected window according to the radiation conditions existing in Israel (latitude 32°N)

b. The percentage of the shade areas, given by various types of fixed shading devices, as a function of the projection depth

c. The intensity of solar radiation on the unshaded part of the window.

In this way, daily curves of the intensities of direct solar radiation falling on windows with various types of shading devices with different orientations for different months were obtained for a variety of fixed shading types. From these curves the total daily quantities of direct radiation falling on the windows were obtained.

The following shading devices were examined by this method:

a. Horizontal shading extending only above the window (H).

b. Horizontal shading extending along the whole facade (H∞).

c. Vertical shading perpendicular to the wall on both sides of the window extending only up to its top (V).

d. Vertical shading as above but extending throughout the whole height of the building (V∞).

e. A frame of perpendicular vertical and horizontal members (H + V).

f. A frame whose vertical members are oblique at 45° towards the south (H + $V_{45°}$).

A summary of the findings will be given according to the orientations.

East and west orientations

Adequate shading for east and west orientations can be provided by an egg-crate shading, especially if the vertical members are oblique at 45° to the south. Horizontal shading is more effective than vertical shading. In fact vertical shading, even with infinite height, provides very poor shading in the summer, while cutting off almost all radiation in winter. These findings are illustrated in Figs. 12.1 and 12.2.

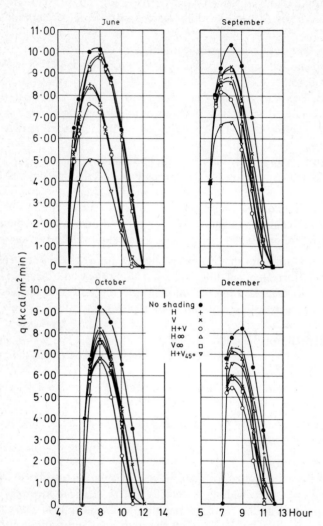

Fig. 12.1.   Diurnal pattern of impinging solar radiation on a square eastern window.

Figure 12.1 shows the daily pattern of intensity of impinging solar radiation on a square eastern window (1 m × 1 m) with the various types of fixed shadings, projecting over the window $\frac{1}{3}$ of its dimensions, in June, September, October and December.

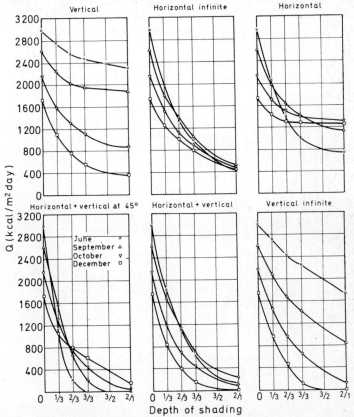

Fig. 12.2.   Effect of projection depth of various fixed shading devices on total radiation impact in east and west orientations.

Figure 12.2 shows the effect of the projection depth of the various shadings on the total radiation impact in east and west orientations.

This study has also shown that horizontal windows are more suitable for east and west elevations than vertical ones.

South, south-east and south-west orientations

For southern, south-east and south-west orientations, horizontal shading is more effective than a vertical one, while the frame shape is the most effective.

Figure 12.3 shows the effect of the projection depth of the various shading on the total radiation impact in southern orientation and Fig. 12.4 shows similar data for south-east or south-west orientations.

This study has demonstrated that in all orientations from east through south to west, horizontal shading is more effective than a vertical one.

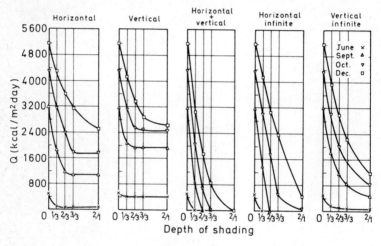

Fig. 12.3. Effect of projection depth of various fixed shading devices on total radiation impact in southern orientation.

12.6. The Thermal Effect of Windows and Shading Devices

The quantitative thermal effects of windows and shading devices depend of course on the size of the windows, relative to the space which is heated by the penetrating radiation. But, in addition, other factors influence the effect of windows and shading such as ventilation conditions, thickness, the thermophysical properties of the materials, etc.

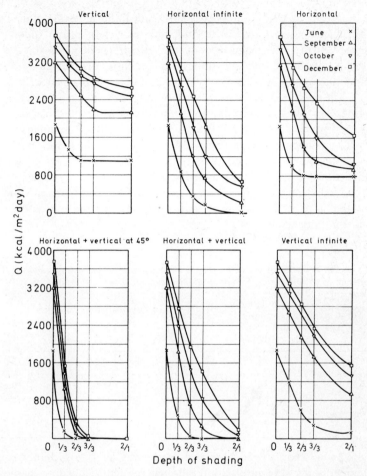

Fig. 12.4.   Effect of projection depth of various fixed shading devices on total
radiation impact in south-east and south-west orientation.

The thermal effect of window size depends mainly on the
shading conditions. When the windows are openable and shaded the
increase in their size brings the indoor temperatures closer to the
outdoor level. This is caused not only by the higher ventilation rate
through the larger windows, but also by the lower thermal resistance
of glass areas as compared with ordinary walls.

But when the windows are not shaded the increase in their size causes higher solar heat gain and thus elevates the indoor temperatures. The magnitude of the elevations depends on the orientation and season, according to the intensity of solar radiation impinging on the windows, as discussed in detail in Chapter 11.

The effect of window size on indoor temperatures, under different ventilation rates and with various types of construction, has been studied by Loudon of the B.R.S. in England [12.10]. A summary of his results is presented in Table 12.IV which gives the indoor maximum temperatures expected in rooms with different sizes of unshaded windows, of a south-facing office building in summer in London. The figures given were derived from the graph presented in Loudon's paper and are expressed as deviations from the outdoor maximum temperatures.

Table 12.IV

Computed deviation of indoor maximum air temperature from outdoor maximum as function of window size, ventilation and constructions, deg C (after Loudon[12.10])

Construction type	Ventilation rate (air change per hour)	Window size relative to wall area					
		0·0	0·2	0·4	0·6	0·8	1·0
Lightweight	2	−4·6	+1·4	+6·4	+11·0	+15·3	+18·0
	10	−2·9	0·0	+2·7	+ 5·3	+ 7·4	+ 9·3
Heavyweight	2	−5·7	−1·4	+2·8	+ 6·7	+ 9·7	+12·1
	10	−4·6	−2·6	−0·7	+ 1·2	+ 2·6	+ 3·8

In a study in the semi-arid Negev region [12.4], indoor air temperatures were measured in full-scale residential buildings with a window-to-floor area ratio of about 8%, when the windows were either closed and shaded, open and shaded or open without shading. The indoor temperatures were higher by about 1½ deg C in the unshaded building, even with the small windows and the cross-ventilation.

In another full-scale study in a region near the sea [12.7] indoor air temperatures were recorded in residential prefabricated buildings with a window-to-floor area ratio of only 6%. The test conditions included various arrangements of the windows and shutters, which were of the external retractable type.

With windows and shutters closed the indoor temperature was kept at an almost constant level, about 2 deg C below the outdoor maximum. With open windows and shutters partially closed, intercepting the radiation and letting in the wind, the range of indoor

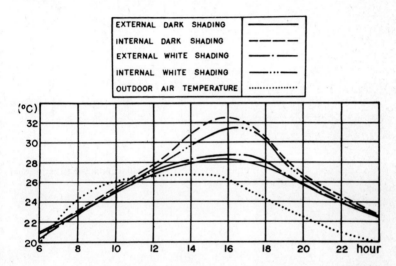

Fig. 12.5. Diurnal pattern of indoor temperatures in models with different shading devices.

temperature was from 2 to 1 deg C below the outdoor maximum. With open windows and shutters the indoor range was about 4 deg C, from about 4 deg C above the outdoor minimum to 1 deg C below the outdoor maximum. With closed windows and open shutters (highest heating by the windows) indoor temperatures were stabilized at about 1 deg C below the outdoor maximum. Thus the provision of unshaded windows, even of very small size, elevated the indoor temperatures by about 1 deg C.

Several laboratory and full-scale experimental studies were carried out on the effect of location and colour of shading devices in Israel. In a laboratory study [12.7], indoor air temperatures of models with a relatively large window-to-wall ratio have been measured

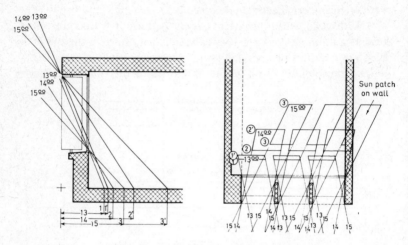

Fig. 12.6.   An example of graphical determination of solar radiation penetration
through a window and a fixed shading device.

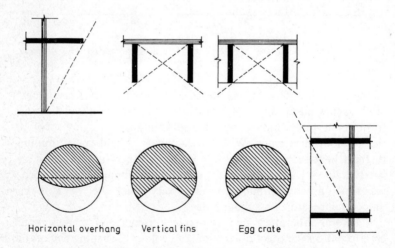

Horizontal overhang   Vertical fins   Egg crate

Fig. 12.7.   Typical masks of various fixed shading devices.

under different shading conditions. Figure 12.5 shows a typical daily pattern of indoor air temperatures in the models facing south-west, under various test conditions. As basis for the evaluation of the efficiency of the various shading devices, a model with complete protection from radiation, by an insulated panel fixed about 10 cm in front of the window, to allow free wind flow over it, was included in the study.

It can be seen that with internal shading, the elevations of the indoor maxima above the outdoor level were 5·5 and 4·5 deg C respectively for green and white venetian blinds, while with external shading the respective elevations were 1·8 and 1·2 deg C. The indoor maximum in the model with complete shading was about the same as that outdoors.

12.7. Computer Aided Design of Fixed Shading

Shaviv has recently suggested a procedure for the design of any fixed external sun-shade [12.13]. The essentials of the method are: (a) Determination of the necessary depth of the sun-shade for full shading and (b) the application of a computer for calculations and graphical presentation of the results.

The steps of the method are as follows: first the times when shading is needed are determined (hours, days, months).

In the second step the window is divided into a fine mesh. Imagine a pole of length l perpendicular to the wall at each mesh point. The length l is calculated in such a way as to give a shadow long enough to reach the frame of the window. The calculation is carried out for the 21st of every month for all the hours for which shading is needed. The distribution of l in the field of the window is the information for the design of the sun-shades.

The third step is to find l_{max} (day)—the maximum of l for every month at each mesh point, and l_{max} (month)—the maximum of l_{max} (day) over all months during which shading is required. The numerical results are presented graphically by means of an axonometric projection plotted by the computer.

A typical example of numerical results and possibilities is shown in Figs. 12.8 and 12.9. Figure 12.8 and Table 12.V show the results

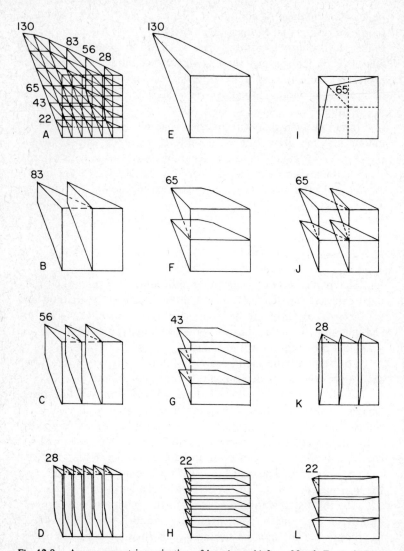

Fig. 12.8.   An axonometric projection of I_{max} (month) for a North-East window.

for a 141 cm/141 cm window on a North-East wall. The results are for latitude 32°N. Shading is required from 8.00 a.m. to 4.00 p.m., and from March 21st to October 21st. Table 12.V gives the results for l_{max} (month) for every point in the grid, as well as the month and hour when it occurred. Note that l_{max} (month), for different points in the grid, occurs at 8.00 a.m. but during different months. The axonometric presentation of the results is given in Fig. 12.8.

Several design alternatives for the North-East window are shown in Fig. 12.8,B,L. Alternatives B, C and D show some possibilities of vertical units. The depth of the units depends on the distance between the units, and is determined by Table 12.V and axonometric

Table 12.V
Results of l_{max} (month) for a North-East window and the period and hours considered.
(Maximum shades needed for window 141·00/141·00 in wall 225·00.)

129·84	126·62	111·18	83·38	55·59	27·79	0·00
7 8	6 8	6 8	6 8	6 8	6 8	10 0
108·20	108·20	105·52	83·38	55·59	27·79	0·00
7 8	7 8	6 8	6 8	6 8	6 8	10 0
86·56	86·56	86·56	83·38	55·59	27·79	0·00
7 8	7 8	7 8	6 8	6 8	6 8	10 0
64·92	64·92	64·92	64·92	55·59	27·79	0·00
7 8	7 8	7 8	7 8	6 8	6 8	10 0
43·28	43·28	43·28	43·28	43·28	27·79	0·00
7 8	7 8	7 8	7 8	7 8	6 8	10 0
21·64	21·64	21·64	21·64	21·64	21·64	0·00
7 8	7 8	7 8	7 8	7 8	7 8	10 0
0·00	0·00	0·00	0·00	0·00	0·00	0·00
10 0	10 0	10 0	10 0	10 0	10 0	10 0

Fig. 12.8,A. All measures in the figures refer to distances in cm from the inner wall of the building. Alternative Fig. 12.8,B demonstrates the possibility of using two identical vertical units, each sheltering half the window. The depth of the sun-shades is 83 cm. When using three vertical units the depth of the shades decreases to 56 cm (Fig. 12.8,C).

Alternative Fig. 12.8,E shows the possibility of using a horizontal unit and a vertical one on the left side of the window. In this case the depth of the shading device is 130 cm (one has to subtract the wall thickness from this depth).

Some possibilities for horizontal sun-shades are shown in Fig.

12.8,F,G and H. The comparison between horizontal and vertical sun-shades shows that the horizontal ones for this window are shorter. A different type of solution is shown in Fig. 12.8,I. Here a tilted sun-shade made of two triangles is proposed. The two triangles meet above the centre of the plane of the window at a distance of 65 cm from the inner wall. A division of the window into four smaller units is shown in Fig. 12.8,J. The maximum depth of the sun-shades is again 65 cm according to the middle point. Finally, Figs. 12.8K and L show the effect of tilting the vertical or horizontal sun-shades. We find the tilted sun-shades to be more economic compared with the non-tilted solution. However, the amount of lighting entering the room in this case is reduced.

Table 12.VI
Results of l_{max} (*month*) *for a South-East window.*
(*Maximum shades needed for window* 141·00/141·00 *in wall* 45·00.)

333·49	333·49	333·49	291·86	221·60	221·60	160·48
10 15	10 15	10 15	10 15	10 14	10 14	10 13
327·88	277·91	277·91	277·91	194·57	184·67	133·74
10 16	10 15	10 15	10 15	10 15	10 14	10 13
327·88	273·23	222·33	222·33	194·57	147·74	106·99
10 16	10 16	10 15	10 15	10 15	10 14	10 13
327·88	273·23	218·59	166·75	166·75	110·80	80·24
10 16	10 16	10 16	10 15	10 15	10 14	10 13
222·88	222·88	218·59	163·94	111·16	97·29	53·49
10 16	10 16	10 16	10 16	10 15	10 15	10 13
111·44	111·44	111·44	111·44	109·29	55·58	26·75
10 16	10 16	10 16	10 16	10 16	10 15	10 13
0·00	0·00	0·00	0·00	0·00	0·00	0·00
10 0	10 0	10 0	10 0	10 0	10 0	10 0

The examples demonstrated in Fig. 12.8 do not exhaust the number of possibilities. All examples comply with the fundamental demand: no penetration of direct sun during the above period and hours.

The results for a 141 cm/141 cm window on a South-West wall are shown graphically in Fig. 12.9,A, while the numerical results for l_{max} (month) are given in Table 12.VI. The maximum of l occurs always in October but at different hours, for different grid points. The sun-shades needed in this case are uncomfortably deep, and it is

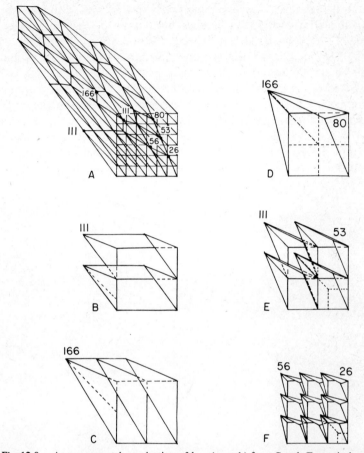

Fig. 12.9.   An axonometric projection of I_{max} (month) for a South-East window.

undesirable to apply a solution of the type Fig. 12.8,E. The alternative solution of several vertical or horizontal units does not improve the situation, since the depth of the sun-shades does not decrease appreciably unless many units are used. The tilted sun-shades offer an economical solution in this case. The shades can be tilted in one direction (Fig. 12.9,B,C) or in two directions (Fig. 12.9,D). Finally, Fig. 12.9,E and F show possibilities of shades made of several units. Clearly, the necessary depth decreases with the increase of the tilt and the number of units. This fact explains why, although the axonometric Fig. 12.9,A implies big single sun-shades, solution Fig. 12.9,F (nine tilted units) is only 56 cm deep.

This method, as demonstrated here, allows the planner to find all possible solutions to the shading problem. The method can be worked out by hand, but this is rather tedious. The application of a computer is desired. The input is the geographical location, the shape of the window (rectangular, triangular, circular, etc.), the orientation of the building and the period and hours during which shading is required. The output is l_{max} (month) for every point in the window which is plotted in an axonometric projection.

Chapter 13

Ventilation Functions and Requirements

The ventilation conditions inside a building are among the primary factors determining human health, comfort and well-being. They have a direct effect on the human body through the physiological effect of air purity and motion, and an indirect effect through their influence on the temperature and humidity of the indoor air and surfaces.

The following chapter deals with the objectives and specific requirements for ventilation under different climatic conditions, while the next two chapters deal with the physical mechanisms causing air flow and the design factors affecting the pattern and velocity of the air flow inside a building, respectively.

Ventilation serves three distinct functions. The first is to maintain the quality of the air in the building above a certain minimum level by replacing indoor air, vitiated in the process of living and occupancy, by fresh outdoor air. This requirement may be termed health ventilation and should be ensured under all climatic conditions.

The second function is to provide thermal comfort by increasing the heat loss from the body and preventing discomfort due to moist skin; this may be termed thermal comfort ventilation. The third is to cool the structure of the building when the indoor temperature is above that out-of-doors, and this may be termed structural cooling ventilation.

The relative importance of each of these functions depends on the climatic conditions prevailing in different seasons and regions, and each involves air flows of a different order of magnitude and their satisfactory use sometimes calls for different design details. Most regions have different requirements during the various seasons, so that details of design should have provisions to satisfy all the requirements.

13.1. Health Ventilation Requirements

The function of "health ventilation" is to provide the necessary amount of oxygen for breathing, cooking, etc., to prevent unduly high levels of carbon dioxide and disagreeable odours. When flueless heating and cooking appliances are used, the ventilation rate should suffice to keep the carbon monoxide and other products of combustion below the level hazardous to health.

Oxygen and carbon dioxide

The outdoor air contains on average about 21% of oxygen, 0·03–0·04% of carbon dioxide, 78% of nitrogen, 1% of inert gases (mainly argon) and between 5 and 25 grams of water vapour per m^3 of air.

In occupied buildings the composition and quality of the air are affected by the living processes and activities of the occupants. Carbon dioxide and water vapour are discharged from the lungs. Bacteria are discharged with breathing, sneezing and coughing. Odour-producing organic materials are given off by the body, to some extent dependent on personal hygiene and diet, and smoking pollutes the air from both the health and odour aspects.

Expired air contains about 16·3% oxygen, 4% carbon dioxide, 79·7% of nitrogen and other gases discharged by the body (mainly ammonia) and about 45 g/m^3 water vapour (saturated air at 37°C).

Oxygen requirements depend primarily on metabolic level. As every litre of oxygen inhaled provides on the average about 5 kcal, the required oxygen (in litres per hour per man) is approximately one-fifth of the metabolic rate (in kcal/h). As the net oxygen intake is about 4·7% of the air (21–16·3%), the air supply (l/h man) required to provide oxygen is about 4·25 times the metabolic rate (in kcal/h). The amount of carbon dioxide released by the body is also proportional to the metabolic rate, the volumetric rate (l/h) being approximately 0·17 M (M in kcal/h). Cooking and heating using gas and oil fuels consume a considerable amount of oxygen and with flueless appliances, release carbon dioxide and other combustion products into the air within the building. The combustion of 1 m^3 of cooking gas produces about 0·6 m^3 of CO_2.

However, in ordinary buildings, such as those for residential, office, school or light industrial use, fluctuations in the oxygen and carbon dioxide content of the air are of little significance. Winslow [13.14], summarizing several physiological studies made by 1925, concluded that harmful effects are only produced when the oxygen content falls below 16–18% and the carbon dioxide rises to 1–2%. The French R.E.E.F. [13.9] summarized more recent studies of the effect of vitiated air and concluded that concentrations of 2–3% carbon dioxide and reductions of 3–4% in oxygen content do not noticeably influence respiratory efficiency, or endanger health. In practice carbon dioxide and oxygen fluctuations in buildings are rarely above 1%. Therefore the concentrations of carbon dioxide and oxygen are not suitable as direct criteria for the specification of ventilation requirements. Air quality, however, is a product of many elements, of which the carbon dioxide concentration is the most easily measured. Thus carbon dioxide can be used to give an indirect indication of the levels of other elements, such as odours, which are more difficult to assess quantitatively. From this point of view, maximum permissible concentrations of carbon dioxide (CO_2) have been suggested in France as 0·1% [13.9] and in the U.S.A. as 0·5% [13.1] (for industrial environments).

It should be borne in mind, however, that there is no constant relationship between the CO_2 concentration and the other factors, but that this depends on personal hygiene, living habits, etc. Therefore to be more useful the actual acceptable level of CO_2 should be determined for different populations.

The volume of fresh air required per person (Q, in m^3/h) to keep the indoor carbon dioxide concentration below 0·5%, when the volume produced per person is q (l/h), is given by:

$$Q = \frac{q \cdot 100}{(0 \cdot 5 - 0 \cdot 05) \cdot 1000} = \frac{q}{4 \cdot 5} \text{ (m}^3\text{/h per person).}$$

For sedentary activity, when the carbon dioxide production is about 18 l/h, Q is 4 m^3/h per person and for manual work at a metabolic rate of 300 kcal/h and carbon dioxide production of 54 l/h the required air supply is about 12 m^3/h per person. But, as will be shown later, air supplies according to these values are not enough to eliminate odours and industrial contaminants and so for practical use a lower maximum concentration should be specified. Thus the

French suggestion of $0 \cdot 1\%$ maximum seems to provide a more adequate indirect criterion for air quality. A level of $0 \cdot 2\%$ carbon dioxide is here tentatively suggested as a criterion for specifying minimum ventilation in residential, office and school buildings.

Odour

To satisfy the requirements of odour level for minimum health, ventilation usually involves a greater air supply than would be indicated by the oxygen and carbon dioxide levels, and therefore is more suitable as a criterion for the ventilation although more difficult to measure. The level of odour is not a health factor in the strict sense but contributes considerably to comfort and well-being in general.

In dealing with odours a distinction should be made between the quantitative aspect (intensity) and the qualitative one (offensiveness or otherwise). The perception of odour intensity follows the Weber–Fechner law of physiological reactions, *i.e.*, it is proportional to the logarithm of the stimulus; the constant of proportionality varies with the odour according to its relative offensiveness.

The odour requirement within a building is simply that disagreeable odours should not be noticeable. This refers to body odours and cooking smells and in some cases to cigarette smoke. The fresh air supply to an occupied room should be sufficient to remove perceptible odours. The amount required varies according to the social standards of acceptability, the number of occupants, their cleanliness and habits, particularly of smoking.

The threshold stimulus for the olfactory sense is extremely low for certain odorous substances and in some cases concentrations well below one part per million can be detected and cause irritation. For this reason the subjective perception of odour is often more sensitive than instrumental detection and forms a more suitable criterion for evaluating air quality.

Adaptation to odour occurs rapidly. As a result, a person remaining in a room where there is a gradual elevation in the level of odour is less sensitive to this change than one just entering the same room. Thus after an adaptation of even a few minutes much higher odour levels can be tolerated.

Several experimental investigations have studied the effect of ventilation on odour intensity and the results of two of these are mentioned here.

Yaglou and Witheridge [13.12] studied ventilation requirements from the odour aspect in relation to the density of occupation (air volume per person) and the presence or absence of smoking. They found that the number of occupants in a room is an important factor in determining the air supply per person required to keep the level of body odours under control. The required ventilation rate varied from 7 ft^3/min per man, with 3 occupants, to 25 ft^3/min per man, with 14 persons. This increase in ventilation rate per person with the number of people in the room they explained by a reduction of the efficiency of ventilation in removing odours. They defined the efficiency of ventilation as the ratio of the effective air flow over the occupied area to the total air supply. This was computed from measurements of the elevation in carbon dioxide concentration in the breathing area according to the formula:

$$\text{Ventilation efficiency} = \frac{(\text{CO}_2 \text{ production per person})}{\left(\dfrac{\text{elevation in CO}_2 \text{ concentration}}{\text{air supply per person}}\right)}.$$

Under full ventilation efficiency the elevation in carbon dioxide concentration should be inversely proportional to the supply rate per person. But it was found that the ratio of the concentration elevation to the ventilation rate increased with the ventilation rate, indicating a reduction in its efficiency.

Yaglou and Witheridge also found a basic difference between body odours and cigarette smell in their spontaneous disappearance.

Body odours were found to be unstable and to disappear with time, even without any air change. In this respect body odours were less stable than odours from chemical materials. The strength of body odours in an unventilated room fell abruptly, within 5 minutes, from very objectionable to perceptible but not objectionable while it took about 6–7 hours for chemical odours to undergo such a reduction.

But the intensity of cigarette smell increased during the first three hours after smoking, and then decreased slowly for a long time, reaching the threshold level only after 17 to 48 hours, depending on the number of cigarettes smoked. It was recommended therefore that in rooms where heavy smoking goes on the ventilation rates required should be much higher than would be necessary to eliminate only body odours.

Consolazio and Pecora [13.2] also studied the effect of ventilation rate on odour level. Forty-five subjects remained in their test chamber for 20 hours daily for 17 days. The odour level was estimated by "judges" according to the following numerical scale:

No odour	0
Threshold odour barely perceptible	1
Definite odour, but not objectionable	2
Strong objectionable odour	3
Very strong disagreeable odour, yet tolerable	4
Overpowering, unbearable and nauseating odour	5

The subjective odour impressions were of two types: instantaneous, upon entrance to the compartment and residual, after one minute of exposure.

A good correlation was found between the instantaneous and residual odour impressions, but the first impression was higher than the later one by about 1·2 points in the subjective scale, indicating adaptation to the odour and fatigue of the olfactory receptors.

The score of instantaneous odour impressions increased arithmetically with the logarithm of the decrease in air supply, in agreement with the Weber–Fechner law of physiological reactions. The effect of adaptation could be seen from the fact that the occupants could detect no odour in their own compartments.

A reduction in air temperature of 16 deg F (from 87° to 71°F) caused a reduction in the perception of odour level equivalent to an increase in the air supply from 5 to 53 ft^3/min per person indicating the increase in odour offensiveness with elevation in temperature.

The bacterial content of the air was also assayed in this investigation. It was found that the bacteria count remained at a constant level and was unaffected by changes in the ventilation rate from 1 to 53 ft^3/min per man. The setting velocity of the bacteria also remains fairly constant.

Carbon dioxide concentration was also measured in this study. The highest concentration found was 0·6%, at a ventilation rate of 1 ft^3/min per man.

Minimum ventilation requirements are of special importance in internal kitchens, bathrooms and lavatories, away from direct outside connection through windows. Estimation of the required ventilation under such conditions can be made when the spontaneous decay rate is disregarded. In this case the pattern of build-up and decay of the concentration of odour-producing gases can be computed mathematically as a function of the ventilation rate.

The concentration of gas emitted at a constant rate is given by the equation:

$$C = \frac{q}{Q} [1 - \exp(-Qt/V)]$$

and its rate of decay after emission is completed, is given by

$$C = C_{\max} \exp(-Qt/V)$$

where:

C = gas concentration ($\%$)
q = rate of emission (m^3/h)
Q = rate of ventilation (m^3/h)
V = room volume (m^3)
t = time (hours)
$\exp$ = exponential function.

Using these equations it is possible either to specify the ventilation rate required to keep the concentration of a given gas, emitted at constant rate, below a predetermined level, or (for intermittent emission, such as in kitchens, bathrooms and W.C.s) to specify the required decay at a given time after cessation of emission.

With constant rates of emission and ventilation and for rooms occupied for several hours, where the value of $\exp(-Qt/V)$ becomes negligible, the first equation reduces to $C = q/Q$ and the required ventilation rate can be computed from the permissible concentration by the equation:

$$Q = q/C.$$

When the outside air contains some of the gas which has to be limited, in the case of carbon dioxide for instance, the equation takes the form:

$$Q = \frac{q}{c_i - c_o}$$

where c_i is the permissible indoor concentration and c_o is the outdoor concentration.

Taking as an example a small bedroom with a volume of 30 m³, occupied by two people, and assuming the maximum permissible concentration of carbon dioxide to be 0·2% with an outdoor concentration of 0·05%, the required ventilation rate is (remembering that the emission rate is 0·17M, or for resting people about 15 1/h):

$$Q = \frac{2 \times 0.015}{0.002 - 0.0005} = 20 \text{ m}^3/\text{h.}$$

Expressing the ventilation in terms of air changes it becomes:

$$n = \frac{20}{30} = 0.67 \text{ air change per hour.}$$

For toilet rooms with permanent ventilation a criterion for minimum ventilation rate could be the decomposition rate of the odours, *e.g.* that ten minutes (one hour/6) after use the concentration would drop to 0·1 of the maximum concentration. In this case the ventilation rate can be computed from the equation:

$$C/C_{max} = 0.1 = \exp(-1/6 \; q/V).$$

With a room of 3 m³ volume this gives:

$$Q = 18 \text{ m}^3/\text{h}$$

or, in terms of air change:

$$n = 18/3 = 6 \text{ complete air changes per hour.}$$

Carbon monoxide (CO)

When flueless heating devices such as petroleum stoves, coal braziers, etc., are used, carbon monoxide may be produced and the odour criterion is not sufficient in the estimation of health hazards. A higher ventilation rate is required, unless provision is made for the evacuation of vitiated air before it can mix with the rest of the indoor air.

Carbon monoxide is produced as a result of incomplete combustion. It has an affinity for the haemoglobin in the blood and forms a compound more stable than that between oxygen and haemoglobin. Thus when carbon monoxide comes into contact with the bloodstream it is readily absorbed, depriving the body of oxygen and causing asphyxia. Van Straaten [13.11] mentions numerous fatal cases in South Africa, among low-income groups using open coal braziers in poorly ventilated buildings.

Carbon monoxide is toxic even at a concentration as low as 0·3%. The highest permissible level suggested in France for residential buildings is 0·003%. The maximum concentration permitted for workshops in the U.S.A. is 100 parts per million (ppm) or 0·01%. As data on the actual rates of CO production of flueless domestic appliances are not available it is not yet possible to compute the required ventilation rate on this basis.

Minimum ventilation rates required in different countries

Many countries have established minimum requirements for permanent ventilation given in terms of either air changes per hour or cubic metres per hour. Table 13.I summarizes the required permanent ventilation rates for different countries.

Table 13.I

Required minimum ventilation rates for different countries

Country	Air changes/hour				m³/h			
	Living room	Kitchen	Bathroom	Toilet	Living room	Kitchen	Bathroom	Toilet
Belgium	1							
Hungary	1	3		5			25	
Poland	0·3–1·0							
Sweden					45			
U.S.S.R.					45	60–90	25	25
France	1–1·5	3–4	3	2				

In practice there is sufficient infiltration of air through the window cracks to provide the necessary air flow for minimum requirements of ordinary families. Even in the absence of wind an air flow of about 1·7 m³/h of air per one metre of crack length (3 ft³/ft) can be expected as a result of temperature gradients. In an average apartment this will amount to about 250 m³/h, *i.e.* much above the minimum requirements.

In an experimental study by Dick *et al.* at the Building Research Station in Great Britain [13.13] air change rates were measured in full-scale buildings. The lowest rate observed (with low wind velocity and small temperature difference) was about 0·7 air change per hour. For an apartment with a volume of 150 m³ this would mean a minimum flow rate of about 100 m³/h which may be sufficient to prevent health hazards.

Only where very effective weather stripping is applied, or where overcrowding results in excessive vapour production from cooking and laundering, is there a need for special provisions for ventilation.

13.2. Thermal Comfort Ventilation

As the term implies, the purpose of thermal comfort ventilation is to provide comfortable indoor thermal conditions. This involves the prevention of discomfort due to feelings of warmth and skin wetness. The physical, physiological and sensory effects of air movement were discussed in Chapters 2, 3 and 4 and here this factor is considered from the point of view of quantitative requirements for thermal comfort ventilation.

While the permanent "health" ventilation is independent of the climatic conditions (although in very cold countries lower requirements might be specified for reasons of fuel economy), the thermal comfort ventilation is not, depending particularly on the temperature and vapour pressure within the building.

It should be appreciated that when high flow rates are involved, as is necessary for thermal comfort, the pattern of velocity distribution is not homogeneous and noticeable variations will exist over the room space. For this reason the ventilation should always be specified in terms of air velocity rather than air supply or air change as there is no direct relationship between quantitative flow and velocity through buildings. For example, a turbulent flow at a low rate might yield higher average velocities in the occupied area of a room than a laminar flow at a higher rate but directed just below the ceiling.

This relation between flow rate and velocity depends also on the geometry of the space and the location of openings. In a long and narrow room having a given rate of air flow, a higher velocity will be obtained when the inlet and outlet windows are located in the narrow walls where the air has a long path to traverse, than when they are in the wide walls, with a shorter path of flow.

From the equations of thermal balance between the body and the environment discussed in detail in Chapter 2, it is possible to compute the air velocity required for comfort under different conditions of temperature, humidity, clothing and metabolic rate, or the velocity for a minimum heat stress at high air temperatures [13.5].

Comfort is associated with a sweat rate lower than 100 g/h and the absence of sensible skin wetness (below 1.0 on the subjective scale of skin wetness—*see* Section 3.7).

From the relationship between skin wetness and the E/E_{max} ratio, discussed in Section 3.7, the air velocity required to prevent moist skin is that yielding a value for E/E_{max} lower than 0.1. The air velocity required to fulfil both conditions, with respect to thermal sensation and skin wetness, can be computed by utilizing the equations of the Index of Thermal Stress (*see* Section 5.6).

At high temperatures, if thermal comfort cannot be achieved, the velocity for minimum thermal stress while the skin remains moist may be lower than that to prevent altogether the subjective discomfort of wet skin (*i.e.* an E/E_{max} ratio of less than 0.1). An increase in the air velocity to achieve dry skin would involve a greater physiological heat load due to convective heat gain. Under such conditions some compromise is advisable and tentatively it is suggested that the air velocity could be increased to an E/E_{max} value of 0.2. The slightly higher physiological strain obtained should then be compensated by an improved subjective comfort.

The air velocity required to attain comfort increases with air temperature because the same cooling effect must be obtained through a smaller temperature difference between body and environment. This relationship holds until the air and skin temperatures are equal, *i.e.* until 35°C (95°F), regardless of the humidity, clothing and work conditions, although these factors determine the magnitude of the required velocity. Above 35°C the increase in air velocity elevates the convective heat gain, but the ultimate effect depends on the level of humidity, metabolic rate and the clothing conditions. At rest and low humidity, especially for the semi-nude or very lightly clothed, a low air velocity is preferable but when the humidity and metabolic rate increase, and heavier clothing is worn, higher air velocities are required to prevent both skin wetness and a reduction of the cooling efficiency of sweating, and a consequent elevation of the sweat rate. Up to a given level the physiological and sensory requirements thus coincide and the optimal velocity can be unequivocably determined. This is so as long as the air velocity required for the prevention of moist skin is lower than that required for the minimum sweat rate. But above certain humidity and metabolic rate levels or in heavier clothing, the lowest sweat rate is achieved when the skin is still wet, and then a compromise should be found, as suggested above.

13.3. Ventilation for Structural Cooling

As an introduction to a discussion of the effect of ventilation on indoor temperature and the ventilation pattern required to achieve optimum conditions, the situation in a building without ventilation will be briefly reviewed, although the subject is treated in more detail in Chapter 7.

Air has a very low heat capacity and therefore when a building is not ventilated the temperature of the indoor air attains that of the surrounding internal surfaces and fluctuates about the average external surface temperature. The relationship between the indoor and outdoor average air temperatures depends mainly on external wall colour, the indoor level being higher as the colour is darkened. The amplitude of fluctuation depends on the product of the structure's heat capacity and thermal resistance as well as on the average range of temperatures of the external surfaces.

When the building is ventilated, air entering the indoor space has its original outdoor temperature, but in traversing the internal space it mixes with indoor air and heat is exchanged with the internal surfaces according to the indoor–outdoor difference.

The quantity of heat removed from or added to the indoor space (Q, kcal/h) is the product of the ventilation rate (V, m^3/h), the volumetric heat capacity of the air (about 0·28 kcal/deg C) and the

Table 13.II

Effect of ventilation on the temperatures of the indoor air and western surface
(deviations from maximum outdoor air temperature, deg C) [13.6]

External colour	Point	Ventilation conditions	Concrete 12 cm	Concrete 22 cm	Hollow concrete blocks 20 cm	Ytong 12 cm	Ytong 22 cm	Ordinary curtain walls 7 cm	Insulated curtain walls 16 cm
Grey	Indoor air	Without ventilation	8·0	3·3	3·5	4·6	2·2	5·8	5·1
		Night ventilation	7·2	1·9	1·7	3·4	0·2	4·8	3·7
		Permanent ventilation	1·0	−0·4	−0·3	0·5	−0·2	0·3	0·4
		Effect of night vent.	−0·8	−1·4	−1·8	−1·2	−2·0	−1·8	−1·4
		Effect of permanent vent.	−7·0	−3·7	−3·8	−4·1	−2·4	−5·5	−4·7
	Western surface	Without ventilation	13·2	6·3	6·8	7·8	2·7	9·3	6·6
		Night ventilation	12·9	4·6	5·2	6·9	0·7	8·4	4·3
		Permanent ventilation	10·1	3·5	2·8	4·5	0·1	3·7	1·7
		Effect of night vent.	−0·3	−1·7	−1·6	−0·9	−2·0	−0·9	−2·3
		Effect of permanent vent.	−3·1	−2·8	−5·0	−3·3	−2·6	−5·6	−4·9
White	Indoor air	Without ventilation	−1·0	−1·8	−2·3	−1·8	−3·2	−1·1	−1·9
		Night ventilation	−2·7	−2·5	−2·8	−2·7	−4·8	−0·5	−3·1
		Permanent ventilation	−1·1	−1·4	−1·4	−0·8	−2·0	0·0	−1·0
		Effect of night vent.	−1·7	−0·7	−0·5	−0·9	−1·6	0·6	−1·2
		Effect of permanent ventilation	−0·1	0·4	0·9	1·0	1·2	1·1	0·9
	Western surface	Without ventilation	−1·1	−1·6	−2·2	−1·7	−3·1	−1·2	−1·8
		Night ventilation	−2·1	−2·8	−2·8	−2·2	−4·5	−0·3	−2·7
		Permanent ventilation	−1·9	−3·1	−2·5	−0·8	−3·6	−0·4	−0·9
		Effect of night vent.	−1·0	−1·2	−0·6	−0·5	−1·4	0·9	−0·9
		Effect of permanent ventilation	−0·8	−1·5	−0·3	0·9	−0·5	0·8	0·9

difference between the outdoor and the average indoor temperatures $(t_i - t_o)$, i.e.

$$Q = 0.28 V (t_i - t_o).$$

Alternatively, it is possible to compute the amount of ventilation required to keep the indoor air temperature within a given limit above the outdoor air temperature in a building subjected to a certain heat flow across the external walls and windows. For example, if the indoor air temperature should not exceed the outdoor level by more than 2 deg C during the time of maximum heat flow the required ventilation rate is:

$$V = \frac{Q_{max}}{0.28 \times 2} = \frac{Q_{max}}{0.56}.$$

It should be emphasized, however, that these equations refer to the temperature of the indoor air which may differ appreciably from temperatures of internal surfaces, especially those of external walls.

An experimental study, dealing with the effect of ventilation on the temperatures of the indoor air and internal surface of the western wall of thermal models, built of different materials and with different external colours, has been conducted at the Building Research Station in Haifa.

Three systems of ventilation timing were examined:

a. Unventilated day and night
b. Ventilated day and night (permanent ventilation)
c. Ventilated only during evening and night (night ventilation).

The results of this study are given in Tables 13.II and 13.III, expressed as average deviations of the internal maximum and minimum temperatures from the corresponding outdoor air temperatures.

It can be seen that when the external colour was grey, ventilation reduced both the indoor air and western surface maxima and minima. When it was white, the maximum temperature was lowered or elevated, according to the wall material. Ventilation lowered the minima in all cases, although to a much lesser degree than with grey surfaces.

The relative effects of permanent versus night ventilation were also affected by the external colour.

Table 13.III

Effect of ventilation on minimum temperatures of indoor air and western surface
(deviations from the minimum outdoor air temperature, deg C) [13.6]

External Colour	Point	Ventilation conditions	Concrete 12 cm	Concrete 22 cm	Hollow concrete blocks 20 cm	Ytong 12 cm	Ytong 22 cm	Ordinary curtain walls 7 cm	Insulated curtain walls 16 cm
Grey	Indoor air	Without ventilation	2·6	4·4	4·4	2·3	4·6	2·0	3·4
		Night ventilation	1·0	2·2	1·7	1·0	1·4	0·8	0·9
		Permanent ventilation	0·6	1·6	1·2	0·7	0·9	0·7	0·7
		Effect of night ventilation	−1·6	−2·2	−2·7	−1·3	−3·2	−1·2	−2·5
		Effect of permanent ventilation	−2·0	−1·8	−3·2	−1·6	−3·7	−1·3	−2·7
	Western surface	Without ventilation	2·1	4·6	4·6	1·7	4·7	1·3	2·9
		Night ventilation	1·7	4·0	3·0	1·2	2·9	0·6	0·9
		Permanent ventilation	0·9	3·1	2·0	0·6	2·1	0·4	0·9
		Effect of night ventilation	−0·4	−0·6	−1·6	−0·5	−1·8	−0·7	−2·0
		Effect of permanent ventilation	−1·2	−1·5	−2·6	−1·1	−2·6	−0·9	−2·0

Table 13.III—*continued*

External colour	Point	Ventilation conditions	Material and thickness						
			Concrete 12 cm	Concrete 22 cm	Hollow concrete blocks 20 cm	Ytong 12 cm	Ytong 22 cm	Ordinary curtain walls 7 cm	Insulated curtain walls 16 cm
White	Indoor air	Without ventilation	2·2	3·7	3·4	2·5	3·4	2·2	3·5
		Night ventilation	0·8	1·7	1·9	1·1	1·0	1·7	0·9
		Permanent ventilation	0·2	0·8	1·1	0·3	0·7	1·0	0·3
		Effect of night ventilation	−1·4	−2·0	−1·5	−1·4	−2·4	−0·5	−2·6
		Effect of permanent ventilation	−2·0	−2·9	−2·3	−2·2	−2·7	−1·2	−3·2
	Western surface	Without ventilation	2·2	3·7	3·3	2·5	3·3	2·2	3·4
		Night ventilation	0·4	2·3	2·1	0·5	1·7	1·0	0·3
		Permanent ventilation	−0·2	1·3	1·1	−0·2	0·8	0·5	−0·1
		Effect of night ventilation	−1·8	−1·4	−1·2	−2·0	−1·6	−1·2	−3·1
		Effect of permanent ventilation	−2·4	−2·4	−2·2	−2·7	−2·7	−1·7	−3·5

When it was grey, permanent ventilation had a much greater cooling effect on the maxima than night ventilation, but with white exterior night ventilation had a greater cooling effect and indoor air temperatures were even elevated when the white models were ventilated during the day.

The quantitative effect of ventilation was dependent also on the material and thickness of the walls, especially when they were painted grey. For each material the cooling effect of permanent ventilation on the maxima was greater when the walls were thinner. For every thickness, the cooling was greater when the material had lower thermal resistance and heat capacity (*see* Chapter 6). Thus grey painted concrete walls were more affected by ventilation than Ytong (lightweight concrete) walls of the same thickness.

Measurements of indoor temperatures in full-scale buildings under different ventilation conditions have been carried out in Israel in several climatic regions [13.4]. In the semi-arid zone of the Negev (Beer-Sheva) measurements of Globe temperature were taken in single-storeyed and in multi-storeyed buildings. The buildings were residentials, built of walls of hollow concrete blocks, plastered on both sides. The external colour was relatively light cream.

The lowest temperatures were obtained when the windows and shutters were closed. Opening one window caused an elevation of about 0·5 deg C and opening two windows caused an elevation of about 1·0 deg C, even when the shutters remained closed.

Opening both windows and shutters caused an elevation of about 3 deg C in the indoor temperature. The opening of a single western (windward) window elevated the indoor maximum Globe temperature by about 2·5 deg C, while the opening of the eastern (leeward) windows caused an elevation only of about 1 deg C.

The difference between the effect of opening the windward and leeward windows is explainable by the fact that the air entering the windward window has previously passed over the external surface of the building and become preheated by contact with it. This phenomenon was much less effective on the leeward wall. Similar results although of a smaller magnitude were obtained in the sea-shore regions of Israel (Acre). Here also lower indoor temperatures were obtained with closed windows and shutters than with open windows and closed shutters.

From the results of these studies it can be concluded that the direction of the ventilation effect, whether of cooling or heating, depends on the pattern of the difference between outdoor and indoor air temperatures in the building, when unventilated, but during the period when ventilation is considered. In buildings, and during hours when the indoor temperature is above the outdoor level, ventilation lowers the indoor temperature, and in reversed conditions the effect is reversed. During the evening and night the indoor temperatures are above the outdoor level in all ordinary conditions so that ventilation at this time always has a cooling effect. On the other hand, the relation between indoor and outdoor temperatures during the daytime depends on the design of the building and in particular on the external colour of walls and on the size and shading of the windows, as discussed in Chapters 7 and 11. Generally speaking, however, it may be assumed that buildings with white or nearly white external colour, medium to high thermal resistance and heat capacity, and relatively small and shaded windows, have daytime indoor temperatures lower than the outdoor. Dark coloured buildings, or those having big, poorly shaded windows, have daytime indoor temperatures above the outdoor.

Thus the direction and magnitude of the ventilation effect on indoor temperature, and the desirable daily pattern of ventilation, depend on the external wall colour and the size and shading of the windows.

When a building is ventilated the internal air changes rapidly and does not have sufficient time to attain the temperature of the surrounding surfaces. Consequently, the internal and external air temperature patterns are close and there is little variation between the indoor air temperatures of ventilated buildings of different materials. The situation is different, however, with respect to the temperature of internal surfaces of the external walls (and roof), when the external colour is dark. Here, too, ventilation brings the temperature of the internal surfaces closer to that of the outside, when compared with unventilated buildings, but the effect is less marked than with indoor air temperature. The quantitative effect also depends on the external colour and wall material.

When the wall colour is dark, ventilation reduces the daytime temperature of the internal surfaces. The relative effect (the ratio of the reduction in temperature by ventilation to the elevation of similar, unventilated surfaces) increases with the thickness of the walls and with their thermal resistance.

13.4. Ventilation Requirements in Relation to Climate

Minimum and optimum ventilation requirements depend on the type of the climate, and may vary according to the seasons within a given region.

Cold dry regions or seasons are characterized by very low outdoor temperatures. Consequently, the outdoor absolute humidity and vapour pressure are also very low. Inhabitants of such regions tend to minimize the entry of outdoor air, in order to save fuel or prevent too low indoor temperatures. Uncontrolled infiltration of cold air causes unpleasant draughts. The indoor relative humidity may be too low, owing to heating of the outdoor air, and may cause irritation. Therefore, humidification is sometimes desirable in these regions. The function of ventilation under such conditions is to ensure a certain minimum rate of air change, to prevent body and other odours from reaching an unpleasant level. This rate will generally be sufficient for the provision of oxygen and prevention of undue concentration of carbon dioxide as well.

The maintenance of a minimum ventilation rate is more complicated in regions with humid winters, not cold enough to make high thermal insulation and central heating indispensable requirements, where low-cost housing exists frequently with high density of occupation, and where flueless devices are a prevalent form of heating.

Under such conditions occupants often tend to reduce the ventilation rate in order not to lower the indoor temperature to an uncomfortable level.

Experience in Israel has shown that in such cases condensation may become a major problem as the ventilation rate required to prevent it is higher than that to dispense only with odours.

The best solution in this case is to provide exhaust ventilation in places where the water vapour is produced, *i.e.* in the kitchens and bathrooms. In this way, vapour is removed before it can disperse and the indoor vapour pressure is reduced with only a low ventilation rate.

In hot regions (or any regions with hot seasons) the ventilation requirements should be based on a different criterion. Here the main function of ventilation is to provide thermal comfort through air motion past the body, sufficient to provide adequate cooling and rapid sweat evaporation, especially under hot-humid conditions.

Volumetric air flow is not a suitable criterion under such conditions and requirements should be specified in terms of the air velocity within the occupied area.

In hot-humid zones, provision should be made to obtain an air velocity of up to 2 m/sec (400 ft/min); as far as possible the prevailing winds should be used to achieve this air movement, by adjustment of design details of the buildings, as discussed in Chapter 15.

In a hot-dry climate it is desirable to reduce to a minimum the ventilation required during the daytime for diluting odours generated in the house. Here the ventilation rate may be even lower than in a cold climate as windows are generally opened in the evening and the time of odour build-up is much shorter. This can be done, however, only if the indoor temperatures are not elevated beyond the level where comfort can be maintained. In the evenings air motion is required to reduce the indoor air temperature and to offset the effect of the warm internal surfaces. As the temperature of the outdoor air in such regions is not usually high in the evenings and nights, the air velocity only needs to reach about 1 m/sec (200 ft/min).

13.5. Methods and Criteria for Evaluating the Ventilation Conditions

Ventilation problems can be studied from measurements taken in full-scale buildings under natural conditions or by model studies in a wind tunnel.

The ventilation in full-size buildings varies continually with the fluctuations in external wind direction and velocity. Therefore it is necessary to repeat measurements over a period of time, in order to obtain a reliable assessment of the conditions.

Ventilation conditions in a building are also affected by nearby structures, and therefore it is difficult to isolate the effect of one given factor from the influence of the surroundings. Because of these difficulties most investigations of ventilation problems are conducted in a wind tunnel using models.

The use of models in ventilation studies

In aeronautical studies, it is normally required that the Reynolds number be the same for the model and the body it represents. In this way air velocity is increased in accordance with their size ratio and similar flow patterns are achieved around the model and the full-scale body. However, it was proved by several investigators (Irminger and Nøkkentved [13.8], Smith [13.10] and Wannenburgh and van Straaten [13.13] that the flow pattern for buildings is independent of the Reynolds number, and that even wide variations in air velocity do not affect flow and pressure distribution over the surfaces. Therefore normal air velocities were used when investigating building ventilation problems.

As criteria for comparing flow patterns Smith [13.10] used the ratios E/h and U/V, the depth of the eddy zone behind the body (E) to the height of the body (h), and the air velocity at a point above the leading edge of the model or building (U) to the undisturbed air velocity (V). He found that, taking into account the length (L) and height (H) of the model in inches, the projected area normal to wind $(A = Lh)$, the perimeter past which the air flows $(P = L + 2h)$ and the free air velocity in ft/min, the flow pattern remains unchanged with variations in the above two criteria when $(2A/P)V$ exceeds 2000, $(2A/P$ being termed the "aerodynamic radius").

Hence, for every model there is a critical air velocity above which the latter does not affect the flow pattern. Under such conditions the flow pattern around buildings can then be inferred from scale model observations.

Wannenburgh and van Straaten [13.13] studied the problem of scale effect by checking the constancy of the flow parameter $\Delta P/\frac{1}{2}\rho V^2$, where:

$$\Delta P = \text{static depression at a given point}$$

$$\tfrac{1}{2}\rho V^2 = \text{dynamic wind pressure.}$$

Studies were made of models with sloping roofs of 10 deg and

35 deg pitch, under two-dimensional flow conditions. They found that ΔP is a linear function of $\frac{1}{2}\rho V^2$ at every point and that their ratio remains constant over a wide range of air velocities, indicating the absence of scale effect in the external flow pattern for the given conditions and criteria.

Criteria for evaluating the ventilation conditions

In dealing with problems of indoor ventilation it should be noted that the relationship between the velocities at various points in the room space is variable and that measurements taken at one "representative" point do not necessarily reflect the conditions in other parts of the room which may be of greater subjective importance.

The criterion for evaluating satisfactory ventilation conditions depends on the type of occupancy and on the climate. The air speed required for comfort depends on the levels of temperature, humidity and physical activity, as discussed above. The desired pattern of air flow and the distribution of velocities in a room vary with the function of the room. For instance, in a living room, where most of the area might be occupied by the people sitting in it, the best distribution would be when the velocities are approximately equal in the various points of the room and the main air flow is at the height of the heads and shoulders of the sitting people, from 70 to 120 cm above the floor. In this case, the best criterion for evaluating the ventilation conditions is the average velocity at the height of 1 metre. In bedrooms, especially in a warm-humid climate, it is important that the main air flow should be at a height a little above the bed level, i.e. from about 50 to 80 cm above the floor. In this case, the best criterion would be the average velocity in that part of the room where the beds will be probably located.

On the other hand, in offices, classrooms, etc., even in hot-humid regions, high air velocity at desk level may disturb work. There the main air stream should be directed at and above the head level, i.e. about 120–150 cm above the floor. In this way the invigorating effect of ventilation can be maintained while minimizing its disturbance to the function of the rooms.

Chapter 14

The Physical Mechanisms of Ventilation

Air flow through a building is induced by pressure gradients across it. Pressure difference builds up from two sources: external wind flow (wind force) and temperature gradients between the indoor and outdoor air (thermal force).

14.1. Ventilation Due to Thermal Force

When the average indoor and outdoor air temperatures are not the same, a difference is created between their densities and the vertical pressure gradients differ correspondingly in and out of doors. The pattern of pressure changes can be described as follows:

When a single opening exists at a certain level in the building, the air pressure on either side of it equalizes, after which no air flow is induced through the aperture in spite of the temperature difference.

The air pressure above and below the aperture varies with height, inside and outside; the rate of variation is proportional to the density of the air. If the indoor air is warmer and therefore less dense, the indoor vertical pressure gradient is less than that outdoors. This means that inside there is an excess pressure at any level above the opening and a depression below it, and these differences increase with vertical distance from the aperture. The indoor air cannot flow out, however, as no aperture is available where the pressure differences exist.

When two openings are provided at different heights and the indoor temperature is again higher than outside, the pressure difference is formed in such a way that excess indoor pressure builds up at the upper opening, where air flows outwards, while a depression is created at the lower level, inducing an inward flow. When the indoor temperature is lower, the positions are interchanged and the flow direction reversed. The total volumetric weight difference between the outdoor and indoor columns of air is proportional to the vertical

281

distance (h) between the two openings and the ratio $\Delta t/T$, where Δt is the indoor–outdoor temperature difference and T is the average absolute temperature ($^\circ K = {^\circ C} + 273$). As the average weight of a 1 cm column of water equals that of 8·5 m of air at ordinary atmospheric temperatures and pressures, the total pressure difference, or pressure "head" (ΔP), is given by:

$$\Delta P = \frac{h\Delta t}{8 \cdot 5T} \text{ (cm } H_2O).$$

For example, with an average indoor temperature of 25°C, outdoor temperature of 30°C and a vertical distance between the centres of the openings of 3·0 m, the pressure head is:

$$\Delta P = \frac{3\,(30-25)}{8 \cdot 5 \left(273 + \dfrac{30+25}{2}\right)} = \frac{3 \times 5}{8 \cdot 5 \times 300 \cdot 5} = 0 \cdot 006 \text{ (cm } H_2O).$$

The air flow (Q) induced by the thermal force is proportional to the square root of the pressure head and the free area of the opening:

$$Q = kA\,(h\Delta t)^{0 \cdot 5}$$

where k is a constant depending on the resistance given by the openings. For standard openings the ASHVE Guide [14.1] suggests the value $k = 9 \cdot 4$ (British units).

Thus the formula becomes:

$$Q = 9 \cdot 4A\,(h\Delta t)^{0 \cdot 5}, \text{ (ft}^3/\text{min/ft}^2)$$

or, in the metric system:

$$Q = 7A\,(h\Delta t)^{0 \cdot 5}, \text{ (m}^3/\text{min/m}^2).$$

14.2. Air Motion Due to Wind Pressure

When wind is blowing against a building, the straight motion of the air is disturbed and deflected around and above the building. The air pressure on the sides facing the wind is elevated above atmospheric pressure (pressure zone) and on the leeward sides it is reduced (suction zone). In this way pressure differences are created over the building.

When wind blows perpendicularly on a rectangular building, the front wall is subject to pressure while the sides and rear are under suction. If the wind direction is oblique, the two upwind sides are under pressure and the others under suction. The roof is subject to suction in all cases. Pressure is not uniformly distributed over the windward surfaces of the building but diminishes outwards from the centre of the pressure zone. Variations in pressure over the wall subject to a perpendicular wind are small, but when the wind flow is oblique there is a sharp drop in pressure from the windward to the leeward corners. When the angle of incidence is about 45°, the pressure at the downwind corners almost disappears and at smaller angles a suction develops there.

Variation of air pressure magnitude in the suction zone is less than in the pressure regions. With a perpendicular wind, the suction on the side walls is greatest upwind, and over the rear wall it diminishes from the centre to the periphery. When the wind is oblique the suction on the two downwind sides and over the roof is reduced downwind.

The pressure difference between any two points on the building envelope determines the potential driving force for ventilation were openings provided at these points. It may be expressed as a dimensionless pressure ratio, when related to the dynamic pressure exerted by the wind. This dynamic pressure, for ordinary temperature conditions, is given by:

$$\Delta P_{(d)}/\tfrac{1}{16}V^2$$

where the pressure, $\Delta P_{(d)}$, is in mm water and the wind velocity (V) in m/sec.

By measuring the actual pressure difference (ΔP) between points on the building envelope with various arrangements of building shape, external wind obstructions and wind direction, and by relating the results to the dynamic pressure of the free wind speed above the building, it is possible to estimate the relative air flow potential if openings were to be provided at the points of reference.

The pressure ratio, $\Delta P/\tfrac{1}{16}V^2$, is a quantitative criterion by which to evaluate the effect of many factors, including wind direction, nearby obstructing structures and trees, building shape, and location of ventilation apertures. Alternatively some schematic distributions of air pressure over the building envelope may be assumed and used to estimate the gradient between points.

The former experimental approach was taken by Irminger and Nøkkentved in Denmark [14.3] and at the N.B.R.I. in Pretoria [14.5, 14.6] where investigations were made on the influence of wind direction, building shape and external obstructions on the pressure ratio. The second, schematic, approach was used by the C.S.T.B. in Paris [14.4] to develop a simplified method for computing approximate pressure gradients.

Irminger and Nøkkentved conducted their experiments in a medium speed wind tunnel (velocity about 20 m/sec) with models of different shapes, including a cube of side 50 mm, and with models of buildings 50 × 50 × 100 mm with various roof slopes (20° to 60°). They found that when the wind was incident normal to the building, the windward wall was subjected to an elevated pressure, averaging 76% of the velocity pressure and decreasing slightly from the centre of the wall (+95%) to the roof (+85%) and sides (+60%). The side walls were subject to a suction averaging −62%, which was highest at the upwind section of the walls (−70%) and decreasing to −30% at the corners. Suction on the leeward wall was almost evenly distributed, averaging −28·5%, and over the roof the average was −65%, decreasing from −70% on the upwind section to −50% downwind.

As the wind turned and became oblique to the building, pressure on the windward wall decreased and the distribution altered. Higher pressure was maintained at the upwind corner, decreasing steeply downwind, so that a marked pressure gradient was established along the windward walls. The suction on the leeward walls was more uniform and was greater as the angle between the wall and the wind increased. Thus the pressure obtained over a wall to which the wind was incident at 60° was +95% of the velocity head at the upwind corner, decreasing downwind to zero, while on the other windward wall (angle of incidence 30°) the pressure ranged from ±30% upwind to − 10% downwind. The average suction was −34·5% on the wall opposite that with wind angle 60°, and was −50·3% on the other leeward wall.

The roof remained under suction, irrespective of the wind direction, with relatively small fluctuations in a magnitude.

Schematic distribution of the pressures around the building, when the building was either normal or oblique (at 60° to one wall, 30° to the other), based on the results obtained by Irminger and Nøkkentved [14.3], is shown in Fig. 14.1.

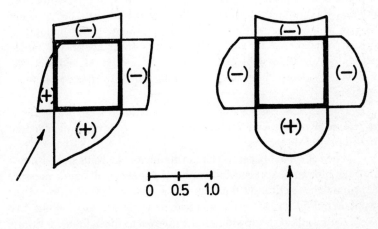

Fig. 14.1.   Schematic distribution of pressure around a building. Based on results of Irminger and Nøkkentved [14.3]. The scale is of $\Delta P / \frac{1}{16} V^2$.

The pressure distribution on the windward walls can be utilized to induce cross-ventilation even in rooms with one external wall, as discussed in Chapter 15.

In the experimental investigation carried out in a low-speed wind tunnel by Richards *et al.* at the N.I.B.R. [14.5] on the effect of wind direction on the pressure ratio, it was found that

". . . in the case of a single-roomed building with windows in two opposite walls . . . changes in wind direction up to 30 degrees either side of the perpendicular have little influence on the value of the pressure ratio." A value of 1·2 was suggested for all wind directions within these limits. For all other wind directions the pressure ratio was found to be linearly related to the angle between the wind and the wall. Analysis of the experimental results of this study, made by the author, yielded the following formula for predicting the pressure ratio (p.r.) as a function of the angle between the wind direction and the wall containing the inlet window (α), for the range $0°$ to $60°$:

$$\text{p.r.} = 0·1 + 0·0183\alpha.$$

Between $60°$ and $90°$ the expected value of p.r. remains at $1·2$.

The pressure distribution over pitched roofs was also studied experimentally at the N.I.B.R. [14.6]. It was found that with a low-pitched roof both the windward the leeward sides of the roof are subject to suction, as the air stream approaching the building is turned upwards at an angle which varies from about $18°$ to $25°$ depending on the height of the wall. With a high-pitched roof, the windward side is under pressure while the leeward side is under suction.

The C.S.T.B. has suggested two schematic pressure distributions over a rectangular building envelope [14.4], for perpendicular and oblique wind directions.

When the wind is perpendicular to one of the walls it is assumed that the pressure over the windward side equals the dynamic pressure (Δp), and the suction on the other three sides is $-0·3\Delta p$. When the wind is oblique at $45°$ it is assumed that the pressure on the two windward walls at the upwind corner is equal to the dynamic pressure, diminishing linearly to zero at the downwind corners; the suction over the two leeward walls is taken to be $-0·5\Delta p$.

The schematic distribution of pressure can be utilized for the estimation of the pressure ratio across any two points. When openings are provided at points subjected to pressure difference, an air flow is initiated between them. The greater the pressure difference the higher the rate of air flow through the building. Even when the windows are closed the pressure difference determines the rate of air flow by infiltration. The magnitude of the infiltration depends not only on the pressure difference but also on the permeability of the openings. The permeability varies according to the type of windows, their details and the quality of their manufacture. For each type this factor must be determined experimentally.

The concept of the pressure ratio is a useful one for estimation of rates of air flow through a building space, which in turn is important in determining air change rates and infiltration heat loss or gain. However, care must be taken in applying it to problems of comfort ventilation, where the air velocity over the occupied space and not the air change rate is significant. For instance, according to the method suggested by the C.S.T.B., when a room has two windows in the centres of opposite walls and the wind is perpendicular to one of them, the pressure ratio is 1·3, and when the wind is oblique at 45° it is only 1·0. But in practice a higher average internal velocity will be obtained in the second case, in spite of the lower pressure difference, on account of the better distribution of air flow (*see* Chapter 15).

14.3. *The Combined Effect and Relative Importance of Wind and Thermal Force*

The actual air flow in buildings results from the combined effect of thermal and wind pressure forces. The gradient obtained across a given opening is the algebraic sum of the pressure differences generated by each force separately. The two forces may operate in the same or in opposite directions, depending on the direction of the wind and on whether the internal or external temperature is the higher. The resulting air flow through the opening is proportional to the square root of the combined pressure difference. Therefore, even when the two forces are operating in the same direction, the resulting air flow can only be slightly higher (at most by 40%) than it would be with the greater force alone [14.2].

As the thermal force of ventilation depends on the product of the indoor–outdoor temperature difference and the height of the ventilation path (*i.e.* vertical distance between apertures), it is of practical importance only when one of these factors is of sufficient magnitude. In residential buildings the effective height of the ventilation path is very small, less than 2 metres in the average single-storeyed apartment, so for an air flow of any practical use to be induced by thermal force there must be an appreciable difference between the indoor and outdoor temperatures. Such differences exist only in winter, and mostly in cold regions. Thus in summer the thermal force is usually too small to have any practical application. Exceptions are kitchens, bathrooms and W.C.s which are ventilated by vertical pipes or ducts. Here the height of the ventilation path may extend through several storeys and the resulting thermal force can be used effectively for natural ventilation.

In addition to the quantitative differences there is also a qualitative difference between the patterns of air flow resulting from the two forces. The thermal force induces an air flow by virtue of the pressure difference alone. The air velocity at the inlet opening is usually very small so that the inertial force is not significant in directing the pattern of flow.

Thus if two rows of openings are placed in all the external walls of a room, at two heights, and the air flow is induced by the thermal force alone, air will enter through lower openings (assuming that the indoor temperature is the higher) and will rise along the wall to leave at the upper openings, producing very little motion of the whole mass of air in the room. On the other hand, an air flow induced by wind pressure causes an air flow across the whole room, the pattern of which is largely determined by the inertia of the incoming air mass, and thus can be controlled by detailed design of the inlet openings. Such an air flow may produce higher velocities (for the same quantity of air moved), on account of its turbulence, than the flow induced by thermal force.

Chapter 15

Design Factors Affecting Ventilation

The pattern of air flow in a room is affected by two factors: the pressure distribution around the building and the inertia of the moving air. When windows are provided in the windward wall of a room, the indoor pressure rises to equal the high external pressure on the wall. If the windows are in a leeward wall, the indoor pressure falls to the level of the lower external pressure. In both cases the average indoor and outdoor pressures equalize, although some difference may exist along the width or the height of the opening.

When windows are opened in both the windward and the leeward sides of the building, a flow of air is induced through the building from the high to the low pressure regions. A mass of air, like any moving mass, is subject to the force of inertia. Therefore the path of an air stream through a room depends mainly on the initial direction of the air mass entering the inlet window. When the direction of the incoming air stream coincides with the line connecting the inlet to the outlet windows, the air stream continues undeflected to the outlet. When the outlet window is not located in the direct path of the incoming air stream, the flow continues its original motion until obstructed by a wall or until its momentum is lost by friction with the air in the room, and only then is the stream deflected towards the lower pressure opening.

15.1. Window Orientation with Respect to the Wind

It is generally believed that to give optimum ventilation conditions the inlet windows should directly face the wind, any deviation from this direction reducing the indoor air speed. However, a recent study [15.2] has shown that this is not always so and that in some cases better conditions can be achieved when the wind is oblique to the inlet windows, particularly when good ventilation conditions are required in the whole area of a room. The study demonstrated that in a room with two windows in opposite walls, where the inlet directly faces the external wind, the main air stream flows straight from inlet to outlet and, apart from local turbulence at the corners of the outlet wall, the rest of the room is only slightly affected. Air flow is slight along the side walls, particularly so at the corners of the inlet window wall. When the wind is oblique (at 45°) to the inlet opening of the same room, most of the air volume takes up a turbulent, circling motion around the room, increasing the air flow along the side walls and in the corners.

On the other hand, if the two windows are located in adjacent walls, better ventilation is obtained with the wind perpendicular to the inlet window than when it is oblique, following the inlet–outlet direction. This pattern is illustrated by Table 15.I which gives average internal air velocities observed in the study, expressed as percentages of the external wind velocity measured at the same height, with window dimensions 1/3 to 3/3 those of the wall.

Table 15.I

Effect of window location and wind direction on average air velocities (per cent of external velocity)

Inlet width	Outlet width	Windows in opposite walls		Windows in adjacent walls	
		Wind perpend.	Wind oblique	Wind perpend.	Wind oblique
1/3	1/3	35	42	45	37
1/3	2/3	39	40	39	40
2/3	1/3	34	43	51	36
2/3	2/3	37	51	—	—
1/3	3/3	44	44	51	45
3/3	1/3	32	41	50	37
2/3	3/3	35	59	—	—
3/3	2/3	36	62	—	—
3/3	3/3	47	65	—	—

From these results it can be concluded that better ventilation conditions are obtained when the air stream has to change direction within the room, than when the flow is direct from inlet to outlet. This conclusion is of great pratical importance in regions where the prevailing wind direction is westerly or easterly, for, as explained earlier (*see* Chapter 11) these building orientations are the most difficult from the point of view of shading. In particular, difficulties may arise with long building blocks where the windows are located in opposite walls of one room, or where two rooms are connected by a hall. Here there may be a conflict between the required orientations from the ventilation and solar radiation aspects.

But from the previous discussion it can be seen that very good ventilation conditions are possible in regions with westerly winds, even when the long facade with the inlet windows is turned by 45° to the north-west or south-west, where the shading is much easier. When the wind direction is north-west or south-west optimum ventilation conditions are achieved when the long facades are orientated towards the north or south, a direction which may also be preferable from the solar radiation viewpoint.

15.2. Window Size

The influence of the size of windows depends to a great extent on whether the room is cross-ventilated. In rooms where windows are only in one wall, the size of the window will have little effect on the internal air velocity. This is illustrated in Table 15.II, which

Table 15.II

Effect of window size in room without cross-ventilation on average air velocities (% of external wind velocity)

Direction of the wind	Width of window		
	1/3	2/3	3/3
Perpendicular to window	13	13	16
Oblique in front	12	15	23
Oblique from rear	14	17	17

gives the average internal velocities observed in a model with a single window, the width of which was varied from 1/3 to the full width of the wall. The experiments were carried out with three window positions with respect to the wind directions: perpendicular, oblique and in the lee of the wind. Average velocity results are given as percentages of the external wind velocity in front of the models, and at the same height.

It may be seen from the table that with the wind oblique to the window there is an appreciable effect when the window size is increased. This is explained by the patterns of pressure distribution discussed earlier (*see* Section 14.2). When the wind is oblique to the window there are greater variations in the air pressure along the width of the wall, and thus the air can enter through one part of the window and leave through another. But when the wind is either perpendicular to or blowing from behind the window, pressure differences along the wall are too small for the increase in window size to have more than a slight effect.

Table 15.III

Effect of inlet and outlet width on average and maximum velocities
(percent of external wind speed)

Wind direction	Outlet size	Inlet size					
		1/3		2/3		3/3	
		Av.	Max.	Av.	Max.	Av.	Max.
Perpendicular	1/3	36	65	34	74	32	49
	2/3	39	131	37	79	36	72
	3/3	44	137	35	72	47	86
Oblique	1/3	42	83	43	96	42	62
	2/3	40	92	57	133	62	131
	3/3	44	152	59	137	65	115

If the room is cross-ventilated, the increase in the size of the windows has a greater effect on the internal air velocity, but only when the inlet and outlet openings are increased simultaneously. Increasing the inlet or outlet alone will only slightly affect the internal air motion. Even when the inlet and outlet are increased simultaneously, the increase in air speed is not proportional to the window size and rate of velocity increase falls off [15.2]. When a room has unequal openings and the outlet is the larger, then much higher maximum velocities and slightly higher average speeds are obtained. This is illustrated in Table 15.III, showing variations in average and maximum internal velocities in a model with inlet and outlet openings of different widths, with inlet/outlet ratios of 1:3 to 3:1. The openings were located in opposite or perpendicular walls.

Experimental results of Givoni [15.3] were analysed mathematically in India [15.1] and the following relationship has been found between the indoor average velocity and the size of the windows (inlet and outlet assumed equal):

$$\overline{V}_{(i)} = 0.45 \, (1 - e^{-3.84X}) \, V_{(o)}$$

where:

$\overline{V}_{(i)}$ = average indoor velocity
X = ratio of window area to wall area
$V_{(o)}$ = outdoor wind speed.

This relationship is applicable for a square room with inlet and outlet windows in opposite walls.

The table shows that the *average* indoor velocity depends mainly on the size of the smaller opening; whether the inlet or the outlet is the smaller makes little difference. On the other hand, the relative

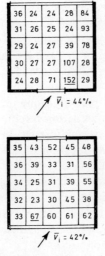

Fig. 15.1.   Distribution of internal air speeds (% of external speed) in models with different ratios of inlet to outlet size.

sizes of the inlet and outlet have a pronounced effect on the *maximum* velocity which in most cases increases with the ratio of outlet to inlet size. Thus the maximum velocity (near the inlet window) in the room with the outlet larger than the inlet is much greater than in the reversed case, but the velocities in other parts of the room are lower, giving little change in the overall average. Therefore the combination of a small inlet with a large outlet produces a concentrated air flow, limited to a small section of the room.

The velocity distribution over the room area is shown in Fig. 15.I [15.2] for inlet/outlet ratios of 1:3 and 3:1 and a wind direction oblique to the inlet wall.

Preference for the type of distribution depends on the function of the room in question, as discussed in Chapter 13, on ventilation requirements.

15.3. Cross-ventilation

The term "cross-ventilation" refers to conditions where a given space is connected by apertures to both pressure and suction areas of the exterior. But sometimes the expression is loosely used whenever the space has more than one access to the outside, regardless of their position in relation to the wind. This may well be misleading, for when all the openings of a space are facing zones at similar air pressures there will be very little internal air flow. Some air motion is caused by the external wind even without cross-ventilation, owing to some differences in air pressure along the height and width of the openings and to the bellows action resulting from pressure fluctuations, which draws air in and out; but this air motion is much smaller than is possible when the location of the same area of openings enables proper cross-ventilation.

Table 15.IV gives some results of a study [15.4] in which the average air velocity in a model of a square room was measured with a constant total area of openings, in the form of a single opening, two openings located in pressure and suction regions, and two openings located in suction areas.

It may be noted from the table that when the room is not cross-ventilated the average indoor velocity is rather low, especially with the wind perpendicular to the inlet window. The provision of cross-ventilation, even without increasing the total area of the openings, more than doubled both the average and maximum velocities.

Table 15.IV

Effect of cross-ventilation on indoor average air velocity
(% of outdoor velocity)

Cross ventilation	Location of openings	Direction of wind	Total width of openings			
			2/3 of the wall		3/3 of the wall	
			Av.	Max.	Av.	Max.
None	Single opening in pressure zone	Perpendicular	13	18	16	20
		Oblique	15	33	23	36
	Single opening in suction zone	Oblique	17	44	17	39
	Two openings in suction zone	Oblique	22	56	23	50
Provided	Two openings in adjacent walls	Perpendicular	45	68	51	103
		Oblique	37	118	40	110
	Two openings in opposite walls	Perpendicular	35	65	37	102
		Oblique	42	83	42	94

15.4. Induced Cross-ventilation in Rooms with One External Wall

Under average conditions, a room with windows on one side only is poorly ventilated because the internal-external pressure gradient across the openings is very small. When the wind direction is oblique to the external wall, there is a flow of air along and parallel to the length of the wall, creating a small pressure gradient in its path and inducing a flow from the high to the low pressure sections. It is possible to utilize this pressure gradient by providing two lateral windows at the upwind and downwind sides of the room, and thus to improve on the ventilation conditions produced by a single window of the same area. But as the pressure gradients are small, the resulting air flow is only moderate.

However, experiments at the B.R.S. in Haifa [15.4] demonstrated
that by adjustment of the details of aperture design a great improvement can be made in the ventilation conditions of rooms with only
one external access. Essentially, this is achieved by creating "artificial"
pressure and suction zones along the external wall. Such pressure
differences can be obtained by providing each of two windows with
a single vertical projection from the internal side, as shown in Fig.
15.2.

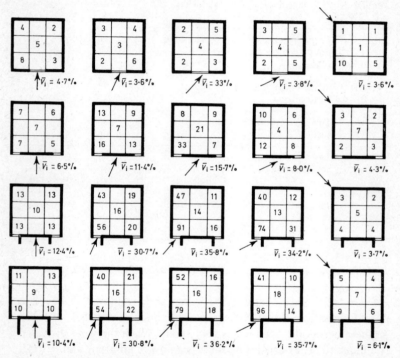

Fig. 15.2. Internal air speeds in models with vertical projections of different
depths, compared with values in models without projections. Window width
⅓ of wall width.

In this way a pressure region is formed in front of the foremost
window (with respect to the wind) and a suction in front of the rear
window. Air then enters the room through the first window and

leaves through the second, in effect creating a cross-ventilation. A similar effect is achieved by incorporating the projections necessary to create the pressure gradient as an integral part of the architectural and functional design. For example, balconies can be designed in conjunction with the openings (windows and doors) to utilize the side walls of the balconies as air flow control devices. The main difference between this arrangement and the previous one is that the positions of the pressure and suction areas are reversed and thus the internal air flow is from the downwind to the upwind window.

Table 15.V gives some observations of the average indoor air velocities (per cent of the outdoor free wind speed, as before) in single rooms with only one exposed wall. Keeping the total area constant (at 1/9 and 2/9 of the wall area) four different window arrangements were used. In the first case one window was placed centrally in the wall; in the second, two windows were used, one at each end of the wall and each with half the area of the first central window. In the third arrangement, the two windows were provided with single vertical projections, and in the fourth case balconies were used in conjunction with the two lateral windows.

It is shown in the table that when the room had a single central window the average indoor air velocity was very low: about 4% of the outdoor free wind speed with the smaller window, and about 10% with the larger. With the two windows at the sides of the wall, of the same total area as that of the single central window, the indoor velocity approximately doubled. When the two windows were provided with vertical projections the indoor velocity reached a level comparable with that existing in rooms with good cross-ventilation, particularly when the wind was oblique to the wall. The balconies were less effective than vertical projections in producing a pressure gradient, but had an effect not to be overlooked. It should be noted however that the provision of two windows and projections had almost no effect when the wind was from the rear, placing the windows in a leeward position.

The conclusion which may be drawn from this study is that a great improvement in ventilation is possible in buildings whose rooms have a single external wall, such as offices, classrooms, etc., provided that there is a prevailing wind direction and the orientation chosen is such that the wind will be oblique to this wall. The angle between

Table 15.V

Average indoor air velocity (% of outdoor free wind speed) in rooms with a single exposure

Window/wall total area	Number and type of windows	Wind direction					
		Perpendicular	Oblique at 22·5°—front	Oblique at 45°—front	Oblique at 67·5°—front	Oblique from the rear
2/9	One central	10·4	10·4	10·4	—	—
	Two lateral	11·8	16·8	17·5	8·9	5·4
	Two at sides with projections	16·0	34·0	38·4	36·2	8·1
1/9	One central	4·7	3·6	3·3	3·8	3·6
	Two lateral	6·5	11·4	15·7	8·0	3·4
	Two lateral with vertical projections	11·4	30·8	36·0	35·0	4·9
	Two lateral with balconies	17·3	—	20·8	—	—

the wall and the wind direction could range from about 20° to 70°.

It should be emphasized that, should the windows be provided with a projection on both sides, the whole effect is lost as the symmetry equalizes the pressure in front of the two windows, and so the driving force for ventilation is greatly reduced. The depth of the projection, for a building containing several rooms, should not be great enough to interfere with the ventilation of adjacent rooms. It appears that it should be no more than one-half the distance between the projection of the outlet window of the first room and the beginning of the inlet of the second room.

15.5. Vertical Location of Windows

While the external wind direction varies considerably in the horizontal plane, variations in the vertical planes are smaller. This is because the free wind, above the level of the buildings, is in most cases nearly horizontal, and the change of vertical direction near a building is almost constant for a given structural and environmental configuration. As a result, the vertical distribution of internal air velocities is much more constant for each arrangement of openings in the buildings than is the horizontal distribution. Therefore, by controlling the design and height of the openings, it is possible to have appreciable control over the vertical velocity distribution.

On account of forces of inertia, the flow pattern of an air mass through a space is primarily determined by its direction on entering. Therefore the vertical location and design of the inlet openings are more critical than the respective characteristics of the outlet.

The height of the outlet window has only a slight effect on the pattern and velocity of the air flow, but in the region of the inlet window there is an abrupt drop in air speed below the level of the window sill, unless this is specifically prevented. The velocities below the sill in a room with cross-ventilation may drop to about 25% of the main air stream velocity. Therefore a change in sill height may significantly alter the velocity at certain levels, although the average air speed in the whole space of the room is only slightly affected. If the height of the window sill in a living room is above that of sedentary occupants, then ventilation will be poor in most of the occupied zone of the room. Sill height in bedrooms is particularly important where the climate is warm, as maximum use must be made of the reduced external air velocity at night.

15.6. Windows—Methods and Positions of Opening

Different types of inlet windows produce characteristic air-flow patterns at various levels in a room space, and thus the window and the way in which it is opened have considerable influence on the ventilation of the living area.

A study of internal flow patterns using several window types was carried out by Holleman [15.5] in Texas, where the patterns were traced by smoke, but no velocity measurements were reported. It was demonstrated that, with double-hung and with horizontal sliding windows, the incoming air stream continues horizontally and in its initial direction, that of the external wind blowing against the building. The maximum free opening with these windows is about one-half of the total glazed area. With vertical pivoted windows it was possible to control the amount of air flow and its horizontal direction, and with standard casement windows opened to the outside this control could be effected by opening both sashes, or one sash only against the wind, or one sash with the wind.

As the air flow is horizontal through all these window types, it is recommended that they be located at the level at which such ventilation is required.

With horizontal projected windows it was found that the air flow is directed upwards at any angle of opening other than the fully open horizontal position. These windows would therefore be most usefully placed below the required level of air movement. With jalousie windows the air flow could be directed either upward or downward on entering, according to the angle of the glass louvres.

Experiments in South Africa by van Straaten et al. [15.6] showed that "... the horizontal centre-pivot-hung sash window is the most suitable for directing the incoming air towards any desired level within the room, particularly if the sashes can be made to open downwards on the room side to 10 degrees below the horizontal. Louvre type windows serve the same purpose." Side-hung windows were found to be less effective in controlling the pattern and speed of the internal air movement.

In Israel, experiments demonstrated [15.4] that altering the angle to which a window is opened shows mainly in the flow pattern and distribution of velocities throughout the room, while the effect on average velocity is more limited. Directing flow downwards from the window greatly increased the speeds in the path of the main air stream, but turbulence produced by the main stream in the rest of the room was only slightly affected.

It is interesting to note that, for every window arrangement tested, the air velocity close to the floor was higher than at upper levels nearer the windows. This is because two main air streams were formed, the initial flow through the inlet and a secondary one along the surfaces of the room, along the walls, floor and ceiling. The air between these two streams remained at lower speeds.

In certain circumstances it is desirable to have a sharp reduction in velocity below a given level. This is so in offices and classrooms, for instance, where the air movement required for comfort might disturb the work, by lifting papers from the desks, etc. The most satisfactory solution would be to direct the air flow in such a way as to obtain a high velocity at the head level (about 120 cm, sitting height) with a sharp decrease at the desk level (about 70 cm).

15.7. Sub-division of the Internal Space

Whenever the width of a building is greater than the depth of its rooms, one room must be ventilated in conjuction with other rooms, either by direct door connections or through an intermediate room such as a hall. If an apartment comprises several interconnected rooms, the incoming air stream may have to change direction a number of times before leaving through the outlet, and these changes impose a higher resistance on the air flow. On the other hand, a greater total area of the apartment may be ventilated by the main stream, making the distribution of air velocities more uniform.

The effect of sub-dividing the internal space into two unequal parts was studied experimentally [15.4]. The arrangement of internal partitions and window location either allowed the air to flow directly from inlet to outlet openings or forced it to change direction up to four times before leaving the room. Wind direction was perpendicular to the windows in all cases and measurements were taken at the level of the window centre. Figure 15.3 shows the distribution of internal air speeds for the arrangements tested, and Fig. 15.4 gives the flow patterns observed in the model by smoke-tracing.

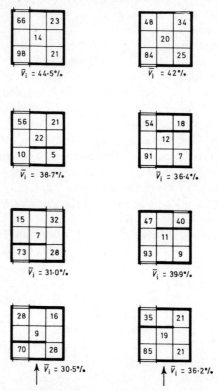

Fig. 15.3.   Effect of sub-division of the interior on the distribution of internal air speeds.

It may be seen that, with the size of internal opening tested, which was designed to avoid appreciable additional resistance to air flow, subdivision moderately reduced the internal velocities on the whole, the greatest reduction in average speed being from 44·5 %

to 30·5%. The velocities were lowest when the partition was in front and nearer to the inlet window, as the air had to change direction upon entering, but better conditions were obtained when the partition was nearer the outlet.

It is inferred therefore that satisfactory ventilation is possible in apartments where air has to pass from one room to another, as

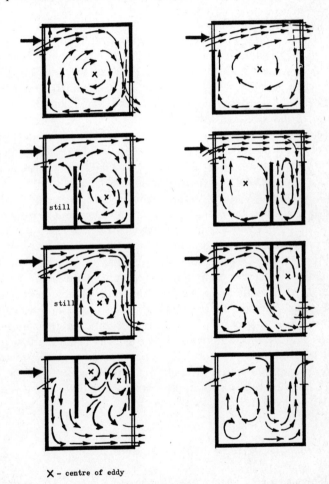

X - centre of eddy

Fig. 15.4. Flow patterns in models with different subdivisions of the internal space.

long as the connections between the rooms remain open when the ventilation is required. It is preferable for the upwind room to be the larger.

15.8. Effect of Fly-screens

Fly-screens are essential in many parts of the world, particularly in the tropics. They may cause considerable reduction in air flow through windows, especially if the external wind is slow. According to van Straaten [15.7] the decrease in total air flow, caused by a 16 mesh, 30 gauge wire screen, is about 60% and 50% when the wind speeds are respectively $1\frac{1}{2}$ and 2 mph, and only about 25% when the speed is 10 mph.

In a wind tunnel study at the B.R.S. in Haifa [15.4] it was found that the effect of fly-screens was dependent on the combination of wind direction and number and position of the inlet windows. The reduction in internal air speed due to the screens over a single central window was greater with an oblique than with a perpendicular wind. It seems that the oblique wind slipped over the screen and did not create an efficient pressure in front of the window. On the other hand this difference was not observed with two lateral inlets.

Application of screens to a whole balcony in front of the openings improved on the ventilation conditions obtained with screens directly applied to the windows. Here the wind was able to penetrate the fly-screen through a large area and then to contract towards the smaller window, free from obstruction. Additional application of screens to the outlet window or a rear balcony produced a smaller effect than the front screens. This supports the hypothesis that the fly-screen does not merely give additional resistance to air flow, but causes the wind to slip over it, preventing the initial entry of the air besides reducing the speed of that air which does pass through.

15.9. Ventilation Problems of Town Planning

Town planning affects several environmental factors important from the point of view of human comfort, in particular the pattern of sun and shade on the various building heights, the degree of protection from solar radiation and rain, dust outside the buildings, and the ventilation conditions around and within houses.

The main planning features which influence these factors are the dimensions and particularly the height of structures in sections of the city, the spacing of the buildings, the homogeneity or variability of the sizes and heights in any one section, the orientation of the street network, and the distribution and extent of open gardens and spaces. In addition, authorities may specify certain design regulations, generally for aesthetic reasons, but this legal right may be utilized to enforce certain features which would contribute to the comfort of the public.

The objectives of town planning for climatic adjustment or control depend on the nature of the prevailing climate. In cold regions, the aim should be to provide protection from wind and rain, and to allow maximum use of sunshine. In warm-humid regions the planning should be directed towards optimum ventilation conditions and maximum protection from solar radiation. In hot-dry areas the main consideration is to reduce the impact of solar radiation on buildings and to provide shade in the streets, playgrounds, etc. Where hot dry winds are associated with dust storms, wind control should be aimed at protection rather than obtaining the best ventilation.

The main effect of building block dimensions is on the ventilation conditions of nearby buildings and their exposure to sunshine and shade. A building standing in the open creates a wind shadow on its lee-side, where the wind velocity is much smaller than in front of the building. In this way the rows of buildings facing the wind cause a reduction in the air velocity around the buildings behind them (with respect to the wind direction). As a result, the wind velocity in a built-up area is generally much lower than in the open country. Streets and other open spaces enable passage of wind among the buildings and so improve the ventilation conditions in the more inner parts of the town. In addition, the air flow above the buildings induces secondary flow at the lower, built-up area and this effect increases along streets and other open spaces.

When the buildings in a city are of approximately the same height, there is a separation between the free air flow above the buildings and that in the built-up zone. The quantitative relationship between the free air stream and the restricted air velocity in the built-up zone depends upon the size, height and spacing of the buildings. In general, as the area is more densely built, and to a greater height, the ground velocity is reduced, relative to the free velocity.

Single buildings projecting above the height of the neighbouring buildings may modify appreciably the pattern and velocity of the air flow near the ground. Although this problem has not been studied sufficiently, there are experimental results of Wise *et al.* [15.8] as well as unpublished data of the author, which indicate that in some cases such high-rise buildings may cause higher air velocity around them, while in other cases they may cause lower air flow.

It seems that this effect depends on the horizontal dimensions of the high buildings and their position with respect to wind direction. When the high buildings are also of large horizontal dimensions they divert the air flow above and over the block and cause "wind shadows" behind them. On the other hand, when the horizontal dimensions are not much larger than those of the lower buildings then the turbulence and pressure difference created around them improve the ventilation conditions of the lower buildings in their neighbourhood.

The environmental conditions around the high buildings may be very different from those prevailing in the "ordinary" zone of the town, especially with regard to ventilation conditions. Wind speed above the level of the bulk of the building blocks in the town, to which the higher buildings are exposed, is much higher. In a hot climate, in particular a humid one, this is obviously an advantage. In hot-dry regions having sand storms, the apartments located at the high floors will be exposed to a much lower concentration of sand, as concentration drops sharply in most cases above the height of about 10 metres from the ground.

In regions with rains accompanied with high winds, the storeys of the high buildings above the level of the rest of the town call for a special measure of wind and water proofing.

Chapter 16

Principles of Design and Choice of Materials to Adapt Building to Climate

GENERAL CONSIDERATIONS

The final two chapters present a synthesis of the numerous systems of interaction between the human comfort and the functional requirements, the architectural features and the characteristics of the structural materials, to form a guide to principles and specifications of building design.

The general principles and methodology involved in determining the interacting factors as functions of the ambient climatic conditions are the considerations of the present chapter. In the following chapter these principles are applied to specific climatic types.

16.1. Range of Climatic Control through Building Design

Specific features of design and of structural materials affect the response of a building to exposure to climatic elements: the quantity of solar radiation absorbed in and penetrating the building, the air and surface temperatures, the air velocity and the vapour pressure. Approximate ranges of variation are summarized below for the relation between indoor and outdoor climatic characteristics.

Solar radiation absorbed in walls
This varies with the absorptivity (colour) of the external surface. Whitewashed surfaces absorb only about 15% of incident radiation; standard light colours, such as cream or light grey, absorb 40–50%, medium dark shades (dark grey, green, red, etc.) 60–70%, and black surfaces 80–90%.

Solar radiation penetrating through windows
This depends on the types of shading employed and to a lesser extent on the composition of the glass. With dark, external shading

as little as 10 % of impinging radiation may enter the building. Using internal shades, 40–70 % enters, and without shading the proportion is about 90 %.

Internal temperatures

The relation of internal to external air and surface temperatures depends on external colour, materials, size and shading of windows and ventilation; it may be expressed by the amplitude ratio, by the deviation of indoor from outdoor maxima and minima, etc. (see Chapter 6).

Using a white exterior with thick walls and small, closed shaded windows it is possible to reduce the internal range to below 10 %, and the internal maximum by 50 % of the outdoor temperature range. The minimum is then elevated by about 40 %. With the addition of ventilation at night the indoor amplitude is slightly increased, as the minimum is subject to further reduction than the maximum. Possible decrease in maximum is then 60 %, and elevation in minimum 20 %, of the outdoor range. In arid regions this reduction in maxima may reach 10 deg C (18 deg F).

To the other extreme, with thin, low resistance and capacity walls, externally dark, and/or with large unshaded windows, indoor temperatures are often more than 10 deg C above the outdoor level; if ventilation is also absent, the elevation of indoor above outdoor maximum may rise above 20 deg C. The amplitude of the interior air temperature is then 1·5–3 that out of doors. Temperature fluctuations of the internal surfaces are even greater than those of the air, elevations in the maxima reaching 30 deg C and over (e.g. for a single layer sheet roof). But the minimum on these surfaces may fall to 8 deg C below the outdoor minimum (where the climate is dry and nights still).

Indoor air velocity

With effective cross-ventilation, average internal air speeds can reach 60 %, and the maximum speed 120 %, of the outdoor free wind speed. If there is no cross-ventilation, even when windows are open, the average may only be 15 % and the minimum 10 %.

Indoor vapour pressure

The vapour pressure in a ventilated building is equal to that outside. In crowded buildings, and in winter when the windows are closed for days on end, the indoor vapour pressure may rise to 7 mm Hg or more above the outdoor level.

The ranges of variation of the indoor climatic elements, which may be expected for different types of buildings, are summarized in Table 16.I.

Table 16.I

Range of variation in indoor climate

The climatic variable	Range of variation
Solar radiation absorbed in the walls	15–90% of incident radiation
Solar radiation penetrating through windows	10–90% of incident radiation
Indoor air temperature amplitude	10–150% of outdoor amplitude
Indoor maximum air temperature	−10 to +10°C from outdoor maximum
Indoor minimum air temperature	0 to +7°C from outdoor minimum
Indoor surface temperature	−8 to + 30°C from outdoor maximum and minimum
Average internal air speed, windows open	15–60% of outdoor wind speed
Actual air speeds at any point in room	10–120% of outdoor wind speed
Indoor vapour pressure	0–7 mm Hg above outdoor level

16.2. Methods to Determine Human Requirements and Satisfactory Design Principles in Relation to Climate

16.2.1. THE METHOD OF OLGYAY.—Olgyay [16.9] was the first to propose a systematic procedure for adapting the design of a building to the human requirements and climatic conditions. His method is based on a "Bioclimatic Chart" showing the zone of human comfort in relation to ambient air temperature and humidity, mean radiant temperature, wind speed, solar radiation and evaporative cooling. On the chart, dry bulb temperature is the ordinate and relative humidity the abscissa. The comfort zone is in the centre, with winter and summer ranges indicated separately (taking seasonal adaptations into account). The lower boundary of the zone is also the limit above which shading is necessary. At temperatures above the comfort level the wind speed required to restore comfort is shown in relation to humidity. Where the ambient conditions are hot and dry, the evaporative cooling necessary for comfort is indicated. Variation in the position of the comfort zone with mean radiant temperature is also marked.

The analysis of climatic data and evaluation of appropriate human requirements and the design principles to satisfy them, proceeds according to the following steps:

a. Compilation of local climatic data, including temperature, wind, radiation and humidity.

b. Tabulation of climatic data on an annual basis, and construction of a series of charts showing annual distribution of the climatic elements.

c. Plotting of the tabulated data on air temperature and humidity on to the bioclimatic chart.

The lower limit of the comfort zone on the chart (70°F) divides the climatic conditions into two categories; the area above this limit is known as the "overheated" period, in which shading from solar radiation is necessary, and below it is the "underheated" period where irradiation is required. Thus the climatic type is determined and, from the other variables shown on the chart, the comfort requirements of ventilation, evaporative cooling, shading or solar radiation can be evaluated.

d. Planning of design factors, such as the building forms and orientation, the location, size and shading of openings and glazed areas, etc., to compensate for disadvantages in the ambient climatic conditions by maximising heating in the underheated period and minimising it in the overheated period. Application of this procedure, for evaluating the performance of fixed shading devices, was demonstrated in Section 11.5.

As mentioned, Olgyay's method was the first attempt to systemize the incorporation of climatic conditions into building design. However, the system is limited in its applicability as the analysis of physiological requirements is based on the outdoor climate and not on that expected within the building in question. It was shown in the previous section that the relation of indoor to outdoor conditions varies widely with different characteristics of the building construction and design. The method is thus suitable for application in humid regions, where ventilation is essential during the day and there is little difference between the indoor conditions and those out of doors. But application in hot dry areas, particularly in the subtropics, could lead to erroneous conclusions.

This important point may be clarified by the following example. Let us consider a sub-tropical inland region where the daytime temperatures are around 32–35°C (90–95°F), the minimum about 17°C (63°F), and the relative humidity about 40%. According to the bioclimatic chart, comfort is unattainable during the day, unless the indoor wind velocity is very high, or evaporative cooling provided. In fact, comfort could easily be achieved, keeping the indoor temperatures below 28°C (82°F), by employing suitable structural materials of white exterior and by closing and efficiently shading the windows.

A similar limitation applies to conditions below the comfort zone, where heating is recommended for periods in which the outdoor temperature is lower than 20°C (70°F); here the actual indoor temperatures may be considerably higher, again depending on the properties and external colour of the structural materials.

16.2.2. METHOD PROPOSED BY THE AUTHOR [16.6].—The method described here uses the Index of Thermal Stress (see *Section* 5.6) to evaluate the human requirements for comfort, from which the necessary features of building design to achieve this comfort are determined; it also involves an estimation of the indoor climate expected under the given ambient conditions. The analysis proceeds as follows.

a. Analysis of the climate

This is carried out on a diurnal basis, for the periods of most extreme physiological stress, enabling the most important aspects of a climate, for considerations of stress, to be specified. These include problems of overheating in the summer, of underheating or excessive cooling in winter, of wetness during rain seasons, etc. In some cases a single aspect is of overriding importance, whereas in others several requirements are of particular significance during different periods of the year. Typical diurnal patterns of outdoor temperature, vapour pressure and wind velocity are compiled and summarized for the hottest and coldest months, and if necessary for other periods of stress conditions, noting features requiring specific attention.

b. Choice of approach in hot climates

The initial examination is a comparison of the indoor conditions of comfort obtained by two methods: by effective ventilation, and by a reduction of the internal temperatures below the outdoor level. The criterion for comparison is the thermal stress of the occupants of the building considered, indicated by their evaporative weight loss: thermal comfort corresponds to a weight loss rate of 40–60 g/h, but provided that the skin remains dry thermal stress is very slight below 100 g/h.

The possibility of achieving thermal comfort during the day using ventilation is examined through the Index of Thermal Stress (*see* Section 5.6), the values of which are computed for the critical hours in the building interior. The assumption is made that, with efficient ventilation, the indoor air temperature and vapour pressure during the day are identical with those outside, and hence only the outdoor values are taken into account. The mean radiant and air temperatures are assumed to be close enough for the additional effect of radiative heat exchange to be neglected, and therefore structural materials must be chosen to justify this assumption. The indoor air speed is taken to be 30% of the free wind speed, with 1·5 m/sec a fixed limit above which the air motion causes annoyance.

At night the required indoor temperatures for comfort are lower than the level necessary during the day, on account of the drop in wind speed and also the higher internal mean radiant temperature which may be maximal at this time. The latter factor requires a compensatory 1–2 deg C reduction in the indoor air temperature.

If it is concluded from the above examination that comfort is attainable using ventilation, under conditions in which the assumptions made are valid, then the primary requirements, to be met through the design of the building and the choice of structural materials, are that these conditions be satisfied (*i.e.* internal surface temperatures below the level causing thermal stress) and that good cross-ventilation be provided.

Application to warm-humid and to Mediterranean marine climates is described in detail in Subsections 17.3.2 and 17.4.2.

If the results of this examination imply that ventilation would not provide the required comfort level, or in cases where ventilation is for some reason undesirable during the day, then a second approach is taken. This involves reduction in indoor temperatures below the outdoor level, effected by the specific selection of building materials.

To obtain this reduction the windows must remain closed and the indoor air is assumed to be still, with the vapour pressure 2 mm Hg higher than that outside. The upper limiting air temperature for comfort is then that temperature producing a weight loss of 100 g/h under the conditions specified, computed from the Index of Thermal Stress. Thus the required reduction in temperature below the outdoor level is evaluated.

The possibility of achieving this temperature with the most favourable design conditions is then examined, i.e. with an externally white building ventilated during the evening and night. The potential reduction varies with the outdoor temperature range, and with suitable materials the indoor maximum may be 50-60% of this range—below the maximum outside. Thus for the ambient internal conditions anticipated, of air temperature, elevated vapour pressure, still air, and elevation of mean radiant temperature above that of the air, the expected sweat rate is computed. If this is below 80 g/h (taking into account the elevated radiant temperature), it is possible to effect the required reduction in internal air temperature by the correct choice of building materials and external colour.

Further details of this procedure are given in Subsection 17.4.1 for a Mediterranean continental climate.

If, however, neither of the above examinations reveals a system able to ensure comfort, or even to come close to it, then the necessity for mechanical thermal control is indicated.

In arid regions this is best provided by either air-conditioning or water evaporation (desert coolers). Where the air is more humid air-conditioning is the only suitable method.

Heating requirements for the winter are determined on the basis of expected indoor temperatures. Those below which heating is necessary are 18°C during the day and 15°C at sunrise, although higher temperatures would be desirable (see Section 17.5).

c. The Building Bioclimatic Chart

As mentioned earlier, the potential reduction of indoor below outdoor temperature increases with the external temperature range. The range, however, is inversely related to the ambient vapour pressure. Thus the upper limit of outdoor temperature at which indoor comfort can be achieved is raised by a drop in the vapour pressure.

The inverse relationship between temperature range and vapour

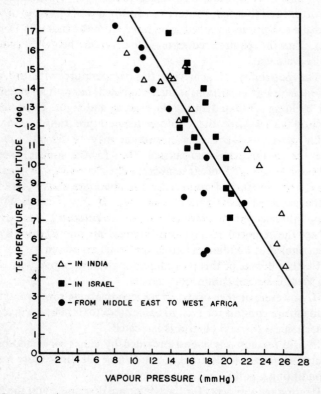

Fig. 16.1.   Relationship between average monthly vapour pressure and temperature amplitude of outdoor air in different regions.

pressure is a global characteristic as well as one shown on large and small regional scales. To illustrate this, Fig. 16.1 shows the inter-relation between the two climatic variables, covering areas of three scales of size: (a) from Bastra and Baghdad in the Middle East to

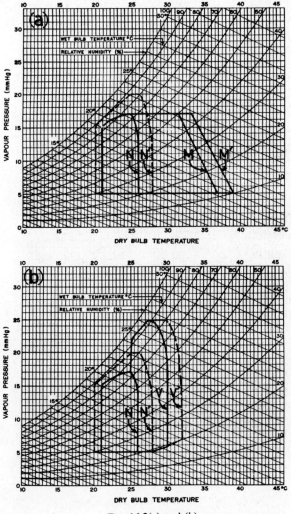

Fig. 16.2(a) and (b)

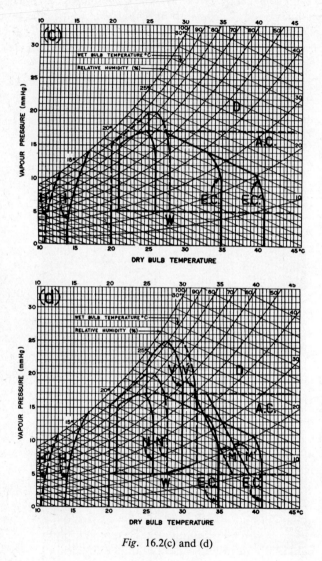

Fig. 16.2(c) and (d)

Fig. 16.2. Building Bioclimatic Chart.

Abidjan and Conakry in West Africa, (b) in several regions in India, and (c) in the relatively small area of Israel, using data derived from various sources. The importance of this interdependence between vapour pressure and temperature range is clear from the correlation between the vastly different areas studied, and quantitatively the relation approximates to:

$$\Delta t \ (^\circ C) = 26 - 0.83 \ \text{v.p. (mm Hg)}.$$

A high humidity necessitates ventilation in a building and, as the corresponding temperature amplitude is low, little reduction in internal temperatures can be obtained. On the other hand, when vapour pressures are low and the temperature range correspondingly high, considerable temperature reductions are possible, and the necessary absence of ventilation is not detrimental at the low humidity. The choice of control method to avoid thermal stress within a building is therefore facilitated to a great extent by considerations of the local temperature range/vapour pressure relation. For the ambient combination of these factors, the indoor climate to be expected using each of the approaches to control can be estimated, and that yielding the most satisfactory thermal conditions selected.

For practical use, the suitability of ventilation, air temperature reduction, evaporative cooling or air-conditioning, for ambient conditions combining different temperature amplitudes and vapour pressures, are plotted on a psychrometric chart to form what has been named a Building Bioclimatic Chart (*see* Fig. 16.2). On each part of the chart is shown the summer comfort or neutral zone, for acclimatized people at rest or engaged in sedentary activity (area bounded by N), and the margin of permissible conditions (area bounded by N'). The temperatures at the upper limit of the acceptable zone are respectively 26° and 28°C for vapour pressures 20 and 5 mm Hg.

In Fig. 16.2 (a) the range of conditions is shown under which comfort is attainable by control of the indoor temperatures alone in the absence of ventilation. The area on the chart in which comfortable conditions can be achieved by this method is marked off by the line M, and the range of attainable acceptable conditions by line M'. Both are found at a vapour pressure below 17 mm Hg. At higher humidities, the still air conditions within a building necessary for the temperature reduction would cause the discomfort of moist skin. The temperature limits of these zones are inversely related to the vapour pressure, varying up to 31° and 33°C at 17 mm Hg and up to 37° and 39°C at 5 mm Hg.

The conditions under which comfort may be achieved using ventilation are shown in Fig. 16.2(b). The zone bounded by the line V applies to buildings not specifically designed to minimize heating (standard buildings), and that enclosed by V' is for structures of medium to high thermal resistance with white external surfaces. The two zones extend respectively to 28° and 30°C at 25 mm Hg and to 30° and 32°C at 5 mm Hg.

Below 17 mm Hg and 32°C there is an overlap area in which the use of ventilation and of temperature control are both applicable, although lower night temperatures might be expected with the former, as less heat is stored within the structure during the day.

The conditions under which neither method is adequate and some system of heating or cooling must be provided are given in Fig. 16.2(c). Such systems can be used of course also at the climatic conditions where comfort is attainable by either ventilation or prevention of undue elevation of the indoor temperatures. EC and EC' mark the regions where evaporative cooling is suitable, for standard and for well-insulated white buildings.

Beyond all these regions in which ventilation, building materials or evaporation can be utilized to ensure thermal comfort within a building, mechanical cooling or air-conditioning must be used. On the chart this zone is marked off by AC. Above 17 mm Hg vapour pressure dehumidification is required and below 8 mm Hg some humidification is advisable. Evaporative coolers provide this increase in humidity but their cooling effect is insufficient outside the range shown on the chart.

At temperatures between 20° and 27°C and v.p. below 5 mm Hg, extra humidification is required to avoid irritation (zone W). Below the neutral zone (20°C) there is a region in which the indoor minimum temperatures are sufficiently higher than the outdoor minima to make heating unnecessary. The limits of this zone (H and H') depend on the structural properties of the building, and extend to include lower temperatures as the humidity falls. This is because of the higher physiological sensitivity to wet-cold than to dry-cold. Below this region some form of artificial heating is required.

The component parts of the chart described above and shown in Fig. 16.2(a), (b) and (c) are recombined in (d) to give the complete chart, from which the alternative methods suitable for comfort provision, under any given combination of temperature and humidity conditions, can be seen simultaneously.

However, the limits of the chart zone should only be considered indicative of the suitability of these thermal control methods, as inaccuracies arise from local deviations in climatic conditions from those assumed for the construction of the chart, particularly in the temperature range and wind velocity. In addition, the effectiveness of the methods suggested also depends on the design and structure of the building.

16.3. Required Thermal Properties of Structure in Relation to Climate

The physical properties of principal interest are the thermal resistance and the heat capacity, and their required characteristics depend of course on the external conditions, giving different criteria for hot and cold climates. Where the annual climate includes only one season of thermal stress, the others being within the comfort range, requirements may be determined according to this season alone. Where two or more such seasons occur during the year, for instance a cold winter and a hot summer, the required resistance and capacity should be evaluated for each period and the most extreme values adopted to comply with both requirements.

The functional requirements for hot and cold climates will be analyzed here, some existing regulations summarized and, in the following section, new formulae presented for evaluating the thermal resistance and heat capacity required according to the climatic conditions.

In a hot climate the function of the building envelope is to moderate the daytime heating effects of the external air and solar radiation on the structure and its interior. At the same time, the rate of cooling during the night should not be over-reduced. When some form of mechanical cooling is employed the "cooling load" should be as low as possible, and when the interior is ventilated during the day provision should be made to minimize any elevation of internal surface temperature above the outdoor level caused by solar radiation.

In the winter of a cold region, heating is always used and the construction of a building must ensure healthy and comfortable indoor thermal conditions, and a reasonable fuel economy with the heating methods locally employed. Structural specifications should be given in terms of two criteria, based on the severity of the climate:

a. The required thermal resistance of the external walls, and possibly of the windows

b. The permissible overall coefficient of heat loss of the building unit (*e.g.* apartment).

The required thermal resistance also depends on the heat capacity of the structure, a relationship discussed in greater detail later.

Regulations specifying minimum thermal requirements for buildings exist in many European countries, but the wide differences between specifications in countries of quite similar climate suggest that local tradition played a considerable part in their designation. However, some of these requirements are summarized below.

Austria

In Austria [16.8] the requirements with respect to thermal insulation are based on the average annual minimum outdoor temperature (or the degree-days) of the locality. The standard used in their formulation was the maintenance of an interior air temperature of 20°C, and the prevention of surface condensation, which is ensured with the internal surfaces of the external walls at a temperature above 10·8°C [16.2]. This last corresponds to the dew point of air at a relative humidity of 55% and temperature 20°C.

The general formula on which the Austrian requirements are based is:

$$R = \frac{20 - t_{(o)\ min}}{5\,(20 - 10\cdot8)} = \frac{20 - t_{(o)\ min}}{46}\ (\text{m}^2\ \text{h deg C/kcal})$$

where R is the required thermal resistance, 20 and 10·8 the temperatures specified above, and $t_{(o)}$ min the outdoor minimum design temperature. The thermal resistance required for roofs is about 1·7 times that for walls.

In addition, requirements are also specified for resistance and heat capacity, combined in the Thermal Time Constant (*see* Section 6.7). The required T.T.C. corresponds to the formula:

$$\text{T.T.C.}_{(req)} = 0.667 \, (20 - t_{(o)min}).$$

For roofs, the value obtained for walls is multiplied by a factor of about 1·6.

The thermal resistance of wall materials (R, m^2 h deg C/kcal) excluding that of the surfaces, the overall thermal transmittance (K, kcal/m^2 h deg C), and the T.T.C. (h) for different design minimum temperatures obtained from the formulae above, are presented in Table 16.II.

Table 16.II
In Austria: Thermal requirements for external walls and roofs [16.8]

Component	Requirement	Design minimum temperature							
		−9	−12	−13	−18	−21	−24	−27	−30
External walls	K	1·59	1·44	1·31	1·21	1·12	1·04	0·98	0·92
	R	0·61	0·49	0·57	0·63	0·70	0·77	0·83	0·89
	T.T.C.	19	21	23	25	27	29	31	33
Roofs	K	0·95	0·86	0·78	0·72	0·67	0·62	0·58	0·55
	R	0·85	0·97	1·09	1·20	1·30	1·41	1·53	1·63
	T.T.C.	31	34	37	40	43	46	49	53

K = overall thermal transmittance (kcal/m^2 h deg C)
R = thermal resistance of wall itself (m^2 h deg C/kcal)
T.T.C. = Thermal Time Constant (h).

Scandinavia

The Scandinavian countries have drawn up joint regulations for the thermal design of buildings [16.10], specified according to the climatic zones within the countries (zone 1: northern and cold regions; zone 4: southern and warmer regions). Specifications refer to the transmittance of windows, according to the window to wall area ratio (f/F), and the transmittance of the walls according to weight and irrespective of the windows.

Table 16.III

In Scandinavia: Requirements for thermal transmittance of window (kcal/m² h deg C) [16.10]

Window to wall area	Climatic zones			
	1	2	3	4
$f/F \leqslant 0.3$	2·7	2·7	3·0	3·0
$0.3 < f/F < 0.6$	2·7	2·7	2·7	3·0
$f/F \geqslant 0.6$	2·1	2·1	2·1	2·7

$K = 2.1$ corresponds to triple glazing
$K = 2.7$ corresponds to double glazing, with at least 12 mm air space
$K = 3.0$ corresponds to double glazing, with minimum spacing 7 mm.

Table 16.IV

In Scandinavia: Specified maximum thermal transmittance and resistance of walls and roofs [16.10]

Requirement	Component	Weight of walls	Climatic zones			
			1	2	3	4
K	Walls	<100 kg/m²	0·4	0·4	0·5	0·5
		>100 kg/m²	0·6	0·7	0·8	0·8
		All bricks	0·8	0·9	1·0	1·1
	Roofs		0·4	0·4	0·5	0·5
R	Walls	<100 kg/m²	2·3	2·3	1·8	1·8
		>100 kg/m²	1·47	1·23	1·05	1·05
		All bricks	1·05	1·05	0·8	0·71
	Roofs	—	2·3	2.3	1·8	1·8

K = overall thermal transmittance (kcal/m² h deg C)
R = Thermal resistance of walls alone, without surface resistance (m² h deg C/kcal).

A summary of these regulation requirements is given in Tables 16.III and 16.IV.

France

In France [16.3] the thermal requirements refer not only to the walls, but also to the global volumetric coefficient of heat loss (the G coefficient). The latter is discussed in detail at a later stage (*see* Section 16.4).

The specifications of thermal transmittance are given according to the climatic regions, the equivalent weight of the walls (relative to standard building materials), and to the quality of the heating system employed. The humidity and ventilation of the indoor air space, and the specific heat and homogeneity of the structure, are taken into account. Three categories of heating system are specified, the superior, average and inferior; as the quality of heating is lower, the thermal transmittance should be reduced (greater insulation).

Table 16.V gives the French regulations concerning thermal transmittance of walls and roofs.

West Germany

In West Germany [16.4], the requirements of thermal resistance for the walls of a structure are specified according to the climatic regions (based on the design outdoor temperature) and the weight of the walls. These are given in Table 16.VI.

Table 16.V

In France: Specifications of maximum thermal transmittance for walls and roofs ($kcal/m^2 h deg C$)

Component	Equivalent weight (kg/m^2)	Climatic zones			
		A	B_1	B_2	C
Roofs	>350	1·2	1·2	1·2	1·2
	250–350	1·1	1·1	1·1	1·0
	150–250	0·9	0·9	1·0	0·8
	75–150	0·8	0·8	0·9	(—)
	<75	0·6	0·6	0·8	(—)

Table 16.V *(continued)*

Com-ponent	Equivalent weight (kg/m^2)	Climatic zones									
		A			B$_1$			B$_2$		C	
		Su.	Av.	In.	Su.	Av.	In.	Su.	Av.	In.	All
Gable walls	>600	1·5	1·5	(—)	1·7	1·5	1·7	1·7	1·7	1·5	1·9
	450–600	1·4	1·4	(—)	1·6	1·4	1·4	1·4	1·6	1·4	1·7
	350–450	1·3	1·3	(—)	1·5	1·3	1·3	1·6	1·6	1·3	1·4
	250–350	1·2	1·2	(—)	1·4	1·2	1·2	1·5	1·5	1·2	1·2
	150–250	1·1	1·1	(—)	1·3	1·1	1·1	1·5	1·5	1·1	(—)
	75–150	1·0	1·0	(—)	1·1	1·0	1·0	1·3	1·3	1·0	(—)
	<75	1·0	1·0	(—)	1·0	1·0	1·0	1·0	1·0	1·0	(—)
Facade walls	>600	1·5	1·5	(—)	1·9	1·7	1·5	1·9	1·9	1·7	2·0
	450–600	1·4	1·4	(—)	1·8	1·6	1·4	1·8	1·8	1·6	1·8
	350–450	1·3	1·3	(—)	1·7	1·5	1·3	1·8	1·8	1·5	1·6
	250–350	1·2	1·2	(—)	1·6	1·4	1·2	1·7	1·7	1·4	1·4
	150–250	1·1	1·1	(—)	1·5	1·3	1·1	1·7	1·7	1·3	1·2
	75–150	1·0	1·0	(—)	1·3	1·2	1·0	1·5	1·5	1·2	1·0
	<75	1·0	1·0	(—)	1·0	1·0	1·0	1·2	1·2	1·0	1·0

(—)　not specified

Climatic zones
    A　= high mountains and severe climate
    B$_1$ = average inland climate
    B$_2$ = Atlantic coast
    C　= Mediterranean coast
Heating quality categories
    Su = superior
    Av = average
    In = inferior.

16.4. *Selection of Materials in Cold Regions*

The characteristic features of the functional thermal require-ments evaluated in the countries mentioned above can be combined

Table 16.VI

In West Germany: Thermal transmittance and resistance requirements [16.4]

Requirement	Weight (kg/m²)	Design outdoor temperature		
		−12°C	−15°C	−18°C
K (kcal/m² deg C h)	20	0·67	0·49	0·36
	50	0·83	0·62	0·45
	100	1·11	0·95	0·67
	150	1·33	1·18	0·91
	200	1·43	1·25	1·05
	300	1·54	1·33	1·18
R (m² deg C h/kcal)	20	1·30	1·85	2·60
	50	1·00	1·40	2·00
	100	0·70	0·95	1·30
	150	0·55	0·65	0·90
	200	0·50	0·60	0·75
	300	0·45	0·55	0·65

K = overall thermal transmittance
R = thermal resistance of walls alone, without surface resistance.

to give a general comprehensive criterion by which to determine the required thermal resistance in relation to climatic conditions. A criterion such as this should have the following features:

a. A quantitative basis on the severity of the outdoor conditions

b. Provision for the damping effect of heat capacity on indoor temperature fluctuations

c. A value suitable to ensure maintenance of desirable indoor thermal conditions (internal air and surface temperatures).

The "design" outdoor temperature

In deciding a temperature to be taken as representative of the severity of a climate, for purposes of calculation and design considerations, several possibilities arise. The average daily minimum of the coldest month of the year is unsuitable because, during this period at least, the temperatures would fall below average level on about one-half of the nights. In the U.S.A. [16.1], the design temperature suggested is based on the lowest minimum temperature expected over periods of 40, 20, 13, 10 and 5 years. For standard structures the 13-year expectancy is recommended; where the structure rapidly responds to fluctuations in outdoor temperature (*e.g.* a lightweight structure) the 40- or 20-year expectancy is considered more suitable.

However, prediction of this nature is only possible in countries where very detailed climatic data and analyses are available. This is not the case in the majority of countries, and an alternative method is put forward here, for more general application.

The average monthly minimum temperature is suggested for the design minimum; this is the lowest temperature reached during the coldest month of the year (*i.e.* that month with the lowest average temperature), averaged over a number of years. In most cases it is also the minimum temperature for the whole year, although occasionally this occurs in a different month.

The difference between the average daily minimum and the actual minimum for the coldest month depends on the degree of fluctuation in the climate of the region in question, but is usually of the order of about 5 deg C (9 deg F). As data on the average daily minimum are generally available at meteorological offices, whereas the average monthly minimum is not, the design minimum temperature can be estimated by reducing the former by 5 deg C.

Desirable indoor conditions

After the design outdoor minimum temperature has been selected, criteria should be established for the indoor conditions desirable for comfort. Even when comfortable air temperatures can be maintained by heating, the properties of the structural materials used are important, not only for considerations of fuel economy, but also for health and comfort.

For instance, if a satisfactory air temperature is maintained in a building of low thermal resistance by a powerful heating system, the internal surface temperatures may fall far enough below those of the air to cause condensation, in addition to the subjective feeling of cold draughts due to radiative heat loss to the cold surfaces. A maximum permissible difference between the temperatures of the indoor air and the internal surfaces of the external walls must therefore be fixed. This limit depends on the ambient vapour pressure within the building, which in turn is determined by several factors. These include the outdoor vapour pressure, the ventilation system, and the density and nature of occupation of the building, as discussed in Chapter 9.

The limiting temperature gradient should therefore be determined for each individual case, taking into account the factors mentioned, or should be fixed at a value low enough to avoid condensation in the most unfavourable conditions possible.

The indoor air temperature satisfactory for comfort (measured 1·5 metres above the floor) is about 20–22°C, but as yet no agreement has been reached concerning the minimum permissible surface temperature. The Austrian regulation requirements discussed in the previous section were based on a minimum of 10·8°C, but in the opinion of the author this value is far too low and may cause discomfort due to radiant heat loss to the cold surfaces, as well as condensation in cases where the indoor humidity level is higher than that assumed in these regulations.

For the air-surface temperature difference, Goromossov [16.7] suggests a maximum value of 3 deg C. Using this criterion, the high thermal resistance required would be very suitable if economic considerations impose no restriction on the thermal quality of the buildings, but it is appreciably higher than that employed in low-cost housing in Germany and Austria for instance. For minimum standards, therefore, a higher air to surface difference must be assumed; the value suggested here is 5 deg C (9 deg F).

Required thermal properties of walls

The maximum required thermal transmittance (K_{max}), when the indoor air temperature ($t_{(i)}$) and air to surface difference ($\Delta t_{(i)}$) are specified, can be evaluated from the formula:

$$K_{max} = \frac{h_{(i)} \times \Delta t_{(i)}}{t_{(i)} - t_{(o)min}}$$

where $h_{(i)}$ is the internal surface coefficient and $t_{(o)min}$ is the design outdoor minimum air temperature. Assuming the surface coefficient to be 7 and the indoor temperature 20°C, the thermal transmittance necessary to ensure an air-surface temperature difference of 3 deg C (desirable) and 5 deg C (permissible) would be:

$$K_{des} = \frac{7 \times 3}{20 - t_{(o)min}} = \frac{21}{20 - t_{(o)min}}$$

$$K_{max} = \frac{7 \times 5}{20 - t_{(o)min}} = \frac{35}{20 - t_{(o)min}}$$

and the thermal resistance of the walls:

$$R_{des} = \frac{20 - t_{(o)min}}{21} = \frac{20 - t_{(o)min}}{20}$$

$$R_{min} = \frac{20 - t_{(o)min}}{35}$$

The above reasoning did not take into account the effect of heat capacity in moderating the influence of external conditions on the interior, which with standard building materials is proportional to the weight per unit area of the walls. As increase in heat capacity reduces the sensitivity of the structure to sharp changes in outdoor temperature, a lower thermal resistance should be permissible when the capacity is high. However, the effect of heat capacity is much smaller in cold climates than in buildings without air-conditioning in warm regions (*see* Section 16.4).

The problem of accounting for the thermal damping effect of heat capacity is approached by compensating for increase in capacity with a corresponding modification of the design minimum temperature assumed. To simplify the procedure, the heat capacity is not referred to directly (as the product of specific heat, density and thickness of the walls), but is expressed in terms of the equivalent weight per unit area of the external walls (kg/m^2). The standards for equivalence are the average inorganic building materials such as concrete products, bricks, stone, etc., and thus for materials like wood products and plastics with specific heat outside the narrow range of the inorganic substances, a correction must be applied to obtain their "equivalent weight".

To modify the design minimum temperature, the following formula is suggested:

$$t'_{(o)min} = t_{(o)min} + 0.01\ W$$

where $t'_{(o)min}$ is the modified design minimum temperature (°C) and W the equivalent weight of the external walls (kg/m^2). The expressions for the desirable and the permissible limiting thermal transmittance and resistance, with the assumptions made before, then become:

$$K_{des} = \frac{20}{20 - (t_{(o)min} + 0.01\ W)}$$

$$K_{max} = \frac{35}{20 - (t_{(o)min} + 0.01\ W)}$$

and

$$R_{des} = \frac{20 - (t_{(o)min} + 0.01\ W)}{20}$$

$$R_{min} = \frac{20 - (t_{(o)min} + 0.01\ W)}{35}.$$

To obtain the resistance of the wall alone, without considering the surface resistance, these values must be reduced by 0.2 (in the metric system).

These formulae are limited in their application only to walls of long building blocks, where the external surface area of each apartment is relatively small. For application to roofs, the values should be increased by about 20%, to account for radiative heat loss to the sky; for the walls of small houses, or of apartments with a large external surface area, the thermal resistance should be increased by 10%.

In the calculation (*see* Section 6.1) the actual thermal conductivities of the materials, based on their moisture content, should be taken into consideration.

Table 16.VII

Desired thermal resistance of walls ($m^2 \times h \times deg\ C/kcal$)

Weight (kg/m²)	Outdoor "design" temperature, $t_{(o)min}$							
	5	0	−5	−10	−15	−20	−25	−30
20	0·74	0·99	1·24	1·49	1·74	1·99	2·24	2·49
50	0·72	0·97	1·22	1·47	1·72	1·97	2·22	2·42
100	0·70	0·95	1·20	1·45	1·70	1·95	2·20	2·45
200	0·65	0·90	1·15	1·40	1·65	1·90	2·15	2·40
300	0·60	0·85	1·10	1·35	1·60	1·85	2·10	2·35
500	0·50	0·75	1·00	1·25	1·50	1·75	2·00	2·25
700	0·40	0·65	0·90	1·15	1·40	1·65	1·90	2·15
900	—	0·55	0·80	1·05	1·30	1·55	1·80	2·05

Table 16.VIII

Minimal thermal resistance of walls ($m^2 \times h \times deg\ C/kcal$)

Weight (kg/m²)	Outdoor "design" temperature, $t_{(o)min}$ °C							
	5	0	−5	−10	−15	−20	−25	−30
20	0·42	0·57	0·71	0·85	0·99	1·14	1·28	1·42
50	0·41	0·56	0·70	0·84	0·98	1·13	1·27	1·41
100	0·40	0·54	0·68	0·83	0·97	1·11	1·26	1·40
200	0·37	0·52	0·66	0·80	0·94	1·09	1·23	1·37
300	0·34	0·49	0·63	0·77	0·91	1·06	1·20	1·34
500	—	0·43	0·57	0·72	0·86	1·00	1·14	1·29
700	—	0·37	0·51	0·56	0·80	0·94	1·09	1·23
900	—	—	0·46	0·60	0·74	0·88	1·03	1·17

For convenience of application, Tables 16.VII and 16.VIII give the desired and minimum permissible thermal resistances (including surface resistance) computed for walls of standard inorganic materials, as a function of the design minimum temperature and weight of the walls.

Required thermal quality of buildings as a whole

The thermal resistance of the external walls is not a sufficient criterion by which to define the thermal quality of a structure. Several important factors differ widely with individual buildings, including the volume to external surface area ratio and the relative size and thermal properties of glazed areas. For economic considerations, the thermal quality requirements specified for the building as a whole should take into account all of these factors.

This may be achieved by formulating a limiting coefficient of volumetric heat loss (G), as a function of the factors mentioned. Using this criterion, it will be seen that to obtain a satisfactory thermal quality in structures with a relatively large exposed area (*e.g.* single one-storeyed houses) and window area, relatively better insulation or more resistant heat loss characteristics of the glazing would be required. The actual requirements assumed for the formulation of the criterion will vary according to the severity of the climate and the degree of fuel economy necessary.

The criterion itself was developed by the C.S.T.B. in France [16.3] and the G coefficient computed using it is defined:

$$G = \frac{Q}{V(t_i - t_e)}$$

where Q is the rate of heat supply to the interior (kcal/h), V is the volume of the interior space and t_i, t_e are the internal and external air temperatures, assumed to be constant.

The evaluation of the G coefficient comprises the three stages described below.

a. Heat loss due to air flow through the building, expressed in the number (N) of total air changes per hour throughout the building. As the heat capacity of 1 m^3 of air is 0·3 kcal, the heat loss through air change is given by:

$$Q_a = 0·3NV(t_i - t_e).$$

N depends on the wind-proofing of the windows, and is assumed to be 1·25 per hour, under standard conditions; the proportion of this component of the G coefficient is:

$$G_a = 0·3N = 0·375.$$

　　b. Heat loss through the walls (Q_w), given by the product of the areas (A_w) and thermal transmittances (K_w), summated for all the external walls, or:

$$Q_w = \sum A_w.K_w (t_i - t_e).$$

The fraction of the G coefficient which it represents is given by:

$$G_w = \frac{1}{V} \sum A_w.K_w.$$

　　c. Heat loss through the glazed areas (Q_g), computed in a similar manner with the formula:

$$Q_g = \sum A_g.K_g (t_i - t_e).$$

The thermal transmittance depends on the type of window and on the shading, as shown in Table 16.IX [16.3]. The fraction of the G coefficient due to the windows is:

$$G_g = \frac{1}{V} \sum A_g.K_g.$$

Table 16.IX

Coefficients of thermal transmittance for
windows of different types and shading [16.3]

Shading	Single windows	Double windows
None	5	3
External shutters	3·8–4·3	2·5–2·7
Internal curtains	3·7–4·0	2·4–2·6
Shutters and curtains	3·3–3·7	2·2–2·4

The overall G coefficient is then computed according to the formula:

$$G = 0\cdot3N + \frac{\Sigma A_{\mathrm{w}}.K_{\mathrm{w}}}{V} + \frac{\Sigma A_{\mathrm{g}}.K_{\mathrm{g}}}{V}.$$

To allow for the smaller heat flow to the ground, compared with that through the external walls, only one-half the area of the ground floor is taken for calculations.

In this form, the concept of overall heat loss excludes the additional influence of thermal capacity, and to take this into account the requirements regarding the G coefficient criterion should be modified by elevating the "design" outdoor temperature, according to the heat capacity of the external structure (in kg/m^2), but such a modification has not been worked out yet.

The ratio of external surface area to volume of the building space, $\dfrac{A_{\mathrm{w}} + u}{V}$ where u is the area of the roof, obviously has a considerable influence on the value of G. The greater the relative exterior area, the higher the potential heat loss per unit volume; if the thermal resistance remains the same, the power of the heating system must be proportionally greater to maintain comfortable conditions. Thus for economical reasons it is necessary to augment the resistance of a structure as the relative exposed area increases, in order to obtain the required G value. In apartment buildings, where the internal flats have only two exterior walls while external and top floor apartments are exposed on three or four surfaces, the thermal resistance should be adjusted to suit each type of apartment, in particular by providing additional insulation on the gables and roof. If individual adjustment is not possible, the requirements for the whole building should be specified to ensure comfortable conditions in the apartments from which heat loss is a maximum.

In specifying building standards for internal thermal comfort, the G coefficient is applied using the general principle that high G values in a building should be mitigated by strong heating, and the reverse. Thus the required G value depends on the necessary heating economy. The capacity of the heating system Q_{max} is given by:

$$Q_{\mathrm{max}} = GV\left(t_{\mathrm{i}} - t_{(\mathrm{o})\mathrm{min}}\right)$$

where t_i is the required indoor temperature and $t_{(o)min}$ the design outdoor minimum temperature.

However, the design minimum temperature does not give sufficient indication of the heating load within a building, as both the duration and average severity of the cold climate also determine the extent of heating required. The extent of these two factors is expressed in concept of "degree-days". The severity of cold on a particular day is represented by the allocation of a number of degree-days, equal to the number of degrees by which the average *outdoor* air temperature on that day falls below a certain threshold level. The threshold temperature is that below which heating is necessary, but is lower than the minimum *indoor* permissible temperature for comfort, as internal temperatures are higher than those out of doors. The number of degree-days throughout a cold season is given by:

$$\sum_{1}^{n} (T - \bar{t}_{(o)}) \text{ deg F}$$

where n is the number of days on which the average outdoor temperature falls below T, the threshold temperature.

Although the threshold temperature in fact depends on the type of building heated, the values of T adopted in several different countries were assumed to be generally applicable. In the U.S.A. a minimum limit of 65°F (18·5°C) has been adopted, but in France a

Table 16.X

In France: Requirements with respect to the volumetric coefficient of heat loss [16.3]

Fuel economy	Climatic zones				
	High mountains	Severe	Average inland	Atlantic coast	Mediter-ranean
Good	0·8	0·95	1·05	1·2	1·3
Average	1·2	1·4	1·6	1·8	2·0
Mediocre	1·6	1·85	2·15	2·4	2·65

lower temperature of 15°C was considered suitable and, after recent studies, this has been further reduced to 11°C.

In France [16.3] the G coefficient requirements are specified according to the necessary heating economy, within certain climatic zones classified by the number of degree-days during the year, taking the threshold temperature as 11°C. The number of days on which the temperature drops below -5°C was also taken into account in classifying a given place to a given climatic zone. These G coefficients are shown in Table 16.X, and figures are also available showing requirements for several building types.

As yet, no general formula is available for the determination of the G coefficient according to both the design minimum temperature and the degree-days of the heating season. However, with modifications according to the type and the heat capacity of the structure, the G coefficient of overall heat loss would provide a basis for evaluation of required thermal resistance, and a criterion for structural thermal quality in cold climates.

16.5. Selection of Materials in Hot Regions

In choosing suitable building materials in hot climates, two ambient characteristics are of primary importance: the maximum temperature and the diurnal range (dependent on the vapour pressure level). A third significant factor is found in the absorbed solar radiation, which depends on the orientation and external colour of the building element in question. The most important thermophysical properties are the thermal resistance (R) and heat capacity (Q), which may often be expressed together by the product QR.

Thermal resistance is necessary to moderate the heat flow from external to internal surfaces, which is determined by the maximum external surface temperature; this in turn is dependent on the maximum outdoor air temperature and the absorption of solar radiation.

The required thermal resistance may therefore be considered as a function of the increase in external surface temperature due to irradiation, and of the elevation of the outdoor maximum above a certain level; this threshold temperature, above which insulation is necessary to reduce inward heat flow, may be taken as 25°C (77°F). But the effects of these two temperature elevations are not equivalent, as the period of the air temperature wave is 24 hours (from minimum to minimum), while the duration of solar heating of the walls is much less, in summer being about 6 hours. As a result the effect of irradiation on internal conditions is smaller than that of an equal increase in the outdoor air temperature.

A high structural heat capacity is effective in moderating the internal response to fluctuations in the external surface temperature, and the required magnitude is therefore more closely related to the temperature elevation with solar radiation and the outdoor *range*, than to the maximum temperature reached. Here again the difference in duration gives these two factors unequal weight in their relation to the compensatory heat capacity necessary. As the temperature amplitude widens, greater advantage can be taken of the effect of heat capacity in controlling the internal temperatures.

As mentioned, the thermal capacity and resistance may be represented together by the QR value, and to a certain extent the effect of the insufficient resistance can be alleviated by an increase in the capacity, and vice versa. But as the mechanisms of heat flow control operating through the two factors are different, the effectiveness, and hence the relative importance, of each with respect to physiological comfort within a building varies differently with the climatic characteristics. Generally speaking, thermal resistance is of greater importance in humid areas where the diurnal range is small, while in a dry climate with a wide temperature range the heat capacity has an increased significance, and the importance of one factor is approximately equal to that of the other.

At present, no adequate standards or formulae are available for evaluating hot-climate requirements of resistance and capacity in buildings without air-conditioning. But from experience gained in Israel [16.6], the author suggests the following formulae as a tentative guide to the selection of suitable materials under these conditions, until further research can provide more exact criteria. Thermal resistance (in deg C m^2 h/kcal, excluding the surface resistance)

for walls: $R_{req} = 0{\cdot}05\,(t_{(o)max}-25) + 0{\cdot}02\left(\dfrac{aI_{max}}{12}\right)$

for roofs: $R_{req} = 0{\cdot}05\,(t_{(o)max}-25) + 0{\cdot}03\left(\dfrac{aI_{max}}{12}\right)$

Table 16.XI

Thermal resistance and heat capacity of walls, required in hot climate, as a function of the outdoor maximum, amplitude and absorption of solar radiation [16.6]

$t_{(o)max}$ (deg C)	$\Delta t_{(o)}$ (deg C)	$\dfrac{aI_{max}}{12}$ (deg C)	R	Q	QR
	5	0	0·25	12·5	3·1
		10	0·45	22·5	10·1
		20	0·65	32·5	21·2
30	10	0	0·25	25·0	6·2
		10	0·45	35·0	15·8
		20	0·65	45·0	29·3
	15	0	0·25	37·5	9·4
		10	0·45	47·5	21·4
		20	0·65	57·5	36·8
	5	0	0·50	12·5	6·2
		10	0·70	22·5	15·8
		20	0·90	32·5	29·3
	10	0	0·50	25·0	12·5
		10	0·70	35·0	24·5
		20	0·90	45·0	40·5
35	15	0	0·50	37·5	18·7
		10	0·70	47·5	31·5
		20	0·90	57·5	51·7
	20	0	0·50	50·0	25·0
		10	0·70	60·0	42·0
		20	0·90	70·0	63·0
	5	0	0·75	12·5	9·4
		10	0·95	22·5	21·4
		20	1·15	32·5	37·5
	10	0	0·75	25·0	18·8
		10	0·95	35·0	33·2
		20	1·15	45·0	51·7
40	15	0	0·75	37·5	28·2
		10	0·95	47·5	45·1
		20	1·15	57·5	66·0
	20	0	0·75	50·0	37·5
		10	0·95	60·0	57·0
		20	1·15	70·0	80·5

Table 16.XII
Computed values of R, Q, and QR for different walls

Wall material	Thickness (cm)	Weight (kg/m^2)	R $\dfrac{m^2 \times h \times \deg C}{kcal}$	Q $\dfrac{kcal}{m^2 \deg C}$	QR (h)
	10	220	0·08	48	4
	15	330	0·12	72	9
	20	440	0·17	97	16
Dense concrete	25	550	0·21	120	25
	30	660	0·25	145	36
	40	880	0·33	194	64
	50	1100	0·42	240	100
	10	60	0·4	14	6
	15	90	0·6	21	13
	20	120	0·8	28	20
Light-weight concrete	25	150	1·0	35	35
	30	180	1·2	42	50
	35	210	1·4	49	69
	40	240	1·6	56	90
	0	330	0·12	72	9
Sandwiched wall with varying insulation thickness	1	330	0·43	72	31
	2	330	0·76	72	55
	3	330	1·09	72	79
	4	330	1·42	72	102
	5	330	1·75	72	126

Heat capacity (in kcal/m^2 deg C)

for walls: $Q_{\text{req}} = 2\cdot5\,(t_{(\text{o})\text{max}} - t_{(\text{o})\text{min}}) + 1\cdot0\left(\dfrac{aI_{\text{max}}}{12}\right)$

for roofs: $Q_{\text{req}} = 2\cdot5\,(t_{(\text{o})\text{max}} - t_{(\text{o})\text{min}}) + 1\cdot5\left(\dfrac{aI_{\text{max}}}{12}\right)$

where: $t_{(\text{o})\text{max}}$ is the expected outdoor air maximum (°C),

$t_{(\text{o})\text{min}}$ is the expected outdoor air minimum (°C), and

aI_{max} is the maximum intensity of incident solar radiation.

Only the surface-to-surface resistance is taken into account, omitting that of the air layers attached to these surfaces, as the internal surface temperature is of primary importance for ensuring comfort; this is particularly so in hot dry areas, where housing is without ventilation during the day.

To illustrate the variations with climatic conditions, the values for R, Q and QR shown in Table 16.XI were computed for several outdoor temperature maxima, diurnal ranges ($\Delta t_{(\text{o})}$) and surface temperature elevations (Δt_{sr}) due to solar radiation absorption. Then to indicate the magnitude of the values for different structural materials, Table 16.XII gives R, Q, and QR computed for walls of various thicknesses of dense and of lightweight concrete, and for composite walls comprising a sandwich of expanded polystyrene insulation between two dense concrete layers, each of 7·5 cm thick, according to the thickness of insulation.

The assumed thermal conductivity of the materials is based on the moisture content expected under summer conditions in subtropical regions (no summer rains): for dense concrete 1·2 and for lightweight concrete 0·25 (kcal/m h deg C).

Chapter 17

Principles of Design and Selection of Materials to Adapt Building to Climate

APPLICATION TO SPECIFIC CLIMATIC TYPES

17.1. Introduction

In this concluding chapter, the aspects of human thermal requirements and the design characteristics aimed to satisfy them will be reviewed and applied to various climatic types. It is of course impossible to deal with every combination of elements which make up the immense variety of weather distributed over the earth, and so certain "ideal" climatic types are considered, to illustrate the application methodology of the principles and approaches discussed in the preceding chapter. As the experience of the author is largely related to sub-tropical and other hot climates, these particular types will serve as primary examples for demonstrating methods of application.

It should be noted that the numerous combinations of climatic variables may be classified according to many different criteria, dependent on the purpose for which such categorization is necessary. As the principal aim of this book is to provide guiding principles for building design for comfort, it is attempted in the classification used here to emphasize those climatic characteristics exerting influence on physiological comfort and, on the other hand, on the thermal response or behaviour of buildings.

From the aspect of building design, the necessary climatic control is entirely different in hot and in cold conditions, and this therefore provides a basic distinction for classification. The thermal effect of materials in buildings without air-conditioning in a warm climate is dependent primarily on the diurnal temperature range, which in turn depends mainly on the vapour pressure level. In this way temperature and humidity are interconnected in determining the type of the climate. Prevention of water penetration is a requirement in all areas with rains, irrespective of the seasons at which they come. Condensation occurs mainly under cold conditions, but the severity of the problem depends on the ambient humidity. Thus wetness (rain) and humidity give two more classifying criteria.

After considering these factors, it was decided to adopt the classification developed by Miller [17.10], with some abbreviation and modification. The following groups of climatic types are specified, for each of which a different approach to thermal design is appropriate.

A. *Hot climates*
  1. Hot-dry: hot deserts
  2. Warm-wet: equatorial- and tropical-marine
  3. Hot-dry and warm-wet: tropical-continental, and monsoon.

B. *Warm-temperate climates*
  4. Western margin type
     i. Mediterranean continental
    ii. Mediterranean marine
   iii. Mediterranean mountains
  5. Eastern margin type.

C. *Cool-temperate climates*
  6. Cool-temperate continental
  7. Cool-temperate marine.

D. *Cold climates*
  8. Cold continental: Siberian
  9. Cold marine: Norwegian
 10. Cold desert
 11. Arctic.

Of these groups, three are discussed in some detail: the hot-dry, the warm-wet, and the Mediterranean climates. For each, the analysis is developed from the point of view of climatic characteristics, through the human requirements, to give principles and certain details for building design and construction.

17.2. Hot-dry Climates (Deserts)

17.2.1. CLIMATIC CHARACTERISTICS AND THEIR GEOGRAPHICAL DISTRIBUTION.—Hot dry deserts are found in the sub-tropical regions of Africa, central and western Asia, north-western and southern America, and in central and western Australia [17.10]. In all these cases the characteristic arid conditions are caused by the Trade winds, blowing south-west and north-west towards the equator, losing most of their water vapour content over the vast continental areas. In addition, the sub-tropics are regions of high barometric pressure, and with the down-flow from the upper atmosphere, which is a characteristic of these regions, the air becomes heated and dried (see Section 1.4).

The aridity mentioned is accompanied by several characteristics of importance to human comfort and to building design. Direct solar radiation is intense, up to 700 or 800 kcal/m^2 h on the horizontal surface, and is further augmented by radiation reflected from the barren, light-coloured terrain. The sky is without cloud for the greater part of the year, but dust haze and storms are frequent, caused by convection currents due to intensive heating of the air near the ground; these occur mainly in the afternoon.

The low humidity and absence of cloud result in a very wide temperature range; in summer the unobstructed solar rays heat the land surface up to about 70°C (158°F) at midday, while at night the rapid loss of this heat by longwave radiation cools the surfaces to 15°C (59°F) or below. The fluctuations in air temperature are much smaller of course, but even so a diurnal range of 20 deg C (36 deg F) is not uncommon; the summer temperatures during the day are around 40–50°C (104–122°F), and at night within the range 15–25°C (59–77°F).

The annual range is influenced by the geographical latitude, with which the summer temperatures vary less than those in winter, so that with increasing latitude the winters become relatively much colder than do the summers, and the annual range therefore greater.

The vapour pressure is fairly steady, varying with the location and season from about 5 to 15 mm Hg. The relative humidity therefore fluctuates with the air temperature, possibly ranging from below 20% in the afternoon to over 40% at night. A change in the wind direction may bring air from the sea and with it a rise in the humidity. Rains are few and far between, and although precipitation sometimes starts at a high altitude, the water usually evaporates completely before reaching the ground. But occasional violent flash storms do occur, breaking suddenly and lasting only a few hours.

The wind speed is generally low in the morning, rising towards noon to reach a maximum in the afternoon, frequently accompanied by whirlwinds of sand and dust.

17.2.2. HUMAN REQUIREMENTS FOR COMFORT.—For physiological comfort in hot dry climates, buildings must be adapted to the summer conditions, as in general the winter requirements will be satisfied by a building in which comfort is ensured for the summer. Reference to the Building Bioclimatic Chart (see Fig. 16.2) shows that the hot-dry conditions are included in area EC, indicating that during the hottest season comfort is not attainable without mechanical means of cooling. However, a bearable interior climate can be achieved, and stress minimized during the hottest period, with careful selection of materials and details of the design.

The natural ventilation provided by open windows greatly reduces this potential control of internal temperatures, which then closely follow the outdoor fluctuations, particularly during the day when wind velocities are high. Convective heat loss from the body is very low at the high daytime temperatures, even when the air speed is high, and when the air temperature is above 35°C convective heat gain increases the physiological load. On the other hand, the low humidity in the desert allows an adequate sweat evaporation rate from the body even in still air, and thus air motion need not be great to prevent discomfort due to most skin.

Natural ventilation during the day is therefore unnecessary for evaporative cooling and undesirable for convective heat exchange, and the ambient air velocity under "still" air conditions may be taken as 15 cm/sec. This slight air movement is the result of convective currents caused by surface temperature discrepancies between differently orientated walls, and by air infiltration through window cracks.

In the evening, with the drop in outdoor air temperature below the level of both internal air and surfaces, ventilation enables rapid cooling of the interior. With the window open during the evening, the air motion indoors depends on the outdoor wind velocity and the quality of cross-ventilation provided. In a building well cross-ventilated, the average indoor speed may be taken as 30 % of the prevailing wind speed quoted in meteorological data. If there is no cross-ventilation, only about 7 % of the free wind speed can be expected indoors (*see* Chapter 15). Thus with a wind velocity of 17 km/h (10 mph) the indoor air speed would be expected to range from 35 cm/sec (70 ft/min) with poor ventilation, to about 150 cm/sec (300 ft/min) with efficient cross-ventilation. Higher velocities are not necessary for comfort and may even be annoying.

At night windless periods are frequent in some regions. The convective currents indoors may cease with the tendency of internal surface temperatures to equalize through radiative heat exchange, and if windows or shutters are closed for privacy the indoor air velocity late at night reaches a minimum level of about 5–7 cm/sec.

The difference between indoor and outdoor vapour pressure depends on the ventilation conditions, as well as on the density of building occupation and the habits concerning vapour-generating processes such as cooking and washing. With open windows there is very little discrepancy, but when these are shut during the day, the indoor vapour pressure may be 1–4 mm Hg above the outdoor level.

The air temperature required for comfort is determined by the pattern of ventilation described above. The relationship has been estimated from Fig. 5.7 as follows.

At the low humidity level the limiting temperature for comfort during the day, when ventilation is inadvisable, is about 27°C, but up to 29°C thermal stress is very slight. In the evening, with poor and with efficient ventilation the limits should be respectively 29° and 32°C, but at this time the internal surface temperatures are higher than that of the air and so a compensatory reduction of 1 deg C should be allowed for when specifying air temperature requirements. In spite of the lower metabolic rate at night, the low air speed and the radiant heat load from the internal surfaces of the external walls and the roof, which reach then their maximum, lower the limiting comfort temperature to about 24–25°C.

In these desert regions the problem of dust entering the buildings is considerable. This problem may be controlled at several levels, through town planning, through organisation of the layout of small neighbourhoods, and through the details of design of the individual buildings.

Comfortable living in such a climate can also be assisted by adaptation of individual living habits, for instance by restricting outdoor activities to the mornings, late afternoon and evening to avoid the intense midday heat; sleeping outdoors in internal courtyards, for example, is also very pleasant.

17.2.3. PRINCIPLES OF BUILDING DESIGN AND CONSTRUCTION IN DESERT REGIONS.—Buildings in the desert are traditionally designed with flat roofs and heavyweight material, and with very small openings. In rural areas, the roofs are composed of a thick layer of dried mud, covered by a second impervious layer. In urban areas reinforced concrete is usually used for roofing contemporary buildings.

The thick exterior walls and roof damp the temperature fluctuations, stabilizing the internal temperatures at a level close to the average external surface temperature.

Both the layout of the buildings and their individual structures are compact, to expose the miminum surface to radiation and the hot air outside. Patios and internal courtyards are often provided for social purposes and also as sleeping areas. Ventilation is reduced to a minimum during the day, to exclude the hot, dust-laden outdoor air from the interior.

However, the aim of this type of design to lower daytime temperatures as far as possible, is achieved at the expense of nocturnal conditions, which are appreciably warmer than those out of doors. In some areas, even the day temperatures are too high during several months of the year, and here true comfort can only be achieved in the traditional buildings by an artificial cooling system. Occasionally underground rooms are provided, in which temperature fluctuations are further stabilized, at a level close to the annual average; the summer temperatures are therefore much lower than in buildings above the ground. But usually where buildings are without mechanical means of cooling, the inhabitants have to sleep on the roofs or in the courtyards.

The use of modern insulating materials in conjunction with

those of high heat capacity allows the openings to be larger while maintaining or even improving on the thermal conditions obtained in the traditional buildings. This is later discussed in detail (Sub-section 17.4.1).

In selecting suitable building orientation in hot-dry areas, the object is to reduce the internal daytime temperatures, and thus minimization of solar heating is the primary concern. A north-south orientation is therefore preferable to one east-west (see Chapter 11). However, although consideration of wind orientation is unnecessary from the point of view of daytime conditions, as windows are to be kept closed at this time, if a slight deviation from a north-south direction would improve the ventilation during the evening and night, this would be advisable.

The low thermal resistance of the windows makes these principal routes of the heat flow to the interior, even when shaded against solar radiation and closed against air flow from outside. The extent of the heat flow and the resulting interior heating are proportional to the size of the windows. The cross-ventilation required during the evening and night necessitates the use of apertures, but the efficiency of ventilation is not proportional to their size (see Chapter 14). With correct coordination of the location and shape of the windows, these may be small enough to minimize heat flow, but still provide efficient ventilation when open.

The windows should be designed and arranged so that approximately equal areas are open on the windward and leeward sides of the building, and so that the air stream is directed to the area and level of occupation. This is particularly important in bedrooms, where two horizontal strips of windows, placed in different walls, provide the most adequate arrangement, one at the height of the beds and the other below the ceiling, thus causing air motion in the room by thermal force during windless hours. The flow at night is inward at the lower level and outward through the upper openings. The horizontal strips generally give a better distribution of air flow in the occupied zone than vertical ones.

With direct and reflected solar radiation the most intensive sources of heating, the effect of a light external colour in minimizing internal daytime temperatures, is far greater than that of increasing either thermal resistance or capacity, with the added advantage that comfort at night is also improved. But if not whitewashed frequently, the building envelope absorbs enormous quantities of solar energy.

The stabilizing influence of a thick envelope results in internal surface temperatures relatively constant and close to the average level of the external surfaces; this level is particularly high for the roof when it is not whitewashed and the ensuing elevation in the average temperature of the ceiling above the level of other internal surfaces makes this an almost continuous heating element in the house.

Composite elements provide a more satisfactory solution to the problem. If a heavyweight layer is provided with an external layer of efficient insulating material, itself protected by a waterproof light-coloured covering, heat flow during the day from external to internal layers is restricted by the insulation and only a small proportion of the potential heat is absorbed in the element. Even this heat can later be removed by ventilating the interior during the evening and night, thus maintaining relatively cool conditions throught the day.

17.2.4. DEVELOPMENT AND APPLICATION OF PRINCIPLES, TO DESIGN NATURALLY COOLED BUILDINGS.—Results of recent investigation at the Building Research Station in Haifa [17.7] indicate the effectiveness of the heavyweight/insulation combination mentioned, when used with certain specific design features, in reducing the overall internal temperatures.

Suitable for this purpose are high heat capacity concrete walls externally insulated by rockwool or expanded plastics and covered by waterproofing materials. The required thickness of these materials may be computed, according to the outdoor maximum and minimum temperatures, using the formulae given earlier (*see* Section 16.5). The roofing should be of a similar composite construction, and the internal partitions of high heat capacity. All external surfaces should be as near to white as possible. The heat entering the building in the day is therefore kept to a minimum, and the high thermal capacity of the concrete layer reduces the effect on internal temperatures of any heat which does penetrate.

Windows may be large but should be protected by movable insulated shutters; apart from small apertures for illumination, both windows and shutters must be closed during the day.

It is advisable to provide an internal or semi-internal courtyard with access to the rooms of the house through large openings, insulated as for the windows. By opening the windows and these apertures during the evening the interior can be cooled rapidly from several sides. The roof should slope down towards the courtyard, and be surrounded by a parapet at the upper edges. Although the temperature of the whitewashed roof will be close to that of the outdoor air during the day, longwave radiation to the sky reduces this to 6–10 deg C below the outdoor level at night. Thus air in contact with the roof will be cooled at night and channelled by the slope into the courtyard and then into the rooms. Heating by warmer external air is restricted by the parapet.

The heat exchange systems involved may be summarized by saying that the building is heated during the day only through the insulated external envelope, but is cooled during the evening and night, primarily through the large openings, by air at temperatures below the ambient outdoor level.

With this type of design it is possible to obtain comfortable conditions in hot-dry regions with summer maximum temperatures up to about 38°C. Where temperatures are higher than this, particularly if the night temperatures are too high, further cooling in the evening and night may be achieved by more efficient use of the cold air in contact with the roof.

This approach to the problem was examined by the B.R.S. in Haifa [17.8] and in the desert region of Elath; two alternative procedures appeared to be applicable. (i) Instead of a courtyard into which the cool air is drained from the roof, windows are provided in the roof itself, at the upper and lower levels of the slope. These windows remain closed in the daytime and open at night. The whole roof is then externally covered by polythene sheeting at a distance of 10–20 cm above the roof surface. Polythene (polyethylene) is chosen because it is transparent to radiation of the wavelength around 10 microns emitted by the roof, placing little restriction on radiative cooling at night.

In this way, the interior is insulated from the air space between the roof and the polythene sheeting while this is subject to solar heating. But when the roof cools during the evening, the skylights are opened to allow cooler air in the space between the polythene and the roof to enter the building through the lower opening, contact with the hot external air being prevented by the polythene. The warm air indoors then rises and flows through the upper window into the space above the roof. The rate of flow in this circuit can be increased by using a small exhaust fan.

The drawback of this method is the deterioration of the polythene sheets with exposure to the sun, so that these have to be replaced at intervals.

(ii) The alternative is to use metal sheeting painted white in the same way as the polythene. This has the advantage of permanence, only requiring a yearly renewal of the whitewash. But as the metal is opaque to radiation, this in effect becomes the external surface of the roof. The daytime temperatures in the air space between the metal sheet and the structural roof are relatively quite low, with a consequent reduction in the heat gain. But during the night the radiating surface is exposed to the ambient air, and the air beneath it cools to a lesser extent than that enclosed by polythene, and the resulting interior cooling is smaller.

17.3. Warm-wet Climates (Equatorial- and Tropical-marine)

17.3.1. CLIMATE CHARACTERISTICS AND THEIR GEOGRAPHICAL DISTRIBUTION.—Two of the climatic types suggested by Miller [17.10] may be termed "warm-wet" from the point of view of building design: the equatorial-marine and the tropical-marine.

The equatorial climate is characteristic of a relatively narrow strip extending along either side of the equator into Africa and South America. Temperatures are high and follow a very constant diurnal pattern throughout the year. The annual mean temperature is about 27°C (80°F) and the range of the average monthly temperature very small, at 1–3 deg C (2–5·5 deg F). The diurnal range, on the other hand, is about 8 deg C (15 deg F). Maximum temperatures are usually about 30°C, with extreme temperature of about 38°C (100°F). In the mountainous areas temperatures are lower, decreasing by about 0·4–0·5 deg C per 100 metres ascent (2·2–2·7 deg F/1000 ft). The average monthly temperature range is very small, but the diurnal amplitude may be more than 15 deg (27 deg F).

Humidity and rainfall are high during most of the year, and the daily incidence of rain is very regular in each particular location, usually occurring in the afternoon. The temperature drops slightly with the rainfall. Precipitation is of a convective nature, caused when air brought with the Trade winds from the north and south hemispheres converges on the equatorial zone and rises at the intertropical front while expanding and cooling at the same time. These rains are accompanied by violent electric storms.

The constant heating and cooling patterns of land and sea create regular land and sea breezes, but these are restricted to the narrow coastal areas. Inland regions may be completely calm and winds, if any, are very slight. However, the annual variation in the location of the low-pressure belt brings each place, for some period of the year, within the range of the Trade winds, when the climate tends to the tropical type described below.

The tropical marine climate is found along the eastern margins of southern Africa and South America. Temperatures and rainfall are similar to those in the equatorial regions, but the winds show different characteristics. In contrast with the calms of the equatorial climate, tropical regions are affected by the Trade winds, which become moist when passing over the ocean and produce rain as they pass over land. Hurricanes are also frequent in these areas.

As the name suggests, the vapour content of the atmosphere in all warm-wet regions is very high, with vapour pressures of about 25 mm Hg which sometimes rise above 30 mm Hg, and a frequent relative humidity of 90% and above. The intensity of direct and diffused solar radiation varies widely with the cloud conditions, and reflected radiation from the ground is usually low as vegetation is dense and the damp soil dark.

The high temperature and humidity levels encourage insect-breeding and the growth of fungi. The termites found in many of these regions necessitate special precautions to protect wooden building components.

17.3.2. HUMAN AND THERMAL REQUIREMENTS.—As the seasonal climatic variations in warm-wet regions are very slight, the physiological thermal requirements, and hence the building characteristics necessary to fulfil them, are similar for the whole year.

The predominance of high humidity necessitates a correspondingly high air velocity to increase the efficiency of sweat evaporation, and to avoid as far as possible discomfort due to moisture on skin and clothes. Continuous ventilation is therefore the primary comfort requirement and affects all aspects of building design, such as orientation, the size and location of windows, layout of the surroundings, etc.

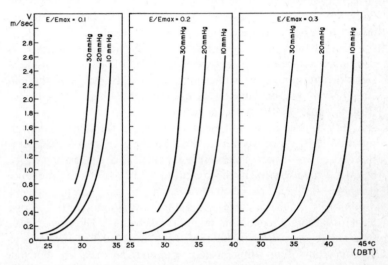

Fig. 17.1.   Air speeds yielding E/E_{max} ratios of 0·1, 0·2 and 0·3 of resting people at different air temperatures and vapour pressures.

In warm-wet areas torrential rains alternate frequently with intense solar irradiation while humidity remains high, and thus provision must be made for protection from rain and sun without impairing ventilation conditions.

When the windows must be open day and night and the diurnal temperature range is small, little reduction in internal temperature is possible; however, if the building is badly designed the internal surface temperature may rise considerably above that outdoors causing discomfort particularly at night with the drop in wind speed.

Even with the maximum ventilation there are limits to the conditions under which comfort can be achieved in a warm-wet climate.

Where a practicable reduction in internal temperatures is impossible, air-conditioning provides the only solution to this problem. An indication of the limiting conditions is to be found by reference to the Building Bioclimatic Chart (*see* Fig. 16.2), from which it will be seen that warm-wet conditions fall into zones V and V' (comfort possible using ventilation) when the vapour pressure is below 25 mm Hg, but above this level extend into zone AC, indicating the necessity for air-conditioning. To fix the limiting temperature for comfort at any given level of vapour pressure, more complex calculations must be made, using one of the thermal indices (*see* Chapter 5).

One of the chief causes of discomfort in warm-wet climates is the subjective feeling of skin wetness. Ventilation should ensure a sweat evaporation rate sufficient not only to maintain thermal equilibrium, but to enable sweat evaporation as the sweat emerges from the pores, without accumulating on the skin.

As discussed in Section 3.7, the wetness of the skin depends on the ratio (E/E_{max}) between heat stress on the body and the evaporative capacity of the air. To ensure a dry skin the E/E_{max} ratio must be below 0·1, and to prevent the condition "skin clammy but moisture invisible" it should be below 0·2. But as in many warm-wet conditions this is unattainable without air-conditioning the limiting level for acceptable conditions might be taken as 0·3. The air velocities required to give E/E_{max} values of 0·1, 0·2 and 0·3, under various combinations of air temperature and vapour pressure, are shown in Fig. 17.1.

17.3.3. PRINCIPLES OF BUILDING DESIGN.—To summarize, the requirements to be satisfied by the design and construction of a building in a warm-wet climate are these: provision of continuous and efficient ventilation; protection from the sun, rain and insects; prevention of internal temperature elevation during the day and minimization during the evening and night.

To adequately cross-ventilate the occupied areas of a house, either all the rooms should be provided with doors, windows, etc., on both windward and leeward sides of the building, or those rooms on the windward or leeward sides only should be given access through large openings to rooms on the opposite pressure-region side (*see* Chapters 14 and 15).

Open planning and wide, free spaces between buildings help to achieve good ventilation. Raising the building on stilts is also advantageous in a warm-wet climate. Firstly, this enables better ventilation by locating the windows above the zone of maximum wind-damping by the surrounding vegetation, and secondly, it enables cooling of the floor from below, which is particularly beneficial at night. In addition, the building is better protected from floods and, with proper detailing, also better protected from termites. High buildings rising above the level of nearby trees and lower buildings, and which can be spaced at wider distances with the same total density, provide improved ventilation conditions for their occupants, and may also improve the ventilation conditions in the smaller buildings around them (see Chapter 15), and thus are preferable in warm-wet climates.

Orientation in a warm-wet climate should be aimed at providing the best possible ventilation and therefore the direction of the prevailing winds should be carefully studied. Contrary to common belief, this does not mean that the wall with the inlet windows should face directly the prevailing winds, as at angles of up to about 50° on either side of the wind direction satisfactory ventilation conditions can be achieved (see Chapter 15). The direction of the storms should be also taken into consideration in order to minimize their impact.

In rooms where the habitable zone is very narrowly defined, as in bedrooms for instance, it is possible to achieve maximum concentration of the wind by providing smaller inlets than outlets and thus concentrating the incoming air flow. But in rooms where the occupied zone may extend over most of their area, as in the case of living rooms, it is preferable to have inlets and outlets of similar size.

Large openings, doors and windows, are of advantage in a warm-wet climate provided that they are effectively protected from penetration of solar radiation, driving rain and intrusion of insects. The advantage of large openings is not only due to the better ventilation conditions that they provide, but also because they enable the achievement of lower temperatures during the night.

When a given room does not have direct cross-ventilation, but the air flow has to pass through another room on its way outwards, it is essential that the openings between the two rooms be at least of the same area as the external inlet and outlet openings. The partition openings should be so placed and detailed as to direct the air flow towards the occupied zone.

The most effective height of the windows from the human comfort aspect is about 0·5–1·5 metres above the floor (the occupied zone). In bedrooms it is particularly important to bring the window sill as close as possible to the height of the beds, thus ensuring adequate air flow around the occupants' sleeping area at those times when the outdoor wind speed is very low. When upper windows have to be used for any reason, it is preferable to use horizontally-pivoted windows with upper hinges which, when open, would direct the air flow downwards.

Large sliding walls which may be kept open most of the time, but closed during storms, may provide good control of the conflicting requirements for maximum ventilation alternating with wind and rain protection during storms. Adjustable or retractable louvres and other shading devices may be equally satisfactory if they are able to withstand the force of the wind.

Fly-screens are essential in most warm-wet regions [17.2], but they may reduce appreciably the air flow. To minimize their blocking effect it is preferable to install them at some distance from the wall, rather than directly on the windows, and extending over a much larger area than the windows. When there is a balcony adjacent to the room it is possible to ensure insect protection with less interference of ventilation by erecting a flyscreen around the balcony, thus enabling the entry of air through a wider free area.

The large area of openings required in a warm-wet climate necessitates adequate shading, otherwise indoor temperatures may rise appreciably above the outdoor level. Shade is required not only against direct solar radiation, but also against diffused radiation from the sky, which in tropical regions may reach very high intensities.

In many instances solar protection may be combined with rain protection, not only with respect to the windows but also for the whole area of the walls, by extending the roof beyond the floor area. This is more necessary in warm-wet regions as tropical rains are very heavy and wind-borne, where the almost horizontal wind-driven rain penetrates through joints and cracks in the walls and fenestration. Unprotected walls may become saturated, and the rapid succession of wetting and drying speeds up deterioration of their component materials, especially on the external surfaces.

Another problem connected with tropical rains concerns the necessity for providing means of disposal of the run-off water and prevention of soil erosion around the buildings. Planning according to the contour lines helps greatly in reducing the erosion hazard [17.2].

The shading devices should not reduce air velocity within the occupied zone. When horizontal adjustable louvres are used they should be constructed so as to enable their opening at an angle of approximately 120°, so that when required they direct the air flow downwards towards the occupied zone. In multi-storeyed buildings, window overhang shades tend to reflect an appreciable amount of solar radiation on to the walls and into the windows of the upper storeys [17.1]. Inclined slats, on the other hand, running parallel to the wall between horizontal beams projecting from the walls, can provide fully effective shading while at the same time reflecting the sun's rays outwards and enabling free air movement over the external surface of the walls. Such slats can be made of precast concrete, asbestos-cement, wood, etc. Moreover, they allow better illumination than do solid overhangs, but provide less protection from the driving rains.

17.3.4. CHOICE OF MATERIALS IN WARM-WET REGIONS.—Because of the permanent ventilation requirements and the small outdoor diurnal temperature range characterizing the warm-wet climate, it is not feasible to utilize the heat capacity and resistance of the walls as a means of reducing the daytime temperatures to those below the outdoor level. Therefore the main criteria in choice of materials are prevention of daytime indoor temperature rise to above outdoor level, and minimization of such elevations during the evening and night hours. Other factors concern the weathering qualities of the materials in a damp and humid environment, and the likelihood of biological attack by insects (*e.g.* termites) and of fungoid growth [17.2]. The heat capacity of the building should be as low as possible in order to prevent accumulation of heat during the daytime, which would elevate the indoor temperature during the night when the external wind speed is usually at its lowest.

Thermal resistance of the external walls is advantageous within certain limits in minimizing the heat flow from the external surfaces warmed by the sun. It is possible by this means to maintain the temperature of the inside surfaces of the external walls very close to the indoor air temperature, which itself is almost level with the outdoor air temperature because of the intensive ventilation. Modern insulating materials, which combine very low weight and heat capacity together with high thermal resistance, may provide the best indoor climatic conditions. It is essential, however, that such materials be protected from biological attack and fire hazard. Although light, reflective external colours would reduce solar heat gain in warm-wet climates, as in any other hot climate, it is much more difficult to maintain these colours because of the high humidity and fungal growth. The thermal resistance should therefore be sufficient to minimize inward heat flow despite the absorbed solar radiation.

When, for structural reasons, heavyweight materials must be used, it is possible to minimize the effect of the heat capacity by covering them with an insulating layer, thereby maintaining the surface temperature very close to the surrounding air temperature. Thus, for instance, when concrete floors are used in multi-storeyed buildings, the corresponding ceilings may be covered by a layer of insulating material so that their temperature at night would closely follow the air temperature.

Lightweight roofs, covered with tiles or sheets of asbestos-cement or aluminium, are preferable in a warm-wet climate owing to their low heat capacity. But such roofs, which are externally usually dark in colour, or at any rate, not whitewashed, are heated by solar radiation and may cause heat stress during the daytime. Therefore thermal insulation either at the ceiling level or beneath the upper roof layer is to be recommended. An effective means of insulation is by placing aluminium foil beneath the roof in order to reduce the radiant heat flow from roof to ceiling. This may be supplemented by an insulating layer above or beneath the ceiling, and by ventilation of the attic space.

Double roofs consisting of two layers with a ventilated air space are desirable not only because of their solar-protecting quality, but also by virtue of the protection they offer from the rain. Care must be exercised, however, in ensuring their resistance to the lifting power of stormy winds.

Ventilation of the attic space without the addition of insulation is inadequate, as the main heat flow from roof to ceiling is by radiation.

When concrete roofs of high heat capacity are constructed, it is preferable to provide an insulating layer below the ceiling, thus reducing heat flow during the day and enabling rapid lowering of the ceiling temperature during the night.

17.4. Mediterranean (Sub-tropical) Climate—General Considerations

The term "Mediterranean climate" is applicable not only to the climatic conditions around the Mediterranean Sea, but also to such regions as California and the coast of Chile [17.10]. The main characteristics of this type are:

a. Concentration of the rains in winter and dry summers
b. Warm to hot summers and cool to cold winters
c. Intensive solar radiation, especially in summer.

The variability of this climate is quite large and when considered from the viewpoint of building design it should be sub-divided at least into three sub-types: continental, marine and mountainous. The transition from one sub-type to another, and also to hot deserts, is observed in many cases within very short distances. Thus the Mediterranean climate presents a good example of the need to consider local conditions and to apply different approaches and architectural solutions within a given geographical zone. and across very small distances.

Although the human thermal requirements and the principles of building design in each of these Mediterranean sub-types are different, there are characteristics and problems common to all of them. In the Mediterranean climate the building should be so designed and built as to provide protection from the heat in summer, and from cold and rain in winter, without the use of expensive mechanical cooling and heating systems. Some heating in winter is usually necessary, and sometimes some cooling in summer also is desirable, but it is possible to design the buildings so that very simple appliances would suffice.

As all these sub-types are found in Israel, with characteristics similar to those in other places as well, they will serve for a detailed illustration of the determination of human requirements and adaptation of various features of design and construction to the specific local characteristics of the Mediterranean climate.

17.4.1. MEDITERRANEAN CONTINENTAL CLIMATE.—The Mediterranean continental climate is found at relatively short distances from the sea. The main characteristics of this type in summer are large diurnal temperature range of about 15–18 deg C; warm daytime temperatures of about 33–37°C, which may rise on hot days to 38–40°C, though for a brief period of time. The nights are cool, with minimum temperatures of about 18–20°C. Vapour pressure is moderately low, about 15 mm Hg in summer, and relative humidity very variable, ranging from about 30–40% at noon to about 80–90% and more at night. The wind is relatively strong, starting in the forenoon, reaching its maximum in the afternoon while accompanied by dust whirls; then declining gradually, preserving relatively high velocity even in the evenings till it ceases at night. Wind direction is mainly westerly, usually from south-west in the forenoon and north-west in the afternoon.

Winter temperatures are usually above freezing point, with an average minimum of about 5°C, but sub-zero temperatures may frequently occur. Average rainfall is small—about 200–300 mm, but very variable.

Human thermal requirements

With reference to Fig. 16.2, it can be seen that the summer conditions are in zone M. This means that daytime thermal comfort can be achieved without ventilation, provided that the indoor air temperature does not rise above about 27°C. To check this point a comparison will be made between the imposed heat stress under two conditions. The first is a well-ventilated building with indoor temperature equal to that outside (35°C) and air velocity of 1·0 m/sec; the second is an unventilated building with an air temperatue of 27°C and air velocity of 0·1 m/sec. Referring back to Chapter 5, Fig. 5.7, it can be seen that in the first case the expected weight-loss is 170 g/h, while in the second case it is about 80 g/h. This indicates that much higher heat stress will be encountered in ventilated buildings as compared with well-built unventilated ones, in which a drop of 8 deg C in the maximum temperature would be realized (47% of the outdoor range).

Other disadvantages of ventilated buildings in such regions are the penetration of dust and the heating of the internal mass of the building by the outdoor warm air, with consequent higher indoor temperatures at night.

The situation is different in buildings where a high level of daylighting is required, such as in schools, offices, etc.; there the windows have to be much larger than in residences. Indoor temperatures cannot be reduced below those outdoors on account of the considerable heat gain through the windows, and in most cases they are even higher. As a result, ventilation would not elevate the indoor temperature and might even reduce it, and at the same time improve the subjective feeling. Although real comfort cannot be attained even if the indoor temperature is not above the outdoor level, the physiological heat stress is reduced owing to the faster rate of evaporation and the higher cooling efficiency of sweating.

This can be verified from Fig. 5.7, from which it can be seen that with an air temperature of 35°C, and a vapour pressure of 15 mm Hg, the expected sweat rate at still air is about 200 g/h, while with an air velocity of 1·0 m/sec it is about 180 g/h. In addition, the skin is kept drier by the higher air velocity so that the subjective discomfort due to moist skin is reduced.

Daytime ventilation in such regions is usually associated with dust penetration. This depends greatly on the height above the ground and the nature of the surroundings. At floors above 10–12 metres height the dust nuisance greatly diminishes, and planting, lawns cultivation and similar treatment of the surroundings can greatly reduce the dust level even at the lower floors.

Principles of design

In this type of climate the details of design and choice of materials determine whether mechanical cooling is needed for the attainment of comfort. Therefore, it is worthwhile even from the economical aspect to take great care in adjusting building construction to the climatic conditions. The main objectives here are to enable a reduction of as much as 8 deg C in the indoor air temperature below the outdoor maximum, and to provide good ventilation in the evenings when the outdoor temperature drops to a comfortable level.

For these objectives to be attained, the building should be so designed and constructed that the heat load operating on it and its rate of heating during the day are minimal and at the same time a much higher rate of cooling during the evening would be possible. These seemingly contradictory characteristics can be obtained by selective ventilation. If the building were not ventilated during the daytime and heat flow through the closed window minimized, its rate of heating would depend only on the thermophysical properties of the external envelope. But during the evening, with open windows, high rate of cooling can be achieved by ventilation.

Choice of materials in Mediterranean continental climate

From Table 16.XI it can be seen that the QR value of the external walls required in this type of climate is about 20–30 hours, depending on the external colour. Such a value can be obtained by various materials, differing in their relative heat capacity and thermal resistance, by providing the necessary thickness.

The preferred materials, from the indoor comfort point of view, depend on the size and shading efficiency of the windows. When the windows are small and well shaded, and consequently the main source of heat gain is that flowing across the wall, thermal resistance is relatively more important than heat capacity in minimizing the rate of daytime heating. In such cases materials like lightweight concrete, with a thickness sufficient to provide the necessary QR value for local conditions (about 20–25 cm; *see* Table 16.XII) may be the simplest and most economical solution.

But when the relative area of the windows is large, or shading is not effective, then a significant portion of the heat gain is that penetrating through the windows either by conduction, solar radiation or hot outdoor air infiltration. Then the heat capacity assumes much greater importance, as lightweight materials would be heated by the penetrating heat more than heavier materials. In this case walls made of bricks, dense concrete or earth, with a thickness of about 20–30 cm, would exhibit better thermal performance [17.8].

Most suitable in this region might be composite walls, incorporating an insulating layer close to the external surface and a heavy layer at the interior. Such walls would provide high thermal resistance in front of the mass of the structure, and so reduce the rate of heat flow from the external surface, and high heat capacity at the interior to absorb any penetrating heat with little elevation in temperature. When the windows are open, such buildings would not be much warmer at night than other types.

Openings

Large openings are not desirable in this type of climate in any building where a high level of daylighting is not specifically required unless special measures are taken, as they provide little thermal resistance to the heat flow from the hot outdoor air to the much cooler indoor air, even when they are well shaded. They are not necessary even at night, as good cross-ventilation can be achieved even with small windows provided that they are placed in the right positions (*see* Chapter 15), and as the outdoor air is cool enough to provide the required cooling. It is preferable to locate the windows in such a way as to direct the main air flow along the internal surfaces, to maximize the rate of heat extraction from the mass of the structure.

However, when movable or adjustable insulated panels are used for shading instead of ordinary shutters, large openings can be used even to advantage in such regions, as the heat flow across them during the day can be reduced to the desired level by the choice of the insulation thickness. Usually a thickness of about 3–5 cm of expanded plastics or mineral wool would be required. Where higher levels of daylight are needed, the window size should be the smallest which would provide the necessary illumination, and all measures should be taken to maximize the illuminating effect of the penetrating radiation, in particular light colours of the internal surfaces.

Orientation

Because the windows in residential buildings should be kept closed during the daytime, the wind direction at that time is not a factor of importance in the choice of orientation in residences. But as dust accompanies the winds in this climate it is preferable to locate the entrances on the leeside of the buildings. The direction of the evening and night winds is of greater importance, although not a major factor as in the more humid zone.

In buildings with a relatively large window area, such as schools and offices, where ventilation is required even during the daytime (*see* above), it would be desirable to orient the building in such a way as to obtain sufficient ventilation while minimizing dust penetration. This problem cannot easily be solved and until now not enough is known on it to enable definite recommendations to be made.

The significance of orientation with respect to the sun depends greatly on the external colour of the walls and the size and shading conditions of the windows. When the walls are whitewashed or nearly white, and the windows small and well shaded, the whole problem of orientation is of little significance, as additional thermal insulation can compensate for slight variations in the temperature elevation of the external surfaces. On the other hand, as the colour is darker and the window area is larger, north and south orientations become preferable to east and west ones.

17.4.2. MEDITERRANEAN MARINE CLIMATE.—The marine sub-type of the Mediterranean climate extends along the seashore. It is characterized by small diurnal range (about 5–10 deg C), with day-time summer temperatures in the range of 25–30°C and night tem-peratures of about 20–23°C. Vapour pressure is high in summer (about 20–22 mm Hg). Wind velocity during the day is relatively low in summer (about 2–3 m/sec), declining in the evening to about 1·5 m/sec and almost to calm at night. Wind direction is mainly westerly, starting from the south-west in the forenoon and changing to western and north-western in the afternoon. The amount of precipitation depends mainly on latitude and decreases from north to south, averaging about 500 mm per annum. The rains are concentrated within periods of a few days of high intensity and are accompanied frequently by storms of high wind velocity. Winter temperatures are usually above freezing point, with an average daily minimum of about 8°C and average monthly minimum of about 3°C.

Human thermal requirements

With reference to Fig. 16.2, it can be seen that the summer conditions in Mediterranean marine climate correspond to zone V, so that the main problem in this climatic type is the provision of good ventilation.

The physiological heat stress encountered in this climate is not high, but moist skin may constitute the principal cause of discomfort. This emphasizes even more the need for good ventilation.

To achieve comfortable indoor climate at the air temperatures and velocities encountered in built-up areas in this climate during the summer, the temperatures of the ceiling and inside surfaces of the external walls should not be elevated greatly above the outdoor air temperature, especially during the evening and nights. Only then can ventilation be relied upon as the main factor in providing comfort. To check these remarks, the physiological heat stress and subjective discomfort due to moist skin will be computed for the "design" summer conditions, which may be assumed in this region, namely: air temperature of about 30°C, vapour pressure of 20 mm Hg, diurnal range of 7 deg C and outdoor wind speed of 3 m/sec. The maximum attainable reduction in indoor air temperature (see Section 16.1) is about $0.5 \times 7 = 3.5$ deg C. This means that the expected indoor air temperature, in a building with high thermal resistance and heat capacity, with whitewashed walls and closed and shaded windows, would be about 26·5°C, with an indoor air velocity of 0·1 m/sec and vapour pressure of about 22 mm Hg. The indoor maximum will lag behind the outdoor maximum and will occur in the evening.

On the other hand, in a well ventilated building the indoor maximum temperature and vapour pressure will equal approximately outdoor conditions. The expected indoor air velocity might be assumed as 1 m/sec (one-third of the outdoor). In a built-up area the expected indoor air velocity might be about 0·5 m/sec.

Referring to Figs. 5.6, 5.7 and 17.1, the physiological heat stress, as manifested by weight loss, and the subjective discomfort due to moist skin, which depends on the E/E_{max} ratio, can be computed and compared under these three conditions. It should be borne in mind that really comfortable conditions correspond to a weight loss of about 60 g/h and an E/E_{max} ratio of less than 0·2, and preferably about 0·1.

In the first case the expected weight loss is about 90 g/h and the E/E_{max} ratio about 0·35. In the second case the expected weight loss is about 80 g/h and the E/E_{max} ratio about 0·09; and in the third case the expected weight loss would be about 85 g/h and the E/E_{max} ratio about 0·12. The significance of these results is that although there is almost no physiological stress (as manifested by weight loss) in all three cases, there would be appreciable discomfort due to moist skin in the first case, where a reduction of the daytime temperature has been attempted, while conditions will be satisfactory in those cases with effective cross-ventilation, even in built-up areas.

These conclusions are valid only as long as the indoor temperatures (air and internal surfaces) can be kept at about the same level as that of the outdoor air. In other words, elevation of temperature of the internal surfaces by solar radiation above the outdoor level should be prevented. This calls for effective shading of the windows, light external colouring and thermal insulation adjusted to the actual elevation of the external surface temperature due to the absorbed solar radiation (*see* Table 16.XI).

As the wind speed during the evenings and nights in this region is very low, the main considerations are to ensure rapid cooling of the interior in the evenings, and to take into account the local directions of the wind at that time.

In winter the main problems in this region are the prevention of water penetration during rain storms and of condensation. As the winter is relatively mild and central heating is not essential, the thermal resistance of the building should suffice to attain comfortable indoor temperatures with inexpensive heating systems.

Principles of design

The main climatic objectives of the architectural design in this climate can be summarized as being the provision of effective ventilation and prevention of overheating of the building in summer, and protection from rain penetration and prevention of condensation in winter.

As the ventilation conditions in a built-up area depend to a great extent on the local town planning, this aspect should be considered carefully. Although not enough is known on this subject to enable detailed recommendations some details can be discussed and analysed.

The height of the buildings above the ground determines greatly their potential for ventilation. Thus buildings which rise above the level of surrounding trees enable better ventilation than single-storeyed structures. "Tower" buildings which rise above the level of nearby lower buildings are not only themselves exposed to much higher wind speeds, but with suitable distribution may improve the ventilation conditions in the lower buildings (see Chapter 15). On the other hand, such buildings are exposed to more violent rain storms in winter; care must be taken in the construction of the walls, and mainly in the details of the windows, to prevent water penetration.

Orientation with respect to the wind is more important in the marine than in the continental sub-type, but it is of equal importance to minimize the impact of solar radiation where the external colour cannot be white, and where fully effective shading of the windows cannot be ensured. As the windows are larger, orientation with respect to the sun assumes greater importance.

The architectural design of the buildings should ensure cross-ventilation through any habitable room, either directly or through other rooms which may be kept open when necessary. Those types of planning in which some apartments may be exposed only to the suction zone of the building (see Chapters 14 and 15) are unsuitable in this type of climate. The size of the windows beyond a certain minimum is not a factor of importance as long as they are well shaded. Effective cross-ventilation may be obtained even with relatively small windows, provided that their location with respect to the wind is suitable. When proper cross-ventilation cannot be secured, large windows may help to cool the building in the evening, but then the question of shading assumes even greater importance.

Care should be taken to see that the main stream of air flow is actually directed toward the people in occupied zone, either by adjusting the height of the window sill or by other details, as discussed in Chapter 15.

Balconies are very useful in this climate both for shading the walls and for providing an area where people can sit during summer evenings in much more comfortable conditions than indoors.

The choice of materials should take into account both the

winter and the summer factors. Thus, by reference to Tables 16.VII and 16.XI, it can be seen that the surface-to-surface thermal resistance required from the summer aspect for walls with medium-light external colouring is from 0·25 to 0·65 (m² h deg C/kcal), depending on the external colour, while from the winter aspect the desirable thermal resistance is from 0·3 to 0·54 depending on the heat capacity of the walls.

Such materials as bricks, concrete, hollow concrete blocks, lightweight concrete and insulated panels might be quite satisfactory in this region, provided that their thickness ensures the required thermal resistance. The heat capacity in this climatic type is of little importance, in contrast with the continental sub-type.

17.4.3. MEDITERRANEAN MOUNTAINOUS CLIMATE.

Climatic characteristics

The Mediterranean mountainous climate is distinguished from the other sub-types by having colder winters, so that the winter aspect becomes the dominant one. Temperatures around and below freezing point are not uncommon, so that the average monthly minimum may be taken as about 0°C. Summer daily average maximum is about 30°C, but occasionally dry-hot spells occur, caused by desert winds, during which the temperature may reach 35°C and more. Temperature amplitude ranges from about 7 deg C in winter to 12 deg C in summer. The vapour pressure is lower than in the marine climate, ranging from about 6–8 mm Hg in winter to 10–15 mm Hg in summer. Rains are heavier than in other parts of the country, and snow is not uncommon. Winds are stronger than at the seashore, particularly in the valleys, and rainstorms are frequent.

A matter of importance from the condensation viewpoint is the relatively higher temperature and vapour pressure during the rains.

Functional and thermal requirements

By reference to Fig. 16.2, it can be seen that the summer conditions fall both in zone V and in zone M, meaning that under ordinary conditions either ventilation or a reduction of the indoor temperatures by suitable choice of materials may be applied in this zone to obtain comfortable indoor climate.

Even when the second method is chosen, ventilation would be necessary in the evenings when the internal surfaces of the relatively heavy walls required for the reduction of the indoor temperature reach their maximum. But during the hot spells, in which the temperature rises to about 35°C, reduction of the indoor maximum is the only approach which may yield satisfactory results.

In fact, at various times either daytime ventilation or a reduction of the indoor temperatures may yield more comfortable conditions, depending on certain other factors, so that provision for both approaches is desirable.

The winter thermal requirements are concerned with maintaining comfortable indoor temperatures and the prevention of rain penetration and condensation. Although these requirements are the same as in the other Mediterranean regions, the environmental conditions under which they have to be satisfied are more severe and call for more careful choice of materials and details of design.

The question of condensation in Mediterranean mountainous climate deserves special attention, as the combination of rain and cold in the winter aggravates the situation. The walls when wetted by the rains are cooled by evaporation due to the wind, and their external surface temperature drops below the outdoor air temperature, while at the same time their thermal resistance is reduced. The outdoor level of vapour pressure during the period of the rains is quite high, and as a result the indoor level of vapour pressure, especially in densely occupied buildings, is elevated so that the dew-point might be only 2–3 deg C below the indoor air temperature.

When the external walls do not have a sufficient thermal resistance to prevent a drop in the internal surface temperature below the dew-point, condensation takes place.

In a field study in Jerusalem [17.3] vapour pressure elevation of up to 7 mm Hg above the outdoor level and a very high prevalence of severe condensation have been observed, in particular in prefabricated buildings whose internal surfaces are made of smooth, dense concrete of very low absorptivity. An additional factor was the use of flue-less heating devices using oil, which produce large quantities of water vapour.

Building design and construction

To enable a significant reduction of the indoor temperatures even during the hot spells, the structure should have sufficient thermal resistance and heat capacity, which would correspond to a QR value of about 25–30 hours (*see* Table 16.XI).

From the winter aspect the required minimum net thermal resistance of the external walls depends on the heat capacity of the materials chosen, and would range from about 0·34 (m^2 h deg C/ kcal) for lightweight concrete walls to about 0·2 for dense concrete walls, while the desirable values range from 0·75 to 0·5, respectively (*see* Tables 16.VII and 16.VIII).

With lightweight concrete walls (density of 600 kg/m^3) these requirements could be met by walls of about 22–25 cm thick. With dense concrete walls the summer requirements could be satisfied by walls about 25–30 cm thick, but the thermal resistance of such walls, although sufficient to satisfy the minimum requirements, is too low in cold winters to satisfy the desirable standards, so that a thickness of about 50 cm would be required for the achievement of really comfortable conditions. For this reason concrete walls are not suitable in this climatic zone.

A solution which might yield satisfactory results is to use composite construction, incorporating dense concrete and an insulating layer (*e.g.* foamed plastics) of about 3 cm thick.

Prevention of condensation can be achieved by the combined application of the following measures (for details *see* Chapter 9):

a. Minimization of the vapour pressure elevation above the out-door level by directed ventilation

b. Provision of thermal resistance sufficient to keep the internal surface temperatures above the dew-point of the indoor air

c. Prevention of cold bridges in the design and construction of the building.

Absorptive internal surfaces may reduce greatly visible condensation.

The ventilation requirements for the prevention of condensation are difficult to achieve by general ventilation through the ordinary windows, as it causes a reduction of the indoor air temperature below the comfort level and produces cold draughts. Therefore there is a need to evacuate the vapour while retaining minimal air flow. This is possible by exhausting the air at places where the vapour is mainly produced, namely in the bathrooms and kitchens.

It is in effect impossible to prevent condensation on the window panes. Such condensation is less annoying, but if not discharged or collected it causes dampness of the surface of the wall below the window. Special details of the windows, for the collection or discharge of the condensed water, are therefore recommended.

17.5. Winter Heating in a Sub-tropical Climate

In contrast with temperate and cold climates on the one hand, where heating is indispensable throughout the winter in all types of occupied buildings, and with tropical climate where heating is not essential, the problem exists in sub-tropical climate of whether heating is necessary in any particular location and type of building, and the time when it is required.

This problem is of particular importance in public buildings, such as schools, hospitals, large offices, etc., where heating cannot be provided conveniently by portable appliances which can be brought to and taken away from any room and are operated by the occupants, but must be designed as an integral part of the building and in many cases operated centrally.

At present, a satisfactory general method by which to determine objectively the necessity of heating in sub-tropical regions is not yet available, but it seems possible, with further research, to develop such a method. A rational approach to this problem requires its breakdown into the following questions:

a. What are the optimal and minimal temperatures required for comfort for different age groups, activities, degree of acclimatization and clothing habits.

b. What are the indoor conditions (indoor air and mean radiant temperatures) which should be considered as the threshold for the provision of heating under the conditions mentioned in (a). It should be taken into account that different types of construction exhibit different relationships between the indoor air and the mean radiant temperatures.

c. What is the relationship between the outdoor conditions of temperature, wind and rain and the indoor thermal conditions, for different types of buildings, taking into account the materials, windows area, orientation, external colour, etc. Although it is a quite complicated matter to solve theoretically these problems, it is possible to establish an empirical relationship between the outdoor and indoor conditions, for any type of building, and thus the practical problem can be solved.

d. What are the *outdoor* conditions under which the *indoor* conditions necessitating heating should be expected in a given type of building, during the periods and hours of its occupancy. In this connection it should be taken into account that the meteorological conditions in any region are subjected to wide fluctuations and, as comfort should be ensured under all conditions which are expected with a reasonable frequency, some accepted extreme conditions rather than long-term averages should be used as a criterion for decision, as discussed in Section 16.4.

It has been demonstrated in South Africa [17.11] that it is possible to establish close correlation for a given type of building between the outdoor-air temperature and the coincident difference between the indoor and outdoor temperatures.

The nature of this correlation depends, however, on the time of the day and is quite different for the period of rise in the outdoor temperature from the morning to about 2–3 p.m. and for the period of decline in outdoor temperature in the afternoon, evening and night. During the first period the coincident temperature difference is usually greater than during the second period. In consequence, two distinct types of correlation have to be established, one for the morning and noon time, and the other for the afternoon and night. In those types of buildings which are occupied only during the day, such as some offices and schools, reference should be made to one type of correlation. On the other hand, in buildings occupied day and night, such as residentials, hospitals, schools, and offices used also during the evening, etc. the two types of correlation should be considered.

Although the optimal comfort temperature in winter is about 20°C (68°F), a certain reduction in temperature can be withstood with relatively little discomfort. The temperature at which heating becomes a necessity depends on many factors, such as activity, age, acclimatization, standard of living, clothing habits, etc., as well as on the humidity, as dry cold is more tolerable than humid cold. In order to take into account the interdependence between the effects of air and mean radiant temperatures, the use of the indoor Globe temperature as a criterion is to be recommended.

In schools, taking into account the higher metabolic rate of children, it seems that daytime indoor Globe temperatures of about 16·5°C (60°F) in dry regions might be considered as the limits below which heating is required. In offices the limit should be higher, about 17° and 18°C, for dry and humid regions, respectively. In residential buildings the limits are similar to those in offices, but the temperatures during the evening and night are of particular importance, and should be taken into account in determining the necessity for heating.

In South Africa the winter heating requirements in schools have been determined with reference to the outdoor air temperature by using the concept of the "equivalent outdoor threshold temperature". It was based on the finding that for a given type of classroom, such as, *e.g.*, north-facing top floor, etc., there exists a clear correlation between average indoor–outdoor temperature difference during the school hours and the coincident outdoor temperature. In the schools of South Africa [17.11], indoor air temperature of 60°F has been suggested as the threshold for cold discomfort necessitating heating. It was thus possible to compute the outdoor air temperature which on the average, is expected to correspond to an indoor temperature of 60°F. Mathematically the "equivalent outdoor threshold temperature", t_{oe}, is computed from the expression

$$t_{oe} = 60 - (t_{ia} - t_{oa})$$

where $(t_{ia} - t_{oa})$ is the average indoor–outdoor temperature difference corresponding to an outdoor temperature t_{oa}. For example, if for a given classroom an outdoor temperature of 40°F corresponds to an average indoor–outdoor temperature difference of 15 deg F then the equivalent outdoor threshold temperature is:

$$t_{oe} = 60 - 15 = 45°F$$

meaning that heating is necessary when the outdoor temperature falls below 45°F.

In order to determine the periods in which heating is required in a given region, the mean hourly air temperatures in that region for the winter season were used to compute the corresponding values of the "equivalent outdoor threshold temperature", *i.e.* the hours in which indoor temperatures below 60°F are expected. In this way the total number of hours during the winter in which heating is required, and the corresponding temperature differences $(60 - t_{oa})$ for each hour, can be computed. The daily sum of the products of hours with required heating and temperature differences, divided by the daily schooling hours (6 hours), gives a quantity termed the "Heating Index" (deg F × days), which is used as a criterion for the necessity of providing heating facilities. The limit beyond which the provision of heating is considered necessary in South Africa is an Index value of about 850.

Caution is required, however, in the author's opinion, in the application of this method, as reliance on computations based on the mean hourly outdoor air temperatures and the average indoor–outdoor temperature differences may involve appreciable departures of the actual from the computed indoor temperatures. Therefore the establishment of the critical "Heating Index" should take into account the extreme conditions which may be expected with a reasonable frequency.

For buildings other than classrooms it would be necessary to determine the specific relationship between the outdoor air temperature and the average indoor–outdoor temperature difference before such method could be used.

Chapter 18

Heating and Cooling of Buildings by Natural Energies—An Overview*

18.1. Introduction

The term "natural energies" applies to those sources of energy which are not derived from fossil or nuclear fuels. There are several natural energy sources which can be utilized for heating and cooling of buildings, or for household water heating [6.7] such as:

Solar radiation
Outgoing longwave radiation
Night convective cooling
Water evaporation

Solar radiation can be utilized for both heating and cooling while the other natural energies only for cooling.

Recently, new interest in the utilization of natural energies for residential uses (as well as heating and cooling of office buildings, schools, etc.) is evident due to two factors. The first is the increased cost and scarcity of the conventional fuels and the second is the desire to reduce the air pollution caused by the combustion of fuels.

The application of solar radiation for heating and cooling of buildings was considered by the U.S. Panel on Solar Energy Utilization to be of the first priority, and in a report to the U.S. Congress it was estimated that at least 35% of all energy needs for heating and cooling of new construction can be supplied from this natural source [18.1].

In many developing countries the rising standard of living is accompanied by an increase in the requirements for thermal comfort, leading to an increase in the consumption of fuel and electricity for winter heating and summer cooling, in the face of limited financial resources for the purchase of fuel. It can be expected that these

* This chapter is based on a research project sponsored by the United States–Israel Binational Science Foundation.

373

trends will continue also in the future. The high proportion of new buildings in developing countries provides a good opportunity for applying new approaches and techniques on a relatively large scale, thus enabling significant energy saving and improvement of the quality of the environment.

Systems utilizing solar radiation and other natural energies for heating and cooling of buildings have some common problems and common features.

The natural phenomena involved are intermittent, both on a diurnal scale, such as the availability of solar radiation only in daytime and cooling by convection and outgoing longwave radiation only at night, and on a larger scale, e.g. during a sequence of several cloudy days. On the other hand the requirements for winter heating, and sometimes also for summer cooling, are continuous. Also there are day to day variations both in the available energy and in the needs for it, and sometimes the needs may be greatest while the supply is absent.

In consequence all systems relying to a significant degree on natural forces have to incorporate as an integral part of the system a considerable capacity for storing thermal energy.

For heating purposes the only available natural energy is solar radiation (except for wind power which is not discussed in this framework). As the primary conversion is from radiant to heat energy, the application for heating is direct. On the other hand, when solar energy is contemplated for cooling, it has to be collected in the form of heat at a relatively high temperature, and then used to operate a heat driven cooling system, such as absorption refrigeration.

The other natural energies, i.e. outgoing longwave radiation, convective cooling at night, and water evaporation, are useful only for cooling purposes. With these energies cold is obtained and can be stored directly. The applicability of the various natural energies for cooling depends upon the characteristics of the summer season in different climatic regions.

Different systems for utilizing natural energies would be suitable for different types of buildings, e.g. for one or two-storey versus multi-storeyed buildings. Furthermore, in different climatic regions different emphasis will be needed on winter heating relative to summer cooling, which may affect the relative advantages of different systems.

The basic components of all heating and cooling systems based on natural energies are:

Collection of the energy
Storage of the energy
Transport of the energy from collection point to storage and from storage to the inhabited space
Control mechanisms over the rates of collection and transport.

Two characteristics of natural energies systems for heating and cooling of buildings may have significant architectural implications. The first is the large exposed areas with suitable orientation which are needed for the collection of the energy. With some systems different areas may be required for the collection of heat and of cold. The second characteristic is the large space required for the storage of thermal energy.

In addition, some systems of natural energies may call for special considerations in relation to the distribution of the energy within the occupied space. For example, by the use of a roof pond, or a roof radiation trap, in one-storeyed buildings, the whole ceiling can serve as a major heating and cooling panel.

The use of natural energies for heating and cooling of buildings may call for specific approaches to the design of the building in order to accommodate them to the intermittent nature of the natural energies. This point may be of particular relevance in the case of multi-storeyed buildings, where space is restricted and expensive. In this case the use of the mass of the building as part of the energy storage system might be considered to be of special advantage.

18.2. Collection of Solar Energy

Solar collectors can be classified as either focusing or non-focusing. For residential uses the latter class is usually applied.

Non-focusing collectors of solar radiation and other natural energies for heating and cooling of buildings can be of several types, such as:

Flat plates with ordinary black or selective surfaces, covered with one or more transparent layers.

Roof ponds in plastic-transparent bags with movable insulation.
Roof radiation traps with fixed or adjustable insulation.
Evaporative cooling and solar heating of roofs.

Each one of these types has advantages and disadvantages, which vary for different applications, types of buildings and climatic conditions.

Flat plate collectors

Flat plate collectors can be divided into two basic types, according to the medium used for the transport of the energy, namely: water systems and air systems. The choice of a given type has direct impact on the energy storage, and its distribution in the occupied space.

Flat plate collectors have been used more than any other type of non-focusing solar collectors, mainly for domestic water heating. Most of the types developed to date consist of a blackened metallic plate from which energy is removed by attached tubes (for liquid heat transport) or fins (for air heat transport). Some air based collectors have special geometrical configurations to increase the heat transfer to the air stream and reduce the radiation loss. The blackened side is exposed to the sun and is covered by one or more of transparent layers (glass or plastics) forming air spaces to reduce the heat loss to the surroundings by convection and radiation.

As the temperature of the collector rises above the ambient temperature, the heat loss by convection and longwave radiation from the collector to the surroundings increases and the efficiency of the collection decreases. Glass, which is opaque to longwave radiation, reduces greatly the radiative component of the heat loss. But, as it is heated itself by the radiant flux and the hot air adjacent to the absorbing surface, there is a significant heat loss to the surroundings by convection and radiation. Consequently, a single glass cover may not reduce sufficiently the heat loss, especially at very high temperatures of the collector.

Two layers of glass (or suitable plastics) can reduce greatly the heat loss even at high temperature but because of the reflections at the air to glass interfaces the amount of radiation impinging on the absorptive surface is also reduced. The reflections can be reduced by special treatments of the surfaces, but this involves a higher cost and the durability of such treatments under the severe conditions of solar collectors are not known sufficiently.

The radiative heat loss from the absorbing surface can be reduced also by using a selective black surface, which combines high absorptivity of solar radiation with low emissivity of longwave radiation, thus increasing the efficiency of the energy collection. Such selective surfaces can be produced by several methods, such as depositing a thin opaque layer (*e.g.* exides) on a reflective substrate (*e.g.* galvanized steel or polished aluminium). The cost of the product is moderate and the initial optical properties good but the durability is not known sufficiently.

For a given intensity of the radiation impinging on the absorptive surface, the efficiency of collection will go up with increasing flow rate of the fluid transporting away the energy, due to the lowering of the collector temperature.

By increasing the storage capacity a larger overall amount of heat can be collected, although at a lower temperature. For residential space heating purposes there is no need for very high temperatures, although for domestic hot water higher temperatures are needed and for operating absorption or ejection air-conditioning, a temperature of 90–95°C or even higher is required, which calls for a specialized collector, low flow rate and smaller storage capacity.

Flat plate collectors can be used for collecting heat only. When cooling is needed they cannot collect "cold" directly, but have to provide the energy at higher temperatures in order to operate a heat driven cooling system. As the efficiency of such cooling systems at the temperatures attainable by flat plate collectors is usually low, the overall efficiency of using flat plate collectors for cooling may be lower than that of other systems which can provide direct cooling by utilizing outgoing longwave radiation and evaporative cooling, such as roof ponds with movable insulation, or night convective and evaporative cooling of the storage, in climatic regions where such systems are effective.

The following factors determine the overall performance of flat plate solar collectors:

The efficiency and durability of the absorptive surfaces.

The number of cover layers as well as the materials of the transparent covers.

The thermal conductivity of the collecting plate and the thermal resistance between the plate and the water pipes (for water base collectors).

The geometrical configuration of the collecting plate (for air based collectors).

The interaction between collectors' type and size, the storage capacity and the flow rate of the fluid transporting the energy.

Architectural problems associated with the visual impact of flat plate collectors over flat roofs, over pitched roofs and over walls.

Maintenance of the collectors.

A detailed discussion of the factors affecting the efficiency of flat plate collectors is presented in Section 18.3.

Concentrating solar collectors

Concentrating solar collectors, mainly in the form of reflecting parabolic cylinders, are used where temperatures above 100°C are required, *e.g.* for operating an absorption cooling device or for producing steam to drive a compression air-conditioner. To be effective, such a collector requires a programmed mechanism to rotate it according to the altitude of the sun.

In addition, it requires constant cleaning and polishing to keep up its reflective properties.

It is doubtful whether a concentrating solar collector is practical for heating and cooling of buildings except for operating absorption or some other heat operated cooling systems.

Roof ponds

Roof ponds can serve for both winter heating and summer cooling. Control of the heating and cooling processes and their diurnal pattern can be achieved by utilizing either movable insulating horizontal panels or by flooding the roof and draining the water according to the needs for heating or cooling.

Roof ponds with movable insulation have been designed and constructed by Hay and Yellott [18.9]. According to their system, for winter heating the water has to be covered by a transparent layer or contained within transparent plastic bags to prevent cooling by evaporation. Heating is provided by absorption of solar radiation during the day when the insulating panels are open. To minimize cooling at night the movable insulating panels are then closed.

For cooling in summer the insulating panels are closed during the days, minimizing heating of the water by the hot air and solar radiation, and are open during the night, enabling cooling of the water by convection and longwave outgoing radiation. Extra cooling can be obtained by flooding the plastic bags or by removing the transparent cover.

In this system the storage of heat and cold is provided by the pond itself, when sufficient quantity of water is available on the roof and its structure can support the load.

Another house utilizing a roof pond with movable insulation has been constructed by Hay in California [18.10]. In this house the pond is insulated by inflated plastic bags, in addition to the movable insulating panels.

In an alternative system of a roof pond the water can be circulated between the roof and a storage tank, which can be located either in the basement or in a special space within the house. In this way the need for the movable insulating panels is eliminated [18.6].

In winter the circulation takes place only during the daytime and the water is heated by the sun. The pond has to be covered by transparent plastic, which can also float over the water, to prevent cooling by evaporation.

In summer the circulation of the water takes place only during the night. If the water is under a polyethylene cover then the cooling is achieved only by longwave radiation and convection. However, in the summer the pond can be uncovered whereby cooling is also obtained by evaporation. In this case, however, the water will contain dust and has to be filtered before draining into the storage.

Roof ponds may provide a relatively inexpensive system for year round air-conditioning for one-storeyed buildings in regions with a mild climate.

There are, however, some factors which limit their efficiency in regions with cold winters and/or humid-hot summers.

The factors which limit the efficiency of heat collection of roof ponds in winter are the low elevation of the sun and the resulting small angle between the horizontal surface of the pond and the sun's rays, as well as the large area of contact between the pond surface and the ambient air. The first factor causes significant reflection of the impinging solar radiation and the second factor causes high heat loss from the pond during the daytime.

The cooling efficiency of roof ponds in regions with hot-humid summers is limited because of the high vapour pressure and cloudiness, which causes a reduction in the heat loss by outgoing longwave radiation as well as a small day-to-night temperature difference.

The effectiveness of evaporative cooling through flooding the plastic bags containing the water is also greatly reduced in such climatic conditions.

From the building design viewpoint the use of roof ponds is limited to buildings with flat roofs of one storey. The roof structure should be able to support the appreciable weight of the water.

Radiation traps

Another approach to the use of the roofs for heating has been developed by the author. A "radiation trap" is constructed over the roof (in the case of a flat roof) or as an integral part of the roof (in the case of a gabled or a pitched roof). The radiation trap consists of a vertical (or slightly inclined) double glazed plane facing the south. An inclined insulated panel extends from the top of the glazing towards the north, extending over the glazing so that in summer the sun is obscured while in winter it penetrates the glass. The triangular sides contain openings, which are closed in winter and opened in summer.

Such radiation traps can form one unit over the whole roof (in small buildings) or a series of successive triangles, to cover the whole roof or any desired part of it. It can also be prefabricated.

The solar radiation which penetrates through the glazing during the day in winter heats the upper surface of the roof and the air above it. Part of the heat is transferred by conduction through the ceiling to the rooms below. The hot air is drawn by a fan to a thermal storage of gravel, or containerized water, in the basement or within the building.

If the roof is made of concrete it may serve as a significant thermal storage by itself. Its thickness can be designed so that the time lag of the temperature wave will result in peak heating during the evening. With lightweight roofs all the storage capacity will have to be supplied by the special storage space.

18.3. Impact of Design on the Efficiency of Flat Plate Collectors

The efficiency of solar energy collection can be defined as the ratio of the useful heat received from the collector to the amount of solar radiation impinging on the surface.

For fixed flat plate collectors the daily amount of radiation impinging on the surface is always less than the radiation falling on a surface normal to the sun's rays, because of the angle between the sun's rays and the collector's surface.

In a sense this factor is also part of the design characteristics of the collector although it is beyond the structural aspect and is related to the choice of the season in which the performance is to be maximized.

The efficiency of solar energy collection by a flat plate depends on many design features, which may affect the thermodynamic process at several of its stages.

From the physical, thermodynamic, viewpoint the following aspects should be considered:

The intensity of solar radiation impinging on the collector surface.
Transmittance of solar energy through the transparent covers.
Absorption of the transmitted solar energy.
Energy loss through the transparent covers.
Resistance to heat flow between the collector plate and the transport fluid.
Energy loss at the back and sides of the collector.
The rate of heat withdrawal from the collector.

From the design viewpoint, different considerations may apply with regard to some factors as to water and to air systems of collection. The following features should be considered in the design of the collectors:

Materials and number of the transparent covers.
Radiative characteristics of the collector plate.
Thermal insulation of the back and sides of the collector.
Material of the collector plate (mainly for water systems).
Material of the water pipes (for water systems).
The thermal bond between the absorbing plate and the water pipes (for water systems).
Geometry of the absorbing plate (for air systems).

From data quoted in the literature it is possible to assume that the average efficiency of flat plate collectors is about 40–45%. On clear days it may rise to 50–55% while on partly cloudy days it may drop down to 30–35%.

The discussion of the efficiency of flat plate collectors will proceed according to the thermodynamical aspects and at each stage the impact of the relevant design features will be considered.

Intensity of the solar radiation impinging on the collector surface

The intensity of solar radiation impinging on the surface of a collector at a given orientation and tilt (elevation of the back of the collector from the horizontal) depends on the intensity of the solar radiation itself (when measured perpendicular to the surface) and the angle in which the sun's rays hit the surface.

Both the intensity of the solar radiation and the path of the sun in the sky vary according to the season. Therefore, for any orientation and tilt of the collector, there would be seasonal variations in the intensity of the impinging radiation. It is possible to choose a tilt which will maximize the impinging radiation in a given season.

In cold climates the interest is to maximize the radiation in winter and a tilt angle equal to the latitude plus 20 degrees might be suitable. For example, for a latitude of 30°N a tilt of 30 + 20 = 50° would be adequate for winter heating.

In hot climates the main interest might be to maximize solar energy collection in summer for utilization in absorption air conditioning. In this case a tilt angle equal to the latitude minus 10 degrees might be suitable (for latitude of 30°N a tilt of 20°, for 50°N a tilt of 40°, etc.). When both winter heating and summer cooling are needed the optimal tilt might be about the latitude plus 10 degrees. Deviation of up to 10 degrees in the tilt has a small effect on the performance.

In most cases the best orientation would be towards the south in the Northern, and to the north in the Southern hemisphere. However, in some places the intensity of solar radiation actually reaching the earth is not symmetrical about noontime. For instance, in many coastal regions (*e.g.* the Californian Coast) the cloudiness is more prevalent in the morning than in the afternoon. In such places the best orientation might be towards the south-south-west. On the other hand, in some tropical regions (*e.g.* in Africa) there is a distinct diurnal pattern of cloudiness and rain. The sky is clear in the morning, becomes cloudy in the afternoon and evening, with intense rains, and clears again late in the night. In such regions an easterly orientation might be better for solar air-conditioning and water heating.

For a given difference between the collection temperature and the outdoor air temperature the efficiency of collection of solar energy increases with the intensity of the radiation. The factor which enables the attainment of a given temperature difference (up to a certain limit) under different intensities of radiation is the flow rate of the medium transporting the energy. Without such a flow, the elevation of the collector temperature above the outdoor level will be such that the amount of solar energy absorbed will equal the heat loss by radiation and convection across the envelope of the collector, mainly across the transparent covers, without any energy gain for utilization. This equilibrium level depends on the overall thermal resistance of the collector's envelope and the rate of radiation transmittance across the transparent layers. There is no energy utilization and the efficiency in this case is zero.

Increasing the intensity of the solar radiation beyond this initial level provides the energy which can be transported and utilized. The ratio of the transported energy to the radiation impinging on the surface of the collector is the efficiency of the collection.

Increasing the flow of the transporting medium carries a greater part of the absorbed energy out of the collector (for utilization), and correspondingly causes a decrease in the temperature of the collector and, in consequence, in the heat loss to the environment, thus increasing the efficiency.

The above discussion shows the dependence of the efficiency of solar energy collection on the interrelationship between the three factors: the intensity of the impinging radiation, the temperature elevation above the ambient air and the flow rate of the transporting medium. For some applications, such as space heating, the main factor is the *amount* of collected energy. In such cases the efficiency can be increased, under given radiation conditions, by increasing the rate of energy transport and correspondingly decreasing the temperature of the collection. For other applications, such as absorption cooling, the *temperature* at which the energy is collected has a decisive influence on the efficiency of the cooling process. In such cases the flow rate, and the collection efficiency, may have to be reduced in order to provide the necessary temperature.

Transmittance of solar energy through the transparent covers of the collector

Of the solar energy impinging on the glass (or plastic) cover of the collector, part is reflected at the air–glass interfaces, part is absorbed in the glass and the rest is transmitted inwards and impinges on the absorbent plate.

The design features which affect solar radiation transmittance through the transparent cover are the angle of incidence of the sun's rays, the number of glass (or plastics) cover plates and the reflectance characteristics of the transparent surfaces.

Each layer of glass reflects some fraction of the radiation impinging on it. The percentage of the reflected energy depends on the angle of incidence. Part of the radiation is absorbed in the glass, and the rest is transmitted across the glass. Maximum transmittance is at normal incidence, but up to an angle of about 40° the transmittance is near maximum. However, a sharp decrease occurs progressively at incidence angles greater than 40°. With ordinary clear glass of low iron content the transmittance at normal incidence is about 0·9 of the impinging radiation and with double glazing it is about 0·8. With incidence angles above 40°, *e.g.* 50, 60, 70 and 80°, the transmittance drops down to about 0·82, 0·77, 0·65 and 0·45, respectively.

It is possible to reduce the reflectance of the glass by special treatment of the surfaces (anti-reflectance), but such treatment involves higher cost and its durability is not fully known.

Absorption of the transmitted solar radiation

The solar radiation which is transmitted through the transparent covers has a spectral distribution of wavelength from 0·4 to about 3·0 microns (μ). Surfaces painted with an ordinary matt black paint absorb about 95% of the impinging radiation, reflecting the remainder. With special carbon-black pigment 98% absorption is obtainable.

These values refer to normal incidence of the radiation. With angles of incidence of up to 50° the absorptivity remains near the maximum value but with longer angles of incidence it drops down progressively. Thus, for incidence angles of 50, 60, 70 and 80° the corresponding absorptivity values will be about 0·90, 0·86, 0·78 and 0·55, respectively. When the effect of angle of incidence of absorption at the blackened plate is coupled with its effect on reflectance, which has been discussed above, the overall effect of the incidence angle becomes a very pronounced one. For practical considerations the heating effect of solar radiation at very large angles of incidence can be discarded.

Selective surfaces

As a result of the absorbed solar radiation the temperature of the absorbing surface is elevated and its potential for emitting longwave radiation is greatly increased.

The intensity of the emitted longwave radiation depends on the radiative properties (emissivity) of the surface, and in some cases of air heaters also on the geometrical configurations. The emissivity of an ordinary matt black paint is about 0·95. In this case the ratio of longwave radiation emissivity (ε) to solar absorptivity (a), $\dfrac{\varepsilon}{a}$ is about 1·0. By special chemical treatment of reflective metal sheets it is possible to produce a so-called "selective surface", which combines high absorptivity with low emissivity, so that the ratio of $\dfrac{\varepsilon}{a}$ is of the order of 0·15–0·30.

Most selective surfaces are based on the deposition of a very thin layer of a black metallic oxide over a highly reflective surface, or on the deposition of successive, very thin layers of reflecting and transparent materials. In this way, the interference effect which occurs between two reflective layers separated by a transparent layer of the proper thickness is utilized to reduce the emission of longwave radiation without great reduction in solar absorption.

However, as the absolute intensity of the impinging solar radiation is much higher than that of the emitted longwave radiation, a unit decrease in the absorptivity has a much greater effect on the radiative balance than a unit decrease in the longwave emissivity but, generally, a selective surface provides a better balance.

By the use of a selective surface the radiant component of the heat loss from the solar absorbing surface decreases and its temperature is elevated. As a result, the convective heat loss increases, and therefore the actual increase in energy gain is not directly proportional to the improved radiative properties.

It is possible to reduce the radiative heat loss of an ordinary black surface by special geometrical configurations. For example, a geometrical configuration of vee-corrugation does not change the absorption, but directs a significant fraction of the emitted and reflected radiation towards the other surfaces, where it is absorbed again. As a result the ratio of the absorbed to the emitted radiation can increase greatly. This configuration is of special interest in the case of air systems, because a vee-corrugated surface provides also an enlarged surface for convective heat transfer from the absorbing surface to the energy transporting stream of air.

The advantage of using a selective surface depends on the temperature difference between the collector and the ambient air and on the number of transparent glass layers. The higher the temperature of the collectors, the greater will be the advantage of using a selective surface, and very high temperatures (*e.g.* 80°C above ambient air) cannot actually be obtained without a selective surface.

This advantage is mostly evident when only a single glass cover is provided. The relative advantage of a selective surface is much smaller when two glass covers are provided.

Energy loss through the transparent covers

The energy loss through the transparent cover depends on the number of cover plates and, to some extent, also on the width of the air gap between the plates.

A single transparent cover plate (glass or plastic) is subjected to intensive heat flow by convection and longwave radiation from the absorbent plate. As a result its temperature is elevated appreciably above the ambient temperature, resulting in a high rate of heat loss to the environment.

By the provision of double glazing the total resistance to heat flow from the absorbing plate to the outdoor air greatly increases. The inner glass effectively intercepts the direct longwave radiant flux from the absorbing plate. The radiation emitted outwards from the inner glass is much lower than that emitted from the absorbing plate due to its lower temperature, and this radiation, in turn, is intercepted by the outer glass. Also the convective heat loss is greatly reduced due to the higher resistance of the two air spaces. The width of the air gaps between the glasses affects the heat flow by conduction across the air space. Thus, a width of 6 mm provides a significantly higher thermal resistance than an air space 3 mm wide. But beyond a width of 12 mm further increase of the distance between the glasses has almost no effect, as convective currents become dominant in the heat transfer.

The higher thermal resistance resulting from the increase in the number of transparent cover plates is counteracted, however, by the increase in the reflection of the radiation at the air–glass interfaces. Anti-reflectance treatment of the glasses can minimize this effect, but at a certain cost.

The use of a selective surface with single glazing results in collection efficiency a little higher than that provided by an ordinary black surface with double glazing.

The average temperature of the absorbing surface, at a given outdoor air temperature, determines the rate of heat loss from the collector. From the energy utilization point of view the temperature that is of interest with regard to the collector is that of the fluid emerging from it. In practice, this temperature is always lower than the collector plate temperature. The difference depends on the resistance to heat flow from the collector plate to the energy transporting medium. In water systems this resistance depends on the materials and design details of the collector, especially the thermal characteristics of the bond between the water tubes and the plate.

In air systems it depends on the geometrical configuration of the collector and the area of contact between the collecting surfaces and the stream of air.

The rate of heat withdrawal from the collectors

When the rate of withdrawal of the solar energy absorbed in the collector is increased, the temperatures of the collector plate and of the air between the plate and the glass cover are lowered. As a result, the heat loss to the environment by convection and radiation is reduced and the efficiency of solar energy collection increases.

However, the effect of increasing the rate of flow is not linear, but diminishes as the flow rate is increased, so that an asymptotic level is reached eventually. For example, in a study by Löf [18.12] it has been found that when the flow rate of an air-based collector has been increased from 0·4 cfm/ft^2 to 0·8, 1·2 and 1·6, the useful heat recovered rose from 400 Btu/ft^2 a day to 650, 800 and 920 Btu/ft^2 a day, respectively (average values for 4 different collectors; total daily incidence was 2200 Btu/ft^2 a day).

Effect of the environment conditions on efficiency of collection

The efficiency of collection increases also with the intensity of the impinging radiation and with the outdoor air temperature. Table 18.I gives results from a study of Löf, for an air-based collector,

Table 18.I

Useful heat recovery (*Btu*/*ft*^{2} *day*)

Outdoor air temperature °F	Total incident radiation (Btu/ft^2 day)			
	1200	1600	2000	2400
70	630	890	1150	1410
50	530	760	1000	1220
30	430	630	850	1050
10	330	510	700	890

on the useful daily heat recovered under different levels of solar radiation and outdoor air temperature (Btu/ft^2 day) (after Löf, [18.12]).

Special factors affecting the efficiency of water-based collectors

Some special features of water-based flat plate collectors have an impact on its efficiency, such as the material of the collector plate and the connection of the plate to the water pipes transporting the energy. Both these factors determine the rate of heat flow from the absorbing plate to the water pipes.

As the material of the absorbing plate is of higher thermal conductivity, and as the connection between the plate and the water pipes provides a better thermal bond, there is less resistance to the heat flow from the plate to the pipes, the water temperature is elevated and the plate's temperature drops. The result is a reduction in the heat loss to the environment and a higher efficiency of solar energy collection.

In the choice of the materials for the collecting plate and the pipes, as well as the method of providing the thermal bond, the danger of corrosion should not be overlooked. In many cases this factor will be the limiting one in the useful lifetime of the system.

Special factors affecting the efficiency of air-based collectors

One of the main features by which air collection systems differ from water systems is the nature of heat transfer from the absorbing plate to the energy transporting fluid.

In the case of air collectors the fluid is in contact with the whole surface of the collecting plate. Therefore, the conductivity of the plate material has much smaller effect on the collection efficiency than with water systems, and even materials like cloth can serve to absorb the solar energy.

Only when the area of heat transfer from the plate to the air is much larger than the area of solar absorption can an advantage be taken of the high thermal conductivity of the collecting plate. By special geometrical configurations, like vee-corrugation, it is possible to reduce appreciably the temperature difference between the plate and the air, lowering that of the plate and raising that of the air. The result is an increase in the collection efficiency.

18.4. Storage of Thermal Energy

Thermal energy can be stored in two forms:

a. Sensible heat, *i.e.* by changing the temperature of inert materials, and
b. by latent heat storage of change of state in reversible chemical and physico-chemical reactions.

Sensible heat can be stored in water, in gravel or pebble bed, and in the mass of the structure itself.

The main problem associated with the storage of sensible heat is that of the space requirements. A cubic metre of water stores 1000 kcal for 1°C change in temperature, while a similar volume of rocks contains about 400 kcal per 1°C. The structure of the building stores about 200 kcal per degree per ton of its mass. In high rise buildings the weight itself may constitute a problem.

One of the main advantages of sensible heat storage is that the same material and accessories can be used both for the storage of heat in winter and the storage of cold in summer. It is usually also less expensive than latent heat storage. However, storage of latent heat requires much less space than that of sensible heat. Thus, for $NaSO_4 . 10H_2O$ (Glauber salt hydrate), which has a melting point at about 32°C, 1 m^3 can store about 4500 kcal while changing its phase from a solid to liquid.

In the following some of the thermodynamical and design aspects of the use of the various storage materials will be discussed.

Thermal storage in water

Water has the highest heat capacity per unit weight of the material, although the difference on the basis of volume is less because of the greater volumetric weight of the other storage materials.

The main problem concerning the use of water for storage of thermal energy is the cost of the container. For heating and cooling of a dwelling unit several cubic metres of water are required and the storage tank should be rust-resistant over a long period. The cost of such tanks is the main expenditure in the use of water as a storage material. On the other hand the comparatively small volume of the space needed for storage in water reduces the cost of the insulation required to conserve the energy within the storage space.

In a large water tank there is a tendency for the water temperature to stratify, with colder water sinking to the bottom and warmer rising to the top. This tendency for stratification can be utilized to retain within the storage space regions of higher temperature, from which heat can be withdrawn for utilization. The stratification can be augmented by introducing the hot water from the collector (in winter) at the top of the storage tank. In this way mixing of the water heated by the collector, with the rest of the storage water, is prevented, and a given volume of the storage is kept at a higher temperature than the rest.

In summer, when the storage is used for cooling, cold water collected during the night should be introduced at the bottom of the tank to ensure the stratification. Advantage can be taken of the thermal stratification when the stored energy is extracted, by withdrawing hot water (during the heating season) from the top of the tank and cold water (during the cooling season) from its bottom.

When the energy is stored in a single large tank, which has a small ratio of surface area to volume, the energy has to be transported in and out of the storage by water flow. In consequence, the whole system of the natural energies becomes a water system, so that also the collection of the energy, as well as its distribution within the occupied space is done by water.

Water solar collectors are usually more complex and expensive than air collectors and, as the cost of the collectors constitutes the main expenditure of solar energy systems, the use of a whole water system may result in a higher total cost. On the other hand such systems can more easily be combined with a conventional energy supply and distribution systems, such as fan-coil heating and cooling.

From the design details viewpoint a large water storage tank is the simplest arrangement. It calls, however, for very careful treatment against leakage. It is easy to check the tank and the pipes under pressure during the initial installation. However, corrosion may cause leakage at a later time and because of the huge quantity of water stored in the tank, the results may be quite severe. Therefore the need for very high quality of materials and waterproofing of the tank.

The shape of the storage tank affects both the total surface of heat loss and thermal stratification of the water. Assuming a cylindrical shape, which from the technological considerations is the easiest to produce, a minimum ratio of surface area to volume is achieved when the diameter of the cylinder equals its height.

When the length of the cylinder is larger than its diameter, the thermal stratification will depend on the position of the tank. An elongated vertical tank will provide the highest stratification while an elongated horizontal tank would provide the lowest stratification, because of the variations in the area of the imaginary layer separating the upper warmer water from the colder water at the bottom of the tank. Stratification can be enhanced, and the mixing of the warmer and colder water reduced by dividing the tank into a series of inter-connected horizontal compartments.

Containerized water storage

Water can be used for thermal storage, in conjunction with air systems for energy collection and distribution, when the water is stored in small containers, of metal or plastics, with air circulating between the containers.

Although the heat transfer coefficient between the air stream and the water containers is rather small, the large surface area of the many small containers can enable an adequate overall rate of heat flow in and out of the storage medium.

The geometry of the containers has a pronounced effect on the surface area available for heat transfer and the development of special containers for this purpose, with high ratio of surface area to volume, would be very useful.

Such a storage system can be incorporated with air solar collectors, thus providing a simpler and less expensive total system than a water system, while requiring less space than gravel storage (although more than a large water tank of the same water capacity).

The consequences of water leakages from the containers are less severe than with a large water tank because of the small quantities involved and the ease by which a damaged container can be replaced.

Thermal storage in gravel

Gravel and pebble beds have many advantages for storing thermal energy when ample space is available (*e.g.* in a basement or underneath the building). The transfer of the energy to and from the storage is done usually by a stream of air. A blower is necessary to produce the air flow to the storage and across it. The required power depends mainly on the resistance of the gravel pile to the air flow.

As the size of the gravel is reduced, the specific surface area of the storage mass is increased and the heat transfer in and out of the material is facilitated but, on the other hand, the resistance to the air flow within the gravel pile increases. Using uniform size of the gravel reduces the resistance. A size of 3–5 cm is a convenient one.

The specific heat of gravel is about 0·22 kcal/kg/°C. The gross density of the storage mass is about 1·2–1·8 kg/litre, depending on the type of the rocks used. Thus, the volumetric heat capacity of the gravel pile is about 0·35 kcal/litre/°C (350 kcal/m^3/°C).

When the storage space is underneath the building and in direct contact with the ground, it is possible to utilize in part also the heat capacity of the earth under the gravel as part of the storage system. In this case the bottom of the storage area should not be insulated but insulation is needed around the periphery of the ground area extending beneath the storage level.

With such an arrangement very large quantities of heat can be stored in the ground–gravel combination. Even seasonal storage, from late summer to the winter, can be contemplated, provided that there is good thermal insulation between the storage and the inhabited space, to prevent overheating in summer.

In a geometrical configuration of the storage space where the height is small in comparison with the horizontal dimensions, the main design problem is to maximize the rate of heat transfer into the gravel bed. The stream of hot (or cold) air, flowing from the collectors to the storage, is confined to its area of contact with the gravel bed. Therefore, either a distribution system of ducts, or a continuous free space, is necessary underneath the gravel bed.

A possible solution, for minimizing the power requirements of the fan, is to provide a strong metal mesh, about 10–20 cm above the ground, and to support over it the gravel bed. In this way a distribution plenum is created underneath the gravel. A similar plenum above the gravel bed can be provided by leaving the upper layer of the storage space free from the gravel.

During the sunny hours in the heating season the hot air from the collectors is directed to the bottom plenum (or distribution ducts). The air infiltrates in the free spaces between the gravel and rises upwards, heating on its way the gravel. This process continues by natural convection during the night and warm air accumulates ultimately at the upper plenum, from which it is withdrawn for utilization in the occupied space.

During the cooling season the pattern is reversed. Cold air is introduced at the upper plenum, sinking down the gravel bed and cooling it on its way. Cool air for utilization is withdrawn from the bottom plenum (or distribution ducts). The cold air can be obtained either by solar absorption cooling (during the day) or by night convective and evaporative cooling.

The gain in the fan power is accompanied, however, by a loss in the ability to get thermal stratification within the gravel bed. From this point of view a better solution is to fill the whole height at the storage space with gravel, and to provide an inlet plenum in front of the gravel, where the hot air is introduced, and an outlet plenum at the end of the space from where the cooler air is returned to the collector.

In this way a horizontal graduation of the gravel temperature is established. When heat is needed it can be withdrawn from the inlet side of the gravel space. In summer the same directions of flow can be maintained, unlike the case of a vertical storage bin, where the flow has to be reversed.

A gravel storage system can usually be provided only with air systems for collection and distribution of the energy, as the heat transfer between a gravel bed and water pipes is very limited.

Water–gravel combination

In some cases, when the solar collection system is based on water but the energy distribution within the building is based on air flow, it is possible to use a combination of an un-insulated water tank and a gravel bed surrounding it for the storage of the thermal energy. With such a combination the rate of heat flow from the collectors to the water storage tank can be much faster than the rate of heat flow from the water tank to the surrounding gravel bed. This latter rate is limited by the low coefficient of surface heat transfer (mainly by natural convection) and the relatively small surface area of a large water tank.

However, the duration of energy flow from the collectors to the storage is limited to only several hours per day. On the other hand, the energy flow from the water tank to the surrounding gravel bed is a continuous process. Therefore, the total energy flows, over the whole day, may balance, and such a combination can perform satisfactorily.

The heat is distributed within the gravel bed by natural convection currents between the tank and the gravel. At the upper layer of the storage space, hot air accumulates and can be withdrawn by a fan and distributed within the occupied space.

During the cooling season, cold water is stored in the tank and the colder air accumulates at the bottom of the storage space. Provision should be made for its withdrawal by perforated ducts located underneath the gravel. From these aspects the design details of the energy withdrawal from a water tank–gravel combination are similar to those of a complete gravel storage, although the details of the energy input into the storage are different.

From the maintenance point of view care should be taken in the design of such a combined system to provide an access to the water tank for repairs, cleaning, etc.

Latent energy storage

Physical changes of state and physico-chemical reactions produced by heat absorption and release involve greater amounts of energy, per volume as well as per weight, than the sensible temperature changes of inert materials. The changes must be reversible for a very large number of cycles. In addition, the kinetics of the reactions should enable rapid heat flow in and out of the storage system. Change of state involves the formation and dissolution of crystals. In some cases the crystallization may not proceed before the liquid is supercooled, unless suitable nucleating agents are added [18.18].

The main problems associated with latent heat storage are: segregation of the two phases and the geometry of the heat-exchange container which must promote the heat and mass transfer during the dissolution-solidification cycles. Different salt hydrates or their eutectics are required for the storage of heat and cold, according to their melting points. Thus, 30–40°C will be suitable for heating in winter and about 5–15°C for cooling in summer. The temperature required for efficient operation of an absorption-cooling system might be about 90°C.

It seems to the author that, at the present, latent energy storage has not reached a stage of development sufficient for application, except for experimental buildings.

Location and design of the storage space

One of the main design problems associated with the storage of thermal energy is its location, either within the space of the building or adjacent to it, *e.g.* in the basement. In one or two storeyed buildings the storage space can be located within the space of the basement or on the roof. In the former case the transport of the energy from the collection point to the storage requires longer routes, but the storage space is better protected from heat loss by suitable insulation. Storage over the roof area is the least efficient from the energy conservation viewpoint, as the ratio of external envelope area to volume is maximized, as well as the temperature gradient between the storage medium and the ambient environment.

From the energy conservation point of view, the best location of the storage is within the inhabited space, as thus all the heat flow in and out, across the container envelope, is utilized for heating or cooling. However, such a location may be the most difficult from the viewpoint of area utilization and might conflict with the functional planning considerations. In the case of multistoreyed buildings the storage space may have to be provided within the inhabited space. In such a case salt hydrates may be more practical because of the saving in valuable space. The mass of the structure may provide partial solution for the storage problem in high rise buildings. A residential unit built of concrete structure may contain a mass of over 100 tons. Such a mass releases 20,000 kcal through a change of 1°C in its average temperature. However, to be effective as a heat storage the mass has to be concentrated mainly within the interior of the building, *i.e.* in the floors and internal partitions, while the external envelope should be of high insulating capacity. Therefore, heat storage within the structure calls for a specific approach to the design and structure of the building.

Another design detail of the storage space affecting its performance is its geometrical shape. For a given volume of storage space the heat loss will be lower as the surface area is smaller. The cost of insulating the storage also is proportional to the surface area of the space.

An exception to these considerations is when the storage space is located within the occupied area of the building. In this case all the "losses" from the storage are "gains" for the occupied space. Therefore, the geometrical configuration is of minor importance. A good solution in such a case is to provide the storage at the centre of the occupied space, preferably at the junction of several rooms, thus facilitating the transport of the heat from the storage to the different rooms.

18.5. General Comparison Between Air and Water Systems

The choice between air and water systems for heating and cooling of buildings involves considerations of all the components of the natural energies systems; the collection of the energy and its transport from the collectors, its storage, as well as the distribution of the heat or cold in the inhabited space.

From the energy collection point of view, air systems are simpler and less expensive than water systems, and complications resulting from leakages are less severe. Leakage of air does not cause damage to the building or the energy system, as is the case with water leakage, although it involves a loss of energy and can not be detected easily.

With air systems, the transport of the energy from the collectors to the storage involves a larger mass transfer and requires ducts which are much bulkier than the pipes needed for water systems and need more insulation. In consequence, the cost of the transport of the energy with air is higher than with water systems. Also, there are technical difficulties in eliminating air leakage.

Solar air-conditioners operating on hot air are presently lacking, but the air systems can be used in summer by utilizing direct night convective and evaporative cooling.

Thermal energy can be stored in water systems either in a water tank or in a combination of a water tank surrounded by a gravel bed. In both cases the collection is done by collectors based on water and the energy is transported, from the collectors to the storage, by means of water flow. However, these two storage methods involve different systems of energy transport from the storage to the useable space, as well as different systems of energy distribution inside the occupied space.

When the storage is in a water tank the energy is transported to the occupied space and distributed within it by water pipes. On the other hand, when the storage is in a combination of a water tank and a surrounding gravel bed, the heat (or cold) is transferred from the water tank to the gravel bed by conduction and convection.

When the stored energy is withdrawn, the air inside and above the gravel bed is heated (or cooled) by heat flow in and out of the gravel. The transport to the occupied space, as well as the distribution within it, is achieved by air flow.

In one-storeyed buildings it is possible to turn the whole ceiling into a heating and cooling panel. Such an arrangement can be done by turning the attic space above the ceiling into an air plenum, where hot air from the collector or cold air from the storage, is discharged. The plenum space should be well insulated and airtight from above, to minimize the heat loss. The excess heat should be transported to a storage space, for utilization at night.

When the building has a flat concrete roof it is possible to cover it with "radiation traps", consisting of a simple solar air heater and a distribution chamber, which are placed right over the concrete, without any insulation in between. In this way the roof is turned into a heating panel and a partial storage element. When the roof is used as the collecting area in high-rise buildings, one of the main factors in the choice between air and water systems is the length of the distribution channels. When these channels are long there would be an advantage for water systems.

In summary, it seems to the author that for single storeyed buildings air systems are preferable to water systems, especially in regions where the main need is for winter heating. On the other hand, in high rise buildings, and in regions where summer cooling is the dominant requirement and night cooling is not sufficient, there would be an advantage with water systems.

18.6. Cooling of Buildings by Natural Energies

Cooling of buildings can be achieved by utilizing several kinds of natural energies, such as:

Absorption cooling operated by solar heat
Solar dehumidification and evaporative cooling
Longwave outgoing radiation at night
Convective cooling during the night
Cooling by water evaporation

Combinations of these cooling forces are also possible, *e.g.* evaporative and convective night cooling, evaporation and outgoing radiation, etc. Such combinations produce higher cooling effects than each one separately.

All cooling methods relying on natural energies require appreciable storage capacity for the cold accumulated, for at least one day, and each of them has some design implications. For example, utilization of longwave outgoing radiative cooling during the night requires a large exposed area of the roof and, when the storage is on the roof, may require protection of the cooled medium from the sun during the day, *e.g.* by moveable insulating panels or by draining the cooled medium (water) into a protected and insulated storage space.

The applicability of each one of these systems depends on one hand on the prevailing climatic conditions and on the other hand on the type of building. All these methods are applicable to one or two storeyed buildings but some might be less suitable for multi-storeyed buildings, *e.g.* the use of outgoing radiation as the cooling force.

Solar absorption cooling

Solar absorption cooling is based on the vaporization of a liquid from a solution by solar energy in the Generator, condensing it by heat removal to the ambient air in the Condenser, evaporating it by drawing energy from the space to be cooled in the Evaporator and absorbing the vapour again in the solution in the Absorber. Solutions suitable for such a cycle are, for example, water and ammonia (H_2O–NH_3) or lithium bromide and water (LiBr–H_2O). In the first case the ammonia, and in the second case the water, serve as the working fluid.

In the LiBr–H_2O system the water vapour pressure of the

solution is considerably lower than that of pure water and a high temperature is required to evaporate the water from the solution. This vaporization can be achieved by heating the solution in the generator with solar energy. The water vapour is then condensed in the condenser, outside the building, by the ambient air or by evaporative cooling. The liquid water then evaporates in the evaporator and the vapour is absorbed in a portion of the rich LiBr solution which is cooled in the absorber by ambient air. The diluted solution is then pumped again to the generator.

One of the attractive features of solar operated air-conditioning is the fact that the largest supply of energy is available at the time of the highest demand for it.

For refrigeration, which requires lower temperatures but smaller quantities of energy, the H_2O–NH_3 system is common. For cooling of buildings, which involves much larger quantities of energy but at a higher temperature, the LiBr–H_2O system is more suitable.

Tabor [18.16] has analysed some thermodynamic aspects of absorption cooling and their implications for the utilization of solar energy for this purpose. His main comments are as follows:

"In all absorption cycles, heat at a temperature T_g—the generator temperature—is supplied whilst heat is extracted at the evaporator where 'cold' is produced at a temperature T_e. Heat is rejected from the system to the surroundings (outside the space to be cooled) from a condenser at temperature T_c and from an absorber, at temperature T_a. T_a and T_c are about equal (and will be referred to as T_c) being a few degrees above ambient for air-cooled condensers and absorbers (and being a few degrees above local wet-bulb temperature for water-cooled systems).

Two important facts emerge from thermodynamic considerations of absorption cycle, which are quite independent of the system or materials used.

    a.   The amount of heat supplied at the hot end will always be more than the amount of 'cold' produced: in an ideal system these quantities approach equality. As the coefficient of performance, COP, of a cooling machine is defined as the ratio of calories extracted at the cold end to the calories of heat supplied, the COP is always less than unity.

b. The temperature 'lift', $i.e.$ $T_g - T_c$ is, in an ideal system, approximately equal to the temperature 'depression', $i.e.$ $T_c - T_e$. In real systems the lift is always a little greater than the depression. For example, when $T_e = 13°C$ and $T_c = 29°C$, $i.e.$ a depression of 16°C, $T_g = 49°C$, $i.e.$ the lift is 20°C: for $T_c = 32°C$ the depression is 20°C and the lift 25°C: for $T_c = 38°C$ the depression is 22°C and the lift is 30°C.

These two facts are vital in appreciating the problem of solar cooling. The first fact indicates the minimum quantity of heat to be supplied from the collector for a given refrigeration effect. Whilst the ideal COP can approach unity, real values are about 0·7 for large industrial plants, falling to about 0·4 for small units.

The second fact fixes the operating temperature for the generator and hence of the collector. For example, normal air-conditioning practice calls for an evaporator temperature of 4–5°C in order to be able to cool the air down with a small heat transfer surface of the evaporator. If the ambient temperature in the summer, is, say, 30°C—and it could easily be more—thus making T_c about 35°C, we see that the depression is $35 - 5 = 30°C$: the lift will therefore be in the region of 40–45°C making the generator temperature 75–80°C: the collector will be a little hotter. This is rather high for a flat plate collector.

As the lift is a little greater than the depression, a rise of 1° in T_c results in a rise of about 2·5° at the generator. With an ambient temperature of 30°C, the use of water cooling might get the condenser temperature to 35°C or even lower: with air-cooling T_c would shoot up to well over 38°C in the summer, thereby requiring generator and collector temperatures considerably higher than 60°C. Thus, by using water cooling—which may not be too popular in some areas—and the highest possible evaporator temperature, it would be possible to consider flat plate collectors where otherwise these could not efficiently have been used.

The relationship of temperature lift to temperature depression makes it virtually impossible to operate a refrigerating cycle ($i.e.$ subzero temperatures) with a flat plate collector".

The COP of absorption cooling goes up with the temperature of the generator. The COP, in turn, determines the required size of the collector. For a reasonable COP, the utilization of solar energy to operate absorption air-conditioning requires at present a heat source at temperatures of 90–98°C, which calls for special and expensive solar collectors. Furthermore, the efficiency of the solar collectors goes down with increasing temperatures because of the increased heat loss. The use of absorption cooling can be greatly enhanced if an absorption system could be developed which works efficiently at lower generator temperatures, *e.g.* by using new working fluids.

An alternative approach for solar energy operated air-conditioning is to utilize solar generated heat to vaporize an organic fluid, *e.g.* R114, in a low temperature boiler of a Rankine cycle engine which in turn will drive the compressor of an ordinary air-conditioner [18.17]. However, there is almost no experience with such systems.

The following factors affect the performance of absorption space cooling, and for determining their quantitative effects additional research seems to be needed:

Intermittent versus continuous operation.
Temperatures of the generator, condenser and evaporator.
Hot-side and cold-side thermal storage.
Air cooling versus water cooling of the condenser.
The working fluids (*e.g.* HN_3–H_2O, $LiBr$–H_2O, etc.).
The need for, and effect on performance of, auxiliary electrical heating (off peak).
Problems resulting from irreversibilities due to temperature drops, pressure drops and mixing.

Solar dehumidification and cooling

An alternative approach to solar adsorption air-conditioning is the use of solar energy for dehumidifying, and subsequent cooling of the air. A system based on this approach has been proposed by Dannies [18.3]. According to this system outdoor air is passing over a bed of solid absorbents, located outside an external wall which is in the shade, on its way indoors. It will be the western wall in the forenoon and the eastern wall in the afternoon. In passing through the adsorbent bed the air is dried excessively, down to a very low relative humidity. The latent heat of condensation released during the adsorption raises the temperature of the adsorbent material, partly raises the temperature of the dry air and partly is transferred outdoors across the outside wall of the adsorbent bed to the cooler outdoor air. The warmed dry air passes over a surface of a water bath and is cooled and rehumidified to the comfortable level before entering the conditioned space in the room.

The room air, on its way outdoors, is passing over a second bed of adsorbent material which is heated by the sun (on the eastern side in the forenoon and on the western side in the afternoon). The solar heated bed has a high vapour pressure and the moisture is extracted by evaporation, regenerating the adsorbent material, to be utilized again later on. The room air can also be heated by solar radiation before entering the exhaust adsorbent bed, thus intensifying the regeneration process.

Tabor [18.16] has commented that such "open systems", in which water is added and subtracted from the atmosphere, involve heating a great mass of air, as well as the adsorbent and the water vapour. In consequence he estimates that the heat supply required for operation of the system is very large and the COP is of the order of 0·10–0·15.

Water evaporation and night convection for cooling of buildings [18.6, 18.7, 18.9, 18.19]

Water evaporation is being used extensively to cool the indoor air of buildings in arid regions (*e.g.* by desert-coolers). However, such systems have to be operated mainly during the day, when the cooling is mostly needed, and consequently have to cool large quantities of very hot air (in the range of 35–42°C). From the physiological viewpoint this approach is not always desirable for two reasons:

a. The cooled indoor air is excessively humid.
b. The high rate of air flow and air change which are necessary for effective cooling, cause very great variation in the air speed, and the associated thermal sensation, within the cooled building, in addition to the waste of energy to cool the air which is subsequently discharged to the outside.

Another possible approach to evaporative cooling is to obtain it during the night hours, sometimes in conjunction with longwave radiant cooling and convection, and to store the cold for daytime or continuous use.

The cooling medium can be water and the location where the

cooling takes place is usually over the roof. A special case of this approach is the roof pond with moveable insulation, where the water mass is stationary and the storage is located also over the roof [18.9, 18.10]. But it is possible to utilize the evaporative and radiative cooling effects to cool running water, which can be stored in the basement or inside the habitable space. From the storage space the cold water (or cold air) is circulated through the inhabited space to cool it [18.6, 18.19]. In this way the need for moveable insulation (which is the costliest item in roof ponds) is eliminated. This system can be applied to buildings with either inclined or flat roofs.

The utilization of evaporative cooling is limited to regions where water is available during the cooling season in quantities of about $0.3–0.5$ m^3 per day per dwelling unit and where the outdoor humidity is sufficiently low. Convective cooling can be effective where night temperatures in the summer are appreciably below the comfort zone, *i.e.* below 19°C and especially where wind speeds during the night are above 5 km/h.

Longwave outgoing radiative cooling is effective mainly from the roof surface, which is the area most exposed to the sky, and in regions with low vapour pressure and a clear sky. In many regions where summer cooling is the dominant requirement, this approach may provide the most practical way to cool houses of one to three storeys high.

Another approach, an air system, for utilizing night convection and radiation for cooling, is to draw air during the night through the storage medium, which in this case is a gravel bed. If the night temperature is not low enough the gravel can be sprinkled, to provide also evaporative cooling. During the day the cooled air from the storage space is circulated through the inhabited space. Such an approach can be applied in conjunction with an air system for solar heating during the winter.

18.7. Architectural Implications of Flat Plate Collectors

Roof mounted collectors

For low-rise buildings the most suitable location of flat plate collectors is over the roof of the building. Their architectural implications differ for flat roofs and for pitched roofs.

In the case of flat roofs the collectors cannot be constructed as an integral part of the roof structure, and consequently may cause aesthetic problems resulting from lack of blending of the collectors with the architectural character of the building, particularly when the facades of the building are not oriented in the position which is optimal for energy collection. However, it seems to the author that this problem could easily be solved by surrounding the roof with a parapet and by arranging the collectors in an orderly way, preferably forming continuous rows. When the orientation of the collectors coincides with that of the building, the blending of the collectors with the roof is, of course, much easier. In such a case the collectors may even be utilized as an architectural feature.

In the case of pitched roofs, the flat plate collectors can be either placed over the roof or form an integral part of it. An aesthetically satisfactory solution is possible only when the orientation of one of the planes of the roof is suitable for efficient collection of solar radiation.

Wall mounted flat collectors

In the case of high rise buildings the roof area may not be sufficient for collecting all the energy required, and use can be made of the southern wall for mounting flat plate collectors. Such collectors can either be attached to the wall or form an integral part of its structure. As the intensity of incident radiation on a southern wall is highest in winter and lowest in summer, such collectors can be used only for winter heating. The efficiency of vertical southern wall collectors increases with higher latitudes due to the lower elevation of the sun.

It is possible to design the collecting wall with an integral storage system. When the wall is a load bearing one, *e.g.* made of concrete with sufficient thickness, its external surface can be painted black, preferably attaching to it a selective black layer. One or two glass layers will render this wall into a combination of absorption and storage unit. In this situation the heat flow from the collecting surface into the storage medium is by direct conduction. This approach has been employed in the solar house built in France [18.22].

Such a system, however, suffers from an inherent drawback with respect to storage efficiency. The exposed area of the wall is very large relative to its heat capacity. Furthermore, the temperature gradient between the external surface and the outdoor air in winter is much greater than the gradient between the internal surface and the indoor air. As a result, a significant fraction of the stored energy is lost to the outdoor environment instead of being utilized to heat the interior of the building.

When the southern wall is not a load bearing one it is possible to construct an integral system of collection and storage by utilizing water (in a tank or in drums) as the storage medium [18.6]. In this way much more heat can be stored per unit volume of the storage space. Such a system could be comprised of ordinary flat plate collectors in front of an insulating layer with the water container behind the insulation.

Even when the orientation of the building block is not towards the south (or any other optimal direction), it is possible, in the design stage, to utilize wall mounted solar collectors by triangular projections from the facade, in which one side is facing the south. Such projections can serve as balconies or even as extensions of the area of the rooms.

Wall mounted collectors do not have to be vertical, because it is possible to mount them on horizontal projections protruding from the facade (*e.g.* canopies), in an inclined position, so as to maximize the incident solar radiation. Wall mounted solar collectors are particularly suitable for high rise buildings, where the area of the roof may be insufficient to supply all the heat required.

In all cases of wall mounted collectors the problem of repair and maintenance should not be overlooked and access to the collectors, either from its front side or from the rear, should be provided. Such access can be easily provided when the collectors are adjacent or below the windows. In this respect, a combination of windows and collectors, or of balconies and collectors, can be satisfactory.

Windows as solar collectors

As southern windows are desirable for both natural lighting and ventilation, the southern wall can be designed as a combination of collecting walls and windows [18.6]. If the windows are double glazed and provided with rollable, insulated shutters, they are in effect solar collectors which admit the sun energy directly and immediately into the inhabited space.

The penetrating solar radiation usually is impinging on the floor. Part of it is absorbed directly in the floor and the rest is reflected onto the other internal surfaces, partly absorbed and partly reflected, and so on. The air in the room is heated by contact with the heated floor, and that heat is partly removed by ventilation and partly transferred to the wall's material.

During the night, when the indoor air temperature is lowered below the level of the internal surfaces, the heat absorbed in the internal walls is released and heats the indoor air.

In consequence of this complex pattern of heat flow, the indoor air temperature is usually higher during the daytime than the internal wall's temperature. The air temperature may reach the upper limit of comfort and this may set the limit to the solar energy which can be collected through southern windows. This limitation can partly be overcome by forced circulation of the heated room air through a storage space, e.g. a gravel filled bin. In this way the excess heat from the daytime sunlight can be stored for use in the night or in a subsequent cloudy day.

The rise in the indoor air temperature depends on the ratio between the rate of penetration of solar radiation through the windows and the rate of heat transfer from the indoor air to the internal walls. This latter rate depends on several factors, such as the area of the surfaces enclosing the indoor space and the thermal conductivity and specific heat of the materials of the internal walls, as well as on the indoor surface coefficient. As the thermal conductivity and heat capacity of the materials of which the internal walls are made are higher—the temperature rise of the indoor air is smaller and more heat can be stored in the internal walls.

Concrete floors can serve as a major element of solar heat storage, especially when the floor colour is dark. Carpeting reduces greatly the rate and amount of solar heat absorption by the floor, and thus causes a rise in the air temperature.

Utilization of windows for the collection of solar energy, and of internal walls for its storage, provides an immediate heating effect, without the time lag which is characteristic of other systems of collection and storage, especially in the external walls. On the other hand, the storage capacity is limited by the small temperature range acceptable for the indoor air and the even smaller temperature range obtained at the internal walls. But in buildings of heavy weight construction, such as concrete, bricks or stone, the total mass of the building is so great that the actual quantities of stored heat can be very significant. If a maximum diurnal range of 5°C is assumed for the average temperature of the building, then for every ton of the building weight a quantity of about 1000 kcal can be stored.

There are problems concerning town planning regulations which will become important if and when the use of natural energies becomes widespread. For example, there is the need to protect a building heated by solar energy from being overshadowed by subsequent newly built nearby buildings or newly planted high trees on a site south to the building in question. Thus the problem of "sun-rights" may have to be dealt with legally.

18.8. Year Round Underground Storage of Solar Energy

Introduction

Most of the solar energy is available in summer while for heating applications it is needed in winter, when its collection potential is minimal. If solar energy is contemplated also as a heat source for absorption air conditioning, high temperatures are required in summer, more than those needed for heating in winter.

Therefore, a system which would enable collection of solar radiation in the spring and summer, in the form of thermal energy at high temperature, and use of it for heating in winter and for air conditioning in summer, would be very valuable.

In the following, a system is proposed for long term storage of solar energy in the underground.

The heat capacity of the ground is very large by any scale. With an average volumetric density of 1800 kg/m^3 and specific heat of 0·22, each cubic metre of the ground, or a rock bed, could store 400 kcal per 1°C temperature change.

In the spring season, when heating requirements are reduced, heat could be stored and the temperature of the storage medium elevated, for utilization in absorption air conditioning in summer. If, for instance, a depth of 10 m could be used for thermal storage, with an annual temperature range of 90–40°C, then every square metre of the storage area could store summer heat for winter use of about 200,000 kcal in addition to the heat used during the summer period.

Heat loss from such an underground reservoir can be rendered relatively small. When the storage is "charged" annually, the heat loss downwards will eventually become zero and, in effect, the layers underneath could serve as an additional reserve for very cold winters. Lateral heat loss to the periphery would decrease year after year, as the average temperature of the underground material surrounding the storage space is raised gradually. The heat loss upwards can be minimized by heavy insulation.

The difficulties in using the underground capacity for thermal storage are mainly with regard to the energy input into the ground in summer and its recovery in winter. In this respect there is a difference in the patterns of heat flow in the two seasons. In the spring and summer, when the reservoir is charged, the heat flow occurs for only several hours every sunny day, with withdrawal during the daytime for the air conditioning. On the other hand, in winter the withdrawal of the heat is a continuous process, accompanied during the days by additional heat inputs. These differences should be taken into account in the design of the system.

The thermal conductivity of the earth is rather low and therefore a large area is needed for the heat transfer between the ground and the energy transporting medium. Furthermore, there is a need to bypass the thermal resistance of the ground to heat flow perpendicular to the surface.

Because of the diurnal fluctuations in the energy needs it would be advantageous to have a storage system which would make it possible to draw heat from a medium with fast response which, in turn, is recharged more slowly from the main ground reservoir. A rock bed above the ground can serve for such regulating purposes.

Based on the above considerations, the following system is proposed for underground year round thermal storage.

Principles of design of an underground thermal storage

From the locational point of view the main factor to consider is the level of the underground water table. Any flow of the underground water will carry away effectively the heat stored underground. Therefore the best locations would be on small hills rising about 10 m or more above the surrounding area, or in other places where there is no likelihood of underground water flow.

It is possible to locate an underground thermal storage either as a separate structure, together with the solar collectors above it, or underneath any building of suitable size, with the collectors over the roof of the building. In the latter case high thermal insulation is needed between the storage and the lowest floor, as well as between the collectors and the upper floor, to minimize heating of the building in the summer.

When the storage is designed as a separate structure, it is suggested that the top layer of the earth is removed and piled like an embankment around the area of the storage, with the east and west wings sloping up to the north at an angle of about 20–30°, so that the northern wing would be higher than the southern wing. This embankment would serve as insulation, to minimize the lateral heat loss from the storage space, as well as to carry away the rain water.

The earth in the area allocated for the underground storage should be compacted as much as possible, to increase its thermal conductivity. Then holes, of a diameter of about 60 cm, should be drilled in the ground at distances of about 2–3 m, to any desired depth. The bottom of the holes should preferably be widened, like holes drilled for foundation piles. The enlarged space at the bottom of the holes should be filled with stones of uniform size of 5–10 cm. Steel pipes of a diameter of 10–20 cm should be inserted in the centres of the holes, and the whole space around them should be filled with gravel.

The pipes should be extended to a height of about 4 m above the ground level and connected to a main distribution duct network, delivering hot air from the solar collectors. The whole space inside the embankment should then be filled with rocks. The top layer of the rock bed should be filled with gravel and smoothed, to form a sloping plane serving as the basis for the absorbers.

In areas where drilling holes in the ground is expensive it is possible to utilize the rock bed as the whole storage space. In such a case the embankment should be higher, to provide the whole depth which is needed for the storage.

In this case the input of the heat could be achieved with horizontal steel pipes placed on the ground below the rock bed and connected to vertical pipes only at one point. Holes could be drilled in the horizontal pipes, or some distances could be left between the sections of the pipes, to facilitate the distribution of the hot air at the bottom of the rock bed.

Within the upper gravel layer, channels should be left for the main distribution ducts, which will be connected to the vertical steel pipes protruding down through the rock bed. The sloping plane formed by the gravel layer should then be covered with a concrete roof, which can serve as a platform on which to place the solar collectors.

It is proposed to use air-type collectors, from which the air will be delivered to the main distribution ducts and then to the vertical steel pipes.

Expected performance

A southern plane with a slope of 20–40 degrees receives annually in Israel, and in other regions with a similar climate, about 2,000,000 kcal/m^2/year. Even with an average collection efficiency of 30%, which is rather low, the thermal yield would be about 600,000 kcal/m^2/year.

Assuming a volumetric heat capacity of the ground to be on the average about 400 kcal/m^3/°C (with volumetric density of 1800 kg/m^3 and a specific heat of 0·22) and a temperature annual range of 40°C, then each square metre of the ground can store about 16,000 kcal/m depth of the storage space. With 5 m depth of the holes plus 5 m thickness of the gravel bed, about 160,000 kcal can be stored in a square metre of the storage area.

Such an annual temperature range can be obtained if the temperature of the collected air charged into the ground in late summer is about 90–100°C, when the outdoor air temperature is about 30°C.

To get a temperature difference of about 70°C, with a collection efficiency of 30% and radiation intensity of about 500 kcal/m^2/h, at least two panes of glass would be required. For the upper section of the collector, where the temperature difference is greatest, three panes of glass or the use of a selective surface might be desired.

With a storage temperature of about 90°C and outdoor temperature of 30°C, the potential for upwards heat loss is very large and a high thermal resistance is required to reduce it to an acceptable level. With a thermal resistance of about $3{\cdot}0 \; \dfrac{m^2 \times h \times {}^{\circ}C}{kcal}$, which corresponds to a layer of expanded polystyrene 10 cm thick, the rate of heat loss would be about 20 kcal/m^2/h or about 500 kcal/m^2/day. Actually, it would be necessary to consider insulating materials which could withstand such high temperatures.

Taking into account a smaller temperature difference in winter, when the heat is withdrawn and the storage temperature is lowered more than the outdoor air temperature, the annual heat loss upwards would be about 170,000 kcal/m^2, out of the collected amount of 600,000 kcal, or nearly 30%.

To minimize lateral heat loss from the periphery, insulation would be desired around the upper level of the periphery, to a depth of about 2 m. Below this level the gradual heating of the ground and its own thermal resistance would render the lateral heat loss very small, especially when a large area is allocated to the storage, and the ratio of the periphery to the total area is small.

Collected solar energy can be utilized also during the summer, e.g. for water heating or as initial heating for steam production and for absorption air conditioning. During the winter there is constant recharge of the storage during sunny days. For these reasons the annual turnover of the stored solar energy would be much larger than with winter utilization only.

Table 18.II

	(kcal/m^2/year)	
Impinging solar radiation	2,000,000	
Efficiency of collection	30%	40%
Collected energy	600,000	800,000
Upwards loss (resistance 3·0)	170,000	190,000
Lateral loss	80,000	90,000
Total loss	250,000	280,000
Total gain	350,000	520,000
Summer use	150,000	250,000
Winter use	200,000	270,000
Energy stored in summer for winter use	160,000	180,000

An expected annual performance of an underground thermal storage could be along breakup given in Table 18.II (per square metre of storage, with 10 m of total depth).

The energy cost of such a system involves the use of the fans needed to deliver the hot air from the collectors to the storage and from the storage to the inhabited spaces, as well as the circulation of the hot water.

No experimental data are available yet for the examination of the projected performance. However, from the theoretical analysis it seems that such a study would be worthwhile.

Architectural aspects of centralized underground storage

A centralized year round thermal storage may have an area of about 30 × 30 to 60 × 60 m and a height of 5–15 m above the surrounding ground level. As a result it forms a structure of considerable size, which might have significant visual impact.

It seems to the author that it is possible to utilize the slopes of the embankments surrounding the storage in several ways, for example:

A sloping garden. For such use of the slopes it is essential to ensure drainage of the water and prevention of their penetration into the underground. This can be achieved by an impervious layer, about 0·5 m below the surface of the top earth layer.
Bleachers for amphitheatres, stadiums, etc.
Low-rise terraced buildings.

Prediction of Indoor Temperature—The Influence of Thermophysical Parameters of Building Elements on Internal Thermal Environments

M. E. HOFFMAN

Building Research Station, Technion, Israel

Many different theoretical and experimental methods have been developed to predict internal temperature patterns in buildings. Some of these methods are described below.

19.1. Harmonic Analysis Method for Internal Surface Temperature Calculation

The problem of heat transfer through a solid was defined by J. Fourier [19.1] in the form of a differential equation, in three dimensions as follows:

$$\nabla (k \, \nabla t) = \rho c \frac{\partial t}{\partial \Theta} \tag{1}$$

The infinitesimal expression $\nabla (k \, \nabla t)$ at a certain place represents the residual heat between entering and leaving flow at this place as a consequence of the gradient of temperature ∇t. This gradient of temperature represents the temperature difference between this place and locations around it in each of the three dimensions. Each direction is characterized by its heat conductivity k.

This residue of heat produces a variation of heat content in time, $\rho c \dfrac{\partial t}{\partial \Theta}$ and, then, a variation of temperature $\dfrac{\partial t}{\partial \Theta}$ with time, where

k = thermal conductivity of the solid (kcal/m h °C)
t = temperature at point (x, y, z) at time Θ (h), (°C)
ρ = density of solid, (kg/m^3)
c = specific heat of the solid, (kcal/kg °C)

If an external building element, such as a wall is considered and a linear heat flow is assumed, the solid being homogeneous over its length, this equation may be written in the form:

$$\frac{\partial^2 t}{\partial x^2} = \frac{\rho c}{k} \frac{\partial t}{\partial \Theta} \tag{2}$$

where $\dfrac{k}{\rho c}$ is called the thermal diffusivity $\left(\dfrac{m^2}{h}\right)$.

For the external element, *e.g.* a wall, assuming a constant internal air temperature, the boundary conditions are:

$$-k \left(\frac{\partial t}{\partial x}\right)_{x=L} = h_{is} (t_{is} - t_{ia}), \text{ at the internal surface} \tag{3}$$

where

$$k \left(\frac{\partial t}{\partial x}\right)_{x=L}$$

represents heat flow at the surface $x = L$ as a consequence of temperature gradient $\dfrac{\partial t}{\partial x}$ to the solid, when k is the thermal conductivity of the solid. $h_{is} (t_{is} - t_{ia})$ represents heat flow by convection between the surface at temperature t_{is} and the contiguous air at temperature t_{ia}. h_{is} = heat transfer coefficient at the internal surface (kcal/m^2 h °C).

Similarly it can be defined at the external surface

$$-k \left(\frac{\partial t}{\partial x}\right)_{x=0} = h_{os} (t_{oa} - t_{os}) + \alpha I - I_{LT} \tag{4}$$

where αI represents solar radiation absorbed at the surface and I_{LT} is the long wave radiation exchange between the surface, the surroundings and, principally, the sky.

According to Mackey and Wright [19.3] the last equation may be written as:

$$-k \left(\frac{\partial t}{\partial x}\right)_{x=0} = h_{os} (t_{sa} - t_{os}) \tag{5}$$

Sol-air temperature, t_{sa}, may be analysed harmonically in terms of a Fourier series in the form:

$$t_{sa} = \bar{t}_{sa} + \sum_{n=1}^{\infty} t_{san} \cos (\omega_n \Theta - \gamma_n) \qquad (6)$$

where

$\bar{t}_{sa}$ = mean value of sol-air temperature

t_{san} = coefficients of successive harmonics

$\omega_n = \dfrac{2\pi n}{24}$, n is the ordinal number of the harmonics

γ_n = retardation of the harmonic with respect to midnight in radians.

Generally a small number of harmonics is more than sufficient for practical purposes. The complete solution for equations (2), (3), (5) and (6) has been given by Alford, Ryan and Urban [19.2] and according to Mackey and Wright [19.3] the inside wall surface temperature may be written:

$$t_{is} = t_{ia} + \frac{U}{h_{is}} (\bar{t}_{sa} - t_{ia}) + \sum_{n=1}^{\infty} \lambda_n t_{san} \cos (\omega_n \Theta - \gamma_n - \phi_n) \qquad (7)$$

where

U = overall conductance of the wall

$$= \left[\sum_{j=1}^{m} \left(\frac{L}{k} \right)_j + \frac{1}{h_{os}} + \frac{1}{h_{is}} \right]^{-1} \left(\frac{\text{kcal}}{\text{m}^2 \text{ h } °\text{C}} \right)$$

They proposed formulae given above in Chapter 6 in order to calculate ϕ_n and λ_n as functions of the product $k\rho c$ and the overall conductance of the wall when it is homogeneous.

According to Dreyfus [6.3] Mackey and Wright's formulae, for a non-homogeneous superposed slab wall or other external element, the decrement in wave amplitude for the nth harmonic may be calculated from:

$$\lambda_n = \exp \left(- \sqrt{\frac{\pi}{T} A^2 B} \right)_n \qquad (8)$$

where

$$T = \text{period of the harmonic } n$$
$$T = \frac{24}{n}$$

and the time-lag of the wave by the formula:

$$\phi_n = \frac{1}{2} \sqrt{\frac{T}{\pi} A^2 B} \tag{9}$$

where

$A^2 B$ is a sort of thermal time constant.

A and B were defined formerly (*see* Section 6.7) as follows:

A is the thermal resistance from the most external layer until the most internal layer of the element (or from surface to surface):

$$A = R_{ss} = \sum_{j=1}^{m} R_j$$

where

j is an ordinal number (index),
l is the most external layer,
m is the most internal layer,
$R_j = \dfrac{L_j}{k_j}$, when a solid slab is considered, or equal to the resistance
of an air space if an air space is considered.
L_j is slab j thickness,
ρ_j is slab j density,
c_j is slab j specific heat,
B, the "equivalent admittivity", is defined as follows:

$$B = \frac{1 \cdot 1}{A} \sum_{j=2}^{m} [R_j (k\rho c)_j] + \frac{(k\rho c)_1}{A} [R_1 - 0 \cdot 1A]$$

In Table 19.I the specific thermal properties of most common building materials are given. In Table 19.Ia the calculated values of the decrement factor and time lag for various types of homogeneous and composite common walls and roofs are given.

Table 19.I
Practical thermal properties of several building materials

Ref.	Component	ρ Specific weight $\dfrac{kg}{m^3}$	k Conductivity $\dfrac{kcal}{m\ h\ deg\ C}$	c^3 Specific heat $\dfrac{kcal}{kg\ deg\ C}$
(1)	Concrete (quality $\geq$ B160)	2350	1·75	0·2
(1)	Concrete (quality $\leq$ B120)		1·30	0·2
(1)	Cement mortar	1500	1·20	0·2
(1)	Lime mortar		0·75	0·2
(1)	Aerated and foamed	600	0·30	0·2
	concrete blocks and	800	0·35	0·2
	lightweight lime concrete blocks steam cured	1000	0·40	0·2
(1)	Plasterboard	1200	0·50	0·2
(1)	Cement mortar	1000	1·20	0·2
(2)	Face brick 10 cm	2000	"1·11"[4]	0·2
(2)	Common brick 10 cm	1600	"0·61"[4]	0·2
(2)	Hollow concrete rectangular core sand and· gravel agg. (20 cm)	1300	"0·87"[4]	0·2
(1)	Window glass (average value)		0·7	0·2
(1)	Asbestos-cement slabs	1800	0·3	0·2
(2)	Cellular glass	·144	0·050	0·2
(2)	Corkboard	104–128	0·036	0·42
(2)	Glassfibre	64–145	0·032	0·2
(2)	Expanded polystyrene, extruded	30	0·032	0·45
(2)	Expanded polyurethane (thickness 1 in and greater)	23–40	0·022	0·45
(2)	Expanded polystyrene, moulded beads	16	0·035	0·45
(1)	Mineral wool with resin binder	240	0·036	0·20
(1)	Mineral wool (glass, slag or rock)	32–80	0·037	

continues

Table 19.I—continued

(2)	Wood (maple, oak, and similar hard woods)	720	0·136	0·42
(2)	Soft woods	510	0·100	0·031
(1)	Wood fibre	51–58		
(1)	Stones			
	Dense (granite, basalt, marble, etc.)		3·0	0·2
	Porous (sandstone, shell lime, braccia, etc.)		2·0	0·2
(1)	Masonry building bricks	1900	0·9	0·2
(1)	Vertically perforated bricks		0·68	0·2
(1)	Solid facing bricks	1000	0·40	0·2
		1200	0·45	0·2
		1400	0·52	0·2
		1800	0·68	0·2

[1] As given in D.I.N. 4108.
[2] As given in ASHRAE. Handbook of Fundamentals 1967, at about 20°C.
[3] Approximated mean values.
[4] The value of "k" for an equivalent value, obtained from thermal resistance.

It may be seen that in a wall (or roof) composed of a heavy layer and a lightweight insulating layer, such as concrete with mineral wool or expanded polystyrene, the location of the insulation has a pronounced effect on the decrement factor. Thus for a composition of 10 cm concrete and 4 cm mineral wool, the placement of the insulation as an external layer results in a decrement factor of only 0·045, while when it is placed as an internal layer the factor is 0·45.

19.2. Thermal Time Constant Method for Amplitude Decrement and Time Lag of Internal Temperature Calculation

Another method for evaluating the total decrement in amplitude and the thermal performance of a structure by a single parameter, termed the thermal time constant, was proposed by Bruckmayer [19.4] from the analogy between the heat flow represented by a "thermal circuit", and the time constant of an electric circuit.

Table 19.Ia

Description of wall	l (thickness)		A	$\sqrt{B}$	$\phi_1 = 1.38\,A\sqrt{B}$	$\lambda_1 = \exp[-0.362\,A\sqrt{B}]$	TTC	$R_{ia\text{-}oa}$	U
Wood shingles (ext.) expanded polystyrene gypsum plasterboard	1 cm d cm→ 1 cm	2 cm 3 cm 4 cm 5 cm 8 cm 10 cm	0·61 0·90 1·18 1·44 2·32 2·90	2·06 2·11 2·16 2·20 2·34 2·42	1·73 h 2·62 3·50 4·36 7·50 9·65	0·64 0·50 0·39 0·32 0·14 0·08	1·9 h 2·9 3·6 4·5 7·5 9·7	0·80 1·09 1·37 1·63 2·51 3·09	1·25 0·92 0·73 0·61 0·40 0·32
Lightweight lime concrete steam cured, plastered on both sides (1 cm each)	20 cm+2×1 cm		0·70	7·1	6·8 h	0·167	14·1 h	0·89	1·12
	15 cm+2×1 cm		0·43		5·0 h	0·256	10·5 h	0·62	1·61
Concrete hollow blocks plastered on both sides (1 cm each)	30 cm+2×1 cm 20 cm+2×1 cm		0·414 0·23	15·2 15·8	8·6 h 5·2 h	0·105 0·256	23·7 h 10·0 h	0·60 0·42	1·22 2·38
Concrete wall cast on site 20 cm	20 cm		0·127	28·8	5·0 h	0·367	11·0 h	0·32	3·03
Concrete with external dense stone covering Air Hollow concrete blocks plastered inside	20 cm 5 cm 7 cm 2 cm		0·41	18·5	10·5 h	0·065	23·8 h	0·60	1·67

Description	Thickness							
Concrete with external dense stone covering	20 cm	0·63	17·1	14·8 h	0·030	18·4 h	0·82	1·22
Air	5 cm							
Lightweight lime conc. steam cured blocks	7 cm							
plastered inside	2 cm							
Face brick	10 cm	0·254	15·2	5·3 h	0·244	11·1 h	0·44	2·28
Common brick inside	10 cm							
Face brick	10 cm	0·54	12·0	9·0 h	0·102	11·4 h	0·73	1·37
Cement mortar	1·5 cm							
Common brick	10 cm							
Air space	5 cm							
Inside plasterboard	1 cm							
Face brick	10 cm	1·71	6·9	16·1 h	0·015	12·2 h	1·90	0·52
Cement mortar	1·5 cm							
Common brick	10 cm							
Expanded polystyrene	5 cm							
Inside plasterboard	1 cm							
Roof rockwool ext.	4 cm	1·11	7·2	11·8 h	0·046	53·5 h	1·30	0·77
concrete int.	10 cm							
Roof concrete ext.	10 cm	1·11	1·96	3·0 h	0·45	4·4 h	1·30	0·77
Rockwool int.	4 cm							

The thermal time constant is a function of the thermal diffusivity and is defined as the ratio:

$$\frac{\text{heat stored}}{\text{heat transmitted}} = \frac{Q}{U}; \quad Q\left(\frac{\text{kcal}}{\text{m}^2 \text{ deg C}}\right) \quad \text{is the heat content}$$

of the external element, a wall for example, per square metre of surface area, for an internal temperature 1°C greater than the external air temperature, and U (kcal/m^2 h °C) is the thermal transmittance.

The physical meaning of Q/U is the time taken in hours for the amount of stored heat to flow through the wall, assuming a constant rate of heat loss and a linear distribution of temperature inside the external element or wall [19.5].

By comparison with the time constant in an electric circuit, the thermal time constant of a multilayer wall is calculated as defined in Section 6.7 as follows:

$$\text{TTC} = Q/U = \sum_i (Q/U)_i \tag{10}$$

where

$$(Q/U)_i = (R_{os} + L_1/k_1 + \ldots + L_i/2k_i).(L_i \rho_i c_i)$$

In Table 19.Ia the thermal time constant for various types of common walls and roofs were calculated.

Raychoudhury et al. [19.6] found a nearly exponential relation between thermal damping (D) and TTC when D is defined as follows:

$$D = \frac{t_{oa} - t_{ia}}{t_{oa}} \quad \text{or} \quad D = \frac{t_{sol} - t_{ia}}{t_{sol}} \tag{11}$$

This exponential relationship can be seen in Fig. 19.4.

As referred to by Raychoudhury and Chaudhoury, Parson (1950) expressed the measure time-lag (t_{24}) between a harmonic temperature variation at the outer surface of a wall and the corresponding variation at the inner face (exposed to a constant temperature sink, i.e. the internal air temperature) as follows:

$$t_{24} = 1 \cdot 18 + \frac{2\pi}{24} \frac{Q}{U} \tag{12}$$

According to Raychoudhury and Chaudhury t_{24} and Q/U were found to correspond significantly only after $Q/U > 7$ in a linear form.

From Fig. 19.1 it is interesting to note that while a 4·5 in brick wall (No. 2) shows a thermal damping of 35%, an addition of outer cladding of 1 in "thermocole" insulation increases the damping to 86% (No. 5) whereas with an inner "thermocole" cladding (No. 6), the damping is only raised to 70%.

In other words the number representing the thermal time constant expresses significantly the insulating layer's position in an external element.

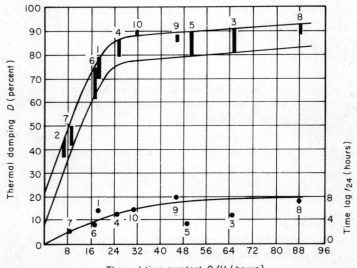

Fig. 19.1.   Relationship between the experimental thermal damping and time-lag values and the computed thermal time constants of various building components tested in experimental test rooms [19.6]. *WALLS:* 1—$\frac{1}{2}$ in plaster, 9 in brickwork, $\frac{1}{2}$ in plaster. 2—$\frac{1}{2}$ in plaster, 4$\frac{1}{2}$ in brickwork, $\frac{1}{2}$ in plaster. 3—$\frac{1}{2}$ in cement concrete plaster, 2 in JAX board, $\frac{1}{2}$ in plaster. 4—$\frac{1}{2}$ in plaster, 4$\frac{1}{2}$ in brickwork, 2 in air space, 4$\frac{1}{2}$ in brickwork, $\frac{1}{2}$ in plaster. 5—1 in plaster over wire netting, 1 in thermocole, 4$\frac{1}{2}$ in brickwork, $\frac{1}{2}$ in plaster. 6—$\frac{1}{2}$ in plaster, 4$\frac{1}{2}$ in brickwork, 1 in thermocole, 1 in plaster over wire netting. *ROOFS:* 7—6$\frac{1}{2}$ in reinforced concrete cement (RCC), $\frac{1}{2}$ in plaster. 8—1$\frac{1}{2}$ in cement concrete, 2 in JAX board, 4$\frac{1}{2}$ in RCC, $\frac{1}{2}$ in plaster. 9—1$\frac{1}{2}$ in cement concrete, 2 in vermiculite concrete, 4$\frac{1}{2}$ in RCC, $\frac{1}{2}$ in plaster. 10—$\frac{1}{4}$ in (water proofing compound, charcoal paper), 1 in thermocole, 2 in shell roof, $\frac{1}{2}$ in plaster.

In the calculation of the thermal time constant neither the external conditions nor the internal ventilation are taken into account. Mackey and Wright's calculation does not take these conditions into account either. Both methods permit the comparison of structures and materials when there is no internal ventilation.

19.3. The Method of Matrices

Another mathematical method, developed by van Gorcum [19.7], transforms input to output values of temperature and heat flow of a building element, representing the thermophysical properties of each building element by the coefficients of a square matrix.

The coefficients of these transfer matrices are computed as known in electric circuit theories (Kirchhoff laws) by considering similar concepts in series and in parallel thermal immittance.

Muncey [19.8] used this method, in successive publications after the year 1953, taking into account periodic and transient heat flow.

The two linear equations that relate input and output values, similar to that of a two-port electric network in assuming linear heat transmission and none or very little loss at the corners, are:

$$t_{os} = At_{is} + Bq_{is}$$

$$q_{os} = Ct_{is} + Dq_{is.} \tag{13}$$

where

t_{os} = temperature at the surface $x = 0$,
q_{os} = the heat flow at the face $x = 0$,
t_{is} = the temperature at the face $x = L$,
q_{is} = the heat flow at the face $x = L$.

This system of equations may be written in matrix form

$$\begin{bmatrix} t_{os} \\ q_{os} \end{bmatrix} = \begin{bmatrix} A & B \\ C & D \end{bmatrix} \begin{bmatrix} t_{is} \\ q_{is} \end{bmatrix} \tag{14}$$

t and q are supposed to be complex terms of harmonic functions at a particular frequency $\omega/2\pi$ with real parts representing temperature and heat flow as a function of time.

The successive transfer matrix coefficients are functions of thermophysical properties of building elements, as follows:

$$A_n = \cosh (1+i)\phi_n$$

$$B_n = R\frac{\sinh (1+i)\phi_n}{(1+i)\phi_n}$$

$$C_n = \frac{(1+i)\phi_n}{R} \sinh (1+i)\phi_n$$

$$D_n = A_n$$

$$\phi_n = \sqrt{\frac{\omega_n CR}{2}} \qquad \omega_n = \frac{2\pi n}{24}$$

L = thickness of the element

$R = \dfrac{L}{k}$ thermal resistance of the element

$C = L\rho c$ heat capacity per unit of area

$$i = \sqrt{-1}; \qquad \sqrt{2i} = (1+i)$$

each term of the several harmonic functions must be multiplied by an exponential time factor $e^{i\omega\theta}$, accounting for transient-state values. Since we are interested in periodic steady-state values, this factor may be not taken into account, as is customary in electric-circuit theory.

Muncey [19.8] used the matrix notation in order to solve the problem for several slabs in series, and several paths for transmission of heat, the elements of which have a small thickness compared to the area (assuming little lateral heat transfer).

According to Dreyfus [19.10] the nth harmonic of the internal temperature, when wall surfaces consist partially of shaded glass, may be given as a function of the nth harmonic of the external air ($t_{oa,n}$) and that of the sol-air radiation component ($t_{sol,n}$) as follows:

$$t_{ia,n} = \frac{\sum_s t_{oa,n}\frac{S_s}{R_0} + \sum_s \left(t_{sol,n}\frac{A_s}{B_n}\right)_s + \sum_s t_{oa,n}\left(\frac{A_s}{B_n}\right)_s + W_n}{\sum_s A_s\left(\frac{A_n}{B_n}\right)_s + \sum_s A_s\left(\frac{C_n}{D_n}\right)_s} \qquad (15)$$

If W_n takes into account ventilation, it is equal to $(t_{oa,n}NVC')$. In this case, the denominator includes a term NVC' as well where,

A_n, B_n, C_n, D_n = above defined matrix elements
$\qquad\qquad R_0$ = thermal resistance of glass from air to air
$\qquad\qquad C'$ = volumetric heat capacity of air
$\qquad\qquad V$ = air volume
$\qquad\qquad N$ = number of air changes per hour
$\qquad\qquad W_n$ may take into account other internal variable heat inputs
$\qquad\qquad s$ = number of the wall.

The solar radiation entering through fenestration is considered as internal varying heat input (a W component too).

Heat resistance and capacity of the common thin glass window panel are not considered because they are relatively small:

S_s = area of glass on wall "s"
A_s = area of wall "s"
$t_{sol,n}$, is the contribution of solar radiation to sol-air temperature
$t_{oa,n}$, is the nth harmonic of external air temperature
$\dfrac{A_s}{B_n}$, is related to the path connected to the outside of the building (both are matrix coefficients as defined above)
$\dfrac{C_n}{D_n}$, is related to internal paths (internal walls or partitions) only, both are matrix coefficients as defined above.

The first term of the series representing internal temperature is:

$$t_{ia} = \frac{\sum_s t_{oa}\dfrac{S_s}{R_0} + \sum_s t_{sol}\dfrac{A_s}{R_s} + \sum_s t_{oa}\dfrac{A_s}{R_s} + \sum \bar{W}}{\sum_s \dfrac{A_s}{R_s}} \qquad (16)$$

where R_s is the total heat resistance of the walls and $\Sigma \bar{W} = t_{oa}NVC'$ + constant heat input or mean in case of varying heat input.

Muncey found good agreement between calculated results and experimental measured values comparing internal temperature of small models, placed in a room the temperature of which was varied cyclically.

However, poor agreement was evident from calculated and measured temperatures, as obtained for actual sized enclosures, by Gupta *et al.* [19.9] using this method, assuming no heat radiation exchange between the internal surfaces of the walls.

Hyperbolic function tables have been prepared by D. G. Stephenson [19.13] to facilitate the computation of the elements of the matrices.

By the matrix method, it is easier to calculate temperature and heat flow for multilayer walls than by the Mackey and Wright formulae. Also internal air temperatures can be calculated, whilst in the case of Mackey and Wright's formulae internal surface temperatures are calculated assuming the internal air to be at a constant temperature.

Muncey and Gupta *et al.* represented heat transfer by convection and radiation at the inside surface by a single coefficient relating an internal surface to the internal air. Heat transfer by radiation from one wall to another may be taken into account for W_n terms.

Computation by matrix methods

The matrix method was developed and written for electronic digital computers by Holden [19.11] for a CSIRAC computer and by Rao and Chandra [19.12] for an IBM 1620 one in Fortran Language.

The purpose of the two methods is different. Holden's programme directly calculates the values of internal temperatures, synthesizing the obtained harmonic components. The harmonic components are calculated in terms of the respective Fourier components of external temperatures and in terms of the building parameters (calculated as matrix transfer coefficients of the enclosure).

In the first step the corresponding complex values $\dfrac{A_n}{B_n}$ and $\dfrac{1}{B_n}$ or $\dfrac{C_n}{D_n}$ are calculated for the successive harmonic terms. Raychoudhury *et al.* [19.14] used this method and computed these values for three harmonics. They considered the enclosure as a cube defined by six

428 MAN, CLIMATE AND ARCHITECTURE

walls and also their interaction. Digital computers allow for more
than three harmonics without great difficulty.

In the second step, the Fourier harmonic analysis is applied for
the external conditions of temperature and solar radiation, considering the steady periodic case only, *i.e.* the external conditions are
considered to repeat themselves endlessly.

In the third step, values of internal temperatures obtained by
equation (15) for different harmonics are calculated by Fourier
harmonic synthesis.

Small differences were found by Muncey and Holden [19.15]
comparing calculated values with measured internal temperatures.
For external temperatures with diurnal ranges of 60°F, the discrepancies in the comparison were of the order of 1°F or less.

Rao and Chandra calculate "thermal systems functions". These
functions are composed of transfer and driving point functions,
computed in terms of transfer matrix coefficients and surface heat
transfer coefficient. From the thermal system functions it is possible
to determine the thermal frequency response characteristics (amplitude decrement and phase-lag) for each harmonic component of
building sections for designing.

Rao and Chandra computed these functions for a large number
of constructions commonly in use, in order to enable easy reference
for predicting indoor air temperatures and air conditioning loads, for
any combination of building sections, under any climatic conditions.
They designed a program for this purpose which takes the basic
thermophysical properties (conductivity, specific heat and density),
the thickness and the surface heat transfer coefficients (h_0 and h_i) as
the input data.

19.4. The Finite Difference Representation for Temperature and Heat Transfer Equations in Buildings

Assuming linear heat flow in solid homogeneous slabs, the
Fourier equation:

$$\nabla k \, \nabla t = \rho c \frac{\partial t}{\partial \Theta} \tag{17}$$

is written in the form:

$$k \frac{\partial^2 t}{\partial x^2} = \rho c \frac{\partial t}{\partial \Theta} \tag{18}$$

In a difference form it can be written, for two consecutive homogeneous internal slabs in a wall, as follows:

$$\frac{\text{Area}_{N+1}}{R_{N+1}} (T_{N+1}{}^M - T_N{}^M) - \frac{\text{Area}_N}{R_N} (T_N{}^M - T_{N-1}{}^M)$$

$$= \left(\text{Area}_N \rho_N c_N \frac{d_N}{2} + \text{Area}_{N+1} \rho_{N+1} c_{N+1} \frac{d_{N+1}}{2} \right) \frac{T_N{}^{M+1} - T_N{}^M}{\Delta \Theta} \tag{19}$$

where $[T_N{}^{M+1} - T_N{}^M]$ is the variation of temperature at the intersurface N in the interval $\Delta \Theta$ between time M and time $M + 1$, as a consequence of the temperature gradient at the intersurfaces $N - 1$, N and $N + 1$, at a distance of d_N between them. R_N is the thermal resistance between intersurfaces $(N-1)$ and (N), ρ_N is the density of this slab and c_N its specific heat.

The solution of this equation for $T_N{}^{M+1}$ at the intersurface N is the form of:

$$T_N{}^{M+1} = A_N T_{N+1}{}^M + B_N T_N{}^M + C_N T_{N-1}{}^M \tag{20}$$

where

$$A_N = \frac{\text{Area}_{N+1}}{R_{N+1}} \frac{\Delta \Theta}{D_N}$$

$$C_N = \frac{\text{Area}_N}{R_N} \frac{\Delta \Theta}{D_N}$$

$$B_N = 1 - (A_N - C_N)$$

$$D_N = \text{Area}_N \rho_N c_N \frac{d_N}{2} \tag{21}$$

R_N is the thermal resistance between the intersurfaces $(N-1)$ and (N), then $R_N = d_N/k_N$, or the thermal resistance due to convection or radiation or both at the surface N if it is the surface in contact with the air.

When N is the internal surface of the wall, facing an enclosure, mechanical heating or cooling of the internal air and the infiltration of the external air into the enclosure can be considered.

When N is the external surface, it is possible to take into account shortwave radiation (from the sun, the sky and that reflected) absorbed at the surface, and longwave radiation exchange with the sky and the ground.

Buchberg et al. [19.19, 19.20, 19.21] used a digital computer with this difference-representation for calculation of changing values of internal temperatures for each slab of each wall all over the structure. The several values of temperatures T_N are calculated by successive computations on the basis of the three temperature groups T_{N-1}, T_N and T_{N+1} previously obtained through the structure, and recycling them for consecutive values Θ of the time by an iteration method.

19.5. Analogue Methods

The method of matrices depicted above was used previously by many authors to design analogue electric computers for heat transfer systems.

Many analogue computers have been built for this purpose. An electric circuit the matrix of which form a two-port electrical network was designed and is used by Vagn Korsgaard [19.16]. Other authors simulate the thermal behaviour of a slab with one-dimensional heat flow by a general resistance–capacitance network. Voltages represent temperatures, and currents represent heat flow. The corresponding electric circuit has the same matrix coefficients as transmission slab matrix [19.17, 19.18].

Other analogue models of the transient phenomena were designed using the Difference Representation. In an electrical analogue, voltages are equivalent to temperature, current to heat-flow per unit time, resistivity to thermal resistivity and capacitance to thermal capacity. Hydraulic analogues may be used as well, the hydraulic resistance being equivalent to thermal resistance, the pressure difference to temperature-difference and the storage capacity to thermal capacity [Leopold, 19.28]. Most publications deal with cooling load estimation [19.22, 19.23, 19.24, 19.25, 19.26].

Because of the inflexibility of the analogue models, some research workers abandoned these methods [19.19].

Buchberg *et al.* worked out basic programs for electronic digital computers. After the year 1964 [19.19, 19.20, 19.21] all their work on environmental design was done in this way, while previous work was done with analogue computers.

19.6. The Response Factor Method*

The response factor method was developed and used by Stephenson and Mitalas [19.41], Mitalas and Arsenault [19.42] and by Kusuda [19.43], in order to evaluate the heat conducted through multilayer building elements under transient (non-steady and non-steady periodic) exposure conditions, utilizing the superposition principle for heat transfer paths and for responses from preceding times.

Rao and Chandra [19.12] wrote explicitly Holden's equations for heat flux in both sides of a slab and defined a system of complex decrement coefficients called "thermal system functions" for each harmonic component of input functions. Stephenson and Mitalas analyse input data in the form of triangular pulses inputs and the response factors are then decay factors for trains of triangular pulses. Kusuda analysed the input values in the form of finite increments transforming them so into a train of trapezoidal pulses. The response factors are then decay factors for trains of trapezoidal pulses.

According to the response factor method, the heat flux at a given time t at the outer as well as the inner surfaces of building elements exposed to the outdoors ($Q_{o,t}$ and $Q_{i,t}$ respectively) can be calculated as follows:

$$Q_{o,t} = \sum_{j=0}^{\infty} T_{o,t-j} X_j - \sum_{j=0}^{\infty} T_{i,t-j} Y_j \tag{22}$$

$$Q_{i,t} = \sum_{j=0}^{\infty} T_{o,t-j} Y_j - \sum_{j=0}^{\infty} T_{i,t-j} Z_j \tag{23}$$

where integrations are done until the moment t, when $j = 0$.

* This subchapter is partially adapted from ASHRAE, 1972, Fundamentals, pp. 355 and 356.

$T_{o,t-j}$ and $T_{i,t-j}$ are outdoor and indoor temperatures values (or outside surface and inside surface temperature, depending upon the heat conduction system) considered as pulses applied at time j hours before t, on the hourly basis. The response factors are three sets of numbers X_j, Y_j and Z_j, applied as decay factors, j hours after the pulses of temperature were applied.

Response factor units are the same as the units for the heat transfer coefficient U. As a matter of fact, when steady state heat conduction situation is considered (*i.e.* when input and output heat flux at outside surface and inside surface are equal, because no heat capacity effect is considered), application of the response factor relations to a steady state heat conduction situation transforms the above equation to the following forms:

$$Q_{o,t} = Q_{i,t} = U(T_o - T_i) \tag{24}$$

and

$$T_o = T_{o,t} \quad \text{for all } t$$

$$T_i = T_{i,t} \quad \text{for all } t$$

then

$$\sum_{j=0}^{\infty} X_j = \sum_{j=0}^{\infty} Y_j = \sum_{j=0}^{\infty} Z_j = U. \tag{25}$$

In order to decrease the maximum number of j, the hourly heat flux history can be added to the temperature history as follows:

$$Q_{o,t} = \sum_{j=0}^{m} T_{o,t-j} X_j = \sum_{j=0}^{m} T_{i,t-j} Y_j - Q_{o,t-m} f_m$$

$$Q_{i,t} = \sum_{j=0}^{m} T_{o,t-j} Y_j - \sum_{j=0}^{m} T_{i,t-j} Z_j - Q_{i,t-m} g_m \tag{26}$$

i.e. the past values of the output are used as input.

In this form, the time of integration is reduced, an important fact when computation is needed, and the number of response factors to be determined is shorter. Stephenson and Mitalas found that m small or equal to 5 is usually sufficient for most building walls response factors when the transient heat conduction is calculated on the hourly basis.

***Table* 19.II**

Tabulation of illustrative wall response factors

Thickness, L (ft)	Thermal conductivity, k (Btu/h) (ft)(F)	Density, ρ (lb/ft³)	Specific heat, c (Btu/(lb F))	Resistance of air layer (h)(ft²)(F) (Btu)	Wall composition
1				0·3333	Outside surface
2 0·3333	0·77	125	0·22		4 in face brick
3				0·842	¾ in air space
4 0·1667	0·025	5·7	0·3		2 in insulation
5 0·0313	0·24	78	0·26		¾ in gypsum bd
6 0·042	0·27	90	0·2		½ in plaster
7				0·833	Inside surface

Overall heat transfer coefficient $U = 0.1060$ (Btu per (h) (ft²) (F))

i	X	Y	Z
0	1·9828631184	0·0000694414	0·7658454069
1	−0·5332548902	0·0032610373	−0·3626101180
2	−0·2897180964	0·0108381158	−0·1594774346
3	−0·2226418777	0·0143821960	−0·0722106733
4	−0·1751782415	0·0141359305	−0·0330527494
5	−0·1381393441	0·0124128118	−0·0153907015
6	−0·1089910981	0·0103599746	−0·0073676305
7	−0·0860172059	0·0084293880	−0·0036792673
8	−0·0678956034	0·0067667191	−0·0019496245
9	−0·0535962455	0·0053921814	−0·0011124022
10	−0·0423104538	0·0042793546	−0·0006875056
11	−0·0334020244	0·0033884423	−0·0004575496
12	−0·0263696421	0·0026795634	−0·0003231437
13	−0·0208180261	0·0021174509	−0·0002380978
14	−0·0164352751	0·0016725725	−0·0001803688
15	−0·0129752460	0·0013208578	−0·0001389992
16	−0·0102436541	0·0010429664	−0·0001082184
17	−0·0080871331	0·0008234788	−0·0000847576
18	−0·0063846118	0·0006501542	−0·0000666111
19	−0·0050405105	0·0005132985	−0·0000524525
20	−0·0039793727	0·0004052451	−0·0000413496
21	−0·0031416279	0·0003199354	−0·0000326175
22	−0·0024802469	0·0002525834	−0·0000257387
23	−0·0019581009	0·0001994098	−0·0000203148
24	−0·0012204372	0·0001242877	−0·0000126587
25	−0·0012204372	0·0001242877	−0·0000126587
26	−0·0009635087	0·0000981225	−0·0000099933
27	−0·0007606692	0·0000774656	−0·0000078893
28	−0·0006005318	0·0000611574	−0·0000062283

Common ratio for $\dfrac{X_{j+1}}{X_j} = \dfrac{Y_{j+1}}{Y_j} = \dfrac{Z_{j+1}}{Z_j} = R$ for $j > 28$

$R = 0.7894782424$

Computer programs have been developed by Mitalas and Arsenault and by Kusuda to calculate response factors from known data, such as the number of composite layers, and for each layer the thermal conductivity, the thermal diffusivity, and the thickness (in the case of an air cavity or air space, only the thermal resistance value is required). The program developed from Kusuda's work [19.43] can also be used to calculate response factors for constructions of cylindrical and spherical shape.

The response factors for a given wall are seen in Table 19.II. The geometrical and heat transfer properties of the wall are given at the head of the table. It is seen that for this particular wall, the response factors for $j > 28$ can be obtained by geometric progression using the common ratio R, as explained in the table.

19.7. The Equivalent Thermal Mass Response Factors Method (an Experimental Method)

Kusuda et al. [19.44] proposed a semi-empirical method for calculating thermal response factors. This method uses an approximated finite difference solution of a differential equation representing the equivalent thermal mass system. Room temperature is predicted using building response factors based upon one parameter, a thermal time constant, provided that the building is subjected only to an outdoor temperature fluctuation. Response factors can be derived from experimental data or from data calculated using an analytical procedure.

The Building Thermal Time Constant is proved in an iterative way until the minimum root mean square value of the deviation between the internal temperature calculated from the finite difference approach (using iteratively the various Thermal Time Constant values) and the measured values or the computed by analytical procedure values, is obtained.

19.8. The Total Thermal Time Constant

A further development of Bruckmayer's thermal time constant concept was given by Raychoudhury [19.29], Chaudhury and Warsi

[19.31, 19.32] and Pratt and Ball [19.33, 19.34]. This is the thermal time constant as a unique thermophysical parameter representing the thermal response of the whole building.

They calculated the internal temperature response solving heat transfer differential equations of the enclosure including heat transfer by ventilation from the outside air. The solutions are obtained as a sum of harmonics in their exponential form in time. Thermal time constant of the enclosure is then defined as the time in which the internal temperature response so obtained rises to 0·6321 (equal to $1 - e^{-1}$) of its final steady state value provided that the external excitation is a unit step function of temperature (for instance from 0 to 1 degree) through all its heat transfer paths. This way is analytically accurate but involves laborious calculation.

Givoni and Hoffman [19.35] developed further the thermal time constant concept for an enclosure, extending Bruckmayer's electric circuit analogy, considering a sink of heat in an internal mass, if any, in the interior of the building, as a thermal condenser.

Bruckmayer defined the thermal time constant of a wall as "the heat stored in the wall per unit of heat transmitted through it". Hoffman [19.36] defined the total thermal time constant of an enclosure (TTTCB), as "the heat stored in the whole enclosure (including the internal air) per unit of heat transmitted to or from the outside through the elements surrounding the enclosure and by ventilation".

In this case, the total thermal time constant so defined measures the ability of the enclosure to admit and to store heat. The shorter the thermal time constant, the smaller the heat flux needed to achieve a unit variation of temperature. The larger it is, the bigger is the heat flux needed to achieve a unit variation of temperature.

The thermal time constant for a wall, according to Bruckmayer, as defined above, is:

$$\text{TTC wall} = \left(\frac{Q}{U}\right)_{\text{wall}} = \sum_{j=i}^{i} \left(\frac{Q}{U}\right)_j, \qquad (27)$$

where i is the index for the wall's most internal layer and, for the layer j:

$$\left(\frac{Q}{U}\right)_j = \left[R_{\text{os}} + \left(\frac{L}{k}\right)_1 + \left(\frac{L}{k}\right)_2 \dots \left(\frac{L}{k}\right)_{j-1} + \frac{1}{2}\left(\frac{L}{k}\right)_j\right](L\rho c)_j \quad (28)$$

(see thermal time constant values calculated for several walls in Table 19.Ia).

Considering this heat path to achieve an internal mass, the total thermal time constant (TTTC) for this heat transfer path until the internal mass is:

$$TTTC = TTC_{wall} + Q_{i\ mass}\ (R_{wall} + R_{si} + \tfrac{1}{4} R_{i\ mass}) \qquad (29)$$

where the heat capacity of the internal mass is

$Q_{i\ mass} = \tfrac{1}{2}$ (weight of internal mass per unit of external surface)
$\times$ (specific heat)

R_{wall}, is the thermal resistance of the wall from the external air until the internal surface,

R_{si}, is the internal surface thermal resistance, and

$R_{i\ mass}$, is the thermal resistance of the internal mass.

Considering all the external input functions to be equal, the total thermal time constant of a whole enclosure was defined as:

$$TTTCB = \frac{\sum\limits_{K} A_K\ (TTTCK)}{\sum\limits_{K} A_K}$$

$$+ Q_{i\ mass} \left(\frac{\sum\limits_{K} A_K R_K}{\sum\limits_{K} A_K} + R_{si} + \frac{1}{4} R_{i\ mass} \right), \qquad (30)$$

where

K identifies the wall,

A_K is the area of wall K surface and $\Sigma_K A_K$ the total external surface area of the enclosure.

If the internal mass is air and all the external elements K are identical, then the TTTCB equals almost the thermal time constant of the identical element, calculated according to Bruckmayer (because of the relative insignificant value of air heat capacity).

If ventilation is considered, Hoffman defined [19.39]:

$$\text{TTTC with ventilation} = \frac{(\text{TTTCB})\,U_\text{T}}{U_\text{T} + N(\rho c)_\text{air}\,\dfrac{V}{A_\text{K}}} \qquad (31)$$

where

U_T is the equivalent overall heat transfer coefficient from the internal mass through the different external elements up to the external air,

N is the number of air changes,

$(\rho c)_\text{air}$ is the heat capacity of air,

V is the internal volume of the room.

The thermal time constant of enclosures given by Raychoudhury, Chaudhury and Warsi, and Pratt and Ball, were recalculated according to the formulae of the total thermal time constant and correspondences can be seen in Table 19.III.

In case the total thermal time constant of an interior partition, internal ceiling or internal floor facing a room and closing its space is needed, the TTTC of this element is calculated from the immediate external element until the partition's slab near the room. If there are more than one external elements on the other side of the partition (e.g. two walls or more) each such external element K is considered to start a new heat transfer path to the partition's slab near the room, independently.

19.9. External Surface Temperature Calculation of Walls; Considering Heat Capacity, Solar Radiation Absorptivity and Longwave Radiation Interchange (Total Thermal Time Constant Method)

Figure 19.2 shows measurements of the external surface temperature patterns of horizontal plates made of different building materials exposed to natural conditions at the Technion's Building Research Station laboratories.

To overcome the difficulty of using the sol-air temperature concept for heat transfer calculations on the external surface, Givoni and Hoffman [19.37] developed a new method, where heat transfer properties of the board under the surface as conductance and heat

Table 19.III

Recalculation of some enclosures thermal time constant

Description of enclosure's walls (from Ref.)		TTTC according to eqns (30) and (31)	Exact TTC (from Ref.)	Reference
(1) 6 identical walls	brick 11·2 cm	4·7	4·0	Choudhuri and Warsi [19.31]
(2) 5 identical walls + internal wall	brick 11·2 cm brick 22·4 cm	9·35	8·38	Choudhuri and Warsi [19.31]
(3) Same as 1 + int. insulation (2·5 cm foam plastic)		4·82	4·80	Choudhuri and Warsi [19.31]
(4) Same as 2 + int. insulation (2·5 cm foam plastic) + internal wall	brick 22·4 cm	16·92	16·20	Choudhuri and Warsi [19.31]
(5) 6 identical walls	brick 22·4 cm	14·70	14·30	Choudhuri and Warsi [19.31]
(6) 5 identical walls + internal wall	brick 22·4 cm brick 22·4 cm	20·30	18·80	Choudhuri and Warsi [19.31]
(7) 6 identical cavity walls	brick 27·4 cm	21·1	17·8	Choudhuri and Warsi [19.31]
(8) 5 identical cavity walls + internal wall	brick 27·4 cm brick 24·4 cm	28·0	24·4	Choudhuri and Warsi [19.31]

(9) Same as 1 + ext. insulation (2·5 cm foam plastic)	42·8	45·2	Choudhuri and Warsi [19.31]
(10) Same as 2 + ext. insulation (2·5 cm foam plastic) + internal wall, brick 22·4 cm	54·9	53·3	Choudhuri and Warsi [19.31]
(11) 6 identical walls, brick 22·86 cm	15·10	15·50	Raychoudhuri [19.29]
(12) 6 identical walls, brick 11·43 cm	4·76	4·90	Raychoudhuri [19.29]
(13) 5 identical walls + internal concrete wall, brick 11·43 cm, brick 5 cm	5·43	5·72	Raychoudhuri [19.29]
(14) 5 identical walls + internal concrete wall, brick 11·43 cm, brick 30·5 cm	7·82	7·02	Raychoudhuri [19.29]
(15) *Ibid.* + 4 air changes/h, Int. vol. / Ext. surf. $= \dfrac{V}{\Sigma A_K} = 0\cdot061$ m	6·82	6·86	Raychoudhuri [19.29]
(16) *Ibid.* + 4 air changes/h, Int. vol. / Ext. surf. $= \dfrac{V}{\Sigma A_K} = 0\cdot61$ m	5·52	5·71	Raychoudhuri [19.29]
(17) *Ibid.* + 4 air changes/h, Int. vol. / Ext. surf. $= \dfrac{V}{\Sigma A_K} = 6\cdot1$ m	1·89	1·78	Raychoudhuri [19.29]

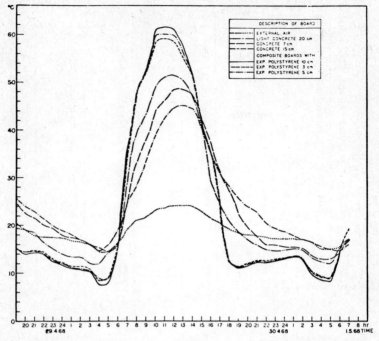

Fig. 19.2. External surface temperature of boards of different materials measured simultaneously [19.37].

capacity, as well as longwave radiation interchange between the surface and the outerspace through the sky, are considered too.

External surface temperatures are calculated from the net radiation exchange obtained between the solar radiation, its diffused component from the sky and that reflected from the environs and the longwave radiation from the surface to the outerspace through the sky, according to formulation developed by the authors [19.35, 19.36, 19.37, 19.39].

The surface temperature of element K, at time i is calculated as follows:

$$t_{sk}(i) = t_{oa}(i) + \sum_{j=i_0}^{i} \frac{1}{\dfrac{1}{R_{os}} + \dfrac{1}{R_s} \exp\left(-\dfrac{i-j}{TTCK}\right)}$$
$$\times \Delta \{\alpha I_{sk}(j) + \sigma T_{oa}^{4}(j)\, [a + bP_w^{\frac{1}{2}}(j) - F\varepsilon]\}_j, \qquad (32)$$

where

$$R_s = \frac{\text{TTCK}}{\sum\limits_{n} L_n \rho_n c_n} \tag{33}$$

TTCK is the thermal time constant of the element K, calculated according to Bruckmayer (see Section 19.8).

$\sum_n L_n \rho_n c_n$ is the heat capacity per unit of external surface of the element K, from its external to its internal layer n

t_a is the air temperature in centigrade

$T_a = t_a + 273°$ is air absolute temperature in Kelvin degrees

P_w is the partial water vapour pressure in the air, mm Hg

ε is the emissivity of the surface (currently, ε is near to 1, about 0·92, for building materials external surface, out of bright polished metals, which commonly are covered with dust—with emissivity as above—especially if they are horizontal or inclined surfaces).

F, correcting operative factor

$F = \left(1 + \dfrac{t_s - t_0}{T_{oa}}\right)^4$, is obtained in an iterative form

j = index of integration (time), i_0, i = limits of integration (time)

In this equation, R_s and TTCK represent the thermophysical properties of the building material under the surface, R_{os} the heat transfer properties at the surface (which depends on the geometrical properties of the surface and the wind velocity) and α is the solar radiation absorption coefficient on the surface (which depends principally on its external colour). a and b are geometrical factors depending on the orientation of the surface with respect to the sky. According to Holden [19.40]:

$$a = 0·32\,(1 - \cos \gamma) - 0·0297\,(\gamma \cos \chi + \sin \gamma \cos \beta) \tag{34}$$
$$b = 0·0323\,(1 - \cos \gamma),\ [\text{mm Hg}]^{-\frac{1}{2}}$$

The angles used in these equations are defined in the Fig. 19.3.

The solar radiation absorption on the surface at time j is represented here by the term $\alpha I_{sk}(j)$.

The longwave radiation interchange between the sky and the surface is represented here by Holden's formulation [19.40]

$$\sigma T_{oa}^{4}\,(a + bP_{w}^{\frac{1}{2}}),$$

and the longwave radiation from the surface to the outer space (supposed to be approximately at the absolute zero temperature) is represented here by Stefan Boltzmann's formulation of radiation emission:

$$\sigma\varepsilon F T_{oa}^{4}.$$

The earlier the i_0 value is considered in calculations, the more accurate the calculations will be. The value of $t_{sk}(i)$ is almost equal to the sol-air temperature in the case where the heat capacity of the slab behind the surface is very low and its thermal resistance is very high.

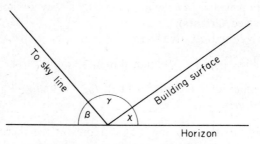

Fig. 19.3.   Definition of surface angles.

The TTCK in equation (32) is considered then to be zero and the t_{sk} transforms into sol-air temperature, *i.e.* sol-air temperature is an ideally insulated wall external surface temperature, where longwave radiation interchange is considered.

19.10. *Use of the Total Thermal Time Constant Method for Internal Temperature Calculations in Buildings*

A method for calculation of internal temperatures in buildings was developed by Hoffman and Givoni [19.39]. This method uses the total thermal time constant concept explained in Section 19.8 for each heat transfer path achieving the different elements closing an internal space in the building (TTTCK).

This method calculates the internal air temperature response to cyclic variations of temperatures of the external air and external surfaces. The external surface temperature patterns are calculated according to the method explained in Section 19.7. Each heat path is represented only by one number, its total thermal time constant.

A fictitious internal layer temperature variation at time i, t_{iK}, is calculated for each heat transfer path K reaching the internal space, as a consequence of an external surface temperature variation $\Delta t(j)_{sk}$ at time j (between i_0 and i). This variation is calculated at any time i by the following matrix multiplication expression, starting from time i_0:

$$\Delta t_{iK} = \sum_{j=i_0}^{i} \Delta t(j)_{sK} \left[1 - \exp\left(-\frac{i-j}{\text{TTTCK}} \right) \right] \qquad (35)$$

then, the corresponding fictitious temperature at any time i will be:

$$t_{iK} = t(i_0)_{sK} + \sum_{j=i_0}^{i} \Delta t(j)_{sK} \left[1 - \exp\left(-\frac{i-j}{\text{TTTCK}} \right) \right]. \qquad (36)$$

Where i is the time of calculation and i_0 is the starting time of calculation. The axiom of superposition is applied then and the following equation for the internal air temperature is obtained:

$$t_{ia} = \frac{\sum_K \left(\frac{S_K}{R_K} t_{iK} \right)}{\sum_K \left(\frac{S_K}{R_K} \right)} \qquad (37)$$

where S_K is the area of the internal surface of heat transfer path K, and R_K is the heat resistance calculated from the middle of the layer of the heat transfer path K, near to the internal space, to the internal air, including the internal surface resistance.

This method was proved successfully with semilaboratory closed models of different building materials and geometries under natural

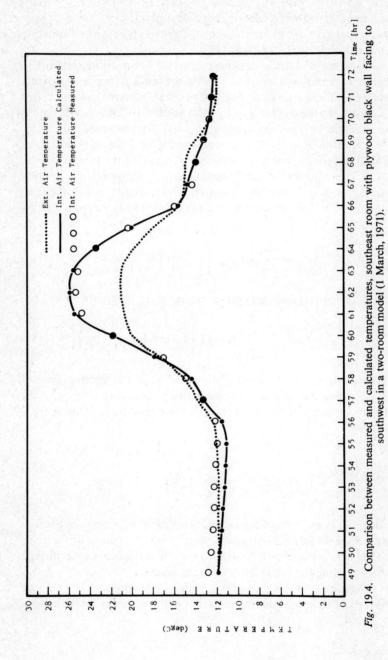

Fig. 19.4. Comparison between measured and calculated temperatures, southeast room with plywood black wall facing to southwest in a two-room model (1 March, 1971).

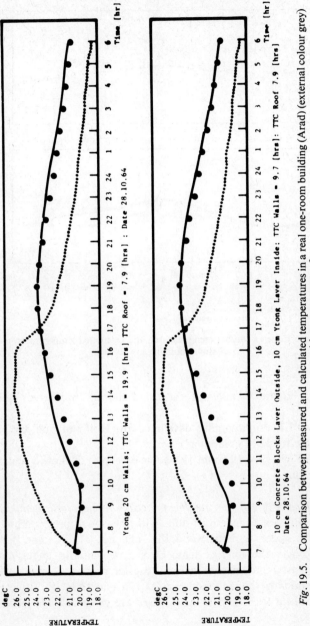

Fig. 19.5. Comparison between measured and calculated temperatures in a real one-room building (Arad) (external colour grey) with a concrete roof.

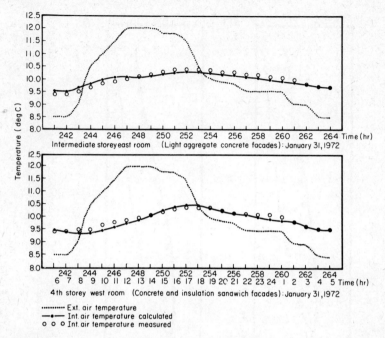

.... Ext. air temperature
—•— Int. air temperature calculated
o o o Int. air temperature measured

Fig. 19.6. Comparison between measured and calculated temperatures in a real 4-storey building in Carmiel.

climatic conditions and with fullscale buildings in different climatic zones.

A PL1 Programming developed by Hoffman and Givoni is available for IBM computers.

In Figs. 19.4, 19.5 and 19.6 some examples of these calculations are given.

The influence of different building materials on the interior temperature

Results of calculations done with the above programming are given in order to understand the influence of different building materials in the interior temperatures of building under natural conditions. Fundamental thermal transfer properties used here for calculations were taken from Tables 19.I and 19.Ia. In Table 19.IV a list of heat transfer paths considered are given and the results are presented in the form of maximum and minimum internal air temperature, together with the TTTCK and R_K of the varying elements used for calculation. The results given here correspond to the west room of a building composed of two rooms. All the external elements are in contact with the outside air (including the floor) and are submitted to solar radiation impinging differently on their exterior surface during the day. The PL1 program used here included solar radiation influence calculated according to the above explained method. Solar radiation influence is considered here, comparing two absorption coefficients: 0·3, which corresponds to the external surface coefficient when the surface is painted light (*e.g.* cream) and 0·6 which corresponds to the external surface coefficient when the surface is painted with a medium colour (*e.g.* the colour of exposed concrete).

Two types of buildings were considered here. One included a heavy internal partition of concrete 20 cm, the other one included a light internal partition of 3 cm expanded polystyrene.

It is seen here that the higher the thermal time constant of the external elements, the lower is the internal air temperature variation (the highest values of thermal time constant are obtained when the insulation layers are given in the outside of the external walls).

But a similar effect can be achieved with well insulated light external elements if heavy internal partitions can be considered. For instance, almost the same maximum and minimum temperatures were obtained in the model built 3 cm expanded polystyrene external elements with the heavy partition and in the model built external elements of 2 cm expanded polystyrene in the outside and 10 cm concrete in the inside with a light partition.

19.11. The Total Thermal Time Constant, The Response Factor and the Equivalent Thermal Mass Response Factor Methods (a Comparison)

The response factor method is conceptually a simple method because, as is the case also with the thermal time constant method, no Fourier analysis of input data is needed, and integrations are done step by step.

The complexity of this method lies in the calculations of the response factors which, because of their long algebraic calculations,

Table 19.IV

Comparison of internal maximum and minimum internal air temperature in buildings of different building materials under natural conditions (external air temperature: max. 35°C; min. 21°C)

Solar radiation external surfaces absorption coefficient (1)		External elements (from outside)					
		Exp. polyst. 3 cm (2)	Concrete 10 cm Exp. polyst. 2 cm (2)	Concrete 10 cm Exp. polyst. 3 cm (2)	Concrete 20 cm	Exp. polyst. 2 cm (2) Concrete 10 cm	Exp. polyst. 3 cm (2) Concrete 10 cm
Temperature (time)		TTTCK = 0·23 h	3·9 h	3·9 h	10·3 h	31·3 h	45·1 h
		RK = 0·58 (m h deg/kcal)	0·44	0·58	0·21	0·18	0·18
Heavy internal partition—Concrete 20 cm (3) RK′ = 0·21 m² h deg/kcal							
		TTTCK′ = 107 h	89 h	116 h	46 h	116 h	158 h
α = 0·3	Min.	22·6 (7·00)	24·4 (8·00)	23·8 (8·00)	24·2 (9·00)	23·7 (8·00)	23·5 (9·00)
	Max.	27·0 (17·00)	28·2 (19·00)	29·0 (19·00)	27·5 (20·00)	25·2 (20·00)	24·7 (20·00)
α = 0·6	Min.	23·7 (7·00)	25·5 (8·00)	24·7 (8·00)	25·4 (9·00)	25·3 (9·00)	25·1 (9·00)
	Max.	29·6 (17·00)	30·6 (19·00)	31·7 (19·00)	30·0 (19·00)	27·4 (20·00)	26·7 (20·00)

Light internal partition—Expanded polystyrene 3 cm (3) $RK' = 0.58$ m² h deg/kcal

		$TTTCK' = 0.94$ h	4·5 h	4·6 h	10·6 h	31·9 h	45·8 h
$\alpha = 0.3$	Min.	18·8 (7^{00})	21·6 (8^{00})	21·6 (8^{00})	23·1 (8^{00})	23·4 (9^{00})	23·5 (8^{00})
	Max.	33·9 (17^{00})	32·6 (19^{00})	32·6 (19^{00})	29·1 (19^{00})	26·2 (19^{00})	25·8 (19^{00})
$\alpha = 0.6$	Min.	18·8 (7^{00})	21·9 (8^{00})	22·0 (8^{00})	24·1 (9^{00})	25·2 (9^{00})	25·5 (8^{00})
	Max.	38·7 (17^{00})	36·3 (19^{00})	36·3 (19^{00})	32·2 (19^{00})	28·9 (19^{00})	28·4 (19^{00})

Programming and calculations were done with an IBM computer by Mr Moshe Feldman (B.Sc.) using the Total Thermal Time Constant Method.

Description of model: Building built—two rooms: 5 m × 5 m × 3 m (height) (east and west) with two 1 m × 1 m shaded windows in each room. Internal temperatures calculated in the west room; latitude 30°N.

(1) α = Solar radiation absorption coefficient.

(2) Expanded polystyrene in a thin (1 mm) aluminium frame on both sides.

(3) RK' and $TTTCK'$ are the corresponding values of external elements through the partition (see text).

can be obtained easily only with the aid of a digital computer program. A building element is represented by a series of three numbers, X_j, Y_j and Z_j (the response factors) where each of them must be calculated until j, a time long enough to assure the integrations to be consistent. In the total thermal time constant method, a heat transfer path is represented by its total thermal time constant and its U value, both easy to calculate, and calibration curves can be plotted for many different values of both numbers and of outside temperature and solar radiation conditions. The main advantage of the response method at the present stage is that using the explicit matrix form for heat flow, the heat flow can be evaluated hour by hour.

Both methods intend to calculate internal temperatures of buildings. The total thermal time constant method was validated with models and real full scale buildings, in situ, under natural conditions of temperature and different impinging solar radiation on the external elements. The response factor method, at least in published reports and papers, was validated essentially with full scale building models subjected to a known cycle of temperature in an experimental climatic chamber, so that all the external elements were influenced simultaneously by the same external input.

The equivalent thermal mass response factor calculates experimentally thermal time constant values of buildings for each thermal input separately, and the authors of this method intend to include internal heating source too. The verification of this method in situ, under natural conditions will conduce from the heat flux evaluation in a building in some climatic place to the evaluation of it under climatic conditions other than the measured conditions (in other seasons of the year or other regions). A simple algebraic equation system easy to calculate by a digital computer, represents the building by this method and allows the prediction of energy requirements for buildings.

Conversion Factors

Linear Measures

Metre (m)	Foot (ft)	Inch (in)	Mile
1	3·281	39·37	0·0006214
0·3048	1	12	0·0001894
0·0254	0·08333	1	0·00001578
1609·35	5280	63360	1

Area

m^2	ft^2	in^2
1	10·7639	1550
0·09290	1	144
0·0006452	0·006944	1

Volume

m^3	ft^3	in^3
1	35·31	61023
0·02832	1	1728
0·00001639	0·0005787	1

Mass

kg	lb
1	2·2
0·454	1

Density

kg/m^3	· g/cm^3	lb/ft^3
1	0·001	0·06243
1000	1	62·4283
16·018	0·0160	1

Speed

m/s	km/h	miles/h	ft/min
1	3·6	2·237	196·85
0·2778	1	0·621	54·68
0·4470	1·6094	1	88·00
0·00508	0·01830	0·0114	1

Energy or Heat

kJ	kcal	Btu	kWh
1	0·239	0·948	0·000278
4·186	1	3·968	0·001163
1·055	0·252	1	0·000293
3600	859·98	3412·66	1

Specific Heat

$$1 \text{ kcal/kg} \times \text{deg C} = 1 \text{ Btu/lb} \times \text{deg F} = 1{\cdot}163 \frac{\text{watt-h}}{\text{kg deg C}}$$

Heat Content

kJ/kg	kcal/kg	Btu/lb
1	0·239	0·72
4·187	1	1·8
2·328	0·556	1

Energy or Heat Flow Rate

Watt/m^2	kcal/m$^2 \times$ h	Btu/ft$^2 \times$ h
1	0·861	0·318
1·163	1	0·369
3·152	2·713	1

Thermal Conductance

Watt/m² × °C	kcal/h × m² × °C	Btu/h × ft² °F
1	0·861	0·176
1·163	1	0·205
5·67	4·88	1

Thermal Conductivity

$\dfrac{\text{Watts}}{\text{m}^2 \times °\text{C/m}}$	$\dfrac{\text{kcal}}{\text{m}^2 \times \text{h} \times °\text{C/m}}$	$\dfrac{\text{Btu}}{\text{ft}^2 \times \text{h} \times °\text{F}}$
1	0·861	6·94
1·163	1	8·064
0·144	0·124	1

Thermal Resistance

$\dfrac{\text{m}^2 \times \text{deg C}}{\text{Watts}}$	$\dfrac{\text{m}^2 \times \text{h} \times \text{deg C}}{\text{kcal}}$	$\dfrac{\text{ft}^2 \times \text{h} \times \text{deg F}}{\text{Btu}}$
1	1·163	5·67
0·861	1	4·88
0·176	0·205	1

Temperatures

$$\text{Degrees C} = 5/9 \text{ (degrees F} - 32)$$
$$\text{Degrees F} = 9/5 \text{ degrees C} + 32$$
$$1°\text{C} = 1·8°\text{F}$$
$$1°\text{F} = 0·556°\text{C}$$

References

Chapter 1

1.1. D. ASHBEL: *Introduction to meteorology*, The University Press, Jerusalem, 1940 (in Hebrew).
1.2. D. ASHBEL: *New world maps of global solar radiation during I.G.Y.*, Hebrew University, Jerusalem, 1961.
1.3. R. GEIGER: *The climate near the ground*, Harvard University Press, Cambridge, Massachusetts, 1959.
1.4. A. A. MILLER: *Climatology*, Methuen & Co. Ltd., London, 1961.
1.5. G. T. TREWARTHA: *An introduction to climate*, McGraw-Hill Book Co. Inc., New York, 1954.

Chapter 2

2.1. E. ASMUSSEN AND E. POULSEN: Energy requirements of practical jobs from pulse increase and ergometer test, *Ergonomics*, Vol. 5, No. 1, London, Jan. 1962.
2.2. H. C. BAZETT: The regulation of body temperatures, contained in ref. 2.10.
2.3. T. BEDFORD: *Basic principles of ventilation and heating*, H. K. Lewis & Co. Ltd., London, 1948.
2.4. H. S. BELDING AND T. F. HATCH: Index of evaluating heat stress in terms of resulting physiological strain, *Heating, Piping & Air Condition. J.*, August 1955.
2.5. H. S. BELDING: Resistance to heat in man and other homeothermic animals, *Thermobiology*, ed. A. H. Rose, Academic Press, London, 1967, pp. 479–510.
2.6. W. BRUCE: Man and his thermal environment, *Division of Building Research, Technical Paper No. 84*, Ottawa, 1960.
2.7. B. GIVONI AND H. S. BELDING: The cooling efficiency of sweat evaporation, *Proceedings 1st International Congress of Bio-Meteorology*, Pergamon Press, London, 1962, pp. 304–314.
2.8. B. GIVONI: The effect of climate on man: development of a new thermal index, *Research Report to UNESCO*, Building Research Station, Technion, Haifa, 1963.
2.9. B. GIVONI AND E. BERNER-NIR: Effect of solar radiation on physiological heat strain in relation to work and clothing, *Research Report to U.S. Public Health Service*, Building Research Station, Technion, Haifa, 1967.
2.10. L. H. NEWBURGH: *Physiology of heat regulation and the science of clothing*, W. B. Saunders Co., Philadelphia, 1949.

Chapter 3

3.1. W. BRUCE: Man and his thermal environment, *Division of Building Research, Technical Paper No. 84*, Ottawa, 1960.
3.2. C. F. CONSOLAZIO, R. E. JOHNSON AND L. J. PECORA: *Physiological*

measurements of metabolic functions in man, McGraw-Hill Book Co., Inc., New York, 1963.

3.3.   T. R. A. DAVIS: Acclimatization to cold in man, contained in ref. 3.11, pp. 443–452.

3.4.   B. GIVONI AND H. S. BELDING: The cooling efficiency of sweat evaporation. *Proceedings 1st International Congress of Bio-meteorology*, Pergamon Press, London, 1962, pp. 304–314.

3.5.   B. GIVONI: The effect of climate on man: development of a new thermal index, *Research Report to UNESCO*, Building Research Station, Technion, Haifa, 1963.

3.6.   B. GIVONI AND E. BERNER-NIR: Effect of solar radiation on physiological heat strain in relation to work and clothing, *Research Report to US Public Health Service*, Building Research Station, Technion, Haifa, 1967.

3.7a.   B. GIVONI AND R. F. GOLDMAN: Predicting metabolic energy cost, *J. Appl. Physiol.*, Vol. 30, No. 3, 1971, pp. 429–433.

3.7b.   B. GIVONI AND R. F. GOLDMAN: Predicting rectal temperature response to work, environment and clothing, *J. Appl. Physiol.*, Vol. 32, No. 6, 1972, pp. 812–822.

3.7c.   B. GIVONI AND R. F. GOLDMAN: Predicting heart rate response to work, environment and clothing, *J. Appl. Physiol.*, Vol. 34, No. 2, 1973, pp. 201–204.

3.7d.   B. GIVONI AND R. F. GOLDMAN: Predicting effects of heat acclimatization on rectal temperature and heart rate responses as functions of activity, environment and clothing conditions, *J. Appl. Physiol.*, Vol. 35, No. 6, 1973, pp. 875–879.

3.8.   N. GLICKMAN, T. INOUYE, R. W. KEETON AND M. K. FAHNESTOCK: Physiologic examination of the effective temperature index, *ASHVE Journal Section*, Heating, Piping and Air Cond. U.S.A., 1950.

3.9.   R. F. GOLDMAN, E. B. GREEN AND P. F. IAMPIETRO: Tolerance of hot, wet environments by resting men, *J. Appl. Physiol*, Vol. 20, No. 2, 1965, U.S.A.

3.10.   M. S. GOROMOSSOV: *The microclimate of dwellings*, State Publishing House for Medical Literature, Moscow, 1963, translated by G. F. Penny, Library Commun. No. 1325, B.R.S., Garston.

3.11.   J. D. HARDY, ed.: *Temperature, its measurement and control in science and industry*, Part 3, Reinhold Pub. Corp., New York, 1963.

3.12.   F. C. HOUGHTEN AND C. P. YAGLOU: Determining lines of equal comfort, *ASHVE Trans.*, Vol. 29, 1923.

3.13.   T. INOUYE, F. K. HICK, S. E. TELSER AND R. W. KEETON: Effect of relative humidity on heat loss of men exposed to environments of 80, 76 and 72°F, *ASHVE Journal Section*, Heating, Piping and Air Cond., Vol. 59, p. 329, U.S.A.

3.14.   D. H. K. LEE: Physiology and the arid zone, contained in ref. 3.26, pp. 15–34.

3.15.   C. S. LEITHEAD AND A. R. LIND: *Heat stress and heat disorders*, Cassel & Co., Ltd., London, 1964.

3.16.   W. V. MACFARLANE: Water and electrolytes of man in hot dry regions, contained in ref. 3.26, pp. 43–50.

3.17.   R. H. MACPHERSON: Physiological responses to hot environments, *Med. Res. Council Sp. Report Series No. 298*, London, H.M.S.O.

3.18.   B. MCARDLE, W. DUNHAM, H. E. HOLLING, W. S. S. LADELL, J. W. SCOTT,

M. L. Thomson and J. S. Weiner: The prediction of the physiological effects of warm and hot environments, *Med. Res. Council R.N.P.*, 47/391, 1947.

3.19. D. Minard and L. Copman: Elevation of body temperature in health, contained in ref. 3.11.

3.20. L. H. Newburgh, ed.: *Physiology of heat regulation and the science of clothing*, W. B. Saunders Co., Philadelphia, 1945.

3.21. S. Robinson: Tropics in laboratory and field studies, contained in ref. 3.20.

3.22. F. Sargent, W. K. Brown, A. T. Pessa, J. Waligora and K. P. Weinman: Observation in dehydration and eccrine sweating, contained in ref. 2.19.

3.23. E. Sohar and R. Adar: Sodium requirements in Israel under conditions of work in hot climate, contained in ref. 3.26, pp. 55–60.

3.24. J. C. Stevens and S. S. Stevens: The dynamics of subjective warmth and cold, contained in ref. 3.11.

3.25. UNESCO Arid Zone Research: Environmental physiology and psychology in arid conditions, *Reviews of Research*, UNESCO, Paris, 1963.

3.26. UNESCO Arid Zone Research: *Proceedings of the Lucknow Symposium on Environmental Physiology and Psychology in Arid Conditions*, UNESCO, Paris, 1964.

3.27. C. E. A. Winslow, L. P. Herrington and A. P. Gagge: Physiological reactions of the human body to varying environmental temperatures, *Am. J. Physiol.*, Vol. 120, 1937.

3.28. C. H. Wyndham, N. B. Strydom, J. F. Morrison, C. G. Williams, G. A. G. Bredell and J. Peter: Fatigue of the sweat gland response, *J. Appl. Physiol.*, 21 (1), 1966, pp. 107–110.

3.29. C. P. Yaglou: A method for improving the effective temperature index, *ASHVE Trans.*, Vol. 53, 1947, pp. 307–309.

Chapter 4

4.1. E. F. Adolph: *Physiology of man in the desert*, Interscience Pub., New York, 1947.

4.2. J. R. Breckenbridge and R. L. Pratt: Effect of clothing colour on solar heat load, *Environmental Protection Research Division, T.R. EP–155*, Q.M.R.E.C. U.S. Army, Natick, 1961.

4.3. A. C. Burton: *Research Report C–2753*, Assoc. Comm. Aviation Medicine, Nov. 1944, p. 159.

4.4. B. Givoni and E. Berner-Nir: Effect of solar radiation on physiological heat strain in relation to work and clothing, *Research Report to U.S. Public Health Service*, Building Research Station, Technion, Haifa, 1967.

4.5. M. S. Goromossov: *The microclimate of dwellings*, Moscow State Publishing House for Medical Literature, 1963 (translated by G. F. Penny), Library Commun. No. 1325, B.R.S., Garston.

4.6. F. C. Houghten, S. B. Gunst and J. Sucin: Radiation as a factor in the sensation of warmth, *ASHVE Trans.*, 1945.

4.7. L. M. Humphreys, O. Imalis and C. Gutberlet: Physiological response of subjects exposed to high effective temperature and elevated mean radiant temperatures, *ASHVE Trans.*, Vol. 52, 1946, pp. 153–166.

4.8. B. H. Jenning and B. Givoni: Environmental reactions in the 80°–105°F zone, *ASHVE Journal*, Jan. 1959, pp. 3–10.

4.9. R. H. MACPHERSON: Physiological responses to hot environments, *Med. Res. Council Sp. Report Series No.* 298, London, H.M.S.O.

4.10. D. MITCHELL, C. H. WYNDHAM AND T. HODGSON: Emissivity and transmittance of excised human skin in its thermal emission wave bond, *Appl. Physiol.* 23 (3), 1967, pp. 390–394.

4.11. L. H. NEWBURGH, ed.: *Physiology of heat regulation and the science of clothing*, W. B. Saunders Co., Philadelphia, Chap. 5, 1949.

4.12. S. ROBINSON AND E. S. TURRELL: C.M.R. Report No. 11, quoted by E. F. Adolph in ref. 4.11.

4.13. M. B. SULZBERGER: The effect of heat and humidity on the skin, *Harefuah, J. Israel Medical Assoc.*, Tel-Aviv, Sept. 1, 1966, pp. 129–131.

Chapter 5

5.1. E. F. ADOLPH, ed.: *Physiology of man in the desert*, Interscience Pub., New York, 1947.

5.2. ASHRAE Guide.

5.3. H. S. BELDING AND T. F. HATCH: Index for evaluating heat stress in terms of resulting physiological strain, *Heating, Piping, Air. Cond.*, Vol. 27, 1955, p. 129.

5.4. W. DUNHAM, H. E. HOLLING, W. S. S. LADELL, B. MCARDLE, J. W. SCOTT, M. L. THOMSON AND J. S. WEINER: The effect of air movement in severe heat, *Med. Res. Council (London)*, R.N.P. 46/316, H.S. 152.

5.5. B. GIVONI: The influence of work and environmental conditions on the physiological responses and thermal equilibrium of man, *Proced. UNESCO · Symposium on Environmental Physiology and Psychology in Arid Conditions*, Lucknow, India, 1962, pp. 199–204.

5.6. B. GIVONI: Estimation of the effect of climate on man: development of a new thermal index, *Research Report to UNESCO*, Building Research Station, Technion, Haifa, Israel, 1963.

5.7. B. GIVONI AND E. BERNER-NIR: Expected sweat rate as function of metabolism in environmental factors and clothing, *Report to the U.S. Department of Health, Education and Welfare*, Haifa, Dec. 1967.

5.8. N. GLICKMAN, T. INOUYE, R. W. KEETON AND M. K. FAHNESTOCK: Physiological examination of the effective temperature index, *ASHVE Trans.*, Vol. 56, 1950, p. 51.

5.9. R. E. GOSSELIN: Rates of sweating, contained in ref. 5.1.

5.10. A. HENSCHEL AND E. H. HANSON: Heat stress in desert environment, *ASME*, Vol. 82, 1960, pp. 57–60.

5.11. F. C. HOUGHTEN AND C. P. YAGLOU: Determining lines of equal comfort, *ASHVE Trans.*, Vol. 29, 1923, p. 163.

5.12. B. H. JENNINGS AND B. GIVONI: Environmental reactions in the 80°–105°F zone, *ASHVE Trans.*, 1959.

5.13. W. KOCH, B. H. JENNINGS AND C. M. HUMPHREYS: Sensation responses, *Presentation at ASHRAE semi-meeting*, Feb. 1960.

5.14. K. K. KRANING, H. S. BELDING AND B. A. HERTIG: Use of sweating rate to predict other physiological responses to heat, *J. Appl. Physiol.*, 21 (1), 1966, pp. 111–117.

5.15. R. H. MACPHERSON: Physiological responses to hot environments, *Med. Res. Council Sp. Report, Series No.* 298, London, H.M.S.O.

5.16. B. McAriel, W. Dunham, H. E. Holling, W. S. S. Ladell, J. W. Scott, M. L. Thomson and J. S. Weiner: The prediction of the physiological effect of warm and hot environments, *Med. Res. Council R.N.P.* 47/391, H.S. 194/1947, London.

5.17. A. Missenard: Equivalences thermiques des ambiences; equivalences de passage; equivalences de sejour, *Chaleur et Industrie*, July-Aug., 1948.

5.18. F. E. Smith: Indices of heat stress, *Med. Res. Council, Memo No.* 29, London, 1955.

5.19. C. P. Yaglou and W. E. Miller: Effective temperature with clothing, *ASHVE Trans.*, Vol. 31, 1925, p. 89.

5.20. C. P. Yaglou: A method for improving the effective temperature index. *ASHVE Trans.*, Vol. 53, 1947, p. 307.

Chapter 6

6.1. ASHRAE Guide and Data Book: Fundamental and equipment, *Am. Soc. Heating, Refrigerating and Air Conditioning Engineers*, 1965.

6.2. F. Bruckmayer: The equivalent brick wall, *Gesundheitsing* 63 (6), 1940, pp. 61–65.

6.3. J. Dreyfus: *Le confort dans l'habitat en pays tropical*, Edition Eyrolls, Paris, 1960.

6.4. C. O. Mackey and L. T. Wright: Periodic heat flow—composite walls or roofs, *Heat, Piping and Air Conditioning*, June 1946.

6.5. B. C. Raychaudhury and N. K. D. Chaudhury: Thermal performance of dwellings in the tropics, *Indian Construction News*, Dec. 1961, pp. 38–42.

6.6. S. J. Richards, J. F. van Straaten and E. N. van Deventer: Some ventilation and thermal considerations in building design to suit climate, *S.A. Architectural Record*, Vol. 45, No. 1, Jan. 1960.

6.7. J. F. van Straaten: *Thermal performance of buildings*, Elsevier Publishing Co. Ltd, 1968.

Chapter 7

7.1. J. Dreyfus: *Le confort dans l'habitat en pays tropical*, Edition Eyrolls, Paris, 1960.

7.2. J. W. Drysdale: *Technical Study No.* 27, Comm. Exp. Bldg. Station, 1948 (Australia).

7.3. J. W. Drysdale: Cooling the home, *Symposium on the Functional Effect of Buildings, Indian Concrete News*, CBRI, Roorkee, India, Nov. 1961, pp. 33–37.

7.4. C. O. Mackey and L. T. Wright: Periodic heat flow—composite walls or roofs, *Heat, Piping and Air Conditioning*, June 1946.

7.5. B. Givoni and E. Hoffman: Effect of building materials on internal temperatures, *Research Report*, Building Research Station, Technion, Haifa, April 1968.

7.6. B. Givoni and E. Hoffman: Effect of materials properties on response of buildings to solar radiation penetration, *Research Report*, Building Research Station, Technion, Haifa, May 1968 (in Hebrew).

7.7. B. Givoni and E. Hoffman: Experimental study of the thermal characteristics of curtain walls in warm climate, *Research Report*, Building Research Station, Technion, Haifa, April 1965.

7.8.   B. C. RAYCHAUDHURY AND N. K. D. CHAUDHURY: Thermal performance of dwellings in the tropics, *Symposium on the Functional Efficiency of Buildings*, CBRI, Roorkee, India, Nov. 1961, pp. 38–42.

Chapter 8

8.1.   G. P. CROWDAN: The height of rooms in dwellings in relation to health and comfort, *J. Roy. San. Inst.*, March 1951.
8.2.   B. GIVONI: The effect of roof construction upon indoor temperatures, *Proceed. 1st Int. Congress of Bio-Climatology*, Pergamon Press, 1962, pp. 237–245.
8.3.   B. GIVONI AND R. SHALON: Influence of ceiling height on thermal conditions in dwelling houses in Beer-Sheva, *Research Paper No.* 10, Building Research Station, Technion, Haifa, 1962.
8.4.   B. GIVONI AND R. SHALON: Influence of type and construction of roof on indoor thermal conditions in Beer-Sheva, *Research Report No.* 11, Building Research Station, Technion, Haifa, 1962.
8.5.   B. GIVONI AND E. HOFFMAN: Experimental study of the thermal characteristics of curtain walls in warm climate, *Research Report to the National Council for Research and Development*, Building Research Station, Technion, Haifa, April 1965.
8.6.   B. GIVONI AND E. HOFFMAN: *Guide to Building Design in Different Climatic Zone*, Building Research Station, Technion, Haifa, 1968 (in Hebrew).
8.7.   C. L. GUPTA AND K. R. RAO: An experimental study for determining adequate ceiling heights of residential buildings in hot-arid region, N.B.O., *J. India*, October 1959.
8.8.   J. HOLMGREN AND T. ISAKSEN: *Ventilated and Unventilated Flat, Compacted Roofs*, Norwegian Building Research Institute, Rapport NR 27, Oslo, 1959.
8.9.   D. H. K. LEE: *Physiological Objectives in Hot Weather Housing*, H.H.F.A., Washington, 1953.
8.10.   F. J. LOTZ: The effect of dust on the efficacy of reflective metal foil used as roof ceiling insulation, *C.S.I.R., Research Report No.* 212, Pretoria, 1964.
8.11.   F. J. LOTZ AND S. J. RICHARDS: The influence of ceiling insulation on indoor thermal conditions in dwellings of heavy-weight construction under South African conditions, *C.S.I.R., Research Report No.* 214, Pretoria, 1964.
8.12.   H. NEUMANN, N. PELEG AND N. ROBINSON: Experiments on thermal protection of concrete roofs, *Report No.* 4, Station for Technical Climatology (Building Research Station), Technion, Haifa, Israel, 1955.
8.13.   S. J. RICHARDS: Minimum ceiling height in South Africa, *Bull. No.* 15, Nat. Build. Res. Inst., Pretoria, Jan. 1957.
8.14.   R. SHALON, A. ALWEYL, R. LANDSBERG, A. MANSFELD, H. NEUMANN, R. C. REINITZ AND B. GIVONI: A study of the influence of ceiling height and dwelling houses, *Research Paper No.* 6, Building Research Station, Technion, Haifa, 1957.
8.15.   G. E. SUTTON: Roof spray for reduction in transmitted solar radiation, *ASHVE Journal Section, Heat, Piping and Air Conditioning*, September 1950, pp. 131–137.

8.16. J. F. VAN STRAATEN: Roof insulation, *South African Architectural Record*, Vol. 49, No. 2, Feb. 1964.

8.17. J. F. VAN STRAATEN, A. J. A. ROUX AND S. J. RICHARDS: The effect of attic ventilation on the indoor thermal and ventilation conditions in dwellings of conventional construction, *N.B.R.I. Bulletin No.* 15, Jan. 1957, pp. 38–64.

8.18. *Woman's Congress on Housing*, H.H.F.A., Washington, October 1956.

Chapter 9

9.1. G. W. ANDERSON: Some moisture problems of contemporary construction, *RILEM/CIB Symposium on Moisture Problems in Buildings*, Helsinki, 1965.

9.2. Ø. BIRKELAND: General report, *RILEM/CIB Symposium on Moisture Problems in Buildings*, Helsinki, 1965.

9.3. D. BISHOP: An interim report of a study of joints between concrete panels, *Proceedings of CIB Conference on Large Concrete Elements*, Stockholm, 1963.

9.4. *Proceedings of CIB Conference on Large Concrete Elements*, Stockholm, 1963.

9.5. B. GIVONI: Field study of wetness conditions in occupied buildings, *RILEM/CIB Symposium on Moisture Problems in Buildings*, Helsinki, 1965.

9.6. T. ISAKSEN: Rain penetration in joints. Influence of dimensions and shape of joints on rain penetration, *RILEM/CIB Symposium on Moisture Problems in Buildings*, Helsinki, 1965.

9.7. REEF, Centre Scientifique et Technique du Batiment, Paris, France, *RILEM/CIB Symposium on Moisture Problems in Buildings*, Helsinki, 1965.

9.8. *RILEM/CIB Symposium on Moisture Problems in Buildings*, Helsinki, 1965.

9.9. I. SOROKA, Water retardant qualities of external coatings, *ASTM Bull. No.* 240, 1959, pp. 40–45, *RILEM/CIB Symposium on Moisture Problems in Buildings*, Helsinki, 1965.

9.10. J. F. VAN STRAATEN: *Thermal performance of buildings*, Elsevier Publishing Co. Ltd, 1968.

Chapter 10

10.1. *ASHRAE Handbook and Product Directory*, 1974 *Applications*, Chapter 59, Am. Soc. Heating, Refrigerating and Air Conditioning Eng., New York.

10.2. H. E. BECKETT AND J. A. GODFREY: *Windows, performance, design and installation*, 1974, Van Nostrand, Reinhold, New York.

10.3. B. J. BRINKWORTH: *Solar energy for man*, 1974, Compton Press, Great Britain.

10.4. JOHN H. CALLENDER: *Time-saver standards for architectural design data*, 1974, McGraw-Hill, Inc., U.S.A.

10.5. FARRINGTON DANIELS: *Direct use of sun's energy*, 1974, Ballantine Books, Inc., New York.

10.6. ERNST DANZ: *Sun protection*, An International Architectural Survey, 1967, Praeger Publishers, Inc., New York.

10.7. JOHN S. FISHER: *Flag pole shadow traces as a means of understanding sun motion*, Office of the Dean, School of Architecture, Syracuse University, Syracuse, New York.

10.8. Libbey-Owens-Ford Glass Company, *Sun angle calculator*, 1975.

10.9. VICTOR OLGYAY: *Design with climate*, Bioclimatic approach to architectural regionalism, 1969, Princeton University Press, New Jersey.

10.10. C. RAMSEY AND H. SLEEPER: *Architectural graphic standards*, 1970, John Wiley & Sons, Inc., New York.

10.11. PHILIP STEADMAN: *Energy, environment and building*, A report to the Academy of Natural Sciences of Philadelphia, 1975, Cambridge University Press, Massachusetts.

10.12. ARTHUR N. STRAHLER: *Physical geography*, 1969, John Wiley & Sons, Inc., New York.

10.13. R. C. WEAST (Ed.): *The Handbook of Chemistry and Physics*, 56th edn, CRC Press, Cleveland, Ohio, 1975.

Chapter 11

11.1. ASHRAE Guide and Data Book, *Fundamental and Equipment*, 1965–1966, Am. Soc. Heating, Refrigerating and Air Conditioning Eng., N.Y., 8–498.

11.2. J. DREYFUS: *Le confort dans l'habitat en pays tropical*, Editions Eyrolles, Paris, 1960.

11.3. B. GIVONI AND E. HOFFMAN: Experimental study of the thermal characteristics of curtain walls in warm climate, *Research Report*, B.R.S., Technion, Haifa, 1965.

11.4. B. GIVONI AND E. HOFFMAN: Effect of orientation of walls and windows on indoor climate, *Research Report*, B.R.S., Technion, Haifa, 1965 (in Hebrew).

11.5. B. GIVONI AND E. HOFFMAN: Effect of window orientation on indoor air temperature, *Architectural Science Review*, Vol. 9, No. 3, Sept. 1966, pp. 80–83.

11.6. V. OLGYAY AND A. OLGYAY: *Solar control and shading devices*, Princeton University Press, Princeton, N.J., 1957.

Chapter 12

12.1. *Architects' Journal*, Jan 12, 1966: Special feature on the sun, pp. 105–149.

12.2. J. F. ARONIN: *Architecture and Climate*, Reinhold Publishing Corp., N.Y., 1953, p. 304.

12.3. BITTER AND IERLAND: Appreciation of sunlight in the home, contained in ref. 12.9.

12.4. B. GIVONI: Window location in residential buildings, *Research Report*, Building Research Station, Technion, Israel Institute of Technology, Haifa, 1961 (in Hebrew).

12.5. B. GIVONI AND M. E. HOFFMAN: Effectiveness of shading devices, *Research Report*, Building Research Station, Technion, Israel Institute of Technology, Haifa, 1964 (in Hebrew).

12.6. B. GIVONI, E. NE'EMAN, M. E. HOFFMAN AND M. BECKER: Effect of orientation and shading of classrooms on thermal and illumination conditions, *Research Report to Ford Foundation*, Building Research Station, Haifa, August 1968.

12.7. B. GIVONI: Unpublished experimental data.

12.8. A. L. JAROS, JR.: Selection of glass and solar shading to reduce cooling demand in: *Solar Effects on Building Design, Pub. No. 1007*, Building Research Institute, Washington, 1963.

12.9. R. G. HOPKINSON, ed.: Sunlight in buildings, *Proceedings C.I.E. Intersessional Conference*, Newcastle-upon-Tyne, April 1965.

12.10. A. G. LOUDON: Window design criteria to avoid overheating by excessive solar heat gains, contained in ref. 12.9.

12.11. A. OLGYAY AND V. OLGYAY: *Solar control and shading devices*, Princeton University Press, 1957, pp. 190.

12.12. P. PETHERBRIDGE: Transmission characteristics of window glasses and sun controls, contained in ref. 12.9.

12.13. E. SHAVIV: A method for the design of fixed external sun-shades, Technion Research and Development Foundation Ltd., Report No. 020-136, December 1974.

12.14. J. F. VAN STRAATEN: *Thermal performance of buildings*, Elsevier Publishing Co. Ltd, 1967.

12.15. J. R. WATERS AND D. A. RICHARDSON: Transmission of glass to solar radiation, contained in ref. 12.9.

Chapter 13

13.1. Am. Soc. Heating, Refrigerating, Ventilating & Air Conditioning, *Guide and Data Book*, 1963, Fundamental and Equipment.

13.2. W. V. CONSOLAZIO AND L. J. PECORA: Minimal replenishment air required for living spaces, *ASHVE Journal Section*, HPAC, March 1947, pp. 103–114.

13.3. J. B. DICK: The fundamentals of natural ventilation for houses, *I.H.V.E. Journal*, 1950 18 (179), pp. 123–134.

13.4. B. GIVONI: Window location in residential buildings, *Research Report*, B.R.S., Technion, Haifa, 1961 (in Hebrew).

13.5. B. GIVONI: Basic study of ventilation problems in housing in hot countries, *Research Report to Ford Foundation*, Building Research Station, Technion, Haifa, 1962.

13.6. B. GIVONI: Ventilation problems in hot countries, *Research Report to Ford Foundation*, Building Research Station, Technion, Haifa, 1968.

13.7. B. GIVONI AND E. HOFFMAN: Effect of building materials on internal temperatures, *Research Report*, Building Research Station, Technion, Haifa, 1968 (in Hebrew with English abstract).

13.8. J. O. V. IRMINGER AND C. NØKKENTVED: *Wind Pressure on Buildings*, Dannmarks Naturvidenskabelige Samfund, Kobenhaven, 1930.

13.9. R.E.E.F. 58, *Sciences du Bâtiment*, Centre Scientifique et Technique du Bâtiment, Paris.

13.10. E. G. SMITH: The feasibility of using models for pre-determining natural ventilation, *Research Report No. 26*, Texas Engineering Experimental Station, College Station, Texas, 1951.

13.11. J. F. VAN STRAATEN: *Thermal performance of buildings*, Elsevier Publishing Co. Ltd, 1967.
13.12. C. P. YAGLOU AND W. N. WITHERIDGE: Ventilation requirements, *ASHVE Trans.*, Vol. 43, 1937, pp. 425–437.
13.13. J. J. WANNENBURGH AND J. F. VAN STRAATEN: Wind tunnel tests on scale model buildings as a means for studying ventilation and allied problems, *J. Inst. Heat. Vent. Engrs.*, March 1957.
13.14. C. E. A. WINSLOW: Objectives and standards of ventilation, *ASHVE Journal*, Vol. 32, March 1926, pp. 113–152.

Chapter 14

14.1. *ASHVE Guide*, American Society of Heating, Ventilating and Air Conditioning Engineers, 1950.
14.2. J. B. DICK: The fundamentals of natural ventilation of houses, *Heating & Ventilating Engineers Journal*, 18 (179), 1950, pp. 123–134.
14.3. J. O. V. IRMINGER AND C. NØKKENTVED: *Wind Pressure on Buildings*, Danmarke Naturvidenskabelige Samfund, Kobenhaven, 1930.
14.4. R.E.E.F. 58, Centre Scientifique et Technique du Bâtiment, Paris.
14.5. S. J. RICHARDS, J. F. VAN STRAATEN AND E. N. VAN DEVENTER: Some ventilation and thermal considerations in building design to suit climate, *S.A. Architectural Record*, Vol. 45, No. 1, Jan. 1960.
14.6. J. F. VAN STRAATEN, S. J. RICHARDS, F. J. LOTZ AND E. N. VAN DEVENTER: *Ventilation and thermal considerations in school building design*, N.B.R.I., Pretoria, 1965.

Chapter 15

15.1. *Building Digest No. 49*, Central Building Research Institute, Roorkee, India, Jan. 1967.
15.2. B. GIVONI: Basic study of ventilation problems in housing in hot countries, *Research Report to Ford Foundation*, Building Research Station, Technion, Haifa, 1962.
15.3. B. GIVONI: Laboratory study of the effect of window size and location on indoor air motion, *Architectural Science Review*, Vol. 8, No. 2, June 1965, pp. 42–46.
15.4. B. GIVONI: Ventilation problems in hot countries, *Research Report to Ford Foundation*, Building Research Station, Technion, Haifa, 1968.
15.5. T. R. HOLLEMEN: Air flow through conventional window openings, *Research Report No. 33*, Texas Engineering Experiment Station, College Station, Texas, 1951.
15.6. J. F. VAN STRAATEN, S. J. RICHARDS, F. J. LOTZ AND E. N. VAN DEVENTER: *Ventilation and thermal considerations in school building design*, N.B.R.I., Pretoria, 1965.
15.7. J. F. VAN STRAATEN: *Thermal performance of buildings*, Elsevier Publishing Co. Ltd, 1967.
15.8. A. F. E. WISE, D. E. SEXTON AND M. S. T. LILLYWHITE: Studies of air flow round buildings, *Architects' Journal*, Vol. 141 (19th May), 1965, pp. 1185–1189.

Chapter 16

16.1. *ASHVAE Guide*, American Society of Heating, Ventilating and Air Conditioning Engineers, New York, 1959.

16.2. F. BRUCKMAYER: Evaluation of prefabricated dwellings with regard to building physics, *Proceedings, CIB 3rd Congress*, Copenhagen, 1965.

16.3. R.E.E.F. 58, Centre Scientifique et Technique du Bâtiment, Paris, pp. 1092.

16.4. DIN 4108, 1960 (West Germany Building Norms).

16.5. B. GIVONI: *Review of Hygienic Requirements in Building as Related to Climate*, Building Research Station, Technion, Haifa, 1965.

16.6. B. GIVONI: *Guide to Building Design for Different Climatic Zones*, Building Research Station, Technion, Haifa, 1968 (in Hebrew).

16.7. M. S. GOROMOSSOV: The physiological basis of health standards for dwellings, *World Health Organization, Public Health Papers No. 33*, Geneva, 1968, p. 99.

16.8. *Hochban Wärmeshutz*, Ö NORM—B 8110 (Austrian Building Norms).

16.9. V. OLGYAY: *Design With Climate*, Princeton University Press, N.J., 1963, pp. 185.

16.10. Private communication from DR. Ø. BIRKELAND, Director, Norwegian Building Research Institute, contained in ref. 16.5.

Chapter 17

17.1. J. DREYFUS: *Le confort dans l'habitat en pays tropical*, Editions Eyrolles, Paris, 1960, p. 363.

17.2. M. FRY AND J. DREW: *Tropical Architecture*, B. T. Bastford Ltd., London, 1964, p. 263.

17.3. B. GIVONI: Comparison and climatic evaluation of buildings with different types of walls in Jerusalem, *Research Report*, Building Research Station, Technion, Haifa, 1964 (in Hebrew).

17.4. B. GIVONI: Indoor climate and dwelling house design in the Negev region, *Research Report*, Building Research Station, Technion, Haifa, 1964 (in Hebrew).

17.5. B. GIVONI: Field study of wetness conditions in occupied buildings, *Proceedings, RILEM/CIB Symposium on Moisture in Buildings*, Helsinki, August 1965, p. 6.

17.6. B. GIVONI: Required thermal characteristics of building in different types of hot climate, *Proceedings, 3rd CIB Congress*, Copenhagen, August 1965, Elsevier Publishing Co. Ltd, 1966, pp. 405–409.

17.7. B. GIVONI: Naturally cooled buildings for hot desert climate, *Proceedings, 4th Int. Congress of Biometeorology*, New Brunswick, U.S.A., Aug. 1966.

17.8. B. GIVONI AND M. E. HOFFMAN: Preliminary experimental study of natural cooling of buildings in deserts by outgoing radiation, *Research Report*, Building Research Station, Technion, Haifa, 1968 (in Hebrew).

17.9. B. GIVONI: Guide to building design for different climatic zones, *Research Report*, Building Research Station, Technion, Haifa, 1968 (in Hebrew).

17.10. A. A. MILLER: *Climatology*, Methuen & Co. Ltd., London, 1961.

17.11. J. F. VAN STRAATEN, S. J. RICHARDS, F. J. LOTZ AND E. N. VAN DEVENTER: *Ventilation and thermal considerations in school building design*, N.B.R.I., Pretoria, 1965.

Chapter 18

18.1.   W. R. CHERRY AND F. H. MORSE: Conclusions and Recommendations of the U.S. Solar Energy Panel (contained in ref. 20), 1973.

18.2.   F. DANIELS: *Direct use of the sun's energy*, Yale University Press, 1964.

18.3.   I. H. DANNIES: Solar air conditioning and solar refrigeration, *Solar energy*, Vol. III, No. 1, 1959, pp. 34–39.

18.4.   E. H. FARBER *et al.*: Operation and performance of the university of Florida—solar air-conditioning system, *Solar Energy*, Vol. 10, No. 2, 1966, pp. 91–95.

18.5.   B. GIVONI: Naturally cooled buildings for hot desert climate, 4th *Int. Congress of Biometeorology*, New Brunswick, U.S.A., August 1966.

18.6.   B. GIVONI: Utilization of natural energies for heating and cooling of houses, *Build International*, Vol. 5, 1974.

18.7.   B. GIVONI: Heating and cooling by natural energies—design implications, Proceedings, Denver, Col., U.S.A., June 1974.

18.8.   B. GIVONI AND S. WEISER: Natural energies for heating and cooling of buildings—analysis and literature survey, Research Report to the Israeli–American Bi-National Foundation (1975).

18.9.   H. R. HAY AND J. I. YELLOTT: A naturally air-conditioned building, *Mech. Engng*, Vol. 92, 1, 1970, pp. 19–25.

18.10. H. R. HAY: *The California solarchitecture house* (contained in ref. 20), 1973.

18.11. J. C. KAPUR: A report on the utilization of solar energy for refrigeration and air-conditioning applications, *Solar Energy*, Vol. 4, 1960, pp. 39–47.

18.12. G. O. G. LOF: House heating and cooling with solar energy, *Solar energy research*, Ed. by Danielas and Duffie, p. 33, University of Wisconsin Press, Madison, Wis., 1955.

18.13. G. O. G. LOF: Use of solar energy for space heating, General Report U.N. Conference on New Sources of Energy, Rome 1961.

18.14. G. O. G. LOF AND R. A. TYBOUT: The design and cost of optimized systems—for cooling dwellings by solar energy (contained in ref. 20), 1973.

18.15. C. PISONI: Examination of some heat storage systems for solar collectors in buildings heating applications (contained in ref. 20), 1973.

18.16. H. TABOR: Use of solar energy for cooling purposes, *Solar Energy*, Vol. 6, No. 4, 1962, pp. 136–142.

18.17. W. P. TEAGAN: A solar powered combined heating cooling system with the air-conditioning unit driven by an organic rankine cycle engine (contained in ref. 20), 1973.

18.18. MARIA TELKES: Storing solar heat in chemicals, *Heat and Vent.*, Nov. 1949, pp. 80–86.

18.19. H. E. THOMASON: Experience with solar houses, *Solar Energy*, Vol. 10, No. 1, 1966, pp. 17–22.

18.20. UNESCO International Congress: *The sun in the service of mankind*, Paris, July 1973.

18.21. J. I. YELLOTT: Utilization of sun and sky radiation for heating and cooling of buildings, *ASHRAE Journal*, December 1973.

18.22. J. D. WALTON, JR: Space heating with solar energy at the C.N.R.S. Laboratory, Odeillo, France, in: *Proceedings of the solar heating and cooling of buildings workshop*, University of Maryland, July 1973.

Chapter 19

19.1. J. FOURIER: *The analytical theory of heat*, Dover, New York, 1955, p. 112.
19.2. S. ALFORD, J. E. RYAN AND F. O. URBAN: Effect of the heat storage and variation in outdoor temperature and solar intensity on heat transfer through walls, *ASHVE Trans.*, Vol. 45, 1939, pp. 387–392.
19.3. C. O. MACKEY AND L. T. WRIGHT: Periodic heat flow composite walls or roofs, *Heating, Piping and Air Conditioning*, Vol. 18, 1946, pp. 107–110.
19.4. F. BRUCKMAYER: The equivalent brick wall, *Gesundheit Ingenieur*, Vol. 63 (6), pp. 61–65.
19.5. B. C. RAYCHOUDHURY: Thermal performance of light weight structures in tropics, *N.B.O. Journal*, October 1961.
19.6. B. C. RAYCHOUDHURY, J. P. JAIN AND K. G. YADVA: Thermal characteristics of unconditioned insulated masonry building in hot arid regions, *Int. J. Biometeor.*, Vol. 21, 1964, pp. 137–145.
19.7. A. H. VAN GORCUM: Theoretical considerations on the conduction of fluctuating heat flow, *Appl. Sci. Res.*, Vol. A2, 1951, pp. 272–280.
19.8. R. W. MUNCEY: The calculation of temperatures inside buildings having variable external conditions, *Aus. J. Appl. Sci.*, Vol. 4, 1953, pp. 189–196.
19.9. C. L. GUPTA, J. P. JAIN AND B. C. RAYCHOUDHURY: Indoor climate prediction by matrix method of circuit analysis, *Indian J. Tech.*, Vol. 3, pp. 166–170.
19.10. J. DREYFUS: Transmission de la chaleur en régime périodique á travers les murs de habitations, *Rev. Gen. de Therm*, Vol. 22, 1963, pp. 1155, 1162.
19.11. T. S. HOLDEN: The calculation of fluctuating heat flow in buildings, *Proceedings Australian Computer Conference*, Melbourne, 1963.
19.12. K. R. RAO AND CHANDRA: Digital computer determination of thermal frequency response of building sections, *Build. Sci.*, Vol. 1, 1963, pp. 299–307.
19.13. D. G. STEPHENSON AND SHIRTELIFFE: *Tabulated values of some special hyperbolic functions*, Tech. Study No. 114, Div. of Bldg Res., National Research Council, Canada, 1961.
19.14. B. RAYCHOUDHURY, S. ALI AND D. P. GARG: Indoor climate of residential buildings in hot arid regions, *Building Sci.*, Vol. 1, 1965, pp. 79–88.
19.15. R. W. MUNCEY AND T. S. HOLDEN: The calculation of internal temperatures—a demonstration experiment, *Build. Sci.*, Vol. 2, 1967, pp. 191–196.
19.16. VAGN KORSGAARD: Thermally equivalent outer walls, *Ingeniøren*, Nr. 11, June 1961.
19.17. W. B. DRAKE, H. BUCHBERG AND D. LEBELL: Load calculations using pretabulated admittance functions, *ASHRAE Journal*, April 1959, pp. 71–74.
19.18. D. G. STEPHENSON AND G. O. STARKE: Design of a π-network for heat flow analog, *J. Appl. Mech.*, Vol. 26, 1959, p. 300.
19.19. H. BUCHBERG, B. BUSSEL AND R. REISMAN: On the determination of optimal stress enclosures, *Int. J. Biometeor*, Vol. 8, 1964, pp. 103–111.
19.20. H. BUCHBERG AND J. NARUISHI: A rational evaluation of thermal protection alternatives for shelters.
19.21. H. BUCHBERG AND J. R. ROULET: *Simulation and optimization of solar collection and storage for house heating* (in press; personal communication by authors).

19.22. H. B. NOTTAGE AND G. V. PARMELEE: Circuit analysis applied to load estimating, *ASHRAE Trans.*, Vol. 60, 1954, p. 59.

19.23. G. LIEBMANN: Solution of transient heat transfer problems by the resistance network analog method, *ASME Trans.*, Vol. 78, 1956, p. 655.

19.24. H. BUCHBERG: Electrical analogue prediction of the thermal behaviour of an inhabitable enclosure, *ASHRAE Trans.*, Vol. 61, 1955, pp. 339–386.

19.25. H. BUCHBERG: Electric analogue studies of single walls, *ASHRAE Trans.*, Vol. 62, 1956, p. 177.

19.26. G. V. PARMALEE, P. VANCE AND CERNY, Analysis of an air conditioning thermal circuit by an electronic differential analyzer, *ASHRAE Trans.*, Vol. 63, 1957, pp. 129–143.

19.27. W. H. MCADAMS: *Heat transmission*, 3rd ed., McGraw-Hill, New York, 1954, pp. 68, 69.

19.28. C. S. LEOPOLD: Hydraulic analogue for the solution of problems of thermal storage, radiation, convection and conduction, *Refrigerating Engineering*, July 1947, p. 33.

19.29. B. C. RAYCHOUDHURY: Transient thermal response of enclosures: the integrated thermal time-constant, *Int. J. Heat Mass Transfer*, Vol. 8, 1965, pp. 1439–1449.

19.30. S. FUJII: Analysis of room temperature by means of weighting functions, *B.R.I. Occasional Report*, Vol. 8, July 1962 (100 pages).

19.31. N. K. D. CHAUDHURY AND Z. U. A. WARSI: Transient thermal response of buildings—Part I, Homogeneous structure, *Int. J. Heat Mass Transfer*, Vol. 7, 1964, pp. 1309–1321.

19.32. *Ibid.*, Part II (Composite Structure), pp. 1323–1334.

19.33. A. W. PRATT AND E. F. BALL: Transient cooling of a heated enclosure, *Int. J. Heat Mass Transfer*, Vol. 6, 1963, pp. 703–718.

19.34. A. W. PRATT: Variable heat flow through walls of cavity construction, naturally exposed, *Int. J. Heat Mass Transfer*, Vol. 8, 1965, pp. 861–872.

19.35. B. GIVONI AND M. E. HOFFMAN: Effect of building materials on internal temperature, Research Report for the Ministry of Housing, B.R.S. Technion, Haifa, April 1968.

19.36. M. E. HOFFMAN: Development of an internal temperature prediction formula for different climatic conditions and experimental examination in closed models, D.Sc. Thesis, July 1970.

19.37. B. GIVONI AND M. E. HOFFMAN: Prediction of the thermal behaviour of full scale buildings, First Research Report to the U.S. National Bureau of Standards, Building Research Station, Technion, Haifa, February 1972.

19.38. M. E. HOFFMAN AND B. GIVONI: Proposal of a method for calculation of external surface temperature, submitted to the U.S. National Bureau of Standards for publication in the final form, January 1973.

19.39. M. E. HOFFMAN AND B. GIVONI: Prediction of internal temperature using the total thermal time constant method as a building parameter, prediction of the thermal behaviour of full scale buildings, 3rd Research Report for the U.S. National Bureau of Standards, Building Research Station, Technion, Haifa, September 1973.

19.40. T. S. HOLDEN: Calculation of incident low temperature radiation upon building surfaces, *ASHRAE Journal*, April 1961, pp. 51–54.

19.41. D. G. STEPHENSON AND G. P. MITALAS: Cooling load calculation by thermal response factors, *ASHRAE Trans.*, Vol. 73, 1967.

19.42. G. P. MITALAS AND J. G. ARSENAULT: Fortran IV program to calculate Z —transfer function for the calculation of transient heat transfer through walls and roofs, Proc. of the First Symposium on the Use of Computers for Environmental Engineering Related to Buildings, Dec. 1970, National Bureau of Standards, Washington.

19.43. T. KUSUDA: Thermal response factors for multi-layer structures of various heat conduction systems, *ASHRAE Trans.*, Vol. 75, 1969, pp. 246–271.

19.44. T. KUSUDA, T. TSUCHIYZ AND F. J. POWELL: Prediction of indoor temperature by using equivalent thermal mass response factors, National Bureau of Standards, Washington, U.S.A., private communication.

Index